James E. Connor, who received a Certificate
of the Russian Institute and a Ph.D. in Public Law and Government from Columbia
University, is Assistant Professor of Government at Columbia College. He has been appointed a White House Fellow for 1968–69.

Lenin

ON POLITICS
AND REVOLUTION

Selected Writings

Edited and Introduced by

JAMES E. CONNOR

PEGASUS

THE BOBBS-MERRILL COMPANY, INC.

PUBLISHERS · INDIANAPOLIS · NEW YORK

Pegasus
A Division of The Bobbs-Merrill Company, Inc.
Library of Congress Catalog Card Number 68-21041
ISBN 0-672-63553-4 (pbk)
ISBN 0-672-53553-x
Printed in the United States of America
Fifth Printing

PREFACE

ALTHOUGH we live in what is reputedly a scientific age, there is considerable evidence that sorcery still holds sway among us. Consider, for example, the marvelous results obtained by adding the magic suffix "ism" to a man's name or a movement's. In a twinkling, gross inconsistencies seem to disappear, radical differences become blurred, and critical faculties are dulled. At such a time even lions and lambs may find it possible to lie down together. Admittedly our contemporary magic lacks the potency of earlier strains; for one thing its effective duration is much shorter. No sooner does one settle down with an "ism" than annoying questions are asked: Is your Marxism early or late, Revisionist or Russian, oriental or existential? Such discomfort occurs, of course, because men and events rarely exhibit the logical coherence that "ism" presumes. Moreover, time as well as circumstance tend to affect both the relevancy and the validity of ideas with the result that a theory emphatically asserted yesterday may be little more than an embarrassing memory today.

The dimensions of the problem are clearly visible in the writings of Lenin. The latest edition of his complete works runs to more than fifty volumes and spans thirty years. When he wrote his earliest pieces, Lenin was merely a minor member of an obscure revolutionary sect. His last works are those of an international figure, the unquestioned leader of the world's first successful "socialist" revolution. Given this enormous mass of material it is not surprising that Leninism has provided a field for virulent and even violent debate from the moment of his death until the present. The amount of writing, however, has had the effect of precluding almost everyone but the committed ideologue or the patient scholar from gaining any more than a passing familiarity with Lenin's ideas.

Sheer bulk, however, is not the only problem encountered in reading Lenin. The fact that he never attempted to set forth an abstract theory of political life presents an equally formidable obstacle. His political theory emerged from his active participation in the innumerable doctrinal squabbles that characterized European socialism in general, and the Russian revolutionary movement in particular. In a very real way he defined himself by first defining his opponents. Unfortunately for many readers the results of this process are clearly visible on almost every page he wrote. He constantly refers to men, parties, organizations, and programs that are familiar often only to the specialist in Russian history. For the nonspecialist to make his way through all of this material is, at best, a tedious task and one that makes Lenin's theoretical arguments extremely difficult to grasp.

The purpose of the present book is twofold. First, to gather into one volume a number of the writings that make up the basis of Lenin's thought, and second, to edit those pieces in order to eliminate as many of the obscure references and passages as possible. Neither aim, it must be confessed, has been wholly achieved. Reducing fifty-five volumes to one without sacrificing important material is impossible. Moreover a conscious choice was made to avoid "snippets," those three- or four-page selections torn from context which are supposed to contain the "great ideas." The selections in this book are, therefore, relatively lengthy. The aim has been to present material that can be analyzed in depth even at the risk of producing a less than perfect sample. As far as the second problem is concerned, no amount of editing could eliminate all of the specific references without rendering Lenin incomprehensible. It is hoped, however, that the introduction and the notes that accompany each selection will smooth the reader's path.

The selections have all been taken from *Lenin: Selected Works in Three Volumes*, Foreign Languages Publishing House, Moscow, 1963 and 1967. That translation, although not elegant, is generally accurate and conveys Lenin's style quite well. Some changes have been made in the translation and spelling to conform to American usage.

A large share of the credit for whatever usefulness this book has must go to some of my students at Columbia College whose answers and questions taught me at least as much about Lenin as I taught them. It is a great pleasure, although hardly an adequate repayment, to acknowledge my debts to Herbert A. Deane, a great teacher and a good friend. Elizabeth Hansot also deserves a special note of recognition. Her analytic skill is matched only by her wit. My thanks go to Stephen F. Cohen who freely shared his extensive knowledge of Soviet political theory with me and who pointed out areas in Lenin's writings which I might otherwise have ignored, and to Joel Linsider, who provided helpful research and stimulating conversations on Lenin. I must also thank Marion Wimbush and Ene Sirvet who took the time to decipher and type my script. Having made these acknowledgments, I find that there is little else for me to claim except the responsibility for selections and errors, which I cheerfully do.

James E. Connor

CONTENTS

INTRODUCTION

LENIN's historical impact has been of such magnitude that even today, nearly half a century after his death, he still evokes extreme reactions from those who study him. He has been praised beyond hyperbole and damned with savage invective; Communists quarrel violently about what he said, and historians learnedly about what he did. Some writers have pictured him as a compulsive revolutionary bent on attaining power regardless of cost, and others as a secular messiah—a prophet and planner of a glorious future. In the midst of such a maelstrom of opinion it is little wonder that the man and his ideas have been frequently obscured.

The selections in the present volume have been chosen in order to convey a fuller picture of Lenin than is usually available. At the very least this has entailed portraying him as a professional revolutionary, a governmental leader, and a political theorist. Within the confines of a brief introduction, however, it is obviously impossible to explore all of these roles in any detail. Attention has been focused, therefore, only on his role as a theorist, since it is the one most frequently neglected.

There are very few political theorists (or philosophers of any sort, for that matter) whose work can be said to be entirely original. Lenin is no exception to the rule. His intellectual obligations are numerous, and for the most part obvious. He claimed to be a Marxist, and clearly he was one. In an uncharacteristic moment of self-deprecation, for example, he even went so far as to call himself a mere "publicist" for Marxian ideas. But Lenin was not only a Marxist, and this he admitted when he acknowledged his debts to earlier generations of Russian revolutionary thinkers.

At first glance a union of Marxian and Russian revolutionary thought seems an unlikely combination. Although both schools preached violent social upheaval, their assumptions, methods, and approaches were vastly different. Marxism presented itself as a coherent, scientific synthesis of all social phenomena; it was concerned with the historical role of the industrial proletariat and its theories were articulated in terms of inevitable developments in the most advanced nations of Europe. Nineteenth-century Russia, however, was a backward, overwhelmingly agrarian country, and most of its revolutionaries directed their attention, not unreasonably, toward the peasantry, an impoverished and angry mass of humanity which accounted for more than eighty per cent of the Russian population. Furthermore, historical inevitability played a relatively minor role in Russian thought. Many Russian revolutionaries envisioned a conspiratorial elite which would seize power and proceed to establish an equitable social order from above. Lenin's major contribution as a political theorist was to reconcile these divergent approaches. In doing so he transformed Marxism from an ideology designed for the most highly industrialized nations into one that provided both a rationale and a strategy for revolution and development in backward areas. In order to illustrate how he accomplished this transformation we must first look briefly at the state of Marxism at the time Lenin entered the movement.

The Marxian Dilemma

On the basis of his examination of the economic processes and the relationships of capitalist society, Marx predicted an inevitable worsening of the lot of the workers, a rapid increase in their number, and an eventual polarization of society into two totally antagonistic classes. At one pole would stand a small, immensely wealthy bourgeoisie dominating all positions of influence in the society; at the other, a huge, impoverished proletariat having neither property nor power. During the process of impoverishment and polarization, the proletariat would gradually come to understand the fundamental relationship between the wretchedness of its condition and the class arrangements of capitalism. It would then arise, overthrow the bourgeoisie, and establish a dictatorship of the proletariat to eliminate the remnants of centuries of bourgeois rule. The traces of the pre-revolutionary class structure would rather quickly be erased, and as this process took place a fundamental change would occur in the governance of men. Throughout history, Marx had argued, the state had served as an instrument used by one class to oppress another. Within a short time after the proletarian revolution, however, society would no longer be composed of antagonistic classes. The state, therefore, would cease to have a function and it could be expected gradually to wither away. In place of the coercive state apparatus there would arise the cooperative institutions of a classless society in which the inequities of private property had been abolished and its limitations transcended.

The foregoing scenario did not depend on the will of individual members of either the proletariat or the bourgeoisie. Marx derived it logically from the ineluctable fall in the profit rate, which, he claimed, invariably accompanied advances in industrial technology.[1] The only way to counter this tendency was to increase the exploitation of labor, either by lowering wages or by extending working hours without increasing pay. The capitalist who did not do this, i.e. the man who attempted to treat his workers fairly, would certainly cease to be a capitalist in short order. Even these extreme measures, however, were no guarantee of survival. Marginal businesses would continue to fail no matter what steps were taken and their owners would fall, along with their more humane brethren, into the swelling ranks of the proletariat.

An aura of comprehensiveness and completeness pervaded the Marxian doctrine. It seemed capable of taking the most diverse social phenomena and weaving them into a tightly-knit historical fabric. No loose threads were apparent, and, although the final tapestry was still unfinished, its outlines were visible for all who chose to see them. But appearances were deceptive. In fact, the Marxian cloth contained a number of flaws which ultimately led to its unraveling. In the main these weak spots were not so much outright mistakes as points where Marx had been vague or ambiguous. For example, he had never stated precisely how the proletariat would come to appreciate the revolutionary role that history had thrust upon it. Did the workers simply have to live under capitalism, to experience its inevitable cruelties, in order to comprehend the fundamental antagonism between their own class interest and the existing social structure? Or must that knowledge be imparted to them by those who had studied the system in detail? A second and related problem arose on the level of action. Would the revolution occur as a spontaneous outburst on the part of the proletariat, or would it require careful planning and organization beforehand? If the former were the case, then it could be plausibly argued that Marxism was little more than an intellectually interesting theory which, like other kinds of deterministic thought, had essentially passive implications. Since the proletarian revolution emerged directly from the structure of capitalism, one need only patiently await it. If, however, the latter were the case, then the doctrine was primarily a call and a guide to action. Theoretically, the revolution was inevitable; in fact, it had to be actively sought after by those who desired it.

The ambiguities of philosophical discourse might permit a conjunction of active and passive voice, but in actual political or

1 For a thorough explication of this process see Marx's pamphlet, *Wages, Prices and Profit.*

social movement it is a highly unstable combination. Continual haggling over questions of purpose and tactics simultaneously frustrates the activists and irritates the determinists. Tempers fray, tolerance wanes, and the movement tends to split, first into factions, and eventually into hostile camps. From its outset the Marxian movement contained within itself the potential for fragmentation along these lines. A partisan of either the active or passive viewpoint could defend his position by citing passages in the work or by pointing to actions in the life of Marx. Yet, despite this potential, fragmentation was postponed for a number of years. External repression, of course, played a major role in maintaining unity. To most Marxists, internal differences in approach seemed less significant and were less of a threat than those between their camp and capitalist society. An equally important, although perhaps not so obvious a factor in keeping the movement together, was the apparent correctness of Marx's predictions—particularly those that dealt with impoverishment and polarization. During the early stages of industrialization, the rapid growth of the working class and the misery in which it lived were facts that few could deny, regardless of political philosophy. Starvation wages, child labor, and dark, satanic mills outraged the sensibilities of socialist and non-socialist alike. Marxists, however, were able to view these horrors as transient stages in a historical process which would ultimately benefit all mankind. Furthermore, their scientific approach to history seemed to differentiate them from other critics of bourgeois society, from the utopian socialists, for example, whose hearts might have been filled with good intentions but whose minds were empty. So long as events continued to validate the predictions there were few occasions for conflict between the activist and determinist wings of the movement. The practicing revolutionary, on the one hand, might work feverishly and see the fruits of his labor in a growing and increasingly oppressed and radicalized working class. The same events, on the other hand, might encourage the determinist to sit back and nod knowingly as the inherent flaws of the capitalist mechanism revealed themselves. There was little need for one side to be overly disturbed by the other, since it appeared that, no matter what the viewpoint, things were turning out as Marx had forecast.

The last decade of the nineteenth century, however, witnessed a relaxation of external repression. In itself, of course, this development hardly gave cause for concern. But it was paralleled by one undeniably ominous trend: as the decade progressed, it became increasingly obvious that events had begun to contradict Marx's predictions. Instead of growing poorer as a result of industrialization, the proletariat was obviously growing richer. By the end of the decade it was evident that industrial workers were living far better lives than had their fathers. Moreover, the bourgeoisie was not contracting; it was expanding both in absolute and relative terms. Finally, the state, which Marx had pictured simply as an instrument of class oppression, was at last recognizing some of the claims of the proletariat. Workers' representatives were entering parliaments in substantial numbers, and these bodies had begun to approve social welfare and insurance legislation as well as restrictions on working hours and conditions.

Marxists were slow to perceive and even slower to admit the widening gap between their theory and reality. Socialist deputies who daily pressed their constituents' interests in parliaments still used inflammatory rhetoric and invoked the specter of class war. In pamphlets, books, and speeches, socialist leaders repeatedly asserted the inevitability of bloody revolution and urged the workers to prepare themselves for it. No one seemed aware of the extensive changes that had occurred over the past decade, and no one seemed willing to offer either theories or policies which took into account such changes. The socialist movement gradually became less relevant to social reality as its leaders became increasingly mesmerized by the coherence of their theory and the violence of their slogans. Reality, however, could not be ignored indefinitely and, when the deficiencies in the theory were finally recognized, the movement was thrown into a state of confusion.

The Bernsteinian Revision

Eduard Bernstein, a leading theoretician of the German Social-Democratic Party and a revered figure in the international socialist movement, was the first to admit the problem openly. In 1899, he published *Evolutionary Socialism,* a work which extensively documented the failure of Marx's predictions and which called upon socialists to reassess their relationship to society and the state. The forecasts proved wrong, Bernstein argued, because they were based on faulty premises, in particular on incorrect concepts of value and profit. The experience of the 1890s had shown that the profit rate did not necessarily fall as an economy matured and, therefore, the Marxian trinity of impoverishment, polarization, and revolution could no longer be regarded as historically inevitable. To be sure, the theoretical weakness of Marxism did not render the socialist movement entirely devoid of value. Socialism's ethical aims—justice, equality, and dignity for all men

—still retained their validity and would continue to do so regardless of flaws in theory. Socialists had already contributed substantially to the welfare of the proletariat by helping to transform an amorphous mass of oppressed workers into a unified and conscious class which was now capable of exerting economic and political pressure in order to better its condition. Granted, much remained to be undone, there was still every reason to believe that further progress would be made. In order to continue advancing, however, socialists had to dismiss visions of a cataclysmic revolution and get on with the far more substantial task of creating and expanding the foundations of a democratic society, one which would benefit not only the proletariat but all social classes.

The reception accorded *Evolutionary Socialism* can best be described as a triumph of irony. Bernstein had tried to revise Marxist doctrine by dispassionately examing new evidence; in other words, he had applied scientific standards to a supposedly scientific body of thought. Yet his effort drew visceral howls of rage from Marxists who had only recently been congratulating one another on their objectivity and scientific outlook. His attempt to persuade socialists to forswear their rhetorical allegiance to violence resulted in new levels of violent abuse within socialist ranks.

Part of the blame for the hostile response must rest with Bernstein himself. By naïvely accepting the scientific claims of Marxism at face value and by treating it as one would any other scientific hypothesis, he showed how fundamentally he misunderstood the real nature of the doctrine. The aura of scientific certainty that surrounded Marxism constituted one of its most potent attractions in an age which equated science with the highest expression of intellectual achievement. But Marxism was never really a science, or perhaps better, it was much more than merely a science. The reader may recall the difficulty with which the Copernican view of the universe replaced the Ptolemaic. Scientific accuracy was not the primary issue, rather the earlier cosmology had become so enmeshed in moral and theological considerations that to reject the geocentric universe was to reject a divinely ordained system of values and ethics. Most men were reluctant to take so drastic a step merely in order to calculate planetary relations more precisely. Marxists faced a similar problem. Their ideology had ossified into a dogma which offered a comforting and comprehensive and integrated view of a chaotic social reality. It enabled them to retain the appearance of objectivity while expressing understandable moral revulsion at the excesses and injustices of nascent capitalism and, finally, it provided a standard of value authenticated by no less an authority than history, against which the presently rich and powerful could be judged and found wanting. The scientific aspect of Marxism, including its predictive apparatus, greatly added to the appeal of the doctrine, but at heart it remained a thoroughgoing ethical and moral critique of bourgeois society. Bernstein's mistake was in assuming that scientific insights and predictions were the primary components of Marxism and that they justified socialist hostility toward the bourgeoisie. In fact, however, the reverse was true. Hostile attitudes toward bourgeois society were prior to the predictions; and no revision in the latter could be expected to alter the former. Indeed, any effort to do so, especially by a socialist, was bound to be construed ultimately as an apology for the bourgeoisie and as such was deserving of a double measure of hostility.

The Leninist Revision

In many ways Lenin's initial reaction to *Evolutionary Socialism* typified the hatred which Bernstein had aroused among his erstwhile comrades. Lenin initially attacked the book on grounds of theoretical impurity. It was, he charged, a worthless, ill-conceived, even potentially dangerous work which relied far more on the ideas of English Fabians than on those of Marx. The author of this heretical text had forfeited his right to the name of socialist. He was in fact nothing more than a cowardly opportunist who must be ousted from socialist ranks at once. But Lenin's reaction was a good deal more complex and less typical than his first outburst indicated. His response, both to the failure of the Marxian predictions and to Bernstein's revision was as much influenced by his position as a Russian revolutionary as it was by his belief in Marxism.

In the last decade of the nineteenth century Russia had begun to undergo intensive industrial development. Economic conditions, therefore, roughly approximated those which existed in Europe when Marx first set down his analysis of capitalism. The costs imposed on the workers in terms of miserable living and working conditions were high and the returns they received in wages and material goods were low. Just as Marx had predicted, the Russian proletariat was growing rapidly and a few individuals were swiftly accumulating vast fortunes. With the exception of some local bodies, no trace of democracy as yet existed in rigidly autocratic Russia. Politics was the prerogative of the Tsar, his favorites, and his bureaucrats. There was little opportunity for political expression let alone organized legislative or group activity. Before 1900, Lenin had spent all but a few months of his life in Russia and thus had not seen direct evidence of either increasing prosperity or the potential for effective political action within the confines of the capitalist system. Unlike European Marxists, therefore, he did not initially perceive *Evolutionary Socialism* as a work which despite some disturbing pretensions to factual accuracy, nevertheless had to be rejected in order to preserve the integrity of the Marxist belief structure. Instead he saw the book as an outright fabrication which could only have been motivated by a sinister desire to prevent revolution by spreading the noxious doctrine of class harmony. Since Lenin considered revolution to be the essential component of Marxist thought he could brook no compromise with the Bernsteinian position nor could he tolerate anyone who espoused that position.

Prior to Bernstein's revision Lenin had little reason to question the revolutionary implications of Marxian thought. From what we know of his early years he seems to have become a Social-Democrat only after satisfying himself that the party, and the doctrine on which it was based, held out the only realistic hope for revolution in Russia. For Lenin, to be a Marxist meant to be a revolutionary. He was, of course, well aware that the converse of this statement was not true. Marxists accounted for a small fraction of the Russian revolutionary movement which was largely dominated by those who rejected Western models and who based their hopes for an uprising on the peasantry. In several of his early works, Lenin pointed out the weaknesses in the position of the peasant oriented revolutionaries. Russia, he argued, was inextricably caught up in the western pattern of development. One could not expect to bypass the capitalist stage no matter how appalling the prospect of industrialization seemed. Neither could one reverse history and return to the simpler life of a pre-capitalist epoch. Anyone seriously interested in revolution must adapt to the realities of developing capitalism and assist in the creation of a strong proletariat, the only real basis for a social revolution. In his early writings, therefore, Lenin concentrated his attacks on revolutionaries who were not Marxists; he scarcely considered the possibility of Marxists who were not revolutionaries.

Under the name of Economism, however, Bernsteinian ideas soon began to gain currency in Russian Marxist circles, and Lenin was forced temporarily to divert his attention from the non-Marxist revolutionaries. The Economists called for an internally democratic, socialist party which would work solely to secure better wages and working conditions for the proletariat and which would put aside both revolutionary sloganeering and conspiratorial methods. In 1902, Lenin issued his reply to the Economists in a lengthy pamphlet entitled *What Is to Be Done?*. He chose to ignore the problems raised by the failure of Marx's predictions. He offered neither a satisfactory refutation of the evidence nor an alternative interpretation of it. He focused instead on those ambiguities in Marx's own thought which held the greatest potential for fragmenting the movement. His aim, however, was not to explore these points in a disinterested intellectual fashion or to find a basis for reconciling divergent positions. Rather he wished to establish once and for all the primacy of the activist view. This he did in a disarmingly simple way by pointing to a fact that many Marxists knew but that few would admit: the socialist and labor movements had grown up independently of each other. Socialist thought had been developed by intellectuals such as Marx and Engels whose social origins were indisputably bourgeois; it had not emerged from the struggles of workers against capitalist oppression. Those who claimed that the proletariat would spontaneously come to appreciate their historically ordained role as a revolutionary class simply deluded themselves. The history of the past half century had shown conclusively that left to its own devices, the proletariat could at best achieve "trade-union consciousness," that is, precisely the limited Bernsteinian vision of a struggle for a fuller pay envelope and some token representation in sham bourgeois parliaments. True "social-democratic consciousness" which recognized the fundamental irreconcilability of classes and the necessity of revolution had to be imparted to the workers from without. Successfully educating the proletariat required both a coherent doctrine and an organization that was capable of spreading the doctrine effectively.

Lenin acknowledged that in the relatively free political environment of western Europe an internally democratic, mass party might be able to impart social-democratic consciousness to the working class. But Russian conditions precluded an open party. Tsarist police agents would immediately penetrate the organization, uncover its plans, identify its members and, when the time was right, destroy it. A truly democratic Russian socialist party would be plagued by harassment, raids and arrests. Many of its members would sit idly by in Siberian exile while the course of the Russian revolution was being charted in St. Petersburg and Moscow. It is important to realize that Lenin shed no tears at the thought of a few socialist intellectuals spending some time in prison. By stupidly or naively demanding adherence to democratic forms, even at the risk of political extinction, they openly invited ruin. The effect of organizational failure on the proletariat was a more serious matter. The relative backwardness of Russia meant that the crucial links between workers and socialists were only just beginning to be forged. These links had to be firmly established if the workers were going to develop into the conscious revolutionary class that history demanded. But what would happen if the first tentative contacts between workers and socialists ended in disaster? How would the workers react if they found themselves face to face with incompetent amateurs or political dilettantes who invariably attracted the attention of the secret police? There could be only one result: the workers would quickly grow wary of social democrats; they would turn away from Marxism and attempt to establish an ideology of their own. Historical experience, however, had shown the proletariat incapable of producing an independent ideology. The only alternative to Marxism was bourgeois thought, and if the workers rejected the former they were bound to fall victim to the latter. At best they might think in trade union terms, accommodating themselves to the capitalist system and trying to squeeze a few extra pennies from it. They would not become the class to abolish the system.

For Lenin, however, the revolution was paramount. Nothing could be permitted to delay or deter it, particularly not the democratic whims of a few intellectuals who fancied themselves Marxists. The revolution depended upon imbuing the workers with social-democratic consciousness which, in turn, depended upon Social Democrats gaining and holding the workers' confidence. Since the all-pervasive tsarist police precluded the possibility of open contact between socialists and workers, only one course was open to the true Marxist. It entailed establishing a party of professional revolutionaries who were skilled enough in the conspiratorial arts to outwit the police, and, it required the formation of a small, disciplined, secret and centralized party capable of operating both independently and through unions and other front organizations. Finally it demanded the ouster of all those fools who mouthed democratic platitudes or who inanely trusted in the spontaneity of the masses. Any other course, Lenin argued, would be tantamount to political suicide.

What Is to Be Done? is now best remembered for its organizational program. The pamphlet presaged the split of the Russian Social-Democratic Party in 1903 into two warring wings, the Bolsheviks, who adhered to the Leninist party model, and the Mensheviks, who sought a less conspiratorial and less overtly revolutionary instrument. Moreover, the party prescribed by Lenin has remained the model for revolutionary Communist parties the world over. But in addition to organizational implications *What*

Is to Be Done? must also be viewed as an important contribution to Marxist theory. By vigorously asserting the legitimacy of the activist interpretation, Lenin took the first step in transforming Marxism into an ideology for underdeveloped areas. Heretofore Marx's observations on revolution had seemed applicable only to those advanced countries in western Europe which were now rapidly exhausting the potential for development within the confines of a capitalist system. In these countries a large proletariat constituted the revolutionary force in reserve which was ready to overthrow the bourgeoisie and proceed onward to the establishment of a just, classless society. A few members of the intelligentsia in backward countries had been impressed by Marx's theoretical coherency, although as a program his work seemed irrelevant to their own societies. As Marxists, the best they might hope to do was to follow events closely in advanced countries and perhaps look fondly on their own emerging proletariat. Lenin provided these Marxists with a rationale for concrete action by arguing that without such action the development of the proletariat into a revolutionary class would be hindered.

In *What Is to Be Done?* Lenin also demonstrated that he had learned an important lesson from Bernstein. One of the major reasons for the hostility that greeted *Evolutionary Socialism* was its author's honesty in proclaiming himself a revisionist. Marxism, as we noted above, was no longer merely an interesting intellectual formulation worthy of discussion and debate. It had achieved the status of dogma and, for that reason, any attempts to revise it were liable to be treated as heresy. In his own revision, which in many ways was as radical as Bernstein's, Lenin overtly denied any claim to theoretical innovation. The activist view of Marx was not novel; it was simply the only correct interpretation. Even where Lenin was undeniably original, as in his call for a tightly-knit conspiratorial party, he was quick to point out that it was only the peculiarity of Russian conditions which permitted a deviation from Marxist norms.

In *What Is to Be Done?* Lenin strode a step closer to his ultimate goal of transforming Marxism into a revolutionary doctrine for backward nations. Nevertheless a great gap continued to separate the ideas of the German philosopher from the reality of tsarist Russia. The chief difficulty was that Russia had not yet gone through its bourgeois revolution. It was still governed by an *ancien régime,* in fact by a regime which was more reactionary that anything the West had known. Yet Marxists were agreed that a genuine socialist revolution would occur only after a bourgeois revolution and a period of bourgeois hegemony. What were

Russian Social-Democrats to do in the meantime? The primarily agrarian character of tsarist Russia presented a second problem. Marx had not assigned the peasantry a central or even a particularly significant role in his formulations. Russian Marxists, however, could hardly ignore the largest single segment of their country's population. They had to take account of it if only for strategic or tactical purposes.

When revolution broke out in Russia in 1905 Lenin seized the opportunity to deal with both of these problems simultaneously. In a pamphlet entitled *Two Tactics of Social-Democracy in the Democratic Revolution* he linked the bourgeois revolution with a role for the peasantry. Russia, he observed, was now finally passing through its bourgeois revolutionary phase, and this most certainly was a progressive step which all socialists must applaud. But Lenin cautioned his comrades to expect crucial differences between the revolutionary experiences of Russia and the West. Backwardness, he claimed, had stunted the Russian bourgeoisie, and as a result it had not matured into a class that was capable of fulfilling the tasks that history had set for it. Unless special steps were taken the revolution now going on in Russia would stop short of completion. Through weakness or cowardice the bourgeosie might compromise with the forces of reaction.

Socialists had good reason to be concerned with a compromise because of its effect on the timing of the proletarian revolution. Marx had stated that a period of bourgeois rule was necessary in order to establish the economic and technical basis for socialism. While frantically chasing after profits, unencumbered by feudal restrictions, capitalists would construct a vast productive network that would ultimately exceed their powers of control. In the process of creating this network they would also whip up that huge wave of social discontent that would inevitably engulf capitalism. The technical achievements of the bourgeoisie, however, would remain and would serve as the basis for further socialist development. But if the bourgeoisie failed to acquire full power, the entrepreneurial spirit would not be given free rein. If, in other words, the bourgeoisie shared power with remnants of the autocracy, the process of economic development might be slowed down, and, from the viewpoint of a practicing revolutionary, the proletarian uprising might be delayed for an intolerably long time. Thus, socialists could not allow the bourgeois revolution to fail. Whatever their feelings toward the bourgeoisie as a class, they had to ensure the success of its revolution.

At the time, however, the Russian proletariat was small, and the number of socialists smaller still. Even if the Social-Democratic

Party could count on the support of all workers (which it could not), it would not be strong enough to affect the course of the revolution. Help was needed from other groups, and the only one which was both large enough to matter and discontented enough to provide assistance was the peasantry. Lenin, therefore, proposed the creation of a "revolutionary dictatorship of the proletariat and peasantry" led, of course, by Social-Democrats. This political hybrid had two major functions; first to blunt the counter-revolutionary thrust of the autocracy by political and military means; and second, to force the bourgeoisie to conclude its revolution without surrender and without compromise. Once the revolution had run its course, Lenin knew full well that the coalition would disintegrate. Important sections of the peasantry would defect to the bourgeois camp. At that point, in order to maintain momentum towards the socialist revolution, the proletariat would have to ally with "the mass of semi-proletarian elements of the population," that is with the poorer strata of the peasantry. But that moment lay in the future. For the time being Lenin was concerned only with the alliance that would protect and extend the bourgeois revolution.

There are some obvious similarities between *Two Tactics* and *What Is to Be Done?* Both works contain specific programmatic suggestions which were implemented in the later history of communism. The Bolsheviks adopted Lenin's proposal for a revolutionary dictatorship of proletariat and peasantry in 1917 when they aligned themselves with radical segments of the peasantry in order to seize control of Russia. Even today the same alliance forms the basis of revolutionary communist strategies in under-developed countries. *Two Tactics,* like *What Is to Be Done?* gave socialists in these countries a rationale for direct revolutionary activity. They had to involve themselves directly in the bourgeois revolution lest that revolution fail and thereby delay the more important socialist revolution. But the real significance of *Two Tactics* lies in its revision of Marxist theory. Lenin called into question three points which most Marxists had, heretofore, accepted without question. First he introduced the concept of the weak or immature bourgeoisie. Prior to 1905 the suggestion of a bourgeoisie which was unable to complete its own revolution would have struck most Marxists as inane, surrounded as they were by a capitalist class that controlled all levers of power in the society. For European socialists the bourgeois revolution was an accomplished fact; their primary task was to prepare for the proletarian revolution while enduring a long period of bourgeois hegemony. Secondly, Lenin sketched out a revolutionary role for the peasantry. Again, although Marxists realized that peasants were capable of sporadic violence, in class terms the peasantry was seen at best as an historical backwater and at worst as a bulwark of reaction. Little thought, certainly, was given to its potential for social revolution. Finally, when Lenin hinted at a socialist revolution made with the help of semi-proletarian elements, he suggested a revolution in a country that had not fully passed through its capitalist stage of development. Yet almost every Marxist had taken it as an article of faith that the proletarian revolution would erupt first in the most advanced countries, in those which had exhausted the possibilities for further progress within the confines of private property relationships. Any one of these changes would have marked a significant departure from what had been considered basic Marxist thought. Together they constituted a revision of major proportions.

Once again, however, Lenin was extremely cautious in proclaiming his originality. At no point did he trumpet the sweep of his revisionary effort. Just as in *What Is to Be Done?* he scrupulously disavowed any claim to originality and presented his modifications simply as responses to the specific peculiarities of tsarist Russia. Nevertheless, despite Lenin's disclaimer, the student of political theory would be wise to examine *Two Tactics* closely, for it is one of the central works in Lenin's transformation of Marxism into a revolutionary doctrine for developing nations.

By focusing on the specific question of revolution in Russia, Lenin had avoided the basic theoretical problems raised by the failure of Marx's predictions. As suggested above, his ability to ignore the improving condition of the European proletariat derived in part from his isolation in Russia prior to 1900. Between 1900 and 1917, however, Lenin spend less that two years in his homeland. The rest of the time he wandered restlessly through European exile, confronted by the same evidence of prosperity and lack of polarization that had earlier disturbed socialists in the West. Moreoever, during the first decade and a half of the twentieth century, the European economy was not stagnant. The trends which Bernstein noted in 1899 were accelerating, and it was becoming increasingly obvious that polarization and impoverishment, the twin preludes to revolution, were not about to occur. With each passing year, therefore, revolutionary Marxism stood in greater need of revision. Without substantial alterations, the theory was in imminent danger of becoming an entirely irrelevant dogma.

World War I provided a second impetus toward revision. When hostilities commenced, workers all over Europe rallied to their respective flags, cheering the mobilizing armies and enthusiastically volunteering for military service. Almost to a man, socialist deputies in the parliaments of the belligerents voted for war credits. Yet Marx had asserted that workers had no country. The socialist movement, he claimed, was international in character because exploitation of the proletariat was an international phenomenon. Nationalism was merely a fig leaf used by the bourgeoisie to cover the naked class bias of the state. Workers had no interest in wars between bourgeois nations, and they would not participate in them. But in 1914 participate they did —with a fervor that matched any class on the continent.

Why had Marx's predictions failed? Why had a major war broken out? Why had the proletariat behaved chauvinistically? If Marxism was to retain any pretensions to intellectual vitality, it had to offer serious answers to all of these questions.

Lenin was aided in his own search for answers by the writings of three men: J. A. Hobson, a British bourgeois economist; Rudolf Hilferding, a German socialist theoretician; and Nikolai Bukharin, a brilliant young Bolshevik theorist. These writers had identified two important tendencies in the political economy of Europe in the late nineteenth and early twentieth centuries. The first was the trend toward imperialism, the mad scramble for colonial acquisition which preoccupied many European statesmen during these years; the second was the growth of industrial and financial monopolies in the most advanced nations. Lenin took these two notions, constructed his own theory of historical development, and presented his results in 1916 in a book entitled *Imperialism, the Highest Stage of Capitalism.*

The monopolistic practices that emerged in the last quarter of the 19th century had resulted, Lenin noted, in the creation of great industrial combinations which were strong enough to suppress competition and ensure stable profit levels regardless of market conditions. The process of monopolization was paralleled and greatly aided by the concentration of enormous amounts of capital in a few large banks. In order to operate efficiently, industrial monopolies required guaranteed reserves of raw materials, as well as markets for their products. Financial institutions, on the other hand, continually had to seek profitable outlets for their capital. Both groups solved their problems by turning to the undeveloped areas of the world. At first privately, and later through their respective governments (which they controlled) the industrial and financial monopolies began to dominate and exploit vast areas of Asia, Africa, and South America. The particular style of domination varied with the circumstances of the countries and .he industries concerned. In some cases it took the form of outright colonization; in others of unequal agreements between powerful western nations and weak backward countries; and in still others of an informal agreement between great powers over spheres of influence. But no matter what the form, the results were the same: the monopolies extracted huge quantities of "super profits" from the colonies and employed these funds to counteract, at least temporarily, Marx's law of falling profit in highly developed economies. The wealth that poured into the mother countries from the colonies was used to fatten the purses of the bourgeoisie and to bribe certain important segments of the working class. These super profits were the reason why Marx's predictions of growing impoverishment and polarization had not been fulfilled in western Europe. The European proletariat had not been radicalized, Lenin argued, because for the last thirty years, real exploitation had been taking place in the least, rather than in the most, advanced areas of the globe.

Thus colonial acquisition was the key to the survival of capitalism. Without the economic cushion of super profits, the bourgeoisie could not hope to forestall social revolution. Yet not all of the powers were equally endowed with colonies. Britain and France, for example, acquired theirs at an early date, while Germany entered the colonial competition only after almost all of the worth while territory had been claimed. The tardy powers then had no choice but to press for a redivision of the colonial status quo. It was this pressure for redivision that had brought on the world war and which would continue to bring on wars so long as the imperialist order flourished, that is, so long as capitalism survived as a social system.

Using the concept of imperialism, Lenin had no difficulty in explaining the patriotic fervor of the European proletariat. Those workers who had been bribed by colonial super profits clearly had a stake in the process of redivision. They constituted a kind of labor aristocracy which, in typical "opportunistic" fashion, sought its own comfort at the expense of the world revolution. Their behavior, although scandalous, was not surprising in men who had supped on scraps from the capitalists' tables.

Although imperialism had delayed the fulfillment of Marx's predictions, it had not, Lenin argued, rendered them permanently invalid. As colonies matured economically, the profit rate would fall just as Marx had forecast. Even before that point was reached, wars would debilitate, perhaps even destroy some of the present powers and reduce them to a semi-colonial status. In certain areas, successful anti-colonial revolution would cut off the flow of funds to the surviving powers. All of these factors would tend to bring about the end of the imperialist epoch. Lenin thus envisaged the Marxian class struggle, with its implications of impoverishment and polarization, reproduced on a gigantic international scale. An increasing number of exploited proletarian nations would confront a handful of the richest and most powerful imperialist states. The end result of this process would be analogous to that which Marx had predicted for individual capitalist countries: a proletariat revolution, now of worldwide dimensions, would over- throw the bourgeoisie and establish the classless society.

There can be little doubt that *Imperialism* was Lenin's most ambitious and most impressive performance as a theorist. He in- corporated the significant events of his age into a Marxian frame- work, while at the same time substantially altering and expanding that framework. Perhaps his most notable achievement, however, was in restoring the sense of the inevitability of revolution, for that was the aspect of the doctrine that had been buffeted most by events after Marx's death. The very scope of Lenin's effort makes it extremely difficult to comment concisely on the work as a whole. One aspect, however, clearly merits attention. *Imperialism* is the most important single step Lenin took in changing Marxism into an ideology that was relevant to the non-industrialized areas of the world. By invoking the notion of proletarian and bourgeois nations, Lenin shifted the attention of Marxists away from Europe and focused it on these backward regions. Here, he implied, was where the energy for social upheaval was stored; here was the stage on which much of the great revolutionary drama would be played out. It is doubtful if a more fundamental change could have been wrought in the Europe-centered thought of Karl Marx.

Limitations of space preclude a detailed examination of Lenin's later works. Our analysis therefore stops before Lenin achieved world notoriety, before he made his own revolution, and before he shepherded that revolution through years of civil war, foreign intervention, and economic collapse. Since successful politicians are not noted for the virtue of consistency, it should surprise no one that these experiences altered some of Lenin's ideas and attitudes. Nevertheless, beneath these changes, beneath, for ex- ample, the euphoria of the months following the Bolshevik power seizure, or the pessimism of his later years, there remained an unchanging core to Lenin's thought. Perhaps this core can best be described as a complete commitment to achieving the socialist revolution in Russia. Prior to October 1917, this commitment re- quired Lenin to justify revolutionary socialist activity in a back- ward society; after October it demanded that he legitimize the revolution he had made.

In order to accomplish his ends Lenin had to alter Marxism drastically. He had to transform it from a doctrine which charted the course of inevitable developments in the most advanced nations into one that set forth a strategy and a rationale for revolutionary activity in the least advanced countries. He did not, however, consciously set out to produce a general revision of Marx. Neither did he cynically use Marx to shield a sinister drive for personal power. Indeed, it is doubtful whether Lenin ever fully comprehended the enormity or the generality of his own revision. When he altered accepted Marxian doctrine, he almost invariably did so in the context of specific Russian peculiarities, and he did not lightly posit general laws for revolutionaries to follow elsewhere. In 1923, for example, when his own revolution had succeeded and the European revolution had failed dismally, Lenin refused to cite Russian success as the sole authority for his actions. Rather, he sought out obscure passages in Marx's letters of 1856 in order to justify the proletarian-peasant coalition which had brought on the revolution in Russia.[2]

Lenin's modesty, however, did not prevent others from generalizing on the basis of his authority and the Russian experience. From Stalin to Mao and beyond, "Leninism" has been used to justify revolution and development in backward countries. In a world in which the majority of mankind still lives in backwardness, Lenin remains an extremely important theorist. The irony of this situation, of course, is that Lenin's thought has lost much of its relevance in its homeland. His ideas offer relatively little help to a soviet society which daily faces problems of nuclear and space technology, and which is now just beginning to confront the dilemmas of automation, mass consumption and excessive leisure time.

James E. Connor

Morningside Heights, 1968

---

2   See "Our Revolution: Apropos of N. Sukhanov's Notes," p. 360.

I.

THE YEARS OF WAITING:
1902–1916

WHAT IS TO BE DONE? (1902)

Burning Questions of Our Movement

> ". . . Party struggles lend a party strength and vitality; the greatest proof of a party's weakness is its diffuseness and the blurring of clear demarcations; a party becomes stronger by purging itself. . . ." (*From a letter of Lassalle to Marx, of June 24, 1852*)

1 Dogmatism and "Freedom of Criticism"

A *What Does "Freedom of Criticism" Mean?*

"FREEDOM of criticism" is undoubtedly the most fashionable slogan at the present time, and the one most frequently employed in the controversies between socialists and democrats in all countries. At first sight, nothing would appear to be more strange than the solemn appeals to freedom of criticism made by one of the parties to the dispute. Have voices been raised in the advanced parties against the constitutional law of the majority of European countries which guarantees freedom to science and scientific investigation? "Something must be wrong here," will be the comment of the onlooker who has heard this fashionable slogan repeated at every turn but has not yet penetrated the essence of the disagreement among the disputants; "evidently this slogan is one of the conventional phrases which, like nicknames, become legitimized by use, and become almost generic terms."

In fact, it is no secret for anyone that two trends have taken form in present-day international Social-Democracy. The conflict between these trends now flares up in a bright flame and now dies down and smoulders under the ashes of imposing "truce resolutions." The essence of the "new" trend, which adopts a "critical" attitude towards "obsolete dogmatic" Marxism, has been clearly enough *presented* by Bernstein and *demonstrated* by Millerand.[1]

---

1 Alexander Millerand (1859–1943), a French socialist who established a precedent in 1899 by becoming a minister in a bourgeois government. [*Ed.*]

Social-Democracy must change from a party of social revolution into a democratic party of social reforms. Bernstein has surrounded this politial demand with a whole battery of well-attuned "new" arguments and reasonings. Denied was the possibility of putting socialism on a scientific basis and of demonstrating its necessity and inevitability from the point of view of the materialist conception of history. Denied was the fact of growing impoverishment, the process of proletarization, and the intensification of capitalist contradictions; the very concept, *"ultimate aim,"* was declared to be unsound, and the idea of the dictatorship of the proletariat was completely rejected. Denied was the antithesis in principle between liberalism and socialism. Denied was *the theory of the class struggle*, on the alleged grounds that it could not be applied to a strictly democratic society governed according to the will of the majority, etc.

Thus, the demand for a decisive turn from revolutionary Social-Democracy to bourgeois social-reformism was accompanied by a no less decisive turn towards bourgeois criticism of all the fundamental ideas of Marxism. In view of the fact that this criticism of Marxism has long been directed from the political platform, from university chairs, in numerous pamphlets and in a series of learned treatises, in view of the fact that the entire younger generation of the educated classes has been systematically reared for decades on this criticism, it is not surprising that the "new critical" trend in Social-Democracy should spring up, all complete, like Minerva from the head of Jove. The content of this new trend did not have to grow and take shape; it was transferred bodily from bourgeois to socialist literature.

To proceed. If Bernstein's theoretical criticism and political yearnings were still unclear to anyone, the French took the trouble strikingly to demonstrate the "new method." In this instance, too, France has justified its old reputation of being "the land where, more than anywhere else, the historical class struggles were each time fought out to a decision . . ." (Engels). The French socialists have begun, not to theorize, but to act. The democratically more highly developed political conditions in France have permitted them to put "Bernsteinism into practice" immediately, with all its consequences. Millerand has furnished an excellent example of practical Bernsteinism; not without reason did Bernstein and Vollmar [2] rush so zealously to defend and laud him. Indeed, if Social-Democracy, in essence, is merely a party of reform and must be bold enough to admit this openly, then not only has a socialist the right to join a bourgeois cabinet, but he must always strive to do so. If democracy, in essence, means the abolition of class domination, then why should not a socialist minister charm

2   George Vollmar (1850–1922), a right-wing German Social-Democratic Party leader. [*Ed.*]

the whole bourgeois world by orations on class collaboration? Why should he not remain in the cabinet even after the shooting-down of workers by gendarmes has exposed, for the hundredth and thousandth time, the real nature of the democratic collaboration of classes? Why should he not personally take part in greeting the Tsar, for whom the French socialists now have no other name than hero of the gallows, knout, and exile (*knouteur, pendeur et déportateur*)? And the reward for this utter humiliation and self-degradation of socialism in the face of the whole world, for the corruption of the socialist consciousness of the working masses—the only basis that can guarantee our victory—the reward for this is pompous *projects* for miserable reforms, so miserable in fact that much more has been obtained from bourgeois governments!

He who does not deliberately close his eyes cannot fail to see that the new "critical" trend in socialism is nothing more nor less than a new variety of *opportunism*. And if we judge people, not by the glittering uniforms they don or by the high-sounding appellations they give themselves but by their actions and by what they actually advocate, it will be clear that "freedom of criticism" means freedom for an opportunist trend in Social-Democracy, freedom to convert Social-Democracy into a democratic party of reform, freedom to introduce bourgeois ideas and bourgeois elements into socialism.

"Freedom" is a grand word, but under the banner of freedom for industry the most predatory wars were waged, under the banner of freedom of labor, the working people were robbed. The modern use of the term "freedom of criticism" contains the same inherent falsehood. Those who are really convinced that they have made progress in science would not demand freedom for the new views to continue side by side with the old, but the substitution of the new views for the old. The cry heard today, "Long live freedom of criticism," is too strongly reminiscent of the fable of the empty barrel.

We are marching in a compact group along a precipitous and difficult path, firmly holding each other by the hand. We are surrounded on all sides by enemies, and we have to advance almost constantly under their fire. We have combined, by a freely adopted decision, for the purpose of fighting the enemy, and not of retreating into the neighboring marsh, the inhabitants of which, from the very outset, have reproached us with having separated ourselves into an exclusive group and with having chosen the path of struggle instead of the path of conciliation. And now some among us begin to cry out: Let us go into the marsh! And when we begin to shame them, they retort: What backward people you are! Are you not ashamed to deny us the liberty to invite you to take a better road! Oh, yes, gentlemen! You are free not only to invite us, but to go yourselves wherever you will, even into the marsh. In fact, we think that the marsh is your proper place, and we are prepared to render *you* every assistance to get there. Only let go of our hands, don't clutch at us and don't besmirch the grand word freedom, for we too are "free" to go where we please, free to fight not only against the marsh, but also against those who are turning toward the marsh! . . .

D Engels on the Importance of the Theoretical Struggle

"Dogmatism, doctrinairism," "ossification of the party—the inevitable retribution that follows the violent strait-lacing of thought"—these are the enemies against which the knightly champions of "freedom of criticism" in *Rabocheye Dyelo* [3] rise up in arms. We are very glad that this question has been placed on the order of the day and we would only propose to add to it one other: . . .

And who are the judges?

We have before us two publishers' announcements. One, "The Program of the Periodical Organ of the Union of Russian Social-Democrats Abroad—*Rabocheye Dyelo*," and the other, the "Announcement of the Resumption of the Publications of the Emancipation of Labor Group." [4] Both are dated 1899, when the "crisis of Marxism" had long been under discussion. And what do we find? We would seek in vain in the first announcement for any reference to this phenomenon, or a definite statement of the position the new organ intends to adopt on this question. Not a word is said about theoretical work and the urgent tasks that now confront it, either in this program or in the supplements to it. . . . During this entire time the editorial board of *Rabocheye Dyelo* ignored theoretical questions, in spite of the fact that these were questions that disturbed the minds of all Social-Democrats the world over.

The other announcement, on the contrary, points first of all to the declining interest in theory in recent years, imperatively demands "vigilant attention to the theoretical aspect of the revolutionary movement of the proletariat," and calls for "ruthless criticism of the Bernsteinian and other anti-revolutionary tendencies" in our movement.

. . . [But these] high-sounding phrases against the ossification of

3 *Rabocheye Dyelo* (*Workers' Cause*), a journal of the Union of Russian Social-Democrats abroad that was published in Geneva from 1899 to 1902. Its politics were on the right wing of the Social-Democratic movement. [*Ed.*]

4 The Emancipation of Labor Group was the first Russian Marxist organization. It was founded by George Plekhanov, the "Father of Russian Marxism," in 1883 and included a number of individuals who were to become prominent figures in the Russian movement. The group was dissolved in 1903. In political outlook it approximated the Menshevik position in the Russian Social-Democratic Party. [*Ed.*]

thought, etc., conceal unconcern and helplessness with regard to the development of theoretical thought. The case of the Russian Social-Democrats manifestly illustrates the general European phenomenon (long ago noted also by the German Marxists) that the much vaunted freedom of criticism does not imply substitution of one theory for another, but freedom from all integral and pondered theory; it implies eclecticism and lack of principle. Those who have the slightest acquaintance with the actual state of our movement cannot but see that the wide spread of Marxism was accompanied by a certain lowering of the theoretical level. Quite a number of people with very little, and even a total lack of, theoretical training joined the movement because of its practical significance and its practical successes. We can judge from that how tactless *Rabocheye Dyelo* is when, with an air of triumph, it quotes Marx's statement: "Every step of real movement is more important than a dozen programs." To repeat these words in a period of theoretical disorder is like wishing mourners at a funeral many happy returns of the day. Moreover, these words of Marx are taken from his letter on the Gotha Program, in which he *sharply condemns* eclecticism in the formulation of principles. If you must unite, Marx wrote to the party leaders, then enter into agreements to satisfy the practical aims of the movement, but do not allow any bargaining over principles, do not make theoretical "concessions." This was Marx's idea, and yet there are people among us who seek—in his name—to belittle the significance of theory!

Without revolutionary theory there can be no revolutionary movement. This idea cannot be insisted upon too strongly at a time when the fashionable preaching of opportunism goes hand in hand with an infatuation for the narrowest forms of practical activity. Yet, for Russian Social-Democrats the importance of theory is enhanced by three other circumstances, which are often forgotten: first, by the fact that our Party is only in process of formation, its features are only just becoming defined, and it has as yet far from settled accounts with the other trends of revolutionary thought that threaten to divert the movement from the correct path. On the contrary, precisely the very recent past was marked by a revival of non-Social-Democratic revolutionary trends. . . . Under these circumstances, what at first sight appears to be an "unimportant" error may lead to most deplorable consequences, and only short-sighted people can consider factional disputes and a strict differentiation between shades of opinion inopportune or superfluous. The fate of Russian Social-Democracy for very many years to come may depend on the strengthening of one or the other "shade."

Second, the Social-Democratic movement is in its very essence an international movement. This means, not only that we must combat national chauvinism, but that an incipient movement in a young country can be successful only if it makes use of the experiences of other countries. In order to make use of these experiences it is not enough merely to be acquainted with them, or simply to copy out the latest resolutions. What is required is the ability to treat these experiences critically and to test them independently. He who realizes how enormously the modern working-class movement has grown and branched out will understand what a reserve of theoretical forces and political (as well as revolutionary) experience is required to carry out this task.

Third, the national tasks of Russian Social-Democracy are such as have never confronted any other socialist party in the world. We shall have occasion further on to deal with the political and organizational duties which the task of emancipating the whole people from the yoke of autocracy imposes upon us. At this point, we wish to state only that the *role of vanguard fighter can be fulfilled only by a party that is guided by the most advanced theory.* . . .

Let us quote what Engels said in 1874 concerning the significance of theory in the Social-Democratic movement. Engels recognizes, *not two* forms of the great struggle of Social-Democracy (political and economic), as is the fashion among us, *but three, placing the theoretical struggle on a par with the first two.* His recommendations to the German working-class movement, which had become strong, practically and politically, are so instructive from the standpoint of present-day problems and controversies, that we hope the reader will not be vexed with us for quoting a long passage. . . .

The German workers have two important advantages over those of the rest of Europe. First, they belong to the most theoretical people of Europe; and they have retained that sense of theory which the so-called 'educated' classes of Germany have almost completely lost. Without German philosophy, which preceded it, particularly that of Hegel, German scientific socialism—the only scientific socialism that has ever existed—would never have come into being. Without a sense of theory among the workers, this scientific socialism would never have entered their flesh and blood as much as is the case. What an immeasurable advantage this is may be seen, on the one hand, from the indifference towards all theory which is one of the main reasons why the English working-class movement crawls along so slowly in spite of the splendid organization of the individual unions; on the other hand, from the mischief and confusion wrought by Proudhonism, in its original form, among the French and Belgians, and in, the form further caricatured by Bakunin, among the Spaniards and Italians.

The second advantage is that, chronologically speaking, the Germans were about the last to come into the workers' movement. Just as German theoretical socialism will never forget that it rests on the shoulders of Saint-Simon, Fourier, and Owen—three men who, in spite of all their fantastic notions and all their utopianism, have their place among the most eminent thinkers of all times, and whose genius anticipated innumerable things, the correctness of which is now being scientifically proved by us—so the practical workers' movement in Germany ought never to forget that it has developed on the shoulders of the English and French movements, that it was able simply to utilize their dearly bought experience, and could now avoid their mistakes, which in their time were mostly unavoidable. Without the precedent of the English trade unions and French workers' political struggles, without the gigantic impulse given especially by the Paris Commune, where would we be now?

It must be said to the credit of the German workers that they have exploited the advantages of their situation with rare understanding. For the first time since a workers' movement has existed, the struggle is being conducted so that its three sides—the theoretical, the political, and the practical-economic (resistance to the capitalists)— form a harmonious and unified system. It is precisely in this, as it were, concentric attack, that the strength and invincibility of the German movement lies.

Due to this advantageous situation, on the one hand, and to the insular peculiarities of the English and the forcible suppression of the French movement, on the other, the German workers have for the moment been placed in the vanguard of the proletarian struggle. How long events will allow them to occupy this post of honor cannot be foretold. But let us hope that as long as they occupy it, they will fill it fittingly. This demands redoubled efforts in every field of struggle and agitation. In particular, it will be the duty of the leaders to gain an ever clearer insight into all theoretical questions, to free themselves more and more from the influence of traditional phrases inherited from the old world outlook, and constantly to keep in mind that socialism, since it has become a science, demands that it be pursued as a science, that is, that it be studied. The task will be to spread with increased zeal among the masses of the workers the ever more clarified understanding thus acquired, to knit together ever more firmly the organization both of the party and of the trade unions. . . .

If the German workers progress in this way, they will not be marching exactly at the head of the movement—it is not at all in the interest of this movement that the workers of any particular country should march at its head—but they will occupy an honorable place in the battle line; and they will stand armed for battle when either unexpectedly grave trials or momentous events demand of them increased courage, increased determination, and energy.

Engels's words proved prophetic. Within a few years the German workers were subjected to unexpectedly grave trials in the form of the Exceptional Law Against the Socialists. And they met those trials armed for battle and succeeded in emerging from them victorious.

The Russian proletariat will have to undergo trials immeasurably graver; it will have to fight a monster compared with which an anti-socialist law in a constitutional country seems but a dwarf. History has now confronted us with an immediate task which is the *most revolutionary* of all the *immediate* tasks confronting the proletariat of any country. The fulfillment of this task, the destruction of the most powerful bulwark, not only of European, but (it may now be said) of Asiatic reaction, would make the Russian proletariat the vanguard of the international revolutionary proletariat. And we have the right to count upon acquiring this honorable title, already earned by our predecessors, the revolutionaries of the seventies, if we succeed in inspiring our movement, which is a thousand times broader and deeper, with the same devoted determination and vigor.

2   The Spontaneity of the Masses and the Consciousness of the Social-Democrats

We have said that our movement, much more extensive and deep than the movement of the seventies, must be inspired with the same devoted determination and energy that inspired the movement at that time. Indeed, no one, we think, has until now doubted that the strength of the present-day movement lies in the awakening of the masses (principally, the industrial proletariat) and that its weakness lies in the lack of consciousness and initiative among the revolutionary leaders.

However, of late a staggering discovery has been made, which threatens to disestablish all hitherto prevailing views on this question. This discovery was made by *Rabocheye Dyelo*, which in its polemic with *Iskra* [5] and *Zarya* [6] did not confine itself to making objections on separate points, but tried to ascribe "general disagreements" to a more profound cause—to the "different appraisals of the *relative* importance of the spontaneous and consciously 'methodical' element." *Rabocheye Dyelo* formulated its indictment as a "*belitting of the significance of the objective or the spontaneous element of development*." To this we say: Had the polemics with *Iskra* and *Zarya* re-

5   *Iskra* (*The Spark*), a Russian Marxist paper founded in 1900 by Lenin and other Russian Social-Democrats. It was published in Western Europe and smuggled into Russia. The paper was conceived by Lenin as the focal point of the revolutionary movement. After the split with the Mensheviks at the Second Party Congress in 1903, Lenin gained almost complete control of the paper. Within three months, however, he was forced to resign his position on the editorial board. *Iskra* then became for all practical purposes a Menshevik paper. In "Two Tactics," Lenin scornfully refers to the "new *Iskra*" which represents the Menshevik position (see pp. 91ff). [*Ed.*]

6   *Zarya* (*Dawn*), a Russian Marxist journal published in Germany during 1901–1902. Lenin contributed several articles to it. [*Ed.*]

sulted in nothing more than causing *Rabocheye Dyelo* to hit upon these "general disagreements," that alone would give us considerable satisfaction, so significant is this thesis and so clear is the light it sheds on the quintessence of the present-day theoretical and political differences that exist among Russian Social-Democrats.

For this reason the question of the relation between consciousness and spontaneity is of such enormous general interest, and for this reason the question must be dealt with in great detail.

A   The Beginning of the Spontaneous Upsurge

In the previous chapter we pointed out how *universally* absorbed the educated youth of Russia was in the theories of Marxism in the middle of the nineties. In the same period the strikes that followed the famous St. Petersburg industrial war of 1896 assumed a similar general character. Their spread over the whole of Russia clearly showed the depth of the newly awakening popular movement, and if we are to speak of the "spontaneous element" then, of course, it is this strike movement which, first and foremost, must be regarded as spontaneous. But there is spontaneity and spontaneity. Strikes occurred in Russia in the seventies and sixties (and even in the first half of the nineteenth century), and they were accompanied by the "spontaneous" destruction of machinery, etc. Compared with these "revolts," the strikes of the nineties might even be described as "conscious," to such an extent do they mark the progress which the working-class movement made in that period. This shows that the "spontaneous element," in essence, represents nothing more nor less than consciousness in an *embryonic form*. Even the primitive revolts expressed the awakening of consciousness to a certain extent. The workers were losing their age-long faith in the permanence of the system which oppressed them and began . . . I shall not say to understand, but to sense the necessity for collective resistance, definitely abandoning their slavish submission to the authorities. But this was, nevertheless, more in the nature of outbursts of desperation and vengeance than of *struggle*. The strikes of the nineties revealed far greater flashes of consciousness; definite demands were advanced, the strike was carefully timed, known cases and instances in other places were discussed, etc. The revolts were simply the resistance of the oppressed, whereas the systematic strikes represented the class struggle in embryo, but only in embryo. Taken by themselves, these strikes were simply trade union struggles, not yet Social-Democratic struggles. They marked the awakening antagonisms between workers and employers; but the workers were not, and could not be, conscious of the irreconcilable antagonism of their interests to the whole of the modern political and social system, that is, theirs was not yet Social-Democratic consciousness. In this sense, the strikes of the nineties, despite the enormous progress they represented as compared with the "revolts," remained a purely spontaneous movement.

We have said that *there could not have been* Social-Democratic consciousness among the workers. It would have to be brought to them from without. The history of all countries shows that the working class, exclusively by its own effort, is able to develop only trade union consciousness, that is, the conviction that it is necessary to combine in unions, fight the employers, and strive to compel the government to pass necessary labor legislation, etc.[7] The theory of socialism, however, grew out of the philosophic, historical, and economic theories elaborated by educated representatives of the propertied classes, by intellectuals. By their social status the founders of modern scientific socialism, Marx and Engels, themselves belonged to the bourgeois intelligentsia. In the very same way, in Russia, the theoretical doctrine of Social-Democracy arose altogether independently of the spontaneous growth of the working-class movement; it arose as a natural and inevitable outcome of the development of thought among the revolutionary socialist intelligentsia. In the period under discussion, the middle nineties, this doctrine not only represented the completely formulated program of the Emancipation of Labor group, but had already won over to its side the majority of the revolutionary youth in Russia.

Hence, we had both the spontaneous awakening of the working masses, their awakening to conscious life and conscious struggle, and a revolutionary youth, armed with Social-Democratic theory and straining towards the workers. In this connection it is particularly important to state the oft-forgotten (and comparatively little-known) fact that, although the *early* Social-Democrats of that period *zealously carried on economic agitation* . . . they did not regard this as their sole task. On the contrary, *from the very beginning* they set for Russian Social-Democracy the most far-reaching historical tasks, in general, and the task of overthrowing the autocracy, in particular. Thus, towards the end of 1895, the St. Petersburg group of Social-Democrats, which founded the League of Struggle for the Emancipation of the Working Class,[8] prepared the first issue of a newspaper called *Rabocheye Dyelo*. This issue was ready to go to press when it was seized by the gendarmes, on the night of December 8, 1895, in a raid on the house of one of the members of the group. . . . This "first effort," if we are not mistaken, of the Russian Social-Democrats of the nineties was not a purely local, or less still, "Economic,"

7   Trade-unionism does not exclude "politics" altogether, as some imagine. Trade unions have always conducted some political (but not Social-Democratic) agitation and struggle. We shall deal with the difference between trade union politics and Social-Democratic politics in the next chapter. [*L.*]

8   Lenin himself was one of the founders of the League. [*Ed.*]

newspaper, but one that aimed to unite the strike movement with the revolutionary movement against the autocracy, and to win over to the side of Social-Democracy all who were oppressed by the policy of reactionary obscurantism. No one in the slightest degree acquainted with the state of the movement at that period could doubt that such a paper would have met with warm response among the workers of the capital and the revolutionary intelligentsia and would have had a wide circulation. The failure of the enterprise merely showed that the Social-Democrats of that period were unable to meet the immediate requirements of the time owing to their lack of revolutionary experience and practical training. . . . Of course, we would not dream of blaming the Social-Democrats of that time for this unpreparedness. But in order to profit from the experience of that movement, and to draw practical lessons from it, we must thoroughly understand the causes and significance of this or that shortcoming. It is therefore highly important to establish the fact that a part (perhaps even a majority) of the Social-Democrats active in the period of 1895–1898 justly considered it possible even then, at the very beginning of the "spontaneous" movement, to come forward with a most extensive program and a militant tactical line.[9] Lack of training of the majority of the revolutionaries, an entirely natural phenomenon, could not have roused any particular fears. Once the tasks were correctly defined, once the energy existed for repeated attempts to fulfill them, temporary failures represented only part misfortune. Revolutionary experience and organizational skill are things that can be acquired, provided the desire is there to acquire them, provided the shortcomings are recognized, which in revolutionary activity is more than half-way towards their removal.

But what was only part misfortune became full misfortune when this consciousness began to grow dim (it was very much alive among the members of the groups mentioned), when there appeared people —and even Social-Democratic organs—that were prepared to regard shortcomings as virtues, that even tried to invent a *theoretical* basis for their *slavish cringing before spontaneity*. It is time to draw con-

9 "In adopting a hostile attitude towards the activities of the Social-Democrats of the late nineties, *Iskra* ignores the absence at that time of conditions for any work other than the struggle for petty demands," declare the Economists. . . . The facts given above show that the assertion about "absence of conditions" is *diametrically opposed to the truth*. Not only at the end, but even in the mid-nineties, all the conditions existed for *other* work, besides the struggle for petty demands—all the conditions except adequate training of leaders. Instead of frankly admitting that we, the ideologists, the leaders, lacked sufficient training—the Economists seek to shift the blame entirely upon the "absence of conditions," upon the effect of material environment that determines the road from which no ideologist will be able to divert the movement. What is this but slavish cringing before spontaneity, what but the infatuation of the "ideologists" with their own shortcomings? [L.]

clusions from this trend, the content of which is incorrectly and too narrowly characterized as Economism.[10]

B   Bowing to Spontaneity: Rabochaya Mysl

. . . . The founding of *Rabochaya Mysl* [11] brought Economism to the light of day, but not at one stroke. We must picture to ourselves concretely the conditions for activity and the short-lived character of the majority of the Russian study circles (a thing that is possible only for those who have themselves experienced it) in order to understand how much there was of the fortuitous in the successes and failures of the new trend in various towns, and the length of time during which neither the advocates nor the opponents of the "new" could make up their minds—and literally had no opportunity of so doing—as to whether this really expressed a distinct trend or merely the lack of training of certain individuals. For example, the first mimeographed copies of *Rabochaya Mysl* never reached the great majority of Social-Democrats. . . . It is well worth dwelling on [the] leading article [in the paper] because it brings out in bold relief *the entire spirit of Rabochaya Mysl* and Economism generally.

After stating that the arm of the "blue-coats" [12] could never halt the progress of the working-class movement, the leading article goes on to say: ". . . The virility of the working-class movement is due to the fact that the workers themselves are at last taking their fate into their own hands, and out of the hands of the leaders"; this fundamental thesis is then developed in greater detail. Actually, the leaders (that is, the Social-Democrats, the organizers of the League of Struggle) were, one might say, torn out of the hands of the workers by the police; yet it is made to appear that the workers were fighting against the leaders and liberated themselves from their yoke! Instead of sounding the call to go forward towards the consolidation of the revolutionary organization and the expansion of political activity, the call was issued for a *retreat* to the purely trade union struggle. It was announced that "the economic basis of the movement is eclipsed by the effort never to forget the political ideal," and that the watchword for the working-class movement was "Struggle for economic conditions" (!) or, better still, "The workers for the workers." It was declared that strike funds "are more valuable to the movement than a hundred other organizations". . . . etc. Catchwords like "We

10   Economism—a tendency in the Russian Social-Democratic Party which stressed the importance of the economic struggle, that is, the struggle to improve wages and working conditions of the proletariat. [*Ed.*]

11   *Rabochaya Mysl* (*Workers' Thought*), The Economists' newspaper published irregularly between 1897 and 1902. [*Ed.*]

12   "Blue-coats" refers to the Tsarist police who wore blue uniforms. [*Ed.*]

must concentrate, not on the 'cream' of the workers, but on the 'average,' mass worker"; "Politics always obediently follows economics," etc., etc., became the fashion, exercising an irresistible influence upon the masses of the youth who were attracted to the movement but who, in the majority of cases, were acquainted only with such fragments of Marxism as were expounded in legally appearing publications.

Political consciousness was completely overwhelmed by spontaneity . . . the spontaneity of those workers who were carried away by the arguments that a kopek added to a ruble was worth more than any socialism or politics, and that they must "fight, knowing that they are fighting, not for the sake of some future generation, but for themselves and their children." . . . Phrases like these have always been a favorite weapon of the West-European bourgeois, who, in their hatred for socialism, strove . . . to transplant English trade-unionism to their native soil and to preach to the workers that by engaging in the purely trade union struggle they would be fighting for themselves and for their children, and not for some future generations with some future socialism. And now . . . [certain Russian Social-Democrats] have set about repeating these bourgeois phrases. It is important at this point to note three circumstances that will be useful to our further analysis of *contemporary* differences.[13]

In the first place, the overwhelming of political consciousness by spontaneity, to which we referred above, also took place *spontaneously*. This may sound like a pun, but, alas, it is the bitter truth. It did not take place as a result of an open struggle between two diametrically opposed points of view, in which one triumphed over the other; it occurred because of the fact that an increasing number of "old" revolutionaries were "torn away" by the gendarmes and increasing numbers of "young" . . . [Economists] of Russian Social-Democracy appeared on the scene. Everyone, who has I shall not say participated in, but at least breathed the atmosphere of, the *present-day* Russian movement, knows perfectly well that this is precisely the case. And if, nevertheless, we insist strongly that the reader be fully clear on this generally known fact, if we cite, for explicitness, as it were, the facts of the first edition of *Rabocheye Dyelo* and of the polemic between the "old" and the "young" at the beginning of 1897, we do this because the people who vaunt their "democracy" speculate on the ignorance of these facts on the part of the broad public (or of the very young generation). We shall return to this point further on.

13 We emphasize the word *contemporary* for the benefit of those who may pharisaically shrug their shoulders and say: It is easy enough to attack *Rabochaya Mysl* now, but is not all this ancient history? *Mutato nomine de te fabula narratur* [change the name and the tale is about you] is our answer to such contemporary Pharisees, whose complete subjection to the ideas of *Rabochaya Mysl* will be *proved* further on. [L.]

Second, in the very first literary expression of Economism we observe the exceedingly curious phenomenon—highly characteristic for an understanding of all the differences prevailing among present-day Social-Democrats—that the adherents of the "labor movement pure and simple," worshippers of the closest "organic" contacts . . . with the proletarian struggle, opponents of any non-worker intelligentsia (even a socialist intelligentsia), are compelled, in order to defend their positions, to resort to the arguments of the bourgeois "pure trade-unionists." This shows that from the very outset Rabochaya Mysl began—unconsciously—to implement the program of the Credo.[14] This shows . . . that all worship of the spontaneity of the working-class movement, all belittling of the role of "the conscious element," of the role of Social-Democracy, means, quite independently of whether he who belittles that role desires it or not, a strengthening of the influence of bourgeois ideology upon the workers. All those who talk about "overrating the importance of ideology," about exaggerating the role of the conscious element, etc., imagine that the labor movement pure and simple can elaborate, and will elaborate, an independent ideology for itself, if only the workers "wrest their fate from the hands of the leaders." But this is a profound mistake. To supplement what has been said above, we shall quote the following profoundly true and important words of Karl Kautsky[15] on the new draft program of the Austrian Social-Democratic Party:

"Many of our revisionist critics believe that Marx asserted that economic development and the class struggle create, not only the conditions for socialist production, but also, and directly, the consciousness [K.K.'s italics] of its necessity. And these critics assert that England, the country most highly developed capitalistically, is more remote than any other from this consciousness. Judging by the draft, one might assume that this allegedly orthodox-Marxist view, which is thus refuted, was shared by the committee that drafted the Austrian program. In the draft program it is stated: 'The more capitalist development increases the numbers of the proletariat, the more the proletariat is compelled and becomes fit to fight against capitalism. The proletariat becomes conscious' of the possibility and of the necessity for socialism. In this connection socialist consciousness appears to be a necessary and direct result of the proletarian class struggle. But this is absolutely untrue. Of course, socialism, as a doctrine, has its roots in modern economic relationships just as the class struggle of the proletariat has, and, like the latter, emerges from the struggle against the capitalist-created poverty and misery of the masses. But socialism and the class struggle arise side by side and not one out of the other; each arises under different conditions. Modern socialist consciousness can arise only on the basis of profound scientific knowledge. Indeed, modern economic science is as much a condition for socialist produc-

14 The Credo was a manifesto of Economism published in 1899. [Ed.]
15 Karl Kautsky (see p. 114n). [Ed.]

tion as, say, modern technology, and the proletariat can create neither the one nor the other, no matter how much it may desire to do so; both arise out of the modern social process. The vehicle of science is not the proletariat, but the *bourgeois intelligentsia* [K.K.'s italics]: it was in the minds of individual members of this stratum that modern socialism originated, and it was they who communicated it to the more intellectually developed proletarians who, in their turn, introduce it into the proletarian class struggle where conditions allow that to be done. Thus, socialist consciousness is something introduced into the proletarian class struggle from without [*von Aussen Hineingetragenes*] and not something that arose within it spontaneously [*urwüchsig*]. Accordingly, the old Hainfeld program quite rightly stated that the task of Social-Democracy is to imbue the proletariat [literally: saturate the proletariat] with the *consciousness* of its position and the consciousness of its task. There would be no need for this if consciousness arose of itself from the class struggle. The new draft copied this proposition from the old program, and attached it to the proposition mentioned above. But this completely broke the line of thought. . . ."

Since there can be no talk of an independent ideology formulated by the working masses themselves in the process of their movement,[16] the *only* choice is—either bourgeois or socialist ideology. There is no middle course (for mankind has not created a "third" ideology, and, moreover, in a society torn by class antagonisms there can never be a non-class or an above-class ideology). Hence, to belittle the socialist ideology *in any way, to turn aside from it in the slightest degree*, means to strengthen bourgeois ideology. There is much talk of spontaneity. But the *spontaneous* development of the working-class movement leads to its subordination to bourgeois ideology, *to its development along the lines of the Credo program*; for the spontaneous working-class movement is trade-unionism, is *Nur-Gewerkschaftlerei*, and trade-unionism means the ideological enslavement of the workers by the bourgeoisie. Hence, our task, the task of Social-Democracy, is *to combat spontaneity, to divert* the working-class movement from this spontaneous, trade-unionist striving to come

16 This does not mean, of course, that the workers have no part in creating such an ideology. They take part, however, not as workers, but as socialist theoreticians, . . . in other words, they take part only when they are able, and to the extent that they are able, more or less, to acquire the knowledge of their age and develop that knowledge. But in order that working men *may succeed in this more often*, every effort must be made to raise the level of the consciousness of the workers in general; it is necessary that the workers do not confine themselves to the artificially restricted limits of "*literature for workers*" but that they learn to an increasing degree to master *general literature*. It would be even truer to say "are not confined," instead of "do not confine themselves," because the workers themselves wish to read and do read all that is written for the intelligentsia, and only a few (bad) intellectuals believe that it is enough "for workers" to be told a few things about factory conditions and to have repeated to them over and over again what has long been known. [*L.*]

under the wing of the bourgeoisie, and to bring it under the wing of revolutionary Social-Democracy.

. . . But why, the reader will ask, does the spontaneous movement, the movement along the line of least resistance, lead to the domination of bourgeois ideology? For the simple reason that bourgeois ideology is far older in origin than socialist ideology, that it is more fully developed, and that it has at its disposal *immeasurably* more means of dissemination.[17] And the younger the socialist movement in any given country, the more vigorously it must struggle against all attempts to entrench non-socialist ideology, and the more resolutely the workers must be warned against the bad counsellors who shout against "overrating the conscious element," etc. The authors of the *Economist* letter, in unison with *Rabocheye Dyelo*, inveigh against the intolerance that is characteristic of the infancy of the movement. To this we reply: Yes, our movement is indeed in its infancy, and in order that it may grow up faster, it must become imbued with intolerance against those who retard its growth by their subservience to spontaneity. Nothing is so ridiculous and harmful as pretending that we are "old hands" who have long ago experienced all the decisive stages of the struggle.

And so, we have become convinced that the fundamental error committed by the "new trend" in Russian Social-Democracy is its bowing to spontaneity and its failure to understand that the spontaneity of the masses demands a high degree of consciousness from us Social-Democrats. The greater the spontaneous upsurge of the masses and the more widespread the movement, the more rapid, incomparably so, the demand for greater consciousness in the theoretical, political, and organizational work of Social-Democracy.

The spontaneous upsurge of the masses in Russia proceeded (and continues) with such rapidity that the young Social-Democrats proved unprepared to meet these gigantic tasks. This unpreparedness is our common misfortune, the misfortune of *all* Russian Social-Democrats. The upsurge of the masses proceeded and spread with uninterrupted continuity; it not only continued in the places where it began, but spread to new localities and to new strata of the population (under the influence of the working-class movement, there

17   It is often said that the working class *spontaneously* gravitates towards socialism. This is perfectly true in the sense that socialist theory reveals the causes of the misery of the working class more profoundly and more correctly than any other theory, and for that reason the workers are able to assimilate it so easily, *provided*, however, this theory does not itself yield to spontaneity, *provided* it subordinates spontaneity to itself. Usually this is taken for granted, but it is precisely this which *Rabocheye Dyelo* forgets or distorts. The working class spontaneously gravitates towards socialism; nevertheless, most widespread (and continuously and diversely revived) bourgeois ideology spontaneously imposes itself upon the working class to a still greater degree. [L.]

was a renewed ferment among the student youth, among the intellectuals generally, and even among the peasantry). Revolutionaries, however, *lagged behind* this upsurge, both in their "theories" and in their activity; they failed to establish a constant and continuous organization capable of *leading* the whole movement. . . .

3 Trade-Unionist Politics and Social-Democratic Politics

A *Political Agitation and Its Restriction by the Economists*

Everyone knows that the economic [18] struggle of the Russian workers underwent widespread development and consolidation simultaneously with the production of "literature" exposing economic (factory and occupational) conditions. The "leaflets" were devoted mainly to the exposure of the factory system, and very soon a veritable passion for exposures was roused among the workers. As soon as the workers realized that the Social-Democratic study circles desired to, and could, supply them with a new kind of leaflet that told the whole truth about their miserable existence, about their unbearably hard toil, and their lack of rights, they began to send in, actually flood us with, correspondence from the factories and workshops. This "exposure literature" created a tremendous sensation, not only in the particular factory exposed in the given leaflet, but in all the factories to which news of the revealed facts spread. And since the poverty and want among the workers in the various enterprises and in the various trades are much the same, the "truth about the life of the workers" stirred *everyone*. Even among the most backward workers, a veritable passion arose to "get into print"—a noble passion for this rudimentary form of war against the whole of the present social system which is based upon robbery and oppression. And in the overwhelming majority of cases these "leaflets" were in truth a declaration of war, because the exposures served greatly to agitate the workers; they evoked among them common demands for the removal of the most glaring outrages and roused in them a readiness to support the demands with strikes. Finally, the employers themselves were compelled to recognize the significance of these leaflets as a declaration of war, so much so that in a large number of cases they did not even wait for the outbreak of hostilities. As is always the case, the mere publi-

18 To avoid misunderstanding, we must point out that here, and throughout this pamphlet, by economic struggle we imply (in keeping with the accepted usage among us) the "practical economic struggle," which Engels, in the passage quoted above, described as "resistance to the capitalists," and which in free countries is known as the organized-labor syndical, or trade union struggle. [*L.*]

cation of these exposures made them effective, and they acquired the significance of a strong moral influence. On more than one occasion, the mere appearance of a leaflet proved sufficient to secure the satisfaction of all or part of the demands put forward. In a word, economic (factory) exposures were and remain an important lever in the economic struggle. And they will continue to retain this significance as long as there is capitalism, which makes it necessary for the workers to defend themselves. Even in the most advanced countries of Europe it can still be seen that the exposure of abuses in some backward trade, or in some forgotten branch of domestic industry, serves as a starting-point for the awakening of class-consciousness, for the beginning of a trade union struggle, and for the spread of socialism.

The overwhelming majority of Russian Social-Democrats have of late been almost entirely absorbed by this work of organizing the exposure of factory conditions. Suffice it to recall *Rabochaya Mysl* to see the extent to which they have been absorbed by it—so much so, indeed, that they have lost sight of the fact that this, *taken by itself*, is in essence still not Social-Democratic work, but merely trade union work. As a matter of fact, the exposures merely dealt with the relations between the workers *in a given trade* and their employers, and all they achieved was that the sellers of labor-power learned to sell their "commodity" on better terms and to fight the purchasers over a purely commercial deal. These exposures could have served (if properly utilized by an organization of revolutionaries) as a beginning and a component part of Social-Democratic activity; but they could also have led (and, given a worshipful attitude towards spontaneity, were bound to lead) to a "purely trade union" struggle and to a non-Social-Democratic working-class movement. Social-Democracy leads the struggle of the working class, not only for better terms for the sale of labor-power, but for the abolition of the social system that compels the propertyless to sell themselves to the rich. Social-Democracy represents the working class, not in its relation to a given group of employers alone, but in its relation to all classes of modern society and to the state as an organized political force. Hence, it follows that not only must Social-Democrats not confine themselves exclusively to the economic struggle, but that they must not allow the organization of economic exposures to become the predominant part of their activities. We must take up actively the political education of the working class and the development of its political consciousness. . . .

The question arises, what should political education consist in? Can it be confined to the propaganda of working-class hostility to the autocracy? Of course not. It is not enough *to explain* to the workers that they are politically oppressed (any more than it is *to explain* to them that their interests are antagonistic to the interests of the employers). Agitation must be conducted with regard to every concrete example of this oppression (as we have begun to carry on agitation based on concrete examples of economic oppression). Inasmuch as *this* oppression affects the most diverse classes of society, inasmuch as it manifests itself in the most varied spheres of life and activity—vocational, civic, personal, family, religious, scientific, etc., etc.—is it not evident that *we shall not be fulfilling our task* of developing the political consciousness of the workers if we do not *undertake* the organization of the *political exposure* of the autocracy *in all its aspects?* In order to carry on agitation based on concrete instances of oppression, these instances must be exposed (as it is necessary to expose factory abuses in order to carry on economic agitation). . . .

Revolutionary Social-Democracy has always included the struggle for reforms as part of its activities. But it utilizes "economic" agitation for the purpose of presenting to the government, not only demands for all sorts of measures, but also (and primarily) the demand that it cease to be an autocratic government. Moreover, it considers it its duty to present this demand to the government on the basis, not of the economic struggle *alone*, but of all manifestations in general of public and political life. In a word, it subordinates the struggle for reforms, as the part to the whole, to the revolutionary struggle for freedom and for socialism. . . .

C Political Exposures and "Training in Revolutionary Activity"

. . . In reality, it is possible to "raise the activity of the working masses" [19] *only* when this activity *is not restricted* to "political agitation on an economic basis." A basic condition for the necessary expansion of political agitation is the organization of *comprehensive* political exposure. *In no way* except by means of such exposures *can* the masses be trained in political consciousness and revolutionary activity. Hence, activity of this kind is one of the most important functions of international Social-Democracy as a whole, for even political freedom does not in any way eliminate exposures; it merely shifts somewhat their sphere of direction. Thus, the German party is especially strengthening its positions and spreading its influence, thanks particularly to the untiring energy with which it is conducting its campaign of political exposure. Working-class consciousness cannot be genuine political consciousness unless the workers are trained to re-

19 A phrase of A.S. Martynov, an Economist-theoretician who argued that the economic struggle, that is, the struggle for better wages and working conditions, was best calculated to increase the political involvement of the worker. [*Ed.*]

spond to *all* cases of tyranny, oppression, violence, and abuse, no matter *what class* is affected—unless they are trained, moreover, to respond from a Social-Democratic point of view and no other. The consciousness of the working masses cannot be genuine class-consciousness, unless the workers learn, from concrete, and above all from topical, political facts and events to observe *every* other social class in *all* the manifestations of its intellectual, ethical, and political life; unless they learn to apply in practice the materialist analysis and the materialist estimate of *all* aspects of the life and activity of *all* classes, strata, and groups of the population. Those who concentrate the attention, observation, and consciousness of the working class exclusively, or even mainly, upon itself alone are not Social-Democrats; for the self-knowledge of the working class is indissolubly bound up, not simply with a fully clear theoretical understanding—or rather, not so much with the theoretical, as with the practical, understanding—of the relationships between *all* the various classes of modern society, acquired through the experience of political life. For this reason the conception of the economic struggle as the most widely applicable means of drawing the masses into the political movement, which our Economists preach, is so extremely harmful and reactionary in its practical significance. In order to become a Social-Democrat, the worker must have a clear picture in his mind of the economic nature and the social and political features of the landlord and the priest, the high state official and the peasant, the student, and the vagabond; he must know their strong and weak points; he must grasp the meaning of all the catchwords and sophisms by which each class and each stratum *camouflages* its selfish strivings and its real "inner workings"; he must understand what interests are reflected by certain institutions and certain laws and how they are reflected. But this "clear picture" cannot be obtained from any book. It can be obtained only from living examples and from exposures that follow close upon what is going on about us at a given moment; upon what is being discussed, in whispers perhaps, by each one in his own way; upon what finds expression in such and such events, in such and such statistics, in such and such court sentences, etc., etc. These comprehensive political exposures are an essential and *fundamental* condition for training the masses in revolutionary activity.

Why do the Russian workers still manifest little revolutionary activity in response to the brutal treatment of the people by the police, the persecution of religious sects, the flogging of peasants, the outrageous censorship, the torture of soldiers, the persecution of the most innocent cultural undertakings, etc.? Is it because the "economic struggle" does not "stimulate" them to this, because such activity does not "promise palpable results," because it produces little that is "positive"? To adopt such an opinion, we repeat, is merely to direct the charge where it does not belong, to blame the working masses for one's own philistinism (or Bernsteinism). We must blame ourselves, our lagging behind the mass movement, for still being unable to organize sufficiently wide, striking, and rapid exposures of all the shameful outrages. When we do that (and we must and can do it), the most backward worker will understand, *or will feel*, that the students and religious sects, the peasants and the authors are being abused and outraged by those same dark forces that are oppressing and crushing him at every step of his life. Feeling that, he himself will be filled with an irresistible desire to react, and he will know how to hoot the censors one day, on another day to demonstrate outside the house of a governor who has brutally suppressed a peasant uprising, on still another day to teach a lesson to the gendarmes in surplices who are doing the work of the Holy Inquisition, etc. As yet we have done very little, almost nothing, *to bring* before the working masses prompt exposures on all possible issues. Many of us as yet do not recognize this as our *bounden duty* but trail spontaneously in the wake of the "drab everyday struggle," in the narrow confines of factory life. Under such circumstances to say that "*Iskra* displays a tendency to minimize the significance of the forward march of the drab everyday struggle in comparison with the propaganda of brilliant and complete ideas" (Martynov) means to drag the Party back, to defend and glorify our unpreparedness and backwardness.

As for calling the masses to action, that will come of itself as soon as energetic political agitation, live and striking exposures come into play. To catch some criminal red-handed and immediately to brand him publicly in all places is of itself far more effective than any number of "calls"; the effect very often is such as will make it impossible to tell exactly who it was that "called" upon the masses and who suggested this or that plan of demonstration, etc. Calls for action, not in the general, but in the concrete, sense of the term can be made only at the place of action; only those who themselves go into action, and do so immediately, can sound such calls. Our business as Social-Democratic publicists is to deepen, expand, and intensify political exposures and political agitation.

D   What Is There in Common between Economism and Terrorism?

. . . [Elsewhere] we cited the opinion of an Economist and of a non-Social-Democratic terrorist, who showed themselves to be accidentally in agreement. Speaking generally, however, there is not an accidental, but a necessary, inherent connection between the two, of which we shall have need to speak later, and which must be mentioned here in connection with the question of education for revolutionary activity. The Economists and the present-day terrorists have one com-

mon root, namely, *subservience to spontaneity*, with which we dealt
in the preceding chapter as a general phenomenon and which we
shall now examine in relation to its effect upon political activity and
the political struggle. At first sight, our assertion may appear paradoxical, so great is the difference between those who stress the "drab
everyday struggle" and those who call for the most self-sacrificing
struggle of individuals. But this is no paradox. The Economists and
the terrorists merely bow to different poles of spontaneity; the Economists bow to the spontaneity of "the labor movement pure and simple," while the terrorists bow to the spontaneity of the passionate
indignation of intellectuals, who lack the ability or opportunity to
connect the revolutionary struggle and the working-class movement
into an integral whole. It is difficult indeed for those who have lost
their belief, or who have never believed, that this is possible, to find
some outlet for their indignation and revolutionary energy other than
terror. Thus, both forms of subservience to spontaneity we have mentioned are nothing but *the beginning of the implementation* of the
notorious *Credo* program: Let the workers wage their "economic
struggle against the employers and the government" . . . and let the
intellectuals conduct the political struggle by their own efforts—with
the aid of terror, of course! This is an absolutely logical and inevitable
conclusion which must be insisted on—*even though those* who are
beginning to carry out this program *do not themselves realize* that it
is inevitable. Political activity has its logic quite apart from the
consciousness of those who, with the best intentions, call either for
terror or for lending the economic struggle itself a political character.
The road to hell is paved with good intentions, and, in this case, good
intentions cannot save one from being spontaneously drawn "along
the line of least resistance," along the line of the *purely bourgeois
Credo* program. Surely it is no accident either that many Russian
liberals—avowed liberals and liberals that wear the mask of Marxism—wholeheartedly sympathize with terror and try to foster the
terrorist moods that have surged up in the present time. . . . Are there
not enough outrages committed in Russian life without special "exci-
tants" having to be invented? On the other hand, is it not obvious
that those who are not, and cannot be, roused to excitement even
by Russian tyranny will stand by "twiddling their thumbs" and
watch a handful of terrorists engaged in single combat with the government? The fact is that the working masses are roused to a high
pitch of excitement by the social evils in Russian life, but we are
unable to gather, if one may so put it, and concentrate all these
drops and streamlets of popular resentment that are brought forth
to a far larger extent than we imagine by the conditions of Russian
life, and that must be combined into a *single* gigantic torrent. That
this can be accomplished is irrefutably proved by the enormous

growth of the working-class movement and the eagerness, noted above, with which the workers clamor for political literature. On the other hand, calls for terror and calls to lend the economic struggle itself a political character are merely two different forms of *evading* the most pressing duty now resting upon Russian revolutionaries, namely, the organization of comprehensive political agitation. . . .

E   The Working Class as Vanguard Fighter for Democracy

We have seen that the conduct of the broadest political agitation and, consequently, of all-sided political exposures is an absolutely necessary and a *paramount* task of our activity, if this activity is to be truly Social-Democratic. However, we arrived at this conclusion *solely* on the grounds of the pressing needs of the working class for political knowledge and political training. But such a presentation of the question is too narrow, for it ignores the general democratic tasks of Social-Democracy, in particular of present-day Russian Social-Democracy. In order to explain the point more concretely we shall approach the subject from an aspect that is "nearest" to the Economist, namely, from the practical aspect. "Everyone agrees" that it is necessary to develop the political consciousness of the working class. The question is, *how* that is to be done and what is required to do it. The economic struggle merely "impels" the workers to realize the government's attitude towards the working class. Consequently, *however much we may try* to "lend the economic struggle itself a political character," we *shall never be able* to develop the political consciousness of the workers (to the level of Social-Democratic political consciousness) by keeping within the framework of the economic struggle, for *that framework is too narrow*. The Martynov formula has some value for us, not because it illustrates Martynov's aptitude for confusing things, but because it pointedly expresses the basic error that all the Economists commit, namely, their conviction that it is possible to develop the class political consciousness of the workers *from within*, so to speak, from their economic struggle, that is, by making this struggle the exclusive (or, at least, the main) starting-point, by making it the exclusive (or, at least, the main) basis. Such a view is radically wrong. Piqued by our polemics against them, the Economists refuse to ponder deeply over the origins of these disagreements, with the result that we simply cannot understand one another. It is as if we spoke in different tongues.

Class political consciousness can be brought to the workers *only from without*, that is, only from outside the economic struggle, from outside the sphere of relations between workers and employers. The sphere from which alone it is possible to obtain this knowledge is the sphere of relationships of *all* classes and strata to the state and the government, the sphere of the interrelations between *all* classes. For that reason, the reply to the question as to what must be done to bring political knowledge to the workers cannot be merely the answer with which, in the majority of cases, the practical workers, especially those inclined towards Economism, mostly content themselves, namely: "To go among the workers." To bring political knowledge to the *workers* the Social-Democrats must *go among all classes of the population*; they must dispatch units of their army *in all directions*. . . .

Let us take the type of Social-Democratic study circle that has become most widespread in the past few years and examine its work. It has "contacts with the workers" and rests content with this, issuing leaflets in which abuses in the factories, the government's partiality towards the capitalists, and the tyranny of the police are strongly condemned. At workers' meetings the discussions never, or rarely ever, go beyond the limits of these subjects. Extremely rare are the lectures and discussions held on the history of the revolutionary movement, on questions of the government's home and foreign policy, on questions of the economic evolution of Russia and of Europe, on the position of the various classes in modern society, etc. As to systematically acquiring and extending contact with other classes of society, no one even dreams of that. In fact, the ideal leader, as the majority of the members of such circles picture him, is something far more in the nature of a trade union secretary than a socialist political leader. For the secretary of any, say English, trade union always helps the workers to carry on the economic struggle, he helps them to expose factory abuses, explains the injustice of the laws and of measures that hamper the freedom to strike and to picket (that is, to warn all and sundry that a strike is proceeding at a certain factory), explains the partiality of arbitration court judges who belong to the bourgeois classes, etc., etc. In a word, every trade union secretary conducts and helps to conduct "the economic struggle against the employers and the government." It cannot be too strongly maintained that *this is still not* Social-Democracy, that the Social-Democrat's ideal should not be the trade union secretary, but *the tribune of the people*, who is able to react to every manifestation of tyranny and oppression, no matter where it appears, no matter what stratum or class of the people it affects; who is able to generalize all these manifestations and produce a single picture of police violence and capitalist exploitation; who is able to take advantage of every event, however small, in order to set forth *before all* his socialist convictions and his democratic demands, in order to clarify for *all* and everyone the world-historic significance of the struggle for the emancipation of the proletariat.

. . . We said that a Social-Democrat, if he really believes it necessary to develop comprehensively the political consciousness of the proletariat, must "go among all classes of the population." This gives rise to the questions: how is this to be done? have we enough forces to do this? is there a basis for such work among all the other classes? will this not mean a retreat, or lead to a retreat, from the class point of view? Let us deal with these questions.

We must "go among all classes of the population" as theoreticians, as propagandists, as agitators, and as organizers. No one doubts that the theoretical work of Social-Democrats should aim at studying all the specific features of the social and political condition of the various classes. But extremely little is done in this direction, as compared with the work that is done in studying the specific features of factory life. In the committees and study circles, one can meet people who are immersed in the study even of some special branch of the metal industry; but one can hardly ever find members of organizations (obliged, as often happens, for some reason or other to give up practical work) who are especially engaged in gathering material on some pressing question of social and political life in our country which could serve as a means for conducting Social-Democratic work among other strata of the population. In dwelling upon the fact that the majority of the present-day leaders of the working-class movement lack training, we cannot refrain from mentioning training in this respect also, for it too is bound up with the Economist conception of "close organic connection with the proletarian struggle." The principal thing, of course, is *propaganda* and *agitation* among all strata of the people. The work of the West-European Social-Democrat is in this respect facilitated by the public meetings and rallies which *all* are free to attend, and by the fact that in parliament he addresses the representatives of *all* classes. We have neither a parliament nor freedom of assembly; nevertheless, we are able to arrange meetings of workers who desire to listen to *a Social-Democrat*. We must also find ways and means of calling meetings of representatives of all social classes that desire to listen to *a democrat*; for he is no Social-Democrat who forgets in practice that "the Communists support every revolutionary movement," that we are obliged for that reason to expound and emphasize *general democratic tasks before the whole people,* without for a moment concealing our socialist convictions. He is no Social-Democrat who forgets in practice his obligation to be *ahead of all* in raising, accentuating, and solving *every* general democratic question. . . .

. . . Have we sufficient forces to direct our propaganda and agitation among *all* social classes? Most certainly. Our Economists, who are frequently inclined to deny this, lose sight of the gigantic progress our movement has made from (approximately) 1894 to 1901. Like real "tail-enders," they often go on living in the bygone stages of the movement's inception. In the earlier period, indeed, we had astonishingly few forces, and it was perfectly natural and legitimate then to devote ourselves exclusively to activities among the workers and to condemn severely any deviation from this course. The entire task then was to consolidate our position in the working class. At the present time, however, gigantic forces have been attracted to the movement. The best representatives of the younger generation of the educated classes are coming over to us. Everywhere in the provinces there are people, resident there by dint of circumstance, who have taken part in the movement in the past or who desire to do so now and who are gravitating towards Social-Democracy (whereas in 1894 one could count the Social-Democrats on the fingers of one's hand). A basic political and organizational shortcoming of our movement is our *inability* to utilize all these forces and give them appropriate work (we shall deal with this more fully in the next chapter). The overwhelming majority of these forces entirely lack the opportunity of "going among the workers," so that there are no grounds for fearing that we shall divert forces from our main work. In order to be able to provide the workers with real, comprehensive, and live political knowledge, we must have "our own people," Social-Democrats, everywhere, among all social strata, and in all positions from which we can learn the inner springs of our state mechanism. Such people are required, not only for propaganda and agitation, but in a still larger measure for organization.

Is there a basis for activity among all classes of the population? Whoever doubts this lags in his consciousness behind the spontaneous awakening of the masses. The working-class movement has aroused and is continuing to arouse discontent in some, hopes of support for the opposition in others, and in still others the realization that the autocracy is unbearable and must inevitably fall. We would be "politicians" and Social-Democrats in name only (as all too often happens in reality) if we failed to realize that our task is to utilize every manifestation of discontent, and to gather and turn to the best account every protest, however small. This is quite apart from the fact that the millions of the laboring peasantry, handicraftsmen, petty artisans, etc., would always listen eagerly to the speech of any Social-Democrat who is at all qualified. Indeed, is there a single social class in which there are no individuals, groups, or circles that are discontented with the lack of rights and with tyranny and, therefore, accessible to the propaganda of Social-Democrats as the spokesmen of the most pressing general democratic needs? To those who desire to have a clear idea of what the political agitation of a Social-Democrat among *all* classes and strata of the population should be like, we would point to *political exposures* in the broad sense of the word as the principal (but, of course, not the sole) form of this agitation. . . .

The ideal audience for political exposure is the working class, which is first and foremost in need of all-round and live political knowledge, and is most capable of converting this knowledge into active struggle, even when that struggle does not promise "palpable results." A tribune for *nation-wide* exposures can be only an all-Russian newspaper.[20] "Without a political organ, a political movement deserving that name is inconceivable in the Europe of today"; in this respect Russia must undoubtedly be included in present-day Europe. The press long ago became a power in our country; otherwise the government would not spend tens of thousands of rubles to bribe it and to subsidize the Katkovs and Meshcherskys.[21] And it is no novelty in autocratic Russia for the underground press to break through the wall of censorship and *compel* the legal and conservative press to speak openly of it. This was the case in the seventies and even in the fifties. How much broader and deeper now are the sections of the people willing to read the illegal underground press, and to learn from it "how to live and how to die," to use the expression of a worker who sent a letter to *Iskra*. Political exposures are as much a declaration of war against the *government* as economic exposures are a declaration of war against the factory owners. The moral significance of this declaration of war will be all the greater, the wider and more powerful the campaign of exposure is, and the more numerous and determined the social *class* that has *declared war in order to begin the war*. Hence, political exposures in themselves serve as a powerful instrument for *disintegrating* the system we oppose, as a means for diverting from the enemy his casual or temporary allies, as a means for spreading hostility and distrust among the permanent partners of the autocracy.

In our time only a party that will *organize* really *nation-wide* exposures can become the vanguard of the revolutionary forces. The word "nation-wide" has a very profound meaning. The overwhelming majority of the nonworking-class exposers (be it remembered that in order to become the vanguard, we must attract other classes) are sober politicians and level-headed men of affairs. They know perfectly well how dangerous it is to "complain" even against a minor official, let alone against the "omnipotent" Russian Government. And they will come *to us* with their complaints only when they see that these complaints can really have effect, and that we represent *a po-*

20 The theme of an all-Russian newspaper dominates the last section of *What Is to Be Done?* and indicates clearly Lenin's concern with matters of practical import in the revolutionary movement. [*Ed.*]

21 M.F. Katkov (1818–1887) and V.P. Meshchersky (1839–1914) were extreme tsarist propagandists whose publications depended heavily on government funds. [*Ed.*]

litical force. In order to become such a force in the eyes of outsiders, much persistent and stubborn work is required *to raise* our own consciousness, initiative, and energy. To accomplish this it is not enough to attach a "vanguard" label to rearguard theory and practice.

But if we have to undertake the organization of a really nation-wide exposure of the government, in what way then will the class character of our movement be expressed?—the overzealous advocate of "close organic contact with the proletarian struggle" will ask us, as indeed he does. The reply is manifold: we Social-Democrats will organize these nation-wide exposures; all questions raised by the agitation will be explained in a consistently Social-Democratic spirit, without any concessions to deliberate or undeliberate distortions of Marxism; the all-round political agitation will be conducted by a party which unites into one inseparable whole the assault on the government in the name of the entire people, the revolutionary training of the proletariat, and the safeguarding of its political independence, the guidance of the economic struggle of the working class, and the utilization of all its spontaneous conflicts with its exploiters which rouse and bring into our camp increasing numbers of the proletariat. . . .

4   The Primitiveness of the Economists and the Organization of the Revolutionaries

. . . [The] assertions, which we have analyzed, that the economic struggle is the most widely applicable means of political agitation and that our task now is to lend the economic struggle itself a political character, etc., express a narrow view, not only of our political, but also of our *organizational* tasks. The "economic struggle against the employers and the government" does not at all require an all-Russian centralized organization, and hence this struggle can never give rise to such an organization as will combine, in one general assault, all the manifestations of political opposition, protest, and indignation, an organization that will consist of professional revolutionaries and be led by the real political leaders of the entire people. This stands to reason. The character of any organization is naturally and inevitably determined by the content of its activity. Consequently . . . the assertions analyzed above [sanctify] and [legitimize] not only narrowness of political activity, but also of organizational work. . . . Yet subservience to spontaneously developing forms of organization, failure to realize the narrowness and primitiveness of our organizational work, of our "handicraft" methods in this most important sphere, failure to realize this, I say, is a veritable ailment from which our movement suffers. It is not an ailment that comes with decline, but one, of course, that comes with growth. It is however at the present time, when the wave of spontaneous indigation, as it were, is sweeping over us, leaders and organizers of the movement, that an irreconcilable struggle must be waged against all defense of backwardness, against any legitimation of narrowness in this matter. It is particularly necessary to arouse in all who participate in practical work, or are preparing to take up that work, discontent with the *amateurism* prevailing among us and an unshakable determination to rid ourselves of it.

A What Is Primitiveness?

We shall try to answer this question by giving a brief description of the activity of a typical Social-Democratic study circle of the period 1894–1901. We have noted that the entire student youth of the period was absorbed in Marxism. Of course, these students were not only, or even not so much, interested in Marxism as a theory; they were interested in it as an answer to the question, "What is to be done?," as a call to take the field against the enemy. These new warriors marched to battle with astonishingly primitive equipment and training. In a vast number of cases they had almost no equipment and absolutely no training. They marched to war like peasants from the plough, armed only with clubs. A students' circle establishes contacts with workers and sets to work, without any connection with the old members of the movement, without any connection with study circles in other districts, or even in other parts of the same city (or in other educational institutions), without any organization of the various divisions of revolutionary work, without any systematic plan of activity covering any length of time. The circle gradually expands its propaganda and agitation; by its activities it wins the sympathies of fairly large sections of workers and of a certain section of the educated strata, which provide it with money and from among whom the "committee" recruits new groups of young people. The attractive power of the committee (or League of Struggle) [22] grows, its sphere of activity becomes wider, and the committee expands this activity quite spontaneously; the very people who a year or a few months previously spoke at the students' circle gatherings and discussed the question, "Whither?," who established and maintained contacts with the workers and wrote and published leaflets, now establish contacts with other groups of revolutionaries, procure literature, set to work to publish a local newspaper, begin to talk of organizing a demonstration, and finally turn to open warfare (which may, according to

22 The "League of Struggle" suggests that Lenin's "typical" case is meant to be autobiographical (see p. 40). [*Ed.*]

circumstances, take the form of issuing the first agitational leaflet or the first issue of a newspaper, or of organizing the first demonstration). Usually the initiation of such actions ends in an immediate and complete fiasco. Immediate and complete, because this open warfare was not the result of a systematic and carefully thought-out and gradually prepared plan for a prolonged and stubborn struggle, but simply the result of the spontaneous growth of traditional study circle work; because, naturally, the police, in almost every case, knew the principal leaders of the local movement, since they had already "gained a reputation" for themselves in their student days, and the police waited only for the right moment to make their raid. They deliberately allowed the study circle sufficient time to develop its work so that they might obtain a palpable *corpus delicti*, and they always permitted several of the persons known to them to remain at liberty "for breeding" (which, as far as I know, is the technical term used both by our people and by the gendarmes). One cannot help comparing this kind of warfare with that conducted by a mass of peasants, armed with clubs, against modern troops. And one can only wonder at the vitality of the movement which expanded, grew, and scored victories despite the total lack of training on the part of the fighters. True, from the historical point of view, the primitiveness of equipment was not only inevitable at first, but *even legitimate* as one of the conditions for the wide recruiting of fighters, but as soon as serious war operations began (and they began in fact with the strikes in the summer of 1896), the defects in our fighting organizations made themselves felt to an ever-increasing degree. The government, at first thrown into confusion and committing a number of blunders (for example, its appeal to the public describing the misdeeds of the socialists, or the banishment of workers from the capitals to provincial industrial centers), very soon adapted itself to the new conditions of the struggle and managed to deploy well its perfectly equipped detachments of *agents provocateurs*, spies, and gendarmes. Raids became so frequent, affected such a vast number of people, and cleared out the local study circles so thoroughly that the masses of the workers lost literally all their leaders, the movement assumed an amazingly sporadic character, and it became utterly impossible to establish continuity and coherence in the work. The terrible dispersion of the local leaders; the fortuitous character of the study circle memberships; the lack of training in, and the narrow outlook on, theoretical, political, and organizational questions were all the inevitable result of the conditions described above. Things have reached such a pass that in several places the workers, because of our lack of self-restraint and the ability to maintain secrecy, begin to lose faith in the intellectuals and to avoid them; the intellectuals, they say, are much too careless and cause police raids! . . .

B Primitiveness and Economism

We must now deal with a question that has undoubtedly come to the mind of every reader. Can a connection be established between primitiveness as growing pains that affect the *whole* movement, and Economism, which is *one* of the currents in Russian Social-Democracy? We think that it can. Lack of practical training, of ability to carry on organizational work is certainly common *to us all*, including those who have from the very outset unswervingly stood for revolutionary Marxism. Of course, were it only lack of practical training, no one could blame the practical workers. But the term "primitiveness" embraces something more than lack of training; it denotes a narrow scope of revolutionary work generally, failure to understand that a good organization of revolutionaries cannot be built on the basis of such narrow activity, and lastly—and this is the main thing—attempts to justify this narrowness and to elevate it to a special "theory," that is, subservience to spontaneity on this question too. Once such attempts were revealed, it became clear that primitiveness is connected with Economism and that we shall never rid ourselves of this narrowness of our organizational activity until we rid ourselves of Economism generally (that is, the narrow conception of Marxist theory, as well as of the role of Social-Democracy and of its political tasks). These attempts manifested themselves in a twofold direction. Some began to say that the working masses themselves have not yet advanced the broad and militant political tasks which the revolutionaries are attempting to "impose" on them; that they must continue to struggle for *immediate* political demands, to conduct "the economic struggle against the employers and the government" (and, naturally, corresponding to this struggle which is "accessible" to the mass movement there must be an organization that will be "accessible" to the most untrained youth). Others, far removed from any theory of "gradualness," said that it is possible and necessary to "bring about a political revolution," but that this does not require building a strong organization of revolutionaries to train the proletariat in steadfast and stubborn struggle. All we need do is to snatch up our old friend, the "accessible" cudgel. To drop [the] metaphor, it means that we must organize a general strike, or that we must stimulate the "spiritless" progress of the working-class movement by means of "excitative terror." Both these trends, the opportunists and the "revolutionists," bow to the prevailing amateurism; neither believes that it can be eliminated; neither understands our primary and imperative practical task to establish *an organization of revolutionaries* capable of lending energy, stability, and continuity to the political struggle. . . .

C *Organization of Workers and Organization of Revolutionaries*

It is only natural to expect that for a Social-Democrat whose conception of the political struggle coincides with the conception of the "economic struggle against the employers and the government," the "organization of revolutionaries" will more or less coincide with the "organization of workers." This, in fact, is what actually happens; so that when we speak of organization, we literally speak in different tongues. I vividly recall, for example, a conversation I once had with a fairly consistent Economist, with whom I had not been previously acquainted. We were discussing the pamphlet, *Who Will Bring About the Political Revolution?* and were soon of a mind that its principal defect was its ignoring of the question of organization. We had begun to assume full agreement between us; but, as the conversation proceeded, it became evident that we were talking of different things. My interlocutor accused the author of ignoring strike funds, mutual benefit societies, etc., whereas I had in mind an organization of revolutionaries as an essential factor in "bringing about" the political revolution. As soon as the disagreement became clear, there was hardly, as I remember, a single question of principle upon which I was in agreement with the Economist!

What was the source of our disagreement? It was the fact that on questions both of organization and of politics the Economists are forever lapsing from Social-Democracy into trade-unionism. The political struggle of Social-Democracy is far more extensive and complex than the economic struggle of the workers against the employers and the government. Similarly (indeed for that reason), the organization of the revolutionary Social-Democratic Party must inevitably be of *a kind different* from the organization of the workers designed for this struggle. The workers' organization must in the first place be a trade union organization; second, it must be as broad as possible; and third, it must be as public as conditions will allow (here, and further on, of course, I refer only to absolutist Russia). On the other hand, the organization of the revolutionaries must consist first and foremost of people who make revolutionary activity their profession (for which reason I speak of the organization of *revolutionaries*, meaning revolutionary Social-Democrats). In view of this common characteristic of the members of such an organization, *all distinctions as between workers and intellectuals*, not to speak of distinctions of trade and profession, in both categories, *must be effaced*. Such an organization must perforce not be very extensive and must be as secret as possible. Let us examine this threefold distinction.

In countries where political liberty exists the distinction between a trade union and a political organization is clear enough, as is the distinction between trade unions and Social-Democracy. The relations between the latter and the former will naturally vary in each country according to historical, legal, and other conditions; they may be more or less close, complex, etc. (in our opinion they should be as close and as little complicated as possible); but there can be no question in free countries of the organization of trade unions coinciding with the organization of the Social-Democratic Party. In Russia, however, the yoke of the autocracy appears at first glance to obliterate all distinctions between the Social-Democratic organization and the workers' associations, since *all* workers' associations and *all* study circles are prohibited, and since the principal manifestation and weapon of the workers' economic struggle—the strike—is regarded as a criminal (and sometimes even as a political!) offense. Conditions in our country, therefore, on the one hand, strongly "impel" the workers engaged in economic struggle to concern themselves with political questions, and, on the other, they "impel" Social-Democrats to confound trade-unionism with Social-Democracy. . . . Indeed, picture to yourselves people who are immersed ninety-nine per cent in "the economic struggle against the employers and the government." Some of them will never, during the *entire* course of their activity (from four to six months), be impelled to think of the need for a more complex organization of revolutionaries. Others, perhaps, will come across the fairly widely distributed Bernsteinian literature, from which they will become convinced of the profound importance of the forward movement of "the drab everyday struggle." Still others will be carried away, perhaps, by the seductive idea of showing the world a new example of "close and organic contact with the proletarian struggle"— contact between the trade union and the Social-Democratic movements. Such people may argue that the later a country enters the arena of capitalism and, consequently, of the working-class movement, the more the socialists in that country may take part in, and support, the trade union movement, and the less the reason for the existence of non-Social-Democratic trade unions. So far the argument is fully correct; unfortunately, however, some go beyond that and dream of a complete fusion of Social-Democracy with trade-unionism. We shall soon see, from the example of the Rules of the St. Petersburg League of Struggle, what a harmful effect such dreams have upon our plans of organization.

The workers' organizations for the economic struggle should be trade union organizations. Every Social-Democratic worker should as far as possible assist and actively work in these organizations. But, while this is true, it is certainly not in our interest to demand that only Social-Democrats should be eligible for membership in the "trade" unions, since that would only narrow the scope of our influence upon the masses. Let every worker who understands the need to unite for the struggle against the employers and the government join the trade unions. The very aim of the trade unions would be impossible to achieve if they did not unite all who have attained at least this elementary degree of understanding, if they were not very *broad* organizations. The broader these organizations, the broader will be our influence over them—an influence due, not only to the "spontaneous" development of the economic struggle, but to the direct and conscious effort of the socialist trade union members to influence their comrades. But a broad organization cannot apply methods of strict secrecy (since this demands far greater training than is required for the economic struggle). How is the contradiction between the need for a large membership and the need for strictly secret methods to be reconciled? How are we to make the trade unions as public as possible? Generally speaking, there can be only two ways to this end: either the trade unions become legalized (in some countries this preceded the legalization of the socialist and political unions), or the organization is kept secret, but so "free" and amorphous, *lose* ["loose"] as the Germans say, that the need for secret methods becomes almost negligible as far as the bulk of the members is concerned. . . .

What, properly speaking, should be the functions of the organization of revolutionaries? We shall deal with this question in detail. First, however, let us examine a very typical argument advanced by our terrorist, who (sad fate!) in this matter also is a next-door neighbor to the Economist. *Svoboda*, a journal published for workers, contains in its first issue an article entitled "Organization," the author of which tries to defend his friends, the Economist workers of Ivanovo-Voznesensk. He writes:

"It is bad when the masses are mute and unenlightened, when the movement does not come from the rank and file. For instance, the students of a university town leave for their homes during the summer and other holidays, and immediately the workers' movement comes to a standstill. Can a workers' movement which has to be pushed on from outside be a real force? No, indeed. . . . It has not yet learned to walk; it is still in leading-strings. So it is in all matters. The students go off, and everything comes to a standstill. The most capable are seized; the cream is skimmed—and the milk turns sour. If the 'committee' is arrested, everything comes to a standstill until a new one can be formed. And one never knows what sort of committee will be set up next—it may be nothing like the former. The first said one thing; the second may say the very opposite. Continuity between yesterday and tomorrow is broken; the experience of the past does not serve as a guide for the future. And all because no roots have been struck in depth, in the masses; the work is carried on not by a hundred fools, but by a dozen wise men. A dozen wise men can be wiped out at a snap, but when the organization embraces masses, everything proceeds from them, and nobody, however he tries, can wreck the cause."

The facts are described correctly. The picture of our amateurism is well drawn. But the conclusions are worthy of *Rabochaya Mysl*, both as regards their stupidity and their lack of political tact. They represent the height of stupidity, because the author confuses the philosophical and social-historical question of the "depth" of the "roots" of the movement with the technical and organizational question of the best method in combating the gendarmes. They represent the height of political tactlessness, because, instead of appealing from bad leaders to good leaders, the author appeals from the leaders in general to the "masses." This is as much an attempt to drag us back organizationally as the idea of substituting excitative terrorism for political agitation drags us back politically. Indeed, I am experiencing a veritable *embarras de richesses*, and hardly know where to begin to disentangle the jumble offered up by *Svoboda*. For clarity, let me begin by citing an example. Take the Germans. It will not be denied, I hope, that theirs is a mass organization, that in Germany everything proceeds from the masses, that the working-class movement there has learned to walk. Yet observe how these millions value their "dozen" tried political leaders, how firmly they cling to them. Members of the hostile parties in parliament have often taunted the socialists by exclaiming: "Fine democrats you are indeed! Yours is a working-class movement only in name; in actual fact the same clique of leaders is always in evidence . . . year in and year out, and that goes on for decades. Your supposedly elected workers' deputies are more permanent than the officials appointed by the Emperor!" But the Germans only smile with contempt at these demagogic attempts to set the "masses" against the "leaders," to arouse bad and ambitious instincts in the former, and to rob the movement of its solidity and stability by undermining the confidence of the masses in their "dozen wise men." Political thinking is sufficiently developed among the Germans, and they have accumulated sufficient political experience to understand that without the "dozen" tried and talented leaders (and talented men are not born by the hundreds), professionally trained, schooled by long experience, and working in perfect harmony, no class in modern society can wage a determined struggle. The Germans too have had demagogues in their ranks who have flattered the "hundred fools," exalted them above the "dozen wise men," extolled the "horny hand" of the masses, and . . . have spurred them on to reckless "revolutionary" action and sown distrust towards the firm and steadfast leaders. It was only by stubbornly and relentlessly combating all demagogic elements within the socialist movement that German socialism has managed to grow and become as strong as it is. Our wiseacres, however, at a time when Russian Social-Democracy is passing through a crisis entirely due to the lack of sufficiently trained, developed, and experienced leaders to guide the spontaneously awakening masses, cry out with the profundity of fools: "It is a bad business when the movement does not proceed from the rank and file."

"A committee of students is of no use; it is not stable." Quite true. But the conclusion to be drawn from this is that we must have a committee of professional *revolutionaries*, and it is immaterial whether a student or a worker is capable of becoming a professional revolutionary. The conclusion you draw, however, is that the working-class movement must not be pushed on from outside! In your political innocence you fail to notice that you are playing into the hands of our Economists and fostering our amateurism. Wherein, may I ask, did our students "push on" our workers? *In the sense* that the student brought to the worker the fragments of political knowledge he himself possesses, the crumbs of socialist ideas he has managed to acquire (for the principal intellectual diet of the present-day student, legal Marxism, could furnish only the rudiments, only scraps of knowledge). There has never been too much of *such* "pushing on from outside"; on the contrary, there has so far been all too little of it in our movement, for we have been stewing too assiduously in our own juice; we have bowed far too slavishly to the elementary "economic struggle of the workers against the employers and the government." We professional revolutionaries must and will make it our business to engage in *this kind* of "pushing on" a hundred times more forcibly than we have done hitherto. But the very fact that you select so hideous a phrase ʌs "pushing on from outside"—a phrase which cannot but rouse in the workers (at least in the workers who are as unenlightened as you yourselves) a sense of distrust towards *all* who bring them political knowledge and revolutionary experience from outside, which cannot but rouse in them an instinctive desire to resist *all* such people—proves you to be *demagogues*, and demagogues are the worst enemies of the working class.

And, please—don't hasten howling about my "uncomradely methods" of debating. I have not the least desire to doubt the purity of your intentions. As I have said, one may become a demagogue out of sheer political innocence. But I have shown that you have descended to demagogy, and I will never tire of repeating that demagogues are the worst enemies of the working class. The worst enemies, because they arouse base instincts in the masses, because the unenlightened worker is unable to recognize his enemies in men who represent themselves, and sometimes sincerely so, as his friends. The worst enemies, because in the period of disunity and vacillation, when our movement is just beginning to take shape, nothing is easier than to employ demagogic methods to mislead the masses, who can realize their error only later by bitter experience. . . .

"A dozen wise men can be more easily wiped out than a hundred fools." This wonderful truth (for which the hundred fools will always applaud you) appears obvious only because in the very midst of the argument you have skipped from one question to another. You began by talking and continued to talk of the unearthing of a "committee," of the unearthing of an "organization," and now you skip to the question of unearthing the movement's "roots" in their "depths." The fact is, of course, that our movement cannot be unearthed, for the very reason that it has countless thousands of roots deep down among the masses; but that is not the point at issue. As far as "deep roots" are concerned, we cannot be "unearthed" even now, despite all our amateurism, and yet we all complain, and cannot but complain, that the "*organizations*" are being unearthed and as a result it is impossible to maintain continuity in the movement. But since you raise the question of *organizations* being unearthed and persist in your opinion, I assert that it is far more difficult to unearth a dozen wise men than a hundred fools. This position I will defend, no matter how much you instigate the masses against me for my "antidemocratic" views, etc. As I have stated repeatedly, by "wise men," in connection with organization, I mean *professional revolutionaries*, irrespective of whether they have developed from among students or working men. I assert: (1) that no revolutionary movement can endure without a stable organization of leaders maintaining continuity; (2) that the broader the popular mass drawn spontaneously into the struggle, which forms the basis of the movement and participates in it, the more urgent the need for such an organization, and the more solid this organization must be (for it is much easier for all sorts of demagogues to side-track the more backward sections of the masses); (3) that such an organization must consist chiefly of people professionally engaged in revolutionary activity; (4) that in an autocratic state, the more we *confine* the membership of such an organization to people who are professionally engaged in revolutionary activity and who have been professionally trained in the art of combating the political police, the more difficult will it be to unearth the organization; and (5) the *greater* will be the number of people from the working class and from the other social classes who will be able to join the movement and perform active work in it.

I invite our Economists, terrorists, and "Economists-terrorists" to confute these propositions. At the moment, I shall deal only with the last two points. The question as to whether it is easier to wipe out "a dozen wise men" or "a hundred fools" reduces itself to the question, above considered, whether it is possible to have a mass *organization* when the maintenance of strict secrecy is essential. We can never give a mass organization that degree of secrecy without which there can be no question of persistent and continuous struggle against the government. To concentrate all secret functions in the hands of as small a number of professional revolutionaries as possible does not mean that the latter will "do the thinking for all" and that the rank and file will not take an active part in the *movement*. On the contrary, the membership will promote increasing numbers of the professional revolutionaries from its ranks; for it will know that it is not enough for a few students and for a few working men waging the economic struggle to gather in order to form a "committee," but that it takes years to train oneself to be a professional revolutionary; and the rank and file will "think," not only of amateurish methods, but of such training. Centralization of the secret functions of the *organization* by no means implies centralization of all the functions of the *movement*. Active participation of the widest masses in the illegal press will not diminish because a "dozen" professional revolutionaries centralize the secret functions connected with this work; on the contrary, it will *increase* tenfold. In this way, and in this way alone, shall we ensure that reading the illegal press, writing for it, and to some extent even distributing it, will *almost cease to be secret work*, for the police will soon come to realize the folly and impossibility of judicial and administrative red-tape procedure over every copy of a publication that is being distributed in the thousands. This holds not only for the press, but for every function of the movement, even for demonstrations. The active and widespread participation of the masses will not suffer; on the contrary, it will benefit by the fact that a "dozen" experienced revolutionaries, trained professionally no less than the police, will centralize all the secret aspects of the work—the drawing up of leaflets, the working out of approximate plans; and the appointing of bodies of leaders for each urban district, for each factory district, and for each educational institution, etc. (I know that exception will be taken to my "undemocratic" views, but I shall reply below fully to this anything but intelligent objection.) Centralization of the most secret functions in an organization of revolutionaries will not diminish, but rather increase the extent and enhance the quality of the activity of a large number of other organizations that are intended for a broad public and are therefore as loose and as nonsecret as possible, such as workers' trade unions; workers' self-education circles and circles for reading illegal literature; and socialist, as well as democratic, circles among *all* other sections of the population; etc., etc. We must have such circles, trade unions, and organizations everywhere in *as large a number as possible* and with the widest variety of functions; but it would be absurd and harmful *to confound* them with the organization of *revolutionaries,* to efface the border-line between them, to make still more hazy the all too faint recognition of the fact that in order to "serve" the mass movement we must have people who will devote themselves exclusively to Social-Democratic activities, and that such people must *train* themselves patiently and steadfastly to be professional revolutionaries.

Yes, this recognition is incredibly dim. Our worst sin with regard to organization consists in the fact that *by our primitiveness we have lowered the prestige of revolutionaries in Russia.* A person who is flabby and shaky on questions of theory, who has a narrow outlook, who pleads the spontaneity of the masses as an excuse for his own sluggishness, who resembles a trade union secretary more than a spokesman of the people, who is unable to conceive of a broad and bold plan that would command the respect even of opponents, and who is inexperienced and clumsy in his own professional art—the art of combating the political police—such a man is not a revolutionary, but a wretched amateur!

Let no active worker take offense at these frank remarks, for as far as insufficient training is concerned, I apply them first and foremost to myself. I used to work in a study circle that set itself very broad, all-embracing tasks; and all of us, members of that circle, suffered painfully and acutely from the realization that we were acting as amateurs at a moment in history when we might have been able to say, varying a well-known statement: "Give us an organization of revolutionaries, and we will overturn Russia!" The more I recall the burning sense of shame I then experienced, the bitterer become my feelings towards these pseudo-Social-Democrats whose preachings "bring disgrace on the calling of a revolutionary," who fail to understand that our task is not to champion the degrading of the revolutionary to the level of an amateur, but *to raise* the amateurs to the level of revolutionaries.

D The Scope of Organizational Work

. . . The scope of revolutionary work is too narrow, as compared with the breadth of the spontaneous basis of the movement. It is too hemmed in by the wretched theory of "economic struggle against the employers and the government." Yet, at the present time, not only Social-Democratic political agitators, but Social-Democratic organizers must "go among all classes of the population." [23] There is hardly a single practical worker who will doubt that the Social-Democrats could distribute the thousand and one minute functions of their organizational work among individual representatives of the most varied classes. Lack of specialization is one of the most serious defects of . . .

---

23 Thus, an undoubted revival of the democratic spirit has recently been observed among persons in military service, partly as a consequence of the more frequent street battles with "enemies" like workers and students. As soon as our available forces permit, we must without fail devote the most serious attention to propaganda and agitation among soldiers and officers, and to the creation of "military organizations" affiliated to our Party. [L.]

our technique, about which [just and bitter complaints are made]. The smaller each separate "operation" in our common cause, the more people we can find capable of carrying out such operations (people who, in the majority of cases, are completely incapable of becoming professional revolutionaries); the more difficult will it be for the police to "net" all these "detail workers," and the more difficult will it be for them to frame up, out of an arrest for some petty affair, a "case" that would justify the government's expenditure on "security." As for the number of people ready to help us, we referred in the preceding chapter to the gigantic change that has taken place in this respect in the last five years or so. On the other hand, in order to unite all these tiny fractions into one whole, in order not to break up the movement while breaking up its functions, and in order to imbue the people who carry out the minute functions with the conviction that their work is necessary and important, without which conviction they will never do the work,[24] it is necessary to have a strong organization of tried revolutionaries. The more secret such an organization is, the stronger and more widespread will be the confidence in the Party. As we know, in time of war, it is not only of the utmost importance to imbue one's own army with confidence in its strength, but it is important also to convince the enemy and all *neutral* elements of this strength; friendly neutrality may sometimes decide the issue. If such an organization existed, one built up on a firm theoretical foundation and possessing a Social-Democratic organ, we should have no reason to fear that the movement might be diverted from its path by the numerous "outside" elements that are attracted to it. (On the contrary, it is precisely at the present time, with amateurism prevalent, that we see many Social-Democrats leaning towards the *Credo* and only imagining that they are Social-Democrats.) In a word, specializa-

24 I recall that once a comrade told me of a factory inspector who wanted to help the Social-Democrats, and actually did, but complained bitterly that he did not know whether his "information" reached the proper revolutionary center, how much his help was really required, and what possibilities there were for utilizing his small and petty services. Every practical worker can, of course, cite many similar instances in which our primitiveness deprived us of allies. These services, each "small" in itself, but invaluable when taken in the mass, could and would be rendered to us by office employees and officials, not only in factories, but in the postal service, on the railways, in the Customs, among the nobility, among the clergy, and in *every* other walk of life, including even the police and the Court! Had we a real party, a real militant organization of revolutionaries, we would not make undue demands on every one of these "aides," we would not hasten always and invariably to bring them right into the very heart of our "illegality," but, on the contrary, we would husband them most carefully and would even train people especially for such functions, bearing in mind that many students could be of much greater service to the Party as "aides" holding some official post than as "short-term" revolutionaries. But, I repeat, only an organization that is firmly established and has no lack of active forces would have the right to apply such tactics. [*L.*]

tion necessarily presupposes centralization, and in turn imperatively calls for it.

To be fully prepared for his task, the worker-revolutionary must likewise become a professional revolutionary. Hence [it] is wrong [to say] that since the worker spends eleven and a half hours in the factory, the brunt of all other revolutionary functions (apart from agitation) "*must necessarily* fall mainly upon the shoulders of an extremely small force of intellectuals." But this condition does not obtain out of sheer "necessity." It obtains because we are backward, because we do not recognize our duty to assist every capable worker to become a *professional* agitator, organizer, propagandist, literature distributor, etc., etc. In this respect, we waste our strength in a positively shameful manner; we lack the ability to husband that which should be tended and reared with special care. Look at the Germans: their forces are a hundredfold greater than ours. But they understand perfectly well that really capable agitators, etc., are not often promoted from the ranks of the "average." For this reason they immediately try to place every capable working man in conditions that will enable him to develop and apply his abilities to the fullest: he is made a professional agitator; he is encouraged to widen the field of his activity, to spread it from one factory to the whole of the industry, from a single locality to the whole country. He acquires experience and dexterity in his profession; he broadens his outlook and increases his knowledge; he observes at close quarters the prominent political leaders from other localities and of other parties; he strives to rise to their level and combine in himself the knowledge of the working-class environment and the freshness of socialist convictions with professional skill, without which the proletariat *cannot* wage a stubborn struggle against its excellently trained enemies. In this way alone do the working masses produce men of the stamp of Bebel and Auer.[25] But what is to a great extent automatic in a politically free country must in Russia be done deliberately and systematically by our organizations. A worker-agitator who is at all gifted and "promising" *must not be left* to work eleven hours a day in a factory. We must arrange that he be maintained by the Party; that he may go underground in good time; that he change the place of his activity, if he is to enlarge his experience, widen his outlook, and be able to hold out for at least a few years in the struggle against the gendarmes. As the spontaneous rise of their movement becomes broader and deeper, the working-class masses promote from their ranks not only an increasing number of talented agitators, but also talented organizers, propagandists, and "practical workers" in the best sense of the term (of whom there are

25 August Bebel (1840–1913), founder and patriarch of the German Social-Democratic Party. Ignaz Auer (1846–1907), official of the German Social-Democratic Party. [*Ed.*]

so few among our intellectuals who, for the most part, in the Russian manner, are somewhat careless and sluggish in their habits). When we have forces of specially trained worker-revolutionaries who have gone through extensive preparation (and, of course, revolutionaries "of all arms of the service"), no political police in the world will then be able to contend with them, for these forces, boundlessly devoted to the revolution, will enjoy the boundless confidence of the widest masses of the workers. We are directly *to blame* for doing too little to "stimulate" the workers to take this path, common to them and to the "intellectuals," of professional revolutionary training, and for all too often dragging them back by our silly speeches about what is "accessible" to the masses of the workers, to the "average workers," etc.

In this, as in other respects, the narrow scope of our organizational work is without a doubt due directly to the fact (although the overwhelming majority of the "Economists" and the novices in practical work do not perceive it) that we restrict our theories and our political tasks to a narrow field. Subservience to spontaneity seems to inspire a fear of taking even one step away from what is "accessible" to the masses, a fear of rising too high above mere attendance on the immediate and direct requirements of the masses. Have no fear, gentlemen! Remember that we stand so low on the plane of organization that the very idea that we *could* rise *too* high is absurd!

E *"Conspiratorial" Organization and "Democratism"*

Yet there are many people among us who are so sensitive to the "voice of life" that they fear it more than anything in the world and charge the adherents of the views here expounded with following a Narodnaya Volya [26] line, with failing to understand "democratism," etc. These accusations . . . need to be dealt with. . . . [They] are the result of a twofold misunderstanding. First, the history of the revolutionary movement is so little known among us that the name "Narodnaya Volya" is used to denote any idea of a militant centralized organization which declares determined war upon tsarism. But the magnificent organization that the revolutionaries had in the seventies, and that should serve us as a model, was not established by the Narodnaya Volya, but by the *Zemlya i Volya*,[27] which split up into the Chernyi

---

26 Narodnaya Volya (Peoples' Will), a tightly-knit, conspiratorial, terrorist organization of the 1870's and 1880's whose major aim was to assassinate high Russian officials, particularly the Tsar. After a number of attempts, the organization succeeded in killing Alexander II in 1883. [*Ed.*]

27 Zemlya i Volya (Land and Liberty), the organizational forerunner of Narodnaya Volya. Its basic premise was that revolutionary hopes for Russia lay in the peasantry. The failure of the peasantry to revolt led to the breakup of the organization in 1879. [*Ed.*]

Peredel [28] and the Narodnaya Volya. Consequently, to regard a militant revolutionary organization as something specifically Narodnaya Volya in character is absurd both historically and logically; for *no* revolutionary trend, if it seriously thinks of struggle, can dispense with such an organization. The mistake the Narodnaya Volya committed was not in striving to enlist *all* the discontented in the organization and to direct this organization to resolute struggle against the autocracy; on the contrary, that was its great historical merit. The mistake was in relying on a theory which in substance was not a revolutionary theory at all, and the Narodnaya Volya members either did not know how, or were unable, to link their movement inseparably with the class struggle in the developing capitalist society. Only a gross failure to understand Marxism . . . could prompt the opinion that the rise of a mass, spontaneous working-class movement *relieves* us of the duty of creating as good an organization of revolutionaries as the Zemlya i Volya had, or, indeed, an incomparably better one. On the contrary, this movement *imposes* the duty upon us; for the spontaneous struggle of the proletariat will not become its genuine "class struggle" until this struggle is led by a strong organization of revolutionaries.

Second, many people . . . misunderstand the polemics that Social-Democrats have always waged against the "conspiratorial" view of the political struggle. We have always protested, and will, of course, continue to protest against *confining* the political struggle to conspiracy. But this does not, of course, mean that we deny the need for a strong revolutionary organization. Thus, [we have elsewhere given] . . . a description . . . (as a Social-Democratic ideal) of an organization so strong as to be able to "resort to . . . rebellion" and to every "other form of attack," in order to "deliver a smashing blow against absolutism." In *form* such a strong revolutionary organization in an autocratic country may also be described as a "conspiratorial" organization, because the French word *conspiration* is the equivalent of the Russian word *zagovor* ("conspiracy"), and such an organization must have the utmost secrecy. Secrecy is such a necessary condition for this kind of organization that all the other conditions (number and selection of members, functions, etc.) must be made to conform to it. It would be extremely naïve indeed, therefore, to fear the charge that we Social-Democrats desire to create a conspiratorial organization. Such a charge should be as flattering to every opponent of Economism as the charge of following a Narodnaya Volya line.

The objection may be raised that such a powerful and strictly secret organization, which concentrates in its hands all the threads of

28 Chernyi Peredel (General Redistribution or Black Repartition), the second offspring, along with Narodnaya Volya, of Zemlya i Volya. Its policies were far more peaceful than those of its terrorist sibling, favoring primarily land reform for the peasantry. [*Ed.*]

secret activities, an organization which of necessity is centralized, may too easily rush into a premature attack, may thoughtlessly intensify the movement before the growth of political discontent, the intensity of the ferment and anger of the working class, etc., have made such an attack possible and necessary. Our reply to this is: Speaking abstractly, it cannot be denied, of course, that a militant organization *may* thoughtlessly engage in battle, which *may* end in a defeat entirely avoidable under other conditions. But we cannot confine ourselves to abstract reasoning on such a question, because every battle bears within itself the abstract possibility of defeat, and there is no way of *reducing* this possibility except by organized preparation for battle. If, however, we proceed from the concrete conditions at present obtaining in Russia, we must come to the positive conclusion that a strong revolutionary organization is absolutely necessary precisely for the purpose of giving stability to the movement and of *safeguarding* it against the possibility of making thoughtless attacks. Precisely at the present time, when no such organization yet exists, and when the revolutionary movement is rapidly and spontaneously growing, we *already observe* two opposite extremes (which, as is to be expected, "meet"). These are: the utterly unsound Economism and the preaching of moderation, and the equally unsound "excitative terror," which strives "artificially to call forth symptoms of the end of the movement, which is developing and strengthening itself, when this movement is as yet nearer to the start than to the end." . . . And . . . *there exist* Social-Democrats who give way to both these extremes. This is not surprising, for, apart from other reasons, the "economic struggle against the employers and the government" can *never* satisfy revolutionaries, and opposite extremes will therefore always appear here and there. Only a centralized, militant organization that consistently carries out a Social-Democratic policy, that satisfies, so to speak, all revolutionary instincts and strivings, can safeguard the movement against making thoughtless attacks and prepare attacks that hold out the promise of success.

A further objection may be raised, that the views on organization here expounded contradict the "democratic principle." Now, while the earlier accusation was specifically Russian in origin, this one is *specifically foreign* in character. And only an organization abroad (the Union of Russian Social-Democrats Abroad) was capable of giving its Editorial Board instructions like the following:

"*Organizational Principle.* In order to secure the successful development and unification of Social-Democracy, the broad democratic principle of Party organization must be emphasized, developed, and fought for; this is particularly necessary in view of the anti-democratic tendencies that have revealed themselves in the ranks of our Party."

. . . Everyone will probably agree that "the broad democratic principle" presupposes the two following conditions: first, full publicity, and second, election to all offices. It would be absurd to speak of democracy without publicity, moreover, without a publicity that is not limited to the membership of the organization. We call the German Socialist Party a democratic organization because all its activities are carried out publicly; even its party congresses are held in public. But no one would call an organization democratic that is hidden from every one but its members by a veil of secrecy. What is the use, then, of advancing "the *broad* democratic principle" when the fundamental condition for this principle *cannot be fulfilled* by a secret organization? "The broad principle" proves itself simply to be a resounding but hollow phrase. Moreover, it reveals a total lack of understanding of the urgent tasks of the moment in regard to organization. Everyone knows how great the lack of secrecy is among the "broad" masses of our revolutionaries. . . . Yet, persons who boast a keen "sense of realities" *urge*, in a situation like this, not the strictest secrecy and the strictest (consequently, more restricted) selection of members, but "the *broad* democratic principle"! This is what you call being wide of the mark.

Nor is the situation any better with regard to the second attribute of democracy, the principle of election. In politically free countries, this condition is taken for granted. "They are members of the Party who accept the principles of the Party program and render the Party all possible support," reads Clause 1 of the Rules of the German Social-Democratic Party. Since the entire political arena is as open to the public view as is a theater stage to the audience, this acceptance or non-acceptance, support or opposition, is known to all from the press and from public meetings. Everyone knows that a certain political figure began in such and such a way, passed through such and such an evolution, behaved in a trying moment in such and such a manner, and possesses such and such qualities; consequently, *all* party members, knowing all the facts, can elect or refuse to elect this person to a particular party office. The general control (in the literal sense of the term) exercised over every act of a party man in the political field brings into existence an automatically operating mechanism which produces what in biology is called the "survival of the fittest." "Natural selection" by full publicity, election, and general control provides the assurance that, in the last analysis, every political figure will be "in his proper place," do the work for which he is best fitted by his powers and abilities, feel the effects of his mistakes on himself, and prove before all the world his ability to recognize mistakes and to avoid them.

Try to fit this picture into the frame of our autocracy! Is it conceivable in Russia for all "who accept the principles of the Party program and render the Party all possible support" to control every action of the revolutionary working in secret? Is it possible for all to elect one of these revolutionaries to any particular office, when, in the very interests of the work, the revolutionary *must* conceal his identity from nine out of ten of these "all"? Reflect somewhat over the real meaning of the high-sounding phrases . . . and you will realize that "broad democracy" in Party organization, amidst the gloom of the autocracy and the domination of gendarmerie, is nothing more than a *useless and harmful toy*. It is a useless toy because, in point of fact, no revolutionary organization has ever practiced, or could practice, *broad* democracy, however much it may have desired to do so. It is a harmful toy because any attempt to practice "the broad democratic principle" will simply facilitate the work of the police in carrying out large-scale raids, will perpetuate the prevailing primitiveness, and will divert the thoughts of the practical workers from the serious and pressing task of training themselves to become professional revolutionaries to that of drawing up detailed "paper" rules for election systems. Only abroad, where very often people with no opportunity for conducting really active work gather, could this "playing at democracy" develop here and there, especially in small groups. . . .

. . . The only serious organizational principle for the active workers of our movement should be the strictest secrecy, the strictest selection of members, and the training of professional revolutionaries. Given these qualties, something even more than "democratism" would be guaranteed to us, namely, complete, comradely, mutual confidence among revolutionaries. This is absolutely essential for us, because there can be no question of replacing it by general democratic control in Russia. It would be a great mistake to believe that the impossibility of establishing real "democratic" control renders the members of the revolutionary organization beyond control altogether. They have not the time to think about toy forms of democratism (democratism within a close and compact body of comrades in which complete, mutual confidence prevails), but they have a lively sense of their *responsibility*, knowing as they do from experience that an organization of real revolutionaries will stop at nothing to rid itself of an unworthy member. Moreover, there is a fairly well-developed public opinion in Russian (and international) revolutionary circles which has a long history behind it, and which sternly and ruthlessly punishes every departure from the duties of comradeship (and "democratism," real and not toy democratism, certainly forms a component part of the conception of comradeship). Take all this into consideration and you will realize that this talk and these resolutions about "antidemocratic tendencies" have the musty odor of the playing at generals which is indulged in abroad. . . .

Conclusion

The history of Russian Social-Democracy can be distinctly divided into three periods:

The first period embraces about ten years, approximately from 1884 to 1894. This was the period of the rise and consolidation of the theory and program of Social-Democracy. The adherents of the new trend in Russia were very few in number. Social-Democracy existed without a working-class movement, and as a political party it was at the embryonic stage of development.

The second period embraces three or four years—1894–1898. In this period Social-Democracy appeared on the scene as a social movement, as the upsurge of the masses of the people, as a political party. This is the period of its childhood and adolescence. The intelligentsia was fired with a vast and general zeal for struggle against Narodism and for going among the workers; the workers displayed a general enthusiasm for strike action. The movement made enormous strides. The majority of the leaders were young people who had not reached "the age of thirty-five." . . . Owing to their youth, they proved to be untrained for practical work and they left the scene with astonishing rapidity. But in the majority of cases the scope of their activity was very wide. Many of them had begun their revolutionary thinking as adherents of Narodnaya Volya. Nearly all had in their early youth enthusiastically worshipped the terrorist heroes. It required a struggle to abandon the captivating impressions of those heroic traditions, and the struggle was accompanied by the breaking off of personal relations with people who were determined to remain loyal to the Narodnaya Volya and for whom the young Social-Democrats had profound respect. The struggle compelled the youthful leaders to educate themselves, to read illegal literature of every trend, and to study closely the questions of legal Narodism. Trained in this struggle, Social-Democrats went into the working-class movement without "for a moment" forgetting either the theory of Marxism, which brightly illumined their path, or the task of overthrowing the autocracy. The formation of the Party in the spring of 1898 was the most striking and at the same time the *last* act of the Social-Democrats of this period.

The third period, as we have seen, was prepared in 1897 and it definitely cut off the second period in 1898 (1898–?). This was a period of disunity, dissolution, and vacillation. During adolescence a youth's voice breaks. And so, in this period, the voice of Russian Social-Democracy began to break, to strike a false note. . . . But it was only the leaders who wandered about separately and drew back; the movement itself continued to grow, and it advanced with enormous strides. The proletarian struggle spread to new strata of the workers and extended to the whole of Russia, at the same time indirectly stimulating the revival of the democratic spirit among the students and among other sections of the population. The political conscious-ness of the leaders, however, capitulated before the breadth and power of the spontaneous upsurge; among the Social-Democrats, another type had become dominant—the type of functionaries, trained almost exclusively on "legal Marxist" literature, which proved to be all the more inadequate the more the spontaneity of the masses demanded political consciousness on the part of the leaders. The leaders not only lagged behind in regard to theory ("freedom of criticism") and practice ("primitiveness"), but they sought to justify their backward-ness by all manner of high-flown arguments. Social-Democracy was degraded to the level of trade-unionism. . . . The *Credo* program be-gan to be put into operation, especially when the "primitive methods" of the Social-Democrats caused a revival of revolutionary non-Social-Democratic tendencies. . . .

The spirit of this third period was exemplified by those who were able properly to express the disunity and vacillation, the readiness to make concessions to "criticism," to "Economism," and to terrorism. Not the lofty contempt for practical work displayed by some wor-shipper of the "absolute" is characteristic of this period, but the com-bination of pettifogging practice and utter disregard for theory. It was not so much in the direct rejection of "grandiose phrases" that the heroes of this period engaged as in their vulgarization. Scientific socialism ceased to be an integral revolutionary theory and became a hodgepodge "freely" diluted with the content of every new German textbook that appeared; the slogan "class struggle" did not impel to broader and more energetic activity but served as a balm, since "the economic struggle is inseparably linked with the political strug-gle"; the idea of a party did not serve as a call for the creation of a militant organization of revolutionaries, but was used to justify some sort of "revolutionary bureaucracy" and infantile playing at "demo-cratic" forms.

When the third period will come to an end and the fourth (now heralded by many portents) will begin we do not know. We are passing from the sphere of history to the sphere of the present and, partly, of the future. But we firmly believe that the fourth period will lead to the consolidation of militant Marxism, that Russian Social-Democracy will emerge from the crisis in the full flower of manhood, that the opportunist rearguard will be "replaced" by the genuine vanguard of the most revolutionary class.

In the sense of calling for such a "replacement" and by way of summing up what has been expounded above, we may meet the question, What is to be done?, with the brief reply:

Put an End to the Third Period.

TWO TACTICS OF SOCIAL-DEMOCRACY IN THE DEMOCRATIC REVOLUTION (1905)

Preface

IN A revolutionary period it is very difficult to keep abreast of events which provide an astonishing amount of new material for an appraisal of the tactical slogans of revolutionary parties. The present pamphlet was written before the Odessa events.[1] . . . Revolution undoubtedly teaches with a rapidity and thoroughness which appear incredible in peaceful periods of political development. And, what is particularly important, it teaches not only the leaders, but the masses as well.

There is not the slightest doubt that the revolution will teach Social-Democratism to the masses of the workers in Russia. The revolution will confirm the program and tactics of Social-Democracy in actual practice by demonstrating the true nature of the various classes of society, by demonstrating the bourgeois character of our democracy and the real aspirations of the peasantry, who, while being revolutionary in the bourgeois-democratic sense, carry within themselves not the idea of "socialization," but the seeds of a new class struggle between the peasant bourgeoisie and the rural proletariat. The old illusions of the old Narodism,[2] so clearly visible, for instance, in the draft program of the "Socialist-Revolutionary Party"[3] on the

1 The reference is to the mutiny on the armored cruiser *Potemkin*. [*L.*]

2 Narodism (Populism), a generic term referring to the revolutionary movement of the eighteen-sixties and seventies which placed its faith in the "people," that is, in the peasantry as the force that would transform Russia. The organizational outgrowths of the movement included Zemlya i Volya, Narodnaya Volya, and Chernyi Peredel (see note on p. 13). [*Ed.*]

3 The Socialist-Revolutionary Party formed in 1901 carried on the heritage of the Populist movement. It was a peasant-oriented revolutionary party which, by 1917, had grown to mass proportions. The SR's played a significant role in the Provisional Government. Their left-wing, however, supported the Bolshevik seizure of power in 1917. [*Ed.*]

question of the development of capitalism in Russia, the question of the democratic character of our "society," and the question of the significance of a complete victory of a peasant uprising—all these illusions will be completely and mercilessly dispelled by the revolution. For the first time, the various classes will be given their real political baptism. These classes will emerge from the revolution with a definite political physiognomy, for they will have revealed themselves not only in the program and tactical slogans of their ideologists but also in open political action by the masses.

Undoubtedly, the revolution will teach us, and will teach the masses of the people. But the question that now confronts a militant political party is: shall we be able to teach the revolution anything? Shall we be able to make use of the correctness of our Social-Democratic doctrine, of our bond with the only thoroughly revolutionary class, the proletariat, to put a proletarian imprint on the revolution, to carry the revolution to a real and decisive victory, not in word but in deed, and to paralyze the instability, half-heartedness, and treachery of the democratic bourgeoisie?

It is to this end that we must direct all our efforts, and the achievement of that end will depend, on the one hand, on the accuracy of our appraisal of the political situation and the correctness of our tactical slogans, and, on the other hand, on whether these slogans will be backed by the real fighting strength of the masses of the workers. All the usual, regular, and current work of all organizations and groups of our Party, the work of propaganda, agitation, and organization, is directed towards strengthening and expanding the ties with the masses. Necessary as this work always is it cannot be considered adequate at a time of revolution. In such a contingency the working class feels an instinctive urge for open revolutionary action, and we must learn to set the aims of this action correctly, and then make these aims as widely known and understood as possible. It must not be forgotten that the current pessimism about our ties with the masses very often serves as a screen for bourgeois ideas regarding the proletariat's role in the revolution. Undoubtedly, we still have a great deal to do in educating and organizing the working class; but now the gist of the matter is: where should we place the main political emphasis in this work of education and organization? On the trade unions and legally existing associations, or on an insurrection, on the work of creating a revolutionary army and a revolutionary government? Both serve to educate and organize the working class. Both are, of course, necessary. But in the present revolution the problem amounts to this: which is to be emphasized in the work of educating and organizing the working class, the former or the latter?

The outcome of the revolution depends on whether the working class will play the part of a subsidiary to the bourgeoisie, a subsidiary that is powerful in the force of its onslaught against the autocracy, but impotent politically, or whether it will play the part of leader of the people's revolution. . . .

. . . It is exceptionally important at the present time for Social-Democrats to have correct tactical slogans for leading the masses. There is nothing more dangerous in a revolutionary period than belittling the importance of tactical slogans that are sound in principle. . . . On the contrary, preparation of correct tactical decisions is of immense importance for a party which desires to lead the proletariat in the spirit of sound Marxist principles, and not merely to lag in the wake of events. In the resolutions of the Third Congress of the Russian Social-Democratic Labor Party and of the Conference of the section that has split away from the Party,[4] we have the most precise, most carefully considered, and most complete expression of tactical views—views not casually expressed by individual writers, but accepted by the responsible representatives of the Social-Democratic proletariat.[5] Our Party is in advance of all the others, for it has a precise and generally accepted program. It must also set the other parties an example of a principled attitude to its tactical resolutions, as distinct from the opportunism of the democratic *Osvobozhdeniye* [6] bourgeoisie, and the revolutionary phrase-mongering of the Socialist-Revolutionaries. It was only during the revolution that they suddenly thought of coming forward with a "draft" program and of investigating for the first time whether it is a bourgeois revolution that is going on before their eyes.

That is why we think it the most urgent task of the revolutionary Social-Democrats carefully to study the tactical resolutions of the Third Congress of the Russian Social-Democratic Labor Party and of the Conference, define what deviations from the principles of Marxism they contain, and get a clear understanding of the Social-Democratic proletariat's concrete tasks in a democratic revolution.

4 The Third Congress of the Russian Social-Democratic Labor Party (London, May 1905) was attended only by Bolsheviks, while Mensheviks alone participated in the "Conference" (Geneva, time the same). In the present pamphlet the latter are frequently referred to as the "new-*Iskra* group" because, while continuing to publish *Iskra*, they declared through their then adherent Trotsky that there was a gulf between the old and the new *Iskra*. [*Lenin's note to the 1907 edition.*]

5 Lenin rather grandly and purposely overemphasizes the significance of the "Third Congress," which was, in fact, a semilegal rump session of Lenin's supporters summoned by Lenin himself to strengthen his hold over his portion of the Russian Social-Democratic Party. [*Ed.*]

6 *Osvobozhdeniye (Emancipation)*, the title of a journal edited by P.B. Struve and published outside of Russia from 1902 to 1905. The primary aim of the journal and the Emancipation League (founded in 1903) was to provide a constitutional monarchy for Russia. [*Ed.*]

It is to this work that the present pamphlet is devoted. The testing
of our tactics from the standpoint of the principles of Marxism and
of the lessons of the revolution is also necessary for those who really
desire to pave the way for unity of tactics as a basis for the future
complete unity of the whole Russian Social-Democratic Labor Party,
and not to confine themselves solely to verbal admonitions.

1 An Urgent Political Question

At the present revolutionary juncture the question of the convocation of a popular constituent assembly is on the order of the day.
Opinions are divided as to how this question should be solved. Three
political trends are taking shape. The tsarist government admits the
necessity of convening representatives of the people, but under no
circumstances does it want to permit their assembly to be popular
and constituent. It seems willing to agree, if we are to believe the
newspaper reports . . . , to a consultative assembly, which is to be
elected without freedom of agitation, and by a system of restrictive
qualifications or one that is restricted to certain social estates. Since
it is led by the Social-Democratic Party, the revolutionary proletariat
demands complete transfer of power to a constituent assembly, and
for this purpose strives to achieve not only universal suffrage and
complete freedom to conduct agitation, but also the immediate overthrow of the tsarist government and its replacement by a provisional
revolutionary government. Finally, the liberal bourgeoisie, expressing its wishes through the leaders of the so-called "Constitutional-
Democratic Party," does not demand the overthrow of the tsarist
government; nor does it advance the slogan of a provisional government, or insist on real guarantees that the elections will be absolutely
free and fair and that the assembly of representatives will be genuinely popular and genuinely constituent. As a matter of fact, the
liberal bourgeoisie, the only serious social support of the *Osvobozhdeniye* trend, is striving to effect as peaceful a deal as possible between
the Tsar and the revolutionary people, a deal, moreover, that would
give a maximum of power to itself, the bourgeoisie, and a minimum
to the revolutionary people—the proletariat and the peasantry.

Such is the political situation at the present time. Such are the
three main political trends, corresponding to the three main social
forces in contemporary Russia. We have already shown on more
than one occasion . . . how the *Osvobozhdeniye* group use pseudo-
democratic phrases to cover up their half-hearted, or, to put it more
bluntly and plainly, their treacherous, perfidious policy towards the
revolution. Let us now see how the Social-Democrats appraise the
tasks of the moment. Excellent material for this is provided by the two

resolutions quite recently adopted by the Third Congress of the Russian Social-Democratic Labor Party and by the "Conference" of the Party's break-away section. The question as to which of these resolutions appraises the political situation more correctly and defines the tactics of the revolutionary proletariat more correctly is of enormous importance, and every Social-Democrat who is anxious to perform his duties intelligently as propagandist, agitator, and organizer must study this question with the closest attention, disregarding all irrelevant considerations.

By the Party's tactics we mean the Party's political conduct, or the character, direction, and methods of its political activity. Tactical resolutions are adopted by Party congresses in order to define accurately the political conduct of the Party as a whole with regard to new tasks or in view of a new political situation. Such a new situation has been created by the revolution that has started in Russia, that is, the complete, decisive, and open break between the overwhelming majority of the people and the tsarist government. The new question concerns the practical methods of convening a genuinely popular and a genuinely constituent assembly (the theoretical question concerning' such an assembly was officially settled by Social-Democracy long ago, before all other parties, in its Party program). Since the people have broken with the government and the masses realize the necessity of setting up a new order, the party which set itself the object of overthrowing the government must necessarily consider what government should replace the old, deposed government. There arises a *new* question concerning a provisional revolutionary government. To give a complete answer to this question the party of the class-conscious proletariat must clarify: 1) the *significance* of a provisional revolutionary government in the revolution now in progress and in the entire struggle of the proletariat in general; 2) its *attitude* towards a provisional revolutionary government; 3) the precise conditions of Social-Democratic *participation* in this government; 4) the conditions under which pressure is to be brought to bear on this government from *below*, that is, in the event of there being no Social-Democrats in it. Only when all these questions have been clarified, will the political conduct of the party in this sphere be principled, clear, and firm.

Let us now consider how the resolution of the Third Congress of the Russian Social-Democratic Labor Party answers these questions. The following is the full text of the resolution:

"*Resolution on a Provisional Revolutionary Government*
"Whereas:
1) both the direct interests of the proletariat and those of its struggle for the ultimate aims of socialism require the fullest possible

measure of political freedom, and, consequently, the replacement of
the autocratic form of government by the democratic republic;

2) the establishment of a democratic republic in Russia is possible only as a result of a victorious popular insurrection whose organ
will be a provisional revolutionary government, which alone will be
capable of securing complete freedom of agitation during the election campaign and of convening a constituent assembly that will really
express the will of the people, an assembly elected on the basis of
universal and equal suffrage, direct elections and secret ballot;

3) under the present social and economic order this democratic
revolution in Russia will not weaken but strengthen the domination
of the bourgeoisie which at a certain juncture will inevitably go to
any length to take away from the Russian proletariat as many of the
gains of the revolutionary period as possible:

"Therefore the Third Congress of the Russian Social-Democratic Labor Party resolves:

a) that it is necessary to spread among the working class a
concrete idea of the most probable course of the revolution, and of
the necessity, at a certain moment in the revolution, for the appearance of a provisional revolutionary government, from which the
proletariat will demand the realization of all the immediate political
and economic demands of our program (the minimum program);

b) that subject to the alignment of forces and other factors which
cannot be exactly predetermined, representatives of our Party may
participate in the provisional revolutionary government for the purpose of waging a relentless struggle against all counter-revolutionary
attempts and of defending the independent interests of the working
class;

c) that an indispensable condition for such participation is strict
control of its representatives by the Party, and the constant safeguarding of the independence of Social-Democracy which strives for
the complete socialist revolution, and, consequently, is irreconcilably
opposed to all the bourgeois parties;

d) that irrespective of whether participation of Social-Democrats in the provisional revolutionary government is possible or not,
we must propagate among the broadest sections of the proletariat the
idea that the armed proletariat, led by the Social-Democratic Party,
must bring to bear constant pressure on the provisional government
for the purpose of defending, consolidating, and extending the gains
of the revolution."

2   What Can We Learn From the Resolution of the Third Congress of the R.S.D.L.P on a Provisional Revolutionary Government?

As is evident from its title, the resolution of the Third Congress of the Russian Social-Democratic Labor Party is devoted wholly and exclusively to the question of a provisional revolutionary government. Hence, the participation of Social-Democrats in a provisional revolutionary government constitutes part of that question. On the other hand, the resolution deals with a provisional revolutionary government only, and with nothing else; consequently, the question of the "conquest of power" in general, etc., does not at all come into the picture. Was the Congress right in eliminating this and similar questions? Undoubtedly it was, because the political situation in Russia does not by any means turn such questions into immediate issues. On the contrary, the whole people have now raised the issue of the overthrow of the autocracy and the convocation of a constituent assembly. Party congresses should take up and decide not issues which this or that writer has happened to mention opportunely or inopportunely, but such as are of vital political importance by reason of the prevailing conditions and the objective course of social development.

Of what signficance is a provisional revolutionary government in the present revolution and in the general struggle of the proletariat? The resolution of the Congress explains this by pointing at the very outset to the need for the "fullest possible measure of political liberty," both from the standpoint of the immediate interests of the proletariat and from the standpoint of the "final aims of socialism." And complete political liberty requires that the tsarist autocracy be replaced by a democratic republic, as our Party program has already recognized. The stress the Congress resolution lays on the slogan of a democratic republic is necessary both as a matter of logic and in point of principle, for it is precisely complete liberty that the proletariat, as the foremost champion of democracy, is striving to attain. Moreover, it is all the more advisable to stress this at the present time, because right now the monarchists, namely, the so-called Constitutional-"Democratic" or the *Osvobozhdeniye* Party in our country, are flying the flag of "democracy." To establish a republic it is absolutely necessary to have an assembly of people's representatives, which must be a popular (that is, elected on the basis of universal and equal suffrage, direct elections, and secret ballot) and constituent assembly. That is exactly what is recognized further on in the Congress resolution. However the resolution does not stop at that. To establish a new order "that will really express the will of the people" it is not enough to term a representative assembly a constituent assembly.

Such an assembly must have the authority and power to "constitute." Conscious of this the Congress resolution does not confine itself to the formal slogan of a "constituent assembly," but adds the material conditions which alone will enable such an assembly to carry out its task properly. This specification of the conditions enabling an assembly that is constituent in name to become one in fact is imperatively necessary, for, as we have more than once pointed out, the liberal bourgeoisie, as represented by the Constitutional-Monarchist Party, is deliberately distorting the slogan of a popular constituent assembly and reducing it to a hollow phrase.

The Congress resolution states that a provisional revolutionary government *alone*, and one, moreover, that will be the organ of a victorious popular insurrection, can secure full freedom to conduct an election campaign and convene an assembly that will really express the will of the people. Is this thesis correct? Whoever took it into his head to dispute it would have to assert that it is possible for the tsarist government not to side with reaction, that it is capable of being neutral during the elections, that it will see to it that the will of the people really finds expression. Such assertions are so absurd that no one would venture to defend them openly; but they are being surreptitiously smuggled in under liberal colors by our *Osvobozhdeniye* gentry. Somebody must convene the constituent assembly; somebody must guarantee the freedom and fairness of the elections; somebody must invest such an assembly with full power and authority. Only a revolutionary government, which is the organ of the insurrection, can desire this in all sincerity, and be capable of doing all that is required to achieve this. The tsarist government will inevitably oppose it. A liberal government which has come to terms with the Tsar and which does not rely in full on the popular uprising cannot sincerely desire this, and could not accomplish it, even if it most sincerely desired to. Therefore, the Congress resolution gives the only correct and entirely consistent democratic slogan.

But an appraisal of a provisional revolutionary government's significance would be incomplete and wrong if the class nature of the democratic revolution were lost sight of. The resolution, therefore, adds that a revolution will strengthen the rule of the bourgeoisie. This is inevitable under the present, that is, capitalist, social and economic, system. And the strengthening of the bourgeoisie's rule over a proletariat that has secured some measure of political liberty must inevitably lead to a desperate struggle between them for power, must lead to desperate attempts on the part of the bourgeoisie "to take away from the proletariat the gains of the revolutionary period." Therefore, the proletariat, which is in the van of the struggle for democracy and heads that struggle, must not for a single moment forget the new antagonisms inherent in bourgeois democracy, or the new struggle.

Thus, the section of the resolution which we have just reviewed fully appraises the significance of a provisional revolutionary government both in its relation to the struggle for freedom and for a republic, in its relation to a constituent assembly, and in its relation to the democratic revolution which clears the ground for a new class struggle.

The next question is that of the proletariat's attitude in general towards a provisional revolutionary government. The Congress resolution answers this first of all by directly advising the Party to spread among the working class the conviction that a provisional revolutionary government is necessary. The working class must be made aware of this necessity. Whereas the "democratic" bourgeoisie keeps in the background the question of the overthrow of the tsarist government, we must bring it to the fore and insist on the need for a provisional revolutionary government. Moreover, we must outline for such a government a program of action that will conform with the objective conditions of the present period and with the aims of proletarian democracy. This program is the *entire* minimum program of our Party, the program of the immediate political and economic reforms which, on the one hand, can be fully realized on the basis of the existing social and economic relationships and, on the other hand, are requisite for the next step forward, for the achievement of socialism.

Thus, the resolution clearly defines the nature and the purpose of a provisional revolutionary government. In origin and basic character such a government must be the organ of a popular uprising. Its formal purpose must be to serve as an instrument for convening a national constituent assembly. The content of its activities must be the implementation of the minimum program of proletarian democracy, the only program capable of safeguarding the interests of a people that has risen in revolt against the autocracy.

It might be argued that a provisional government, being only provisional, cannot carry out a constructive program that has not yet received the approval of the entire people. Such an argument would merely be the sophistry of reactionaries and "absolutists." To refrain from carrying out a constructive program means tolerating the existence of the feudal regime of a corrupt autocracy. Such a regime could be tolerated only by a government of traitors to the cause of the revolution, but not by a government that is the organ of a popular insurrection. It would be mockery for anyone to propose that we should refrain from exercising freedom of assembly pending the confirmation of such freedom by a constituent assembly, on the plea that the constituent assembly might not confirm freedom of assembly. It is equal mockery to object to the immediate execution of the minimum program by a provisional revolutionary government.

Finally, we will note that the resolution, by making implementation of the minimum program the provisional revolutionary government's task, eliminates the absurd and semianarchist ideas of giving immediate effect to the maximum program, and the conquest of power for a socialist revolution. The degree of Russia's economic development (an objective condition) and the degree of class-consciousness and organization of the broad masses of the proletariat (a subjective condition inseparably bound up with the objective condition) make the immediate and complete emancipation of the working class impossible. Only the most ignorant people can close their eyes to the bourgeois nature of the democratic revolution which is now taking place; only the most naïve optimists can forget how little as yet the masses of the workers are informed about the aims of socialism and the methods of achieving it. We are all convinced that the emancipation of the working classes must be won by the working classes themselves; a socialist revolution is out of the question unless the masses become class-conscious and organized, trained and educated in an open class struggle against the entire bourgeoisie. Replying to the anarchists' objections that we are putting off the socialist revolution, we say: we are not putting it off, but are taking the first step towards it in the only possible way, along the only correct path, namely, the path of a democratic republic. Whoever wants to reach socialism by any other path than that of political democracy will inevitably arrive at conclusions that are absurd and reactionary both in the economic and the political sense. If any workers ask us at the appropriate moment why we should not go ahead and carry out our maximum program we shall answer by pointing out how far from socialism the masses of the democratically-minded people still are, how undeveloped class antagonisms still are, and how unorganized the proletarians still are. Organize hundreds of thousands of workers all over Russia; get the millions to sympathize with our program! Try to do this without confining yourselves to high-sounding but hollow anarchist phrases—and you will see at once that achievement of this organization and the spread of this socialist enlightenment depend on the fullest possible achievement of democratic transformations.

Let us continue. Once the significance of a provisional revolutionary government and the attitude of the proletariat towards it have been made clear, the following question arises: is it permissible for us to participate in such a government (action from above) and, if so, under what conditions? What should be our action from below? The resolution supplies precise answers to both these questions. It emphatically declares that it is *permissible* in principle for Social-Democrats to participate in a provisional revolutionary government (during the period of a democratic revolution, the period of struggle for a republic). By this declaration we once and for all dissociate ourselves both from the anarchists, who answer this question in the negative in principle, and from the tail-enders [7] in Social-Democracy . . . who have *tried to frighten* us with the prospect of a situation in which it might prove necessary for us to participate in such a government. By this declaration the Third Congress of the Russian Social-Democratic Labor Party irrevocably rejected the new-*Iskra* idea that the participation of Social-Democrats in a provisional revolutionary government would be a variety of Millerandism, that it is impermissible in principle, as sanctifying the bourgeois order, etc.

It stands to reason, however, that the question of permissibility in principle does not solve the question of practical expediency. Under what conditions is this new form of struggle—the struggle "from above," recognized by the Party Congress—expedient? It goes without saying that it is impossible at present to speak of concrete conditions, such as the relation of forces, etc., and the resolution, naturally, refrains from defining these conditions in advance. No intelligent person would venture at present to predict anything on this subject. What we can and must do is to determine the nature and aim of our participation. That is what is done in the resolution, which points to the two purposes for which we participate: 1) a relentless struggle against counter-revolutionary attempts, and 2) the defense of the independent interests of the working class. At a time when the liberal bourgeoisie is beginning to talk with such zeal about the psychology of reaction . . . in an attempt to frighten the revolutionary people and induce it to show compliance towards the autocracy—at such a time it is particularly appropriate for the party of the proletariat to call attention to the task of waging a real war against counter-revolution. In the final analysis force alone settles the great problems of political liberty and the class struggle, and it is our business to prepare and organize this force and to employ it actively, not only for defense but also for attack. The long reign of political reaction in Europe, which has lasted almost uninterruptedly since the days of the Paris Commune, has made us too greatly accustomed to the idea that action can proceed only "from below," has too greatly inured us to seeing only defensive struggles. We have now undoubtedly entered a new era—a period of political upheavals and revolutions has begun. In a period such as that which Russia is now passing through, it is impermissible to confine ourselves to old, stereotyped formulas. We must propagate the idea of action from above, must prepare for the most energetic, offensive action, and must study the conditions for and forms of such action. The Congress resolution brings two of these conditions into the forefront: one refers to the formal aspect of Social-Democratic participation in a provisional revolutionary government

---

7 Tail-enders are those who lag behind events. The Russian word for tail is "*khovst*" and "khovstism" is one of Lenin's favorite targets. [*Ed.*]

(strict control by the Party over its representatives), the other, to the nature of such participation (without for an instant losing sight of the aim of effecting a complete socialist revolution).

Having thus explained all aspects of the Party's policy with regard to action "from above"—this new, hitherto almost unprecedented method of struggle—the resolution also provides for the eventuality that we shall not be able to act from above. We must in any case exercise pressure on the provisional revolutionary government from below. To be able to exercise this pressure from below, the proletariat must be armed—for in a revolutionary situation matters develop with exceptional rapidity to the stage of open civil war—and must be led by the Social-Democratic Party. The object of its armed pressure is "to defend, consolidate, and extend the gains of the revolution," that is, those gains which from the standpoint of the proletariat's interests must consist in fulfilling the whole of our minimum program. . . .

6 Whence Is the Proletariat Threatened with the Danger of Finding Itself with Its Hands Tied in the Struggle Against the Inconsistent Bourgeoisie?

Marxists are absolutely convinced of the bourgeois character of the Russian revolution. What does that mean? It means that the democratic reforms in the political system, and the social and economic reforms that have become a necessity for Russia, do not in themselves imply the undermining of capitalism, the undermining of bourgeois rule; on the contrary, they will, for the first time, really clear the ground for a wide and rapid, European, and not Asiatic, development of capitalism; they will, for the first time, make it possible for the bourgeoisie to rule as a class. The Socialist-Revolutionaries cannot grasp this idea, for they do not know the ABC of the laws of development of commodity and capitalist production; they fail to see that even the complete success of a peasant insurrection, even the redistribution of the whole of the land in favor of the peasants and in accordance with their desires ("general redistribution" or something of the kind) will not destroy capitalism at all, but will, on the contrary, give an impetus to its development and hasten the class disintegration of the peasantry itself. Failure to grasp this truth makes the Socialist-Revolutionaries unconscious ideologists of the petty bourgeoisie. Insistence on this truth is of enormous importance for Social-Democracy not only from the standpoint of theory but also from that of practical politics, for it follows therefrom that complete class independence of the party of the proletariat in the present "general democratic" movement is an indispensable condition.

But it does not by any means follow that a *democratic* revolution (bourgeois in its social and economic essence) would not be of *enormous* interest to the proletariat. It does not follow that the democratic revolution could not take place both in a form advantageous mainly to the big capitalist, the financial magnate, and the "enlightened" landlord, and in a form advantageous to the peasant and the worker.

The new-*Iskra* [8] group completely misunderstands the meaning and significance of bourgeois revolution as a category. The idea that is constantly running through their arguments is that a bourgeois revolution is one that can be advantageous only to the bourgeoisie. And yet nothing can be more erroneous than such an idea. A bourgeois revolution is a revolution which does not depart from the framework of the bourgeois, that is, capitalist, socio-economic system. A bourgeois revolution expresses the needs of capitalist development, and, far from destroying the foundations of capitalism, it effects the contrary—it broadens and deepens them. This revolution, therefore, expresses the interests not only of the working class but of the entire bourgeoisie as well. Since the rule of the bourgeoisie over the working class is inevitable under capitalism, it can well be said that a bourgeois revolution expresses the interests not so much of the proletariat as of the bourgeoisie. But it is quite absurd to think that a bourgeois revolution does not at all express proletarian interests. This absurd idea boils down either to the hoary Narodnik theory that a bourgeois revolution runs counter to the interests of the proletariat, and that, therefore, we do not need bourgeois political liberty; or to anarchism which denies any participation of the proletariat in bourgeois politics, in a bourgeois revolution, and in bourgeois parliamentarism. From the standpoint of theory this idea disregards the elementary propositions of Marxism concerning the inevitability of capitalist development on the basis of commodity production. Marxism teaches us that at a certain stage of its development a society which is based on commodity production and has commercial intercourse with civilized capitalist nations must inevitably take the road of capitalism. Marxism has irrevocably broken with the Narodnik and anarchist gibberish that Russia, for instance, can by-pass capitalist development, escape from capitalism, or skip it in some way other than that of the class struggle, on the basis and within the framework of this same capitalism.

All these principles of Marxism have been proved and explained in minute detail in general and with regard to Russia in particular. And from these principles it follows that the idea of seeking salvation for the working class in anything save the further development

8 See note on p. 38. [*Ed.*]

of capitalism is *reactionary*. In countries like Russia the working class suffers not so much from capitalism as from the insufficient development of capitalism. The working class is, therefore, *most certainly interested* in the broadest, freest, and most rapid development of capitalism. The removal of all the remnants of the old order which hamper the broad, free, and rapid development of capitalism is of absolute *advantage* to the working class. The bourgeois revolution is precisely an upheaval that most resolutely sweeps away survivals of the past, survivals of the serf-owning system (which include not only the autocracy but the monarchy as well), and most fully guarantees the broadest, freest, and most rapid development of capitalism.

That is why a *bourgeois* revolution is *in the highest degree advantageous to the proletariat*. A bourgeois revolution is *absolutely* necessary in the interests of the proletariat. The more complete, determined, and consistent the bourgeois revolution, the more assured will the proletariat's. struggle be against the bourgeoisie and for socialism. Only those who are ignorant of the ABC of scientific socialism can regard this conclusion as new, strange, or paradoxical. And from this conclusion, among other things, follows the thesis that *in a certain sense* a bourgeois revolution is *more advantageous* to the proletariat than to the bourgeoisie. This thesis is unquestionably correct in the following sense: it is to the advantage of the bourgeoisie to rely on certain remnants of the past, as against the proletariat, for instance, on the monarchy, the standing army, etc. It is to the advantage of the bourgeoisie for the bourgeois revolution not to sweep away all remnants of the past too resolutely, but keep some of them, that is, for this revolution not to be fully consistent, not to be complete, and not to be determined and relentless. Social-Democrats often express this idea somewhat differently by stating that the bourgeoisie betrays its own self, that the bourgeoisie betrays the cause of liberty, that the bourgeoisie is incapable of being consistently democratic. It is of greater advantage to the bourgeoisie for the necessary changes in the direction of bourgeois democracy to take place more slowly, more gradually, more cautiously, less resolutely, by means of reforms and not by means of revolution; for these changes to spare the "venerable" institutions of the serf-owning system (such as the monarchy) as much as possible; for these changes to develop as little as possible the independent revolutionary activity, initiative, and energy of the common people, that is, the peasantry and especially the workers, for otherwise it will be easier for the workers, as the French say, "to change the rifle from one shoulder to the other," that is, to turn against the bourgeoisie the weapon the bourgeois revolution will supply them with, the liberty the revolution will bring, and the democratic institutions that will spring up on the ground cleared of the serf-owning system.

On the other hand, it is more advantageous to the working class for the necessary changes in the direction of bourgeois democracy to take place by way of revolution and not by way of reform, because the way of reform is one of delay, procrastination, the painfully slow decomposition of the putrid parts of the national organism. It is the proletariat and the peasantry that suffer first of all and most of all from that putrefaction. The revolutionary path is one of rapid amputation, which is the least painful to the proletariat, the path of the immediate removal of what is putrescent, the path of least compliance with and consideration for the monarchy and the abominable, vile, rotten, and noxious institutions that go with it.

So it is not only because of the censorship, not only "for fear of the Jews," that our bourgeois-liberal press deplores the possibility of the revolutionary path, fears the revolution, tries to frighten the Tsar with the bogey of revolution, seeks to avoid revolution, and grovels and toadies for the sake of miserable reforms as the foundation of the reformist path. . . . The very position the bourgeoisie holds as a class in capitalist society inevitably leads to its inconsistency in a democratic revolution. The very position the proletariat holds as a class compels it to be consistently democratic. The bourgeoisie looks backward in fear of democratic progress which threatens to strengthen the proletariat. The proletariat has nothing to lose but its chains, but with the aid of democratism it has the whole world to win. That is why the more consistent the bourgeois revolution is in achieving its democratic transformations, the less will it limit itself to what is of advantage exclusively to the bourgeoisie. The more consistent the bourgeois revolution, the more does it guarantee the proletariat and the peasantry the benefits accruing from the democratic revolution.

Marxism teaches the proletarian not to keep aloof from the bourgeois revolution, not to be indifferent to it, not to allow the leadership of the revolution to be assumed by the bourgeoisie but, on the contrary, to take a most energetic part in it, to fight most resolutely for consistent proletarian democratism, for the revolution to be carried to its conclusion. We cannot get out of the bourgeois-democratic boundaries of the Russian revolution, but we can vastly extend these boundaries, and within these boundaries we can and must fight for the interests of the proletariat, for its immediate needs and for conditions that will make it possible to prepare its forces for the future complete victory. There is bourgeois democracy and bourgeois democracy. The Zemstvo [9] monarchist who favors an upper chamber and

9   Zemstvos were representative organs of "local self-government" created in 1864 by Tsar Alexander II. Property qualifications and indirect voting ensured the dominance of the wealthy in the zemstvos. Nevertheless these institutions became centers for the liberal movement in tsarist Russia. [Ed.]

"asks" for universal suffrage, while secretly, on the sly, striking a bargain with tsarism for a docked constitution, is a bourgeois democrat too. The peasant, who has taken up arms against the landlords and the government officials, and with a "naïve republicanism" proposes "to send the Tsar packing," is also a bourgeois democrat. There are bourgeois-democratic regimes like the one in Germany, and also like the one in England; like the one in Austria and also like those in America and Switzerland. He would be a fine Marxist indeed who in a period of democratic revolution failed to see this difference between the degrees of democratism and the difference between its forms, and confined himself to "clever" remarks to the effect that, after all, this is "a bourgeois revolution," the fruit of "bourgeois revolution." . . .

The . . . new-Iskrists' . . . [point] to the danger of Social-Democracy tying its own hands in the struggle against the inconsistent policy of the bourgeoisie, of its becoming dissolved in bourgeois democracy. The thought of this danger pervades all specifically new-Iskrist literature; it lies at the very heart of the principle involved in our Party split (ever since the bickering in the split was completely overshadowed by the turn towards Economism). Without any equivocation we admit that this danger really exists, that just at the present time, at the height of the Russian revolution, this danger has become particularly grave. The pressing and extremely responsible duty that devolves on all of us theoreticians or—as I should prefer to say of myself—publicists of Social-Democracy is to find out *from what direction* this danger actually threatens. For the source of our disagreement is not a dispute as to whether such a danger exists, but the dispute as to whether it is caused by the so-called tail-ism of the "Minority" or the so-called revolutionism of the "Majority."

To remove all misinterpretations and misunderstandings let us first of all note that the danger to which we are referring lies not in the subjective, but in the objective aspect of the matter, not in the formal stand which Social-Democracy will take in the struggle, but in the material outcome of the entire present revolutionary struggle. The question is not whether this or that Social-Democratic group will want to dissolve in bourgeois democracy, or whether they realize that they are doing so. Nobody suggests that. We do not suspect any Social-Democrat of harboring such a desire, and this is not at all a matter of desire. Nor is it a question of whether this or that Social-Democratic group will formally retain its separate identity, individuality, and independence of bourgeois democracy throughout the course of the revolution. They may not merely proclaim such "independence" but may even retain it formally, and yet *it may turn out* that their hands will nevertheless be tied in the struggle against the inconsistency of the bourgeoisie. The ultimate political outcome of the revolution may prove to be that, despite the formal "independence" of Social-Démocracy, despite its complete organizational individuality as a separate party, it will in fact not be independent; it will not be able to place the imprint of its proletarian independence on the course of events; it will prove so weak that, on the whole and in the last analysis, its "dissolution" in bourgeois democracy will nevertheless be a historical fact.

That is what constitutes the real danger. Now let us see from what direction the danger threatens—from the deviation of Social-Democracy, as represented by the new *Iskra*, to the Right, as we believe; or from the deviation of Social-Democracy, as represented by the "Majority," [10] . . . to the Left—as the new-*Iskra* group believes.

The answer to this question, as we have pointed out, is determined by the objective combination of the operation of the various social forces. The character of these forces has been defined theoretically by the Marxist analysis of Russian life; at present it is being determined in practice by open action by groups and classes in the course of the revolution. Now the entire theoretical analysis made by the Marxists long before the period we are now passing through, as well as all the practical observations of the development of revolutionary events, show that, from the standpoint of objective conditions, there are two possible courses and two possible outcomes of the revolution in Russia. The transformation of the economic and political system in Russia along bourgeois democratic lines is inevitable and inescapable. No power on earth can prevent such a transformation, but the combined action of the existing forces which are effecting it may result in either of two things, may bring about either of two forms of that transformation. Either 1) matters will end in "the revolution's decisive victory over tsarism," or 2) the forces will be inadequate for a decisive victory, and matters will end in a deal between tsarism and the most "inconsistent" and most "self-seeking" elements of the bourgeoisie. By and large, all the infinite variety of details and combinations, which no one is able to foresee, lead to one outcome or the other.

Let us now consider these two possibilities, first, from the standpoint of their social significance and, second, from the standpoint of the position of Social-Democracy (its "dissolution" or "having its hands tied") in one outcome or the other.

What is meant by "the revolution's decisive victory over tsarism"? We have already seen that in using this expression the new-*Iskra* group fail to grasp even its immediate political significance. Still less do they seem to understand the class essence of this concept. Surely, we Marxists must not under any circumstances allow ourselves to be

10   That is, the Bolsheviks, Lenin's wing of the Party. [*Ed.*]

deluded by *words*, such as "revolution" or "the great Russian revolution," as do many revolutionary democrats. . . . We must be perfectly certain in our minds as to what real social forces are opposed to "tsarism" (which is a real force perfectly intelligible to all) and are capable of gaining a "decisive victory" over it. The big bourgeoisie, the landlords, the factory owners, the "society" which follows the *Osvobozhdeniye* lead, cannot be such a force. We see that they do not even want a decisive victory. We know that owing to their class position they are incapable of waging a decisive struggle against tsarism; they are too heavily fettered by private property, by capital and land to enter into a decisive struggle. They stand in too great need of tsarism, with its bureaucratic, police, and military forces for use against the proletariat and the peasantry, to want it to be destroyed. No, the only force capable of gaining "a decisive victory over tsarism" is the *people,* that is, the proletariat and the peasantry, if we take the main, big forces, and distribute the rural and urban petty bourgeoisie (also part of "the people") between the two. "The revolution's decisive victory over tsarism" means the establishment of the *revolutionary-democratic dictatorship of the proletariat and the peasantry*. Our new-*Iskra* group cannot escape from this conclusion, which *Vperyod* [11] indicated long ago. No other force is capable of gaining a decisive victory over tsarism.

And such a victory will be precisely a dictatorship, that is, it must inevitably rely on military force, on the arming of the masses, on an insurrection, and not on institutions of one kind or another established in a "lawful" or "peaceful" way. It can be only a dictatorship, for realization of the changes urgently and absolutely indispensable to the proletariat and the peasantry will evoke desperate resistance from the landlords, the big bourgeoisie, and tsarism. Without a dictatorship it is impossible to break down that resistance and repel counter-revolutionary attempts. But of course it will be a democratic, not a socialist dictatorship. It will be unable (without a series of intermediary stages of revolutionary development) to affect the foundations of capitalism. At best, it may bring about a radical redistribution of landed property in favor of the peasantry, establish consistent and full democracy, including the formation of a republic, eradicate all the oppressive features of Asiatic bondage, not only in rural but also in factory life, lay the foundation for a thorough improvement in the conditions of the workers and for a rise in their standard of living, and—last but not least—carry the revolutionary conflagration into Europe. Such a victory will not yet by any means

11 *Vperyod (Forward)*, the newspaper started by Lenin after the Mensheviks gained control of *Iskra*, the official party paper (thus Lenin's ironic remarks about the new *Iskra*). The title of *Vperyod* seems a conscious attempt to copy the German Social-Democrats whose paper, *Vorwärts*, was one of the most influential voices in European socialism. [*Ed.*]

transform our bourgeois revolution into a socialist revolution; the democratic revolution will not immediately overstep the bounds of bourgeois social and economic relationships; nevertheless, the significance of such a victory for the future development of Russia and of the whole world will be immense. Nothing will raise the revolutionary energy of the world proletariat so much, nothing will shorten the path leading to its complete victory to such an extent, as this decisive victory of the revolution that has now started in Russia.

How far such a victory is probable is another question. We are not in the least inclined to be unreasonably optimistic on that score; we do not for a moment forget the immense difficulties of this task, but, since we are out to fight, we must desire victory and be able to point out the right road to it. Trends capable of leading to such a victory undoubtedly exist. True, our influence on the masses of the proletariat—the Social-Democratic influence—is as yet very, very inadequate; the revolutionary influence on the mass of the peasantry is quite insignificant; the proletarians, and especially the peasants, are still frightfully disunited, backward, and ignorant. However, revolution unites rapidly and enlightens rapidly. Every step in its development rouses the masses and attracts them with irresistible force to the side of the revolutionary program, as the only program that fully and consistently expresses their real and vital interests.

According to a law of mechanics, action and reaction are always equal. In history too, the destructive force of a revolution is to a considerable degree dependent on how strong and protracted the suppression of the striving for liberty has been, and how profound is the contradiction between the outmoded "superstructure" and the living forces of our times. The international political situation, too, is in many respects taking shape in a way most advantageous to the Russian revolution. The workers' and peasants' insurrection has already begun; it is sporadic, spontaneous, and weak, but it unquestionably and undoubtedly proves the existence of forces capable of waging a decisive struggle and marching towards a decisive victory.

If these forces prove inadequate, tsarism will have time to conclude a deal, which is already being prepared. . . . Then the whole matter will end in a docked constitution, or, if the worst comes to the worst, even in a travesty of a constitution. This, too, will be a "bourgeois revolution," but it will be a miscarriage, a premature birth, an abortion. Social-Democracy entertains no illusions on that score; it knows the treacherous nature of the bourgeoisie; it will not lose heart or abandon its persistent, patient, and sustained work of giving the proletariat class training, even in the most drab, humdrum days of bourgeois-constitutional . . . bliss. Such an outcome would be more or less similar to that of almost all the nineteenth-century democratic revolutions in Europe, and our Party development would then proceed along the arduous, long, but familiar and beaten track.

The question now arises: in which outcome of the two possible will Social-Democracy find its hands actually tied in the struggle against the inconsistent and self-seeking bourgeoisie, find itself actually "dissolved," or almost so, in bourgeois democracy?

It is sufficient to put this question clearly to have a reply without a moment's difficulty.

If the bourgeoisie succeeds in frustrating the Russian revolution by coming to terms with tsarism, Social-Democracy will find its hands actually tied in the struggle against the inconsistent bourgeoisie; Social-Democracy will find itself "dissolved" in bourgeois democracy in the sense that the proletariat will not succeed in placing its clear imprint on the revolution, will not succeed in settling accounts with tsarism in the proletarian or, as Marx once said, "in the plebeian manner."

If the revolution gains a decisive victory—then we shall settle accounts with tsarism in the Jacobin, or, if you like, in the plebeian way. "The whole French terrorism," wrote Marx in 1848 . . . "was nothing but a plebeian manner of settling accounts with the enemies of the bourgeoisie, with absolutism, feudalism, and philistinism." . . . Have those people who in a period of a democratic revolution try to frighten the Social-Democratic workers in Russia with the bogey of "Jacobinism" ever given thought to the significance of these words of Marx?

The new-*Iskra* group, the Girondists of contemporary Russian Social-Democracy, does not merge with the *Osvobozhdeniye* group, but actually, by reason of the nature of its slogans, it follows in the wake of the latter. And the *Osvobozhdeniye* group, that is, the representatives of the liberal bourgeoisie, wishes to settle accounts with the autocracy in a reformist manner, gently and compliantly, so as not to offend the aristocracy, the nobles, or the Court—cautiously, without breaking anything—kindly and politely as befits gentlemen in white gloves. . . .

The Jacobins of contemporary Social-Democracy—the Bolsheviks . . . —wish by their slogans to raise the revolutionary and republican petty bourgeoisie, and especially the peasantry, to the level of the consistent democratism of the proletariat, which fully retains its individuality as a class. They want the people, that is, the proletariat and the peasantry, to settle accounts with the monarchy and the aristocracy in the "plebeian way," ruthlessly destroying the enemies of liberty, crushing their resistance by force, making no concessions whatever to the accursed heritage of serf-ownership, Asiatic barbarism, and human degradation.

This, of course, does not mean that we necessarily propose to imitate the Jacobins of 1793, and borrow their views, program, slogans, and methods of action. Nothing of the kind. Our program is not an old one but a new—the minimum program of the Russian Social-Democratic Labor Party. We have a new slogan: the revolutionary-democratic dictatorship of the proletariat and the peasantry. If we live to see the real victory of the revolution, we shall also have new methods of action in keeping with the nature and aims of the working-class party that is striving for a complete socialist revolution. By our parallel we merely want to explain that the representatives of the progressive class of the twentieth century, the proletariat, that is, the Social-Democrats, are divided into two wings (the opportunist and the revolutionary) similar to those into which the representatives of the progressive class of the eighteenth century, the bourgeoisie, were divided, that is, the Girondists and the Jacobins.

Only in the event of a complete victory of the democratic revolution will the proletariat have its hands free in the struggle against the inconsistent bourgeoisie; only in that event will it not become "dissolved" in bourgeois democracy, but will leave its proletarian, or rather proletarian-peasant, imprint on the whole revolution.

In a word, to avoid finding itself with its hands tied in the struggle against the inconsistent bourgeois democracy, the proletariat must be class-conscious and strong enough to rouse the peasantry to revolutionary consciousness, guide its assault, and thereby independently pursue the line of consistent proletarian democratism.

That is how matters stand in the question—so ineptly dealt with by the new-*Iskra* group—of the danger of our hands being tied in the struggle against the inconsistent bourgeoisie. The bourgeoisie will always be inconsistent. There is nothing more naïve and futile than attempts to set forth conditions and points which, if satisfied, would enable us to consider that the bourgeois democrat is a sincere friend of the people. Only the proletariat can be a consistent fighter for democracy. It can become a victorious fighter for democracy only if the peasant masses join its revolutionary struggle. If the proletariat is not strong enough for this, the bourgeoisie will be at the head of the democratic revolution and will impart an inconsistent and self-seeking nature to it. Nothing but a revolutionary-democratic dictatorship of the proletariat and the peasantry can prevent this.

Thus, we arrive at the indubitable conclusion that it is the new-*Iskra* tactic which, by its objective significance, is *playing into the hands of the bourgeois democrats*. The preaching of organizational diffuseness which goes to the length of plebiscites, the principle of compromise, and the divorcement of Party literature from the Party; [the] belittling of the aims of insurrection; [the] confusing of the popular political slogans of the revolutionary proletariat with those of the monarchist bourgeoisie; [the] distortion of the requisites for "revolution's decisive victory over tsarism"—all these taken together

produce that very policy of tail-ism in a revolutionary period which
bewilders the proletariat, disorganizes it, confuses its understanding,
and belittles the tactics of Social-Democracy instead of pointing out
the only way to victory and getting all the revolutionary and republican elements of the people to adhere to the proletariat's slogan. . . .

10   "Revolutionary Communes" and the Revolutionary-Democratic Dictatorship of the Proletariat and the Peasantry

. . . [The Mensheviks have stated that]:

"Only in one event should Social-Democracy on its own initiative direct its efforts towards seizing power and holding it as long as
possible—namely, in the event of the revolution spreading to the advanced countries of Western Europe, where conditions for the
achievement of socialism have already reached a certain [?] degree of
maturity. In that event the limited historical scope of the Russian
revolution can be considerably widened and the possibility will arise
of entering on the path of socialist reforms.

"By basing its tactics on the expectation that during the entire
revolutionary period the Social-Democratic Party will retain its stand
of extreme revolutionary opposition to all governments that may succeed one another in the course of the revolution, Social-Democracy
will best be able to prepare itself to utilize governmental power if it
falls (??) into its hands."

The basic idea here is the one repeatedly formulated by *Vperyod*,
which has stated that we must not be afraid . . . of Social-Democracy's
complete victory in a democratic revolution, that is, of a revolutionary-democratic dictatorship of the proletariat and the peasantry, for
such a victory will enable us to rouse Europe; after throwing off the
yoke of the bourgeoisie, the socialist proletariat of Europe will in its
turn help us to accomplish the socialist revolution. But see how the
. . . [Menshevik] rendering impairs this idea. We shall not dwell on
details; on the absurd assumption that power could "fall" into the
hands of a class-conscious party which considers seizure of power
harmful tactics; on the fact that in Europe the conditions for socialism have reached not a certain degree of maturity, but maturity in
general; on the fact that our Party program knows no socialist reforms, but only the socialist revolution. Let us take the principal and
basic difference between *Vperyod*'s idea and the one presented . . .
[by the Mensheviks]. *Vperyod* set the revolutionary proletariat of
Russia an active task: winning the battle for democracy and using
this victory to bring the revolution into Europe. The . . . [Menshevik
statement] fails to grasp this link between our "decisive victory" . . .

and the revolution in Europe, and, therefore, it does not speak of the tasks of the proletariat or the prospects of the *latter*'s victory, but of one of the possibilities in general: "in the event of the revolution spreading. . . ." *Vperyod* pointedly and definitely indicated—and this was incorporated in the resolution of the Third Congress of the Russian Social-Democratic Labor Party—how "governmental power" can and must "be utilized" in the interests of the proletariat, bearing in mind what can be achieved immediately, at a given stage of social development, and what must first be achieved as a democratic prerequisite of the struggle for socialism. Here, too, the [Menshevik] resolution lags hopelessly behind when it states: "will be able to prepare itself to utilize," but fails to say *how* it will be able, *how* it will prepare itself, and to utilize *for what purpose*. We have no doubt, for instance, that the new-Iskrists may be "able to prepare themselves to utilize" their leading position in the Party, but the point is that so far their experience of that utilization, their preparation, does not hold out much hope of possibility becoming reality. . . .

Vperyod stated quite definitely wherein lies the real "possibility of retaining power"—namely, in the revolutionary-democratic dictatorship of the proletariat and the peasantry; in their joint mass strength, which is capable of outweighing all the forces of counter-revolution; in the inevitable concurrence of their interests in *democratic* reforms. Here, too, the . . . [Menshevik statement] gives us nothing positive; it merely evades the issue. Surely, the possibility of retaining power in Russia must be determined by the composition of the social forces in Russia herself, by the circumstances of the democratic revolution now taking place in our country. A victory of the proletariat in Europe (it is still quite a far cry from bringing the revolution into Europe to the victory of the proletariat) will give rise to a desperate counter-revolutionary struggle on the part of the Russian bourgeoisie. . . . If, in our fight for a republic and democracy, we could not rely upon the peasantry as well as upon the proletariat, the prospect of our "retaining power" would be hopeless. But if it is not hopeless, if the "revolution's decisive victory over tsarism" opens up such a possibility, then we must indicate it, call actively for its transformation into reality, and issue practical slogans not only *for the contingency* of the revolution being brought into Europe, but also *for the purpose* of taking it there. The reference made by tail-ist Social-Democrats to the "limited historical scope of the Russian revolution" merely serves to cover up their limited understanding of the aims of this democratic revolution, and of the proletariat's leading role in it!

One of the objections raised to the slogan of "the revolutionary-democratic dictatorship of the proletariat and the peasantry" is that dictatorship presupposes a "single will" . . . and that there can be no single will of the proletariat and the petty bourgeoisie. This objection is unsound, for it is based on an abstract, "metaphysical" interpretation of the term "single will." There may be a single will in one respect and not in another. The absence of unity on questions of socialism and in the struggle for socialism does not preclude singleness of will on questions of democracy and in the struggle for a republic. To forget this would be tantamount to forgetting the logical and historical difference between a democratic revolution and a socialist revolution. To forget this would be tantamount to forgetting the character of the democratic revolution as one *of the whole people*: if it is "of the whole people," that means that there *is* "singleness of will" precisely in so far as this revolution meets the needs and requirements of the whole people. Beyond the bounds of democratism there can be no question of the proletariat and the peasant bourgeoisie having a single will. Class struggle between them is inevitable, but it is in a democratic republic that this struggle will be the most thoroughgoing and widespread struggle of the people *for socialism*. Like everything else in the world, the revolutionary-democratic dictatorship of the proletariat and the peasantry has a past and a future. Its past is autocracy, serfdom, monarchy, and privilege. In the struggle against this past, in the struggle against counter-revolution, a "single will" of the proletariat and the peasantry is possible, for here there is unity of interests.

Its future is the struggle against private property, the struggle of the wage-worker against the employer, the struggle for socialism. Here singleness of will is impossible.[12] Here the path before us lies not from autocracy to a republic, but from a petty-bourgeois democratic republic to socialism.

Of course, in actual historical circumstances, the elements of the past become interwoven with those of the future; the two paths cross. Wage-labor with its struggle against private property exists under the autocracy as well; it arises even under serfdom. But this does not in the least prevent us from logically and historically distinguishing between the major stages of development. We all [contrast] bourgeois revolution and socialist revolution; we all insist on the absolute necessity of strictly distinguishing between them; however, can it be denied that in the course of history individual, *particular* elements of the two revolutions become interwoven? Has the period of democratic revolutions in Europe not been familiar with a number of socialist movements and attempts to establish socialism? And will not the future socialist revolution in Europe still have to complete a great deal left undone in the field of democratism?

12 The development of capitalism, more extensive and rapid in conditions of liberty, will inevitably soon put an end to singleness of will; that will take place the sooner, the earlier counter-revolution and reaction are crushed. [*L.*]

A Social-Democrat must never for a moment forget that the proletariat will inevitably have to wage a class struggle for socialism even against the most democratic and republican bourgeoisie and petty bourgeoisie. This is beyond doubt. Hence, the absolute necessity of a separate, independent, strictly class party of Social-Democracy. Hence, the temporary nature of our tactics of "striking a joint blow" with the bourgeoisie and the duty of keeping a strict watch "over our ally, as over an enemy," etc. All this also leaves no room for doubt. However, it would be ridiculous and reactionary to deduce from this that we must forget, ignore, or neglect tasks which, although transient and temporary, are vital at the present time. The struggle against the autocracy is a temporary and transient task for socialists, but to ignore or neglect this task in any way amounts to betrayal of socialism and service to reaction. The revolutionary-democratic dictatorship of the proletariat and the peasantry is unquestionably only a transient, temporary socialist aim, but to ignore this aim in the period of a democratic revolution would be downright reactionary.

Concrete political aims must be set in concrete circumstances. All things are relative, all things flow, and all things change. German Social-Democracy does not put into its program the demand for a republic. The situation in Germany is such that this question can in practice hardly be separated from that of socialism (although with regard to Germany too, Engels . . . in 1891 warned against belittling the importance of a republic and of the struggle for a republic!). In Russian Social-Democracy the question of eliminating the demand for a republic from its program and its agitation has never even arisen, for in our country there can be no talk of an indissoluble link between the question of a republic and that of socialism. It was quite natural for a German Social-Democrat of 1898 not to place special emphasis on the question of a republic, and this evokes neither surprise nor condemnation. But in 1848 a German Social-Democrat who would have relegated to the background the question of a republic would have been a downright traitor to the revolution. There is no such thing as abstract truth. Truth is always concrete.

The time will come when the struggle against the Russian autocracy will end, and the period of democratic revolution will have passed in Russia; it will then be ridiculous even to speak of "singleness of will" of the proletariat and the peasantry, about a democratic dictatorship, etc. When that time comes we shall deal directly with the question of the socialist dictatorship of the proletariat and speak of it in greater detail. At present the party of the advanced class cannot but strive most energetically for the democratic revolution's decisive victory over tsarism. And a decisive victory means nothing

else than the revolutionary-democratic dictatorship of the proletariat
and the peasantry. . . .

12   Will the Sweep of the Democratic Revolution Be Diminished if the Bourgeoisie Recoils From It?

. . . [The new-Iskrists believe] that the formation of a provisional
government by Social-Democrats, or their entering such a government,
would lead, on the one hand, to the masses of the proletariat becoming disappointed in the Social-Democratic Party and abandoning
it, because the Social-Democrats, despite the seizure of power, would
not be able to satisfy the pressing needs of the working class, including the establishment of socialism (a republic is not a pressing need!
The authors in their innocence do not notice that they are speaking
purely anarchist language, as if they were repudiating participation
in bourgeois revolutions!), and, on the other hand, *would cause the
bourgeois classes to recoil from the revolution and thus diminish
its sweep.*"

That is the crux of the matter. That is where anarchist ideas
become interwoven . . . with the sheerest opportunism. Just imagine:
these people will not enter a provisional government because that
would cause the bourgeoisie to recoil from the revolution, thereby
diminishing the sweep of the revolution! Here, indeed, we have the
new-*Iskra* philosophy as a whole, in a pure and consistent form:
since the revolution is a bourgeois revolution, we must bow to bourgeois philistinism and make way for it. If we are even in part, even
for a moment, guided by the consideration that our participation may
cause the bourgeoisie to recoil, we thereby simply hand over leadership of the revolution entirely to the bourgeois classes. We thereby
place the proletariat entirely under the tutelage of the bourgeoisie
(while retaining complete "freedom of criticism"!!), compelling the
proletariat to be moderate and meek, so that the bourgeoisie should
not recoil. We emasculate the most vital needs of the proletariat,
namely, its political needs—which the Economists and their imitators
have never properly understood—so as not to make the bourgeoisie
recoil. We go over completely from the platform of revolutionary
struggle for the achievement of democracy to the extent required
by the proletariat, to a platform of haggling with the bourgeoisie,
buying the bourgeoisie's voluntary consent ("so that it should not
recoil") at the price of our principles, by betraying the revolution. . . .

Social-Democrats, who write such disgraceful things . . . are so
blinded by sophistry, which has utterly driven the living spirit out of
Marxism, that they fail to notice that these resolutions turn all their
other fine words into empty phrases. Take any of their articles in

Iskra . . .—there you will read about a *popular* insurrection, about carrying the revolution to *completion*, about striving to rely upon the *common people* in the struggle against the inconsistent bourgeoisie. However, all these excellent things become miserable phrases as soon as you accept or approve the idea that "the sweep of the revolution" will be "diminished" as a consequence of the bourgeoisie's alienation. These are the alternatives, gentlemen: either we, together with the people, must strive to carry out the revolution and win complete victory over tsarism *despite* the inconsistent, self-seeking, and cowardly bourgeoisie, or else we do not accept this "despite" and are afraid that the bourgeoisie may "recoil" from the revolution; in the second case we are betraying the proletariat and the people to the bourgeoisie —the inconsistent, self-seeking, and cowardly bourgeoisie.

Don't take it into your heads to misinterpret my words. Don't shrill that you are being accused of deliberate treachery. No, you have always crawled towards the marsh and have at last crawled into it, just as unconsciously as the Economists of old, who were irresistibly and irrevocably drawn down the inclined plane of "deeper" Marxism, until it at last became an anti-revolutionary, soulless, and lifeless intellectual pose.

Have you, gentlemen, ever given thought to real social forces that determine "the sweep of the revolution"? Let us disregard the foreign political forces, the international combinations, which have developed very favorably for us at the present time, but which we all leave out of the discussion, and rightly so, inasmuch as we are concerned with the question of Russia's internal forces. Examine these internal social forces. Aligned against the revolution are the autocracy, the imperial court, the police, the bureaucracy, the army, and a handful of the aristocracy. The deeper the indignation of the people grows, the less reliable the troops become, and the more the bureaucracy wavers. Moreover, the bourgeoisie, on the whole, is now in favor of revolution, zealously speechifying about liberty and holding forth more and more frequently in the name of the people and even in the name of the revolution. But we Marxists all know from theory and from daily and hourly observation of our liberals, Zemstvo people, and *Osvobozhdeniye* supporters that the bourgeoisie is inconsistent, self-seeking, and cowardly in its support of the revolution. The bourgeoisie, in the mass, will inevitably turn towards counter-revolution, towards the autocracy, against the revolution, and against the people, as soon as its narrow, selfish interests are met, as soon as it "recoils" from consistent democracy (*and it is already recoiling from it!*). There remains the "people," that is, the proletariat and the peasantry: the proletariat alone can be relied on to march on to the end, for it goes far beyond the democratic revolution. That is why the proletariat fights in the forefront for a republic and contemptuously rejects stupid and unworthy advice to take into account the possibility of the bourgeoisie recoiling. The peasantry includes a great number of semi-proletarian as well as petty-bourgeois elements. This makes it also unstable, compelling the proletariat to rally in a strictly class party. However, the instability of the peasantry differs radically from that of the bourgeoisie, for at present the peasantry is interested not so much in the absolute preservation of private property as in the confiscation of the landed estates, one of the principal forms of private property. Without thereby becoming socialist, or ceasing to be petty-bourgeois, the peasantry is capable of becoming a wholehearted and most radical adherent of the democratic revolution. The peasantry will inevitably become such if only the course of revolutionary events, which brings it enlightenment, is not prematurely cut short by the treachery of the bourgeoisie and the defeat of the proletariat. Subject to this condition the peasantry will inevitably become a bulwark of the revolution and the republic, for only a completely victorious revolution can give the peasantry *everything* in the sphere of agrarian reforms—*everything* that the peasants desire, dream of, and truly need, not for the abolition of capitalism as the "Socialist-Revolutionaries" imagine, but, in order to emerge from the mire of semi-serfdom, from the gloom of oppression and servitude, in order to improve their living conditions, as much as they can be improved within the system of commodity production.

Moreover, it is not only by the prospect of radical agrarian reform that the peasantry is attached to the revolution, but by all its general and permanent interests as well. Even when fighting with the proletariat, the peasantry stands in need of democracy, for only a democratic system is capable of accurately expressing its interests and ensuring its predominance as a mass, as the majority. The more enlightened the peasantry becomes (and since the war with Japan it is becoming enlightened at a pace unsuspected by many who are accustomed to measure enlightenment with the school yardstick), the more consistently and resolutely will it stand for a thoroughgoing democratic revolution; for, unlike the bourgeoisie, it has nothing to fear from the people's supremacy, but on the contrary stands to gain by it. A democratic republic will become the peasantry's ideal as soon as it begins to throw off its naïve monarchism, because the conscious monarchism of the bourgeois stockjobbers (with an upper chamber, etc.) implies for the peasantry the same absence of rights and the same oppression and ignorance as it suffers today, only slightly polished over with the varnish of European constitutionalism.

That is why, as a class, the bourgeoisie naturally and inevitably tends to come under the wing of the liberal-monarchist party, while the peasantry, in the mass, tends to come under the leadership of the revolutionary and republican party. That is why the bourgeoisie

is incapable of carrying through the democratic revolution to its consummation, while the peasantry is capable of doing so, and we must
exert all our efforts to help it do so.

The objection may be raised that this goes without saying, is all
ABC, something that all Social-Democrats understand perfectly well.
No, that is not the case; it is not understood by those who can talk
about "the diminishing sweep" of the revolution as a consequence of
the bourgeoisie falling away from it. Such people repeat the words of
our agrarian program, which they have learned by rote without understanding their meaning, for otherwise they would not be frightened
by the concept of the revolutionary-democratic dictatorship of the
proletariat and the peasantry, which inevitably follows from the entire
Marxist world outlook and from our program; otherwise they would
not restrict the sweep of the great Russian revolution to the limits
to which the bourgeoisie is prepared to go. Such people defeat their
abstract Marxist revolutionary phrases by their concrete anti-Marxist
and anti-revolutionary resolutions.

Those who really understand the role of the peasantry in a victorious Russian revolution would not dream of saying that the sweep
of the revolution will be diminished if the bourgeoisie recoils from
it. For, in actual fact, the Russian revolution will begin to assume its
real sweep, and will really assume the widest revolutionary sweep
possible in the epoch of bourgeois-democratic revolution, only when
the bourgeoisie recoils from it and when the masses of the peasantry
come out as active revolutionaries side by side with the proletariat.
To be consistently carried through to the end, our democratic revolution must rely on forces capable of paralyzing the inevitable inconsistency of the bourgeoisie (that is, capable precisely of "making
it recoil from the revolution" . . .).

*The proletariat must carry the democratic revolution to comple-
tion, allying to itself the mass of the peasantry in order to crush the
autocracy's resistance by force and paralyze the bourgeoisie's instability. The proletariat must accomplish the socialist revolution, allying
to itself the mass of the semiproletarian elements of the population,
so as to crush the bourgeoisie's resistance by force and paralyze the
instability of the peasantry and the petty bourgeoisie. . . .*

One circumstance, however, should not be forgotten, one that is
frequently lost sight of in discussions about the "sweep" of the revolution. It should not be forgotten that it is not a question of the difficulties presented by this problem, but of the way in which its solution
is to be sought and attained. It is not a question of whether it is easy
or difficult to render the sweep of the revolution mighty and invincible, but of how to act so as to make that sweep more powerful. It is
on the fundamental nature of our activities, the direction they should
follow, that our views differ. We emphasize this because inattentive

and unscrupulous people only too frequently confuse two different problems, namely, that of the direction to be followed, that is, the choice of one of two different roads, and that of the ease of attaining our goal, or the nearness of its attainment along a given road.

In the foregoing we have not dealt with this last problem at all because it has not evoked any disagreement or differences in the Party. The problem itself is, of course, extremely important and deserving of the most serious attention from all Social-Democrats. It would be unforgivable optimism to forget the difficulties involved in drawing into the movement the masses not only of the working class, but also of the peasantry. These difficulties have more than once wrecked efforts to carry through a democratic revolution to completion, the inconsistent and self-seeking bourgeoisie triumphing most of all, because it has "made capital" in the shape of monarchist protection against the people, at the same time "preserving the virginity" of liberalism . . . or of the *Osvobozhdeniye* trend. However, difficulty does not imply impossibility. The important thing is to be confident that the path chosen is the right one, this confidence multiplying a hundredfold revolutionary energy and revolutionary enthusiasm, which can perform miracles. . . .

13   Conclusion. Dare We Win?

. . . The democratic revolution is bourgeois in nature. The slogan of a general redistribution, or "land and freedom"—that most widespread slogan of the peasant masses, downtrodden and ignorant, yet passionately yearning for light and happiness—is a bourgeois slogan. But we Marxists should know that there is not, nor can there be, any other path to real freedom for the proletariat and the peasantry than the path of bourgeois freedom and bourgeois progress. We must not forget that there is not, nor can there be at the present time, any other means of bringing socialism nearer than complete political liberty, than a democratic republic, than the revolutionary-democratic dictatorship of the proletariat and the peasantry. As representatives of the advanced and only revolutionary class, revolutionary without any reservations, doubts, or looking back, we must confront the whole of the people with the tasks of the democratic revolution as extensively and boldly as possible and with the utmost initiative. To disparage these tasks means making a travesty of theoretical Marxism, distorting it in philistine fashion, while in practical politics it means placing the cause of the revolution into the hands of the bourgeoisie, which will inevitably recoil from the task of consistently effecting the revolution. The difficulties that lie on the road to complete victory of the revolution are very great. No one will be able to blame the proletariat's representatives if, when they have done everything in their power, their efforts are defeated by the resistance of reaction, the treachery of the bourgeoisie, and the ignorance of the masses. But everybody, and, above all, the class-conscious proletariat, will condemn Social-Democracy if it curtails the revolutionary energy of the democratic revolution and dampens revolutionary ardor because it is afraid to win, because it is actuated by the consideration: lest the bourgeoisie recoil.

Revolutions are the locomotives of history, said Marx. Revolutions are festivals of the oppressed and the exploited. At no other time are the mass of the people in a position to come forward so actively as creators of a new social order as at a time of revolution. At such times the people are capable of performing miracles, if judged by the limited, philistine yardstick of gradualist progress. But it is essential that leaders of the revolutionary parties, too, should advance their aims more comprehensively and boldly at such a time, so that their slogans shall always be in advance of the revolutionary initiative of the masses, serve as a beacon, reveal to them our democratic and socialist ideal in all its magnitude and splendor, and show them the shortest and most direct route to complete, absolute, and decisive victory. Let us leave to the opportunists of the *Osvobozhdeniye* bourgeoisie the task of inventing roundabout, circuitous paths of compromise, out of fear of the revolution and of the direct path. If we are forcibly compelled to drag ourselves along such paths we shall be able to fulfill our duty in petty, everyday work also. But first let the choice of path be decided in ruthless struggle. We shall be traitors, betrayers of the revolution, if we do not use this festive energy of the masses and their revolutionary ardor to wage a ruthless and self-sacrificing struggle for the direct and decisive path. Let the bourgeois opportunists contemplate the future reaction with craven fear. The workers will not be intimidated either by the thought that reaction intends to be terrible, or that the bourgeoisie proposes to recoil. The workers do not expect to make deals; they are not asking for petty concessions. What they are striving towards is ruthlessly to crush the reactionary forces, that is, to set up a *revolutionary-democratic dictatorship of the proletariat and the peasantry*.

Of course, in stormy times greater dangers threaten the ship of our Party than in periods of the smooth "sailing" of liberal progress, which means the painfully steady sucking of the working class's lifeblood by its exploiters. Of course, the tasks of the revolutionary-democratic dictatorship are infinitely more difficult and more complex than the tasks of an "extreme opposition," or of an exclusively parliamentary struggle. But whoever is consciously capable of preferring smooth sailing and the course of safe "opposition" in the present revolutionary situation had better abandon Social-Democratic work for a while, had better wait until the revolution is over, until the festive days have passed, when humdrum, everyday life starts again, and his narrow routine standards no longer strike such an abominably discordant note or constitute such an ugly distortion of the tasks of the advanced class.

At the head of the whole people, and particularly of the peasantry —for complete freedom, for a consistent democratic revolution, for a republic! At the head of all the toilers and the exploited—for socialism! Such in practice must be the policy of the revolutionary proletariat; such is the class slogan which must permeate and determine the solution of every tactical problem, every practical step of the workers' party during the revolution.

IMPERIALISM, THE HIGHEST STAGE OF CAPITALISM (1916)

A Popular Outline

Preface

THE PAMPHLET here presented to the reader was written in the spring of 1916, in Zurich. In the conditions in which I was obliged to work there I naturally suffered somewhat from a shortage of French and English literature and from a serious dearth of Russian literature. However, I made use of the principal English work on imperialism, the book by J. A. Hobson, with all the care that, in my opinion, that work deserves.

This pamphlet was written with an eye to the tsarist censorship. Hence, I was not only forced to confine myself strictly to an exclusively theoretical, specifically economic analysis of facts, but to formulate the few necessary observations on politics with extreme caution, by hints, in an allegorical language—in that accursed Aesopian language—to which tsarism compelled all revolutionaries to have recourse whenever they took up the pen to write a "legal" work.

It is painful, in these days of liberty, to re-read the passages of the pamphlet which have been distorted, cramped, compressed in an iron vice on account of the censor. That the period of imperialism is the eve of the socialist revolution; that social-chauvinism (socialism in words, chauvinism in deeds) is the utter betrayal of socialism, complete desertion to the side of the bourgeoisie; that this split in the working-class movement is bound up with the objective conditions of imperialism, etc.—on these matters I had to speak in a "slavish" tongue. . . . I was forced to quote as an example—Japan! The careful reader will easily substitute Russia for Japan, and Finland, Poland, Courland, the Ukraine, Khiva, Bokhara, Estonia [1] or other regions peopled by non-Great Russians, for Korea.

I trust that this pamphlet will help the reader to understand the

---

1 All non-Russian areas included in the Russian Empire. [*Ed.*]

fundamental economic question, that of the economic essence of imperialism, for unless this is studied, it will be impossible to understand and appraise modern war and modern politics.

Author

Petrograd. April 26, 1917

Preface to the French and German Editions

I

As was indicated in the preface to the Russian edition, this pamphlet was written in 1916, with an eye to the tsarist censorship. I am unable to revise the whole text at the present time, nor, perhaps, would this be advisable, since the main purpose of the book was, and remains, to present, on the basis of the summarized returns of irrefutable bourgeois statistics, and the admissions of bourgeois scholars of all countries, a *composite picture* of the world capitalist system in its international relationships at the beginning of the twentieth century—on the eve of the first world imperialist war.

To a certain extent it will even be useful for many Communists in advanced capitalist countries to convince themselves by the example of this pamphlet, *legal from the standpoint of the tsarist censor*, of the possibility, and necessity, of making use of even the slight remnants of legality which still remain at the disposal of the Communists, say, in contemporary America or France, after the recent almost wholesale arrests of Communists, in order to explain the utter falsity of social-pacifist views and hopes for "world democracy." The most essential of what should be added to this censored pamphlet I shall try to present in this preface.

II

It is proved in the pamphlet that the war of 1914–1918 was imperialist (that is, an annexationist, predatory war of plunder) on the part of both sides; it was a war for the division of the world, for the partition and repartition of colonies and spheres of influence of finance capital, etc.

Proof of what was the true social, or rather, the true class character of the war is naturally to be found, not in the diplomatic history of the war, but in an analysis of the *objective* position of the ruling *classes* in *all* the belligerent countries. In order to depict this objective position one must not take examples or isolated data (in view of the extreme complexity of the phenomena of social life it is always possible to select any number of examples or separate data to prove any proposition), but *all* the data on the *basis* of economic life in *all* the belligerent countries and the *whole* world.

It is precisely irrefutable summarized data of this kind that I quoted in describing the *partition of the world* in 1876 and 1914 . . . and the division of the world's *railways* in 1890 and 1913. . . . Railways are a summation of the basic capitalist industries, coal, iron, and steel; a summation and the most striking index of the development of world trade and bourgeois-democratic civilization. How the railways are linked up with large-scale industry, with monopolies, syndicates, cartels, trusts, banks, and the financial oligarchy is shown in the preceding chapters of the book. The uneven distribution of the railways—their uneven development—sums up, as it were, modern monopolist capitalism on a world-wide scale. And this summary proves that imperialist wars are absolutely inevitable under *such* an economic system, *as long as* private property in the means of production exists.

The building of railways seems to be a simple, natural, democratic, cultural, and civilizing enterprise; that is what it is in the opinion of the bourgeois professors who are paid to depict capitalist slavery in bright colors and in the opinion of petty-bourgeois philistines. But as a matter of fact the capitalist threads, which in thousands of different intercrossings bind these enterprises with private property in the means of production in general, have converted this railway construction into an instrument for oppressing *a thousand million* people (in the colonies and semi-colonies), that is, more than half the population of the globe that inhabits the dependent countries, as well as the wage-slaves of capital in the "civilized" countries.

Private property based on the labor of the small proprietor, free competition, democracy—all the catchwords with which the capitalists and their press deceive the workers and the peasants—are things of the distant past. Capitalism has grown into a world system of colonial oppression and of the financial strangulation of the overwhelming majority of the population of the world by a handful of "advanced" countries. And this "booty" is shared between two or three powerful world plunderers armed to the teeth (America, Great Britain, Japan), who are drawing the whole world into *their* war over the division of *their* booty.

III

The Treaty of Brest-Litovsk dictated by monarchist Germany, and the subsequent much more brutal and despicable Treaty of Versailles dictated by the "democratic" republics of America and France and also by "free" Britain, have rendered a most useful service to humanity by exposing both imperialism's hired coolies of the pen and petty-bourgeois reactionaries who, although they call themselves pacifists and socialists, sang praises to "Wilsonism" and insisted that peace and reforms were possible under imperialism.

The tens of millions of dead and maimed left by the war—a war to decide whether the British or German group of financial plunderers is to receive the most booty—and those two "peace treaties" are with unprecedented rapidity opening the eyes of the millions and tens of millions of people who are downtrodden, oppressed, deceived, and duped by the bourgeoisie. Thus, out of the universal ruin caused by the war a world-wide revolutionary crisis is arising which, however prolonged and arduous its stages may be, cannot end otherwise than in a proletarian revolution and in its victory. . . .

V

A few words must be said about Chapter VIII, "Parasitism and Decay of Capitalism." As already pointed out in the text, Hilferding,[2] ex-"Marxist," and now a comrade-in-arms of Kautsky [3] and one of the chief exponents of bourgeois, reformist policy in the Independent Social-Democratic Party of Germany, has taken a step backward on this question compared with the *frankly* pacifist and reformist Englishman, Hobson. The international split of the entire working-class movement is now quite evident (the Second and the Third Internationals).[4]

2 Rudolf Hilferding (1877–1941), a major Austrian Social-Democratic theorist. His book, *Finanzkapital* (Finance Capital), strongly influenced Lenin's *Imperialism*. [*Ed.*]

3 Karl Kautsky (1854–1938), a German Social-Democrat and a major party theoretician. Lenin quoted Kautsky approvingly in *What Is To Be Done* for his attack on Bernstein. In 1914, however, Kautsky, Hilferding, and the bulk of the German Social-Democrats became anathema because of their attitude towards German involvement in the war. Lenin's most direct attack on Kautsky appears in his book, *The Proletarian Revolution and the Renegade Kautsky* (1918). [*Ed.*]

4 The Second (or Socialist) International was formed in 1889 by representatives of the European Socialist parties. The International all but collapsed as a result of World War I when the European parties supported the war effort in their respective countries. The divisions in European socialism were further widened by the Bolshevik Revolution on the one hand and the participation by German Social-Democrats in the German government on the other. In 1919 the Soviets convened the Third (or Communist) International in Moscow. The delegates (in many cases foreign nationals who found themselves in Russia at the time) issued a manifesto denouncing the reformist trend in European socialism and establishing an alternative organization for communists and left-wing Socialists. Within a short time the Communist International fell completely under Soviet dominance and served as one of Moscow's major levers in foreign affairs until it was dismantled in 1943 as gesture of the "allied" spirit during the Second World War. [*Ed.*]

It is precisely the parasitism and decay of capitalism, characteristic of its highest historical stage of development, that is, imperialism. As this pamphlet shows, capitalism has now singled out a *handful* (less than one-tenth of the inhabitants of the globe; less than one-fifth at a most "generous" and liberal calculation) of exceptionally rich and powerful states which plunder the whole world simply by "clipping coupons." Capital exports yield an income of eight to ten thousand million francs per annum, at pre-war prices and according to pre-war bourgeois statistics. Now, of course, they yield much more.

Obviously, out of such enormous *superprofits* (since they are obtained over and above the profits which capitalists squeeze out of the workers of their "own" country) it is *possible to bribe* the labor leaders and the upper stratum of the labor aristocracy. And that is just what the capitalists of the "advanced" countries are doing: they are bribing them in a thousand different ways, direct and indirect, overt and covert.

This stratum of workers-turned-bourgeois, or the labor aristocracy, who are quite philistine in their mode of life, in the size of their earnings and in their entire outlook, is the principal prop of the Second International, and in our days, the principal *social* (not military) *prop of the bourgeoisie*. For they are the real *agents of the bourgeoisie in the working-class* movement, the labor lieutenants of the capitalist class, real vehicles of reformism and chauvinism. In the civil war between the proletariat and the bourgeoisie they inevitably, and in no small numbers, take the side of the bourgeoisie, the "Versailles" against the "Communards."

Unless the economic roots of this phenomenon are understood and its political and social significance is appreciated, not a step can be taken towards the solution of the practical problems of the communist movement and of the impending social revolution.

Imperialism is the eve of the social revolution of the proletariat. This has been confirmed since 1917 on a world-wide scale.

July 6, 1920

During the last fifteen to twenty years, especially since the Spanish-American War (1898) and the Anglo-Boer War (1899–1902), the economic and also the political literature of the two hemispheres has more and more often adopted the term "imperialism" in order to describe the present era. In 1902, a book by the English economist J. A. Hobson, *Imperialism*, was published in London and New York. This author, whose point of view is that of bourgeois social-reformism and pacifism which, in essence, is identical with the present point of view of the ex-Marxist, Karl Kautsky, gives a very good and comprehensive description of the principal specific economic and political features of imperialism. In 1910, there appeared in Vienna the work of the Austrian Marxist, Rudolf Hilferding, *Finance Capital*. . . . In spite of the mistake the author makes on the theory of money, and in spite of a certain inclination on his part to reconcile Marxism with opportunism, this work gives a very valuable theoretical analysis of "the latest phase of capitalist development," as the subtitle runs. Indeed, what has been said of imperialism during the last few years . . . has scarcely gone beyond the ideas expounded, or more exactly, summed up by the two writers mentioned above. . . .

Later on, I shall try to show briefly, and as simply as possible, the connection and relationships between the *principal* economic features of imperialism. I shall not be able to deal with the non-economic aspects of the question, however much they deserve to be dealt with. . . .

1   Concentration of Production and Monopolies

The enormous growth of industry and the remarkably rapid concentration of production in ever-larger enterprises are one of the most characteristic features of capitalism. Modern production censuses give most complete and most exact data on this process.

In Germany, for example, out of every 1,000 industrial enterprises, large enterprises, that is, those employing more than 50 workers, numbered three in 1882, six in 1895, and nine in 1907; and out of every 100 workers employed, this group of enterprises employed 22, 30, and 37, respectively. Concentration of production, however, is much more intense than the concentration of workers, since labor in the large enterprises is much more productive. This is shown by the figures on steam-engines and electric motors. If we take what in Germany is called industry in the broad sense of the term, that is, including commerce, transport, etc., we get the following picture. Large-scale enterprises, 30,588 out of a total of 3,265,623, that is to say, 0.9 per cent. These enterprises employ 5,700,000 workers out of a total of 14,400,000, that is, 39.4 per cent; they use 6,600,000 steam horse power out of a total of 8,800,000, that is, 75.3 per cent, and 1,200,000 kilowatts of electricity out of a total of 1,500,000, that is, 77.2 per cent.

Less than one-hundredth of the total number of enterprises utilize *more than three-fourths* of the total amount of steam and electric power! Two million nine hundred and seventy thousand small enterprises (employing up to five workers), constituting 91 per cent of the total, utilize only 7 per cent of the total amount of steam and electric power! Tens of thousands of huge enterprises are everything; millions of small ones are nothing.

In 1907, there were in Germany 586 establishments employing

one thousand and more workers, nearly *one-tenth* (1,380,000) of the total number of workers employed in industry, and they consumed *almost one-third* (32 per cent) of the total amount of steam and electric power. As we shall see, money capital and the banks make this superiority of a handful of the largest enterprises still more overwhelming, in the most literal sense of the word, that is, millions of small, medium and even some big "proprietors" are in fact in complete subjection to some hundreds of millionaire financiers.

In another advanced country of modern capitalism, the United States of America, the growth of the concentration of production is still greater. . . .

Almost half the total production of all the enterprises of the country was carried on by *one-hundredth part* of these enterprises! These 3,000 giant enterprises embrace 258 branches of industry. From this it can be seen that, at a certain stage of its development, concentration itself, as it were, leads straight to monopoly, for a score or so of giant enterprises can easily arrive at an agreement, and on the other hand, the hindrance to competition, the tendency towards monopoly, arises from the huge size of the enterprises. This transformation of competition into monopoly is one of the most important —if not the most important—phenomena of modern capitalist economy, and we must deal with it in greater detail. But first we must clear up one possible misunderstanding.

American statistics speak of 3,000 giant enterprises in 250 branches of industry, as if there were only a dozen enterprises of the largest scale for each branch of industry.

But this is not the case. Not in every branch of industry are there large-scale enterprises; and moreover, a very important feature of capitalism in its highest stage of development is so-called *combination* of production, that is to say, the grouping in a single enterprise of different branches of industry, which either represent the consecutive stages in the processing of raw materials (for example, the smelting of iron ore into pig iron, the conversion of pig iron into steel, and then, perhaps, the manufacture of steel goods)—or are auxiliary to one another (for example, the utilization of scrap or of by-products, the manufacture of packing materials, etc.).

"Combination," writes Hilferding, "levels out the fluctuations of trade and therefore assures to the combined enterprises a more stable rate of profit. Second, combination has the effect of eliminating trade. Third, it has the effect of rendering possible technical improvements, and, consequently, the acquisition of superprofits over and above those obtained by the 'pure' [that is, noncombined] enterprises. Fourth, it strengthens the position of the combined enterprises relative to the 'pure' enterprises, strengthens them in the competitive struggle in periods of serious depression, when the fall in prices of raw materials does not keep pace with the fall in prices of manufactured goods." . . .

Half a century ago, when Marx was writing *Capital*, free competition appeared to the overwhelming majority of economists to be a "natural law." Official science tried, by a conspiracy of silence, to kill the works of Marx, who by a theoretical and historical analysis of capitalism had proved that free competition gives rise to the concentration of production, which, in turn, at a certain stage of development, leads to monopoly. Today, monopoly has become a fact. Economists are writing mountains of books in which they describe the diverse manifestations of monopoly and continue to declare in chorus that "Marxism is refuted." But facts are stubborn things, as the English proverb says, and they have to be reckoned with, whether we like it or not. The facts show that differences between capitalist countries, for example, in the matter of protection or free trade, give rise to only insignificant variations in the form of monopolies or in the moment of their appearance; and that the rise of monopolies, as the result of the concentration of production, is a general and fundamental law of the present stage of development of capitalism.

For Europe, the time when the new capitalism *definitely* superseded the old can be established with fair precision; it was the beginning of the twentieth century. In one of the latest compilations on the history of the "formation of monopolies," we read:

"Isolated examples of capitalist monopoly could be cited from the period preceding 1860; in these could be discerned the embryo of the forms that are so common today; but all this undoubtedly represents the prehistory of the cartels. The real beginning of modern monopoly goes back, at the earliest, to the sixties. The first important period of development of monopoly commenced with the international industrial depression of the seventies and lasted until the beginning of the nineties." "If we examine the question on a European scale, we will find that the development of free competition reached its apex in the sixties and seventies. It was then that Britain completed the construction of her old-style capitalist organization. In Germany, this organization had entered into a fierce struggle with handicraft and domestic industry and had begun to create for itself its own forms of existence.

"The great revolution commenced with the crash of 1873, or rather, the depression which followed it and which, with hardly discernible interruptions in the early eighties, and the unusually violent, but short-lived boom round about 1889, marks twenty-two years of European economic history." "During the short boom of 1889–1890, the system of cartels was widely resorted to in order to take advantage of favorable business conditions. An ill-considered policy drove prices up still more rapidly and still higher than would have been the case if there had been no cartels, and nearly all these cartels perished ingloriously in the smash. Another five-year period of bad trade and low prices followed, but a new spirit reigned in industry; the depression was no longer regarded as something to be taken for granted: it was regarded as nothing more than a pause before another boom.

"The cartel movement entered its second epoch: instead of being a transitory phenomenon, the cartels have become one of the foundations of economic life. They are winning one field of industry after another, primarily, the raw materials industry. At the beginning of the nineties the cartel system had already acquired—in the organization of the coke syndicate on the model of which the coal syndicate was later formed—a cartel technique which has hardly been improved on. For the first time the great boom at the close of the nineteenth century and the crisis of 1900–1903 occurred entirely—in the mining and iron industries at least—under the aegis of the cartels. And while at that time it appeared to be something novel, now the general public takes it for granted that large spheres of economic life have been, as a general rule, removed from the realm of free competition."

Thus, the principal stages in the history of monopolies are the following: (1) 1860–1870, the highest stage, the apex of development of free competition; monopoly is in the barely discernible, embryonic stage. (2) After the crisis of 1873, a lengthy period of development of cartels; but they are still the exception. They are not yet durable. They are still a transitory phenomenon. (3) The boom at the end of the nineteenth century and the crisis of 1900–1903. Cartels become one of the foundations of the whole of economic life. Capitalism has been transformed into imperialism.

Cartels come to an agreement on the terms of sale, dates of payment, etc. They divide the markets among themselves. They fix the quantity of goods to be produced. They fix prices. They divide the profits among the various enterprises, etc. . . .

Competition becomes transformed into monopoly. The result is immense progress in the socialization of production. In particular, the process of technical invention and improvement becomes socialized.

This is something quite different from the old free competition between manufacturers, scattered and out of touch with one another, and producing for an unknown market. Concentration has reached the point at which it is possible to make an approximate estimate of all sources of raw materials (for example, the iron ore deposits) of a country and even, as we shall see, of several countries, or of the whole world. Not only are such estimates made, but these sources are captured by gigantic monopolist associations. An approximate estimate of the capacity of markets is also made, and the associations "divide" them up amongst themselves by agreement. Skilled labor is monopolized; the best engineers are engaged; the means of transport are captured—railways in America, shipping companies in Europe and America. Capitalism in its imperialist stage leads directly to the most comprehensive socialization of production; it, so to speak, drags the capitalists, against their will and consciousness, into some sort of a new social order, a transitional one from complete free competition to complete socialization.

Production becomes social, but appropriation remains private. The social means of production remain the private property of a few. The general framework of formally recognized free competition remains, and the yoke of a few monopolists on the rest of the population becomes a hundred times heavier, more burdensome, and intolerable. . . .

Here we no longer have competition between small and large, between technically developed and backward enterprises. We see here the monopolists throttling those who do not submit to them, to their yoke, to their dictation. This is how this process is reflected in the mind of a bourgeois economist:

"Even in the purely economic sphere," writes Kestner, "a certain change is taking place from commercial activity in the old sense of the word towards organizational-speculative activity. The greatest success no longer goes to the merchant whose technical and commercial experience enables him best of all to estimate the needs of the buyer, and who is able to discover and, so to speak, 'awaken' a latent demand; it goes to the speculative genius [?!] who knows how to estimate, or even only to sense in advance, the organizational development and the possibilities of certain connections between individual enterprises and the banks. . . ."

Translated into ordinary human language this means that the development of capitalism has arrived at a stage when, although commodity production still "reigns" and continues to be regarded as the basis of economic life, it has in reality been undermined and the bulk of the profits go to the "geniuses" of financial manipulation. At the basis of these manipulations and swindles lies socialized production; but the immense progress of mankind, which achieved this socialization, goes to benefit . . . the speculators. . . .

Monopoly! This is the last word in the "latest phase of capitalist development." But we shall only have a very insufficient, incomplete, and poor notion of the real power and the significance of modern monopolies if we do not take into consideration the part played by the banks.

2   Banks and Their New Role

The principal and primary function of banks is to serve as middlemen in the making of payments. In so doing they transform inactive money capital into active, that is, into capital yielding a profit; they collect all kinds of money revenues and place them at the disposal of the capitalist class.

As banking develops and becomes concentrated in a small number of establishments, the banks grow from modest middlemen into powerful monopolies having at their command almost the whole of the money capital of all the capitalists and small businessmen and also the larger part of the means of production and sources of raw materials in any one country and in a number of countries. This transformation of numerous modest middlemen into a handful of monopolists is one of the fundamental processes in the growth of capitalism into capitalist imperialism; for this reason we must first of all examine the concentration of banking.

In 1907–1908, the combined deposits of the German joint-stock banks, each having a capital of more than a million marks, amounted to 7,000 million marks; in 1912–1913, these deposits already amounted to 9,800 million marks, an increase of 40 per cent in five years; and of the 2,800 million increase, 2,750 million was divided among 57 banks, each having a capital of more than 10 million marks. The distribution of the deposits between big and small banks was as follows:

PERCENTAGE OF TOTAL DEPOSITS

	In 9 big Berlin banks	In the other 48 banks with a capital of more than 10 million marks	In 115 banks with a capital of 1-10 million marks	In small banks (with a capital of less than 1 million marks)
1907-08	47	32.5	16.5	4
1912-13	49	36	12	3

The small banks are being squeezed out by the big banks, of which only nine concentrate in their hands almost half the total deposits. But we have left out of account many important details, for instance, the transformation of numerous small banks into actual branches of the big banks, etc. Of this I shall speak later on.

At the end of 1913, Schulze-Gaevernitz estimated the deposits in the nine big Berlin banks at 5,100 million marks, out of a total of about 10,000 million marks. Taking into account not only the deposits, but the total bank capital, this author wrote: "At the end of 1909, the nine big Berlin banks, *together with their affiliated banks*, controlled 11,300 million marks, that is, about 83 per cent of the total German bank capital. The Deutsche Bank, which *together with its affiliated banks* controls nearly 3,000 million marks, represents, parallel to the Prussian State Railway Administration, the biggest and also the most decentralized accumulation of capital in the Old World."

I have emphasized the reference to the "affiliated" banks because it is one of the most important distinguishing features of modern capitalist concentration. The big enterprises, and the banks in particular, not only completely absorb the small ones, but also "annex" them, subordinate them, bring them into their "own" group or "concern" (to use the technical term) by acquiring "holdings" in their capital, by purchasing or exchanging shares, by a system of credits, etc., etc. . . .

The Deutsche Bank "group" is one of the biggest, if not the biggest, of the big banking groups. In order to trace the main threads which connect all the banks in this group, a distinction must be made between holdings of the first and second and third degree, or what amounts to the same thing, between dependence (of the lesser banks on the Deutsche Bank) in the first, second, and third degree. We then obtain the following picture:

THE DEUTSCHE BANK HAS HOLDINGS

	Direct or first-degree dependence	Second-degree dependence	Third-degree dependence
Permanently	in 17 other banks	9 of the 17 have holdings in 34 other banks	4 of the 9 have holdings in 7 other banks
For an indefinite period	in 5 other banks	—	—
Occasionally	in 8 other banks	5 of the 8 have holdings in 14 other banks	2 of the 5 have holdings in 2 other banks
Totals	in 30 other banks	14 of the 30 have holdings in 48 other banks	6 of the 14 have holdings in 9 other banks

Included in the eight banks "occasionally" dependent on the Deutsche Bank in the "first degree" are three foreign banks: one Austrian . . . and two Russian. . . . Altogether, the Deutsche Bank group comprises, directly and indirectly, partially and totally, 87 banks; and the total capital—its own and that of others which it controls—is estimated at between two and three thousand million marks.

It is obvious that a bank which stands at the head of such a group, and which enters into agreement with half a dozen other banks only slightly smaller than itself for the purpose of conducting exceptionally big and profitable financial operations like floating state loans, has already outgrown the part of "middleman" and has become an association of a handful of monopolists.

The rapidity with which the concentration of banking proceeded in Germany at the turn of the twentieth century is shown by the following data:

SIX BIG BERLIN BANKS

Year	Branches in Germany	Deposit banks and exchange offices	Constant holdings in German joint-stock banks	Total establishments
1895	16	14	1	42
1900	21	40	8	80
1911	104	276	63	450

We see the rapid expansion of a close network of channels which cover the whole country, centralizing all capital and all revenues, transforming thousands and thousands of scattered economic enterprises into a single national capitalist, and then into a world capitalist, economy. The "decentralization" that . . . exponent[s] of present-day bourgeois political economy, speak of . . . really means the subordination to a single center of an increasing number of formerly relatively "independent," or rather, strictly local economic units. In reality it is *centralization*, the enhancement of the role, importance and power of monopolist giants. . . .

These simple figures show perhaps better than lengthy disquisitions how the concentration of capital and the growth of bank turnover are radically changing the significance of the banks. Scattered capitalists are transformed into a single collective capitalist. When carrying the current accounts of a few capitalists, a bank, as it were, transacts a purely technical and exclusively auxiliary operation. When, however, this operation grows to enormous dimensions we find that a handful of monopolists subordinate to their will all the operations, both commercial and industrial, of the whole of capitalist society; for they are enabled—by means of their banking connections, their current accounts, and other financial operations—first, to *ascertain exactly* the financial position of the various capitalists, then to *control* them, to influence them by restricting or enlarging, facilitating or hindering credits, and finally to *entirely determine* their fate, determine their income, deprive them of capital, or permit them to increase their capital rapidly and to enormous dimensions, etc. . . .

The banking system "possesses, indeed, the form of universal bookkeeping and distribution of means of production on a social scale, but solely the form," wrote Marx in *Capital* half a century ago. . . . The figures we have quoted on the growth of bank capital, on the increase in the number of the branches and offices of the biggest banks, the increase in the number of their accounts, etc., present a concrete picture of this "universal bookkeeping" of the *whole* capitalist class; and not only of the capitalists, for the banks collect, even though temporarily, all kinds of money revenues—of small businessmen, office clerks, and of a tiny upper stratum of the working class. "Universal distribution of means of production"—that, from the formal aspect, is what *grows* out of the modern banks, which, numbering some three to six of the biggest in France, and six to eight in Germany, control millions and millions. In *substance*, however, the distribution of means of production is not at all "universal," but private, that is, it conforms to the interests of big capital, and primarily, of huge, monopoly capital, which operates under conditions in which the masses live in want, in which the whole development of agriculture hopelessly lags behind the development of industry, while within industry itself the "heavy industries" exact tribute from all other branches of industry. . . .

In other words, the old capitalism, the capitalism of free competition . . . is passing away. A new capitalism has come to take its place, bearing obvious features of something transient, a mixture of free competition and monopoly. The question naturally arises: *into what* is this new capitalism "developing"? . . .

Among the few banks which remain at the head of all capitalist economy as a result of the process of concentration, there is naturally to be observed an increasingly marked tendency towards monopolist agreements, towards a *bank trust*. In America, not nine, but *two* very big banks, those of the multimillionaires Rockefeller and Morgan, control a capital of eleven thousand million marks. In Germany the absorption of the Schaaffhausenscher Bankverein by the Disconto-Gesellschaft . . . was commented on in the following terms by the *Frankfurter Zeitung*, an organ of Stock Exchange interests:

"The concentration movement of the banks is narrowing the circle of establishments from which it is possible to obtain credits, and is consequently increasing the dependence of big industry upon a small number of banking groups. In view of the close connection between industry and the financial world, the freedom of movement of industrial companies which need banking capital is restricted. For this reason, big industry is watching the growing trustification of the banks with mixed feelings. Indeed, we have repeatedly seen the beginnings of certain agreements between the individual big banking concerns, which aim at restricting competition."

Again and again, the final word in the development of banking is monopoly.

As regards the close connection between the banks and industry, it is precisely in this sphere that the new role of the banks is, perhaps, most strikingly felt. When a bank discounts a bill for a firm, opens a current account for it, etc., these operations, taken separately, do not in the least diminish its independence, and the bank plays no other part than that of a modest middleman. But when such operations are multiplied and become an established practice, when the bank "collects" in its own hands enormous amounts of capital, when the running of a current account for a given firm enables the bank—and this is what happens—to obtain fuller and more detailed information about the economic position of its client, the result is that the industrial capitalist becomes more completely dependent on the bank.

At the same time a personal link-up, so to speak, is established between the banks and the biggest industrial and commercial enterprises, the merging of one with another through the acquisition of shares, through the appointment of bank directors to the Supervisory Boards (or Boards of Directors) of industrial and commercial enterprises, and vice versa. The German economist, Jeidels, has compiled most detailed data on this form of concentration of capital and of enterprises. Six of the biggest Berlin banks were represented by their directors in *344* industrial companies and by their board members in *407* others, making a total of *751* companies. In *289* of these companies they either had two of their representatives on each of the respective Supervisory Boards, or held the posts of chairmen. We find these industrial and commercial companies in the most diverse branches of industry: insurance, transport, restaurants, theaters, art industry, etc. On the other hand, on the Supervisory Boards of these six banks (in 1910) were fifty-one of the biggest industrialists. . . . From 1895 to 1910, each of these six banks participated in the share and bond issues of many hundreds of industrial companies (the number ranging from 281 to 419).

The "personal link-up" between the banks and industry is supplemented by the "personal link-up" between both of them and the government. "Seats on Supervisory Boards," writes Jeidels, "are freely offered to persons of title, also to ex-civil servants, who are able to do a great deal to facilitate [!!] relations with the authorities." . . . "Usually, on the Supervisory Board of a big bank, there is a member of parliament, or a Berlin city councillor."

The building and development, so to speak, of the big capitalist monopolies is therefore going on full steam ahead in all "natural" and "supernatural" ways. A sort of division of labor is being systematically developed among the several hundred kings of finance who reign over modern capitalist society. . . .

At precisely what period were the "new activities" of the big banks finally established? Jeidels gives us a fairly exact answer to this important question:

"The connections between the banks and industrial enterprises, with their new content, their new forms and their new organs, namely, the big banks which are organized on both a centralized and a decentralized basis, were scarcely a characteristic economic phenomenon before the nineties; in one sense, indeed, this initial date may be advanced to the year 1897, when the important 'mergers' took place and when, for the first time, the new form of decentralized organization was introduced to suit the industrial policy of the banks. This starting-point could perhaps be placed at an even later date, for it was the crisis of 1900 that enormously accelerated and intensified the process of concentration of industry and of banking, consolidated that process, for the first time transformed the connection with industry into the actual monopoly of the big banks, and made this connection much closer and more active."

Thus, the twentieth century marks the turning-point from the old capitalism to the new, from the domination of capital in general to the domination of finance capital.

3   Finance Capital and the Financial Oligarchy

"A steadily increasing proportion of capital in industry," writes Hilferding, "ceases to belong to the industrialists who employ it. They obtain the use of it only through the medium of the banks which, in relation to them, represent the owners of the capital. On the other hand, the bank is forced to sink an increasing share of its funds in industry. Thus, to an ever greater degree the banker is being transformed into an industrial capitalist. This bank capital, that is, capital in money form, which is thus actually transformed into industrial capital, I call 'finance capital.' " "Finance capital is capital controlled by banks and employed by industrialists."

This definition is incomplete insofar as it is silent on one extremely important fact—on the increase of concentration of production and of capital to such an extent that concentration is leading, and has led, to monopoly. But throughout the whole of his work, and particularly in the two chapters preceding the one from which this definition is taken, Hilferding stresses the part played by *capitalist monopolies*.

The concentration of production; the monopolies arising therefrom; the merging or coalescence of the banks with industry—such is the history of the rise of finance capital and such is the content of that concept.

We now have to describe how, under the general conditions of commodity production and private property, the "business operations" of capitalist monopolies inevitably lead to the domination of a financial oligarchy. . . .

But the monstrous facts concerning the monstrous rule of the financial oligarchy are so glaring that in all capitalist countries, in America, France and Germany, a whole literature has sprung up, written from the *bourgeois* point of view, but which, nevertheless, gives a fairly truthful picture and criticism—petty-bourgeois, naturally —of this oligarchy.

Paramount importance attaches to the "holding system." . . . The German economist, Heymann, probably the first to call attention to this matter, describes the essence of it in this way:

"The head of the concern controls the principal company [literally: the "mother company"]; the latter reigns over the subsidiary companies ["daughter companies"] which in their turn control still other subsidiaries ["grandchild companies"], etc. In this way, it is possible with a comparatively small capital to dominate immense spheres of production. Indeed, if holding 50 per cent of the capital is always sufficient to control a company, the head of the concern needs only one million to control eight million in the second subsidiaries. And if this 'interlocking' is extended, it is possible with one million to control sixteen million, thirty-two million, etc."

As a matter of fact, experience shows that it is sufficient to own 40 per cent of the shares of a company in order to direct its affairs, since in practice a certain number of small, scattered shareholders find it impossible to attend general meetings, etc. The "democratization" of the ownership of shares, from which the bourgeois sophists and opportunist so-called "Social-Democrats" expect (or say that they expect) the "democratization of capital," the strengthening of the role and significance of small-scale production, etc., is, in fact, one of the ways of increasing the power of the financial oligarchy. . . .

But the "holding system" not only serves enormously to increase the power of the monopolists; it also enables them to resort with impunity to all sorts of shady and dirty tricks to cheat the public, because formally the directors of the "mother company" are not legally responsible for the "daughter company," which is supposed to be "independent," and *through the medium* of which they can "pull off" *anything.* . . .

4 Export of Capital

Typical of the old capitalism, when free competition held undivided sway, was the export of *goods.* Typical of the latest stage of capitalism, when monopolies rule, is the export of *capital.*

Capitalism is commodity production at its highest stage of development, when labor-power itself becomes a commodity. The growth of internal exchange, and, particularly, of international exchange, is a characteristic feature of capitalism. The uneven and spasmodic development of individual enterprises, individual branches of industry, and individual countries is inevitable under the capitalist system. England became a capitalist country before any other, and by the middle of the nineteenth century, having adopted free trade, claimed to be the "workshop of the world," the supplier of manufactured goods to all countries, which in exchange were to keep her provided with raw materials. But in the last quarter of the nineteenth century, *this* monopoly was already undermined; for other countries, sheltering themselves with "protective" tariffs, developed into independent capitalist states. On the threshold of the twentieth century we see the formation of a new type of monopoly: first, monopolist associations of capitalists in all capitalistically developed countries; second, the monopolist position of a few very rich countries, in which the accumulation of capital has reached gigantic proportions. An enormous "surplus of capital" has arisen in the advanced countries.

It goes without saying that if capitalism could develop agriculture, which today is everywhere lagging terribly behind industry, if it could raise the living standards of the masses, who in spite of the amazing technical progress are everywhere still half-starved and poverty-stricken, there could be no question of a surplus of capital. This "argument" is very often advanced by the petty-bourgeois critics of capitalism. But if capitalism did these things it would not be capitalism; for both uneven development and a semi-starvation level of existence of the masses are fundamental and inevitable conditions and constitute premises of this mode of production. As long as capitalism remains what it is, surplus capital will be utilized not for the purpose of raising the standard of living of the masses in a given country, for this would mean a decline in profits for the capitalists, but for the purpose of increasing profits by exporting capital abroad to the backward countries. In these backward countries profits are usually high, for capital is scarce, the price of land is relatively low, wages are low, raw materials are cheap. The export of capital is made possible by a number of backward countries having already been drawn into world capitalist intercourse; main railways have either been or are being built in those countries; elementary conditions for industrial development have been created, etc. The need to export capital arises from the fact that in a few countries capitalism has become "overripe" and (owing to the backward state of agriculture and the poverty of the masses) capital cannot find a field for "profitable" investment.

Here are approximate figures showing the amount of capital invested abroad by the three principal countries:

CAPITAL INVESTED ABROAD: (000,000,000 francs)

Year	Great Britain	France	Germany
1862	3.6	—	—
1872	15.0	10(1869)	—
1882	22.0	15(1880)	?
1893	42.0	20(1890)	?
1902	62.0	27-37	12.5
1914	75-100.0	60	44.0

This table shows that the export of capital reached enormous dimensions only at the beginning of the twentieth century. Before the war the capital invested abroad by the three principal countries amounted to between 175,000 million and 200,000 million francs.

At the modest rate of 5 per cent, the income from this sum should reach from 8,000 to 10,000 million francs a year—a sound basis for the imperialist oppression and exploitation of most of the countries and nations of the world, for the capitalist parasitism of a handful of wealthy states!

How is this capital invested abroad distributed among the various countries? *Where* is it invested? Only an approximate answer can be given to these questions, but it is one sufficient to throw light on certain general relations and connections of modern imperialism.

DISTRIBUTION (APPROXIMATE) OF FOREIGN CAPITAL IN DIFFERENT PARTS OF THE GLOBE
(circa 1910)

	Great Britain	France	Germany	Total
		(000,000,000 marks)		
Europe	4	23	18	45
America	37	4	10	51
Asia, Africa and Australia . .	29	8	7	44
Total	70	35	35	140

The principal spheres of investment of British capital are the British colonies, which are very large also in America (for example, Canada), not to mention Asia, etc. In this case, enormous exports of capital are bound up most closely with vast colonies, of the importance of which for imperialism I shall speak later. In the case of France the situation is different. French capital exports are invested mainly in Europe, primarily in Russia (at least ten thousand million francs). This is mainly *loan* capital, government loans, and not capital invested in industrial undertakings. Unlike British colonial imperialism, French imperialism might be termed usury imperialism. In the case of Germany, we have a third type; colonies are inconsiderable, and German capital invested abroad is divided most evenly between Europe and America.

The export of capital influences and greatly accelerates the development of capitalism in those countries to which it is exported. While, therefore, the export of capital may tend to a certain extent to arrest development in the capital-exporting countries, it can only do so by expanding and deepening the further development of capitalism throughout the world. . . .

Finance capital has created the epoch of monopolies, and monopolies introduce everywhere monopolist principles: the utilization of "connections" for profitable transactions takes the place of competition on the open market. The most usual thing is to stipulate that part of the loan granted shall be spent on purchases in the creditor country, particularly on orders for war materials, or for ships, etc. In the course of the last two decades (1890–1910), France has very often resorted to this method. The export of capital thus becomes a means of encouraging the export of commodities. In this connection, transactions between particularly big firms assume a form which, as Schilder "mildly" puts it, "borders on corruption." Krupp in Germany, Schneider in France, Armstrong in Britain are instances of firms which have close connections with powerful banks and governments and which cannot easily be "ignored" when a loan is being arranged. . . .

Thus finance capital, literally, one might say, spreads its net over all countries of the world. An important role in this is played by banks founded in the colonies and by their branches. German imperialists look with envy at the "old" colonial countries which have been particularly "successful" in providing for themselves in this respect. In 1904, Great Britain had 50 colonial banks with 2,279 branches (in 1910 there were 72 banks with 5,449 branches); France had 20 with 136 branches; Holland, 16 with 68 branches; and Germany had "only" 13 with 70 branches. The American capitalists, in their turn, are jealous of the English and German: "In South America," they complained in 1915, "five German banks have forty branches and five British banks have seventy branches. . . . Britain and Germany have invested in Argentina, Brazil, and Uruguay in the last twenty-five years approximately four thousand million dollars, and as a result together enjoy 46 per cent of the total trade of these three countries."

The capital-exporting countries have divided the world among themselves in the figurative sense of the term. But finance capital has led to the *actual* division of the world.

5 Division of the World Among Capitalist Associations

Monopolist capitalist associations, cartels, syndicates and trusts first divided the home market among themselves and obtained more or less complete possession of the industry of their own country. But under capitalism the home market is inevitably bound up with the foreign market. Capitalism long ago created a world market. As the export of capital increased, and as the foreign and colonial connections and "spheres of influence" of the big monopolist associations expanded in all ways, things "naturally" gravitated towards an international agreement among these associations, and towards the formation of international cartels. . . .

Certain bourgeois writers (now joined by Karl Kautsky, who has completely abandoned the Marxist position he had held, for example, in 1909) have expressed the opinion that international cartels, being one of the most striking expressions of the internationalization of capital, give the hope of peace among nations under capitalism. Theoretically, this opinion is absolutely absurd, while in practice it is sophistry and a dishonest defense of the worst opportunism. International cartels show to what point capitalist monopolies have developed, and *the object* of the struggle between the various capitalist associations. This last circumstance is the most important; it alone shows us the historico-economic meaning of what is taking place; for the *forms* of the struggle may and do constantly change in accordance with varying, relatively specific, and temporary causes, but the *substance* of the struggle, its class *content*, positively *cannot* change while classes exist. Naturally, it is in the interests of, for example, the German bourgeoisie . . . to obscure the *substance* of the present economic struggle (the division of the world) and to emphasize now this and now another *form* of the struggle. . . . Of course, we have in mind not only the German bourgeoisie, but the bourgeoisie all over the world. The capitalists divide the world, not out of any particular malice, but because the degree of concentration which has been reached forces them to adopt this method in order to obtain profits. And they divide it "in proportion to capital," "in proportion to strength," because there cannot be any other method of division under commodity production and capitalism. But strength varies with the degree of economic and political development. In order to understand what is taking place, it is necessary to know what questions are settled by the changes in strength. The question as to whether these changes are "purely" economic or *non*economic (for example, military) is a secondary one, which cannot in the least affect fundamental views on the latest epoch of capitalism. To substitute the question of the form of the struggle and agreements (today peaceful, tomorrow warlike, the next day warlike again) for the question of the *substance* of the struggle and agreements between capitalist associations is to sink to the role of a sophist.

The epoch of the latest stage of capitalism shows us that certain relations between capitalist associations grow up, *based* on the economic division of the world; while parallel to and in connection with it, certain relations grow up between political alliances, between states, on the basis of the territorial division of the world, of the struggle for colonies, of the "struggle for spheres of influence."

6 Division of the World Among the Great Powers

In his book, on "the territorial development of the European colonies," A. Supan, the geographer, gives the following brief summary of this development at the end of the nineteenth century:

PERCENTAGE OF TERRITORY BELONGING TO THE EUROPEAN
COLONIAL POWERS (INCLUDING THE UNITED STATES)

	1876	1900	Increase or decrease
Africa	10.8	90.4	+79.6
Polynesia	56.8	98.9	+42.1
Asia	51.5	56.6	+ 5.1
Australia	100.0	100.0	—
America	27.5	27.2	— 0.3

"The characteristic feature of this period," he concludes, "is, therefore, the division of Africa and Polynesia." As there are no unoccupied territories—that is, territories that do not belong to any state—in Asia and America, it is necessary to amplify Supan's conclusion and say that the characteristic feature of the period under review is the final partitioning of the globe—final, not in the sense that *repartition* is impossible; on the contrary, repartitions are possible and inevitable—but in the sense that the colonial policy of the capitalist countries has *completed* the seizure of the unoccupied territories on our planet. For the first time the world is completely divided up, so that in the future *only* redivision is possible, that is, territories can only pass from one "owner" to another, instead of passing as ownerless territory to an "owner."

Hence, we are living in a peculiar epoch of world colonial policy, which is most closely connected with the "latest stage in the development of capitalism," with finance capital. For this reason, it is essential first of all to deal in greater detail with the facts, in order to ascertain as exactly as possible what distinguishes this epoch from those preceding it, and what the present situation is. In the first place, two questions of fact arise here: is an intensification of colonial policy, a sharpening of the struggle for colonies, observed precisely in the epoch of finance capital? And how, in this respect, is the world divided at the present time?

The American writer, Morris, in his book on the history of colonization, made an attempt to sum up the data on the colonial possessions of Great Britain, France and Germany during different periods of the nineteenth century. The following is a brief summary of the results he has obtained:

COLONIAL POSSESSIONS

YEAR	GREAT BRITAIN		FRANCE		GERMANY	
	Area (000,000 sq. m.)	Pop. (000,000)	Area (000,000 sq. m.)	Pop. (000,000)	Area (000,000 sq. m.)	Pop. (000,000)
1815-30	?	126.4	0.02	0.5	—	—
1860	2.5	145.1	0.2	3.4	—	—
1880	7.7	267.9	0.7	7.5	—	—
1899	9.3	309.0	3.7	56.4	1.0	14.7

For Great Britain, the period of the enormous expansion of colonial conquests was that between 1860 and 1880, and it was also very considerable in the last twenty years of the nineteenth century. For France and Germany this period falls precisely in these twenty years. We saw above that the development of premonopoly capitalism, of capitalism in which free competition was predominant, reached its limit in the 1860s and 1870s. We now see that it is *precisely after that period* that the tremendous "boom" in colonial conquests begins, and that the struggle for the territorial division of the world becomes extraordinarily sharp. It is beyond doubt, therefore, that capitalism's transition to the stage of monopoly capitalism, to finance capital, *is connected* with the intensification of the struggle for the partitioning of the world.

Hobson, in his work on imperialism, marks the years 1884–1900 as the epoch of intensified "expansion" of the chief European states. According to his estimate, Great Britain during these years acquired 3,700,000 square miles of territory with 57,000,000 inhabitants; France, 3,600,000 square miles with 36,500,000; Germany, 1,000,000 square miles with 14,700,000; Belgium, 900,000 square miles with 30,000,000; Portugal, 800,000 square miles with 9,000,000 inhabitants. The scramble for colonies by all the capitalist states at the end of the nineteenth century and particularly since the 1880s is a commonly known fact in the history of diplomacy and of foreign policy.

In the most flourishing period of free competition in Great Britain, that is, between 1840 and 1860, the leading British bourgeois politicians were *opposed* to colonial policy and were of the opinion that the liberation of the colonies, their complete separation from Britain, was inevitable and desirable. M. Beer, in an article, "Modern British Imperialism," published in 1898, shows that in 1852, Disraeli, a statesman who was generally inclined towards imperialism, declared: "The colonies are millstones round our necks." But at the end of the nineteenth century the British heroes of the hour were Cecil Rhodes and Joseph Chamberlain, who openly advocated imperialism and applied the imperialist policy in the most cynical manner!

It is not without interest to observe that even then these leading British bourgeois politicians saw the connection between what might be called the purely economic and the socio-political roots of modern imperialism. Chamberlain advocated imperialism as a "true, wise and economical policy" and pointed particularly to the German, American, and Belgian competition which Great Britain was encountering in the world market. Salvation lies in monopoly, said the capitalists as they formed cartels, syndicates, and trusts. Salvation lies in monopoly, echoed the political leaders of the bourgeoisie, hastening to appropriate the parts of the world not yet shared out. And Cecil Rhodes . . . expressed his imperialist views . . . in 1895 in the following terms: "I was in the East End of London [a working-class quarter] yesterday and attended a meeting of the unemployed. I listened to the wild speeches, which were just a cry for 'bread! bread!' and on my way home I pondered over the scene and I became more than ever convinced of the importance of imperialism. . . . My cherished idea is a solution for the social problem, that is, in order to save the 40,000,000 inhabitants of the United Kingdom from a bloody civil war, we colonial statesmen must acquire new lands to settle the surplus population, to provide new markets for the goods produced in the factories and mines. The Empire, as I have always said, is a bread and butter question. If you want to avoid civil war, you must become imperialists."

To present as precise a picture as possible of the territorial division of the world and of the changes which have occurred during the last decades in this respect, I shall utilize the data furnished by Supan in the work already quoted on the colonial possessions of all the powers of the world. Supan takes the years 1876 and 1900; I shall take the year 1876—a year very aptly selected, for it is precisely by that time that the premonopolist stage of development of West-European capitalism can be said to have been, in the main, completed —and the year 1914. . . . I [also] think it useful, in order to present a complete picture of the division of the world, to add brief data on noncolonial and semicolonial countries, in which category I place Persia, China, and Turkey; the first of these countries is already almost completely a colony; the second and third are becoming such.

We thus get the following result:

COLONIAL POSSESSIONS OF THE GREAT POWERS
(000,000 SQUARE KILOMETERS AND 000,000 INHABITANTS)

| | COLONIES | | | | METROPOLITAN COUNTRIES | | TOTAL | |
| | 1876 | | 1914 | | 1914 | | 1914 | |
	Area	Pop.	Area	Pop.	Area	Pop.	Area	Pop.
Great Britain	22.5	251.9	33.5	393.5	0.3	46.5	33.8	440.0
Russia	17.0	15.9	17.4	33.2	5.4	136.2	22.8	169.4
France	0.9	6.0	10.6	55.5	0.5	39.6	11.1	95.1
Germany	—	—	2.9	12.3	0.5	64.9	3.4	77.2
United States	—	—	0.3	9.7	9.4	97.0	9.7	106.7
Japan	—	—	0.3	19.2	0.4	53.0	0.7	72.2
Total for 6 Great Powers	40.4	273.8	65.0	523.4	16.5	437.2	81.5	960.6
Colonies of other powers (Belgium, Holland, etc)							9.9	45.3
Semi-colonial countries (Persia, China, Turkey)							14.5	361.2
Other countries							28.0	289.9
Total for the world							133.9	1,657.0

We clearly see from these figures how "complete" was the partition of the world at the turn of the twentieth century. After 1876 colonial possessions increased to enormous dimensions, by more than fifty per cent, from 40,000,000 to 65,000,000 square kilometers for the six biggest powers; the increase amounts to 25,000,000 square kilometers, fifty per cent more than the area of the metropolitan countries (16,500,000 square kilometers). In 1876 three powers had no colonies, and a fourth, France, had scarcely any. By 1914 these four powers had acquired colonies with an area of 14,100,000 square kilometers, that is, about half as much again as the area of Europe, with a population of nearly 100,000,000. The unevenness in the rate of expansion of colonial possessions is very great. If, for instance, we compare France, Germany and Japan, which do not differ very much in area and population, we see that the first has acquired almost three times as much colonial territory as the other two combined. In regard to finance capital, France, at the beginning of the period we are considering, was also, perhaps, several times richer than Germany and Japan put together. In addition to, and on the basis of, purely economic conditions, geographical and other conditions also affect the dimensions of colonial possessions. However strong the process of leveling the world, of leveling the economic and living conditions in different countries, may have been in the past decades as a result of the pressure of large-scale industry, exchange, and finance capital, considerable differences still remain; and among the six countries mentioned we see, first, young capitalist countries (America, Germany, Japan) whose progress has been extraordinarily rapid; second, countries with an old capitalist development (France and Great Britain), whose progress lately has been much slower than that of the previously mentioned countries, and third, a country most backward economically (Russia), where modern capitalist imperialism is enmeshed, so to speak, in a particularly close network of precapitalist relations.

Alongside the colonial possessions of the Great Powers, we have placed the small colonies of the small states, which are, so to speak, the next objects of a possible and probable "redivision" of colonies. These small states mostly retain their colonies only because the big powers are torn by conflicting interests, friction, etc., which prevent them from coming to an agreement on the division of the spoils. As to the "semicolonial" states, they provide an example of the transitional forms which are to be found in all spheres of nature and society. Finance capital is such a great, such a decisive, you might say, force in all economic and in all international relations that it is capable of subjecting, and actually does subject, to itself even states enjoying the fullest political independence; we shall shortly see examples of this. Of course, finance capital finds most "convenient," and derives the greatest profit from, a *form* of subjection which involves the loss of the political independence of the subjected countries and peoples. In this respect, the semicolonial countries provide a typical example of the "middle stage." It is natural that the struggle for these semidependent countries should have become particularly bitter in the epoch of finance capital, when the rest of the world has already been divided up.

Colonial policy and imperialism existed before the latest stage of capitalism, and even before capitalism. Rome, founded on slavery, pursued a colonial policy and practiced imperialism. But "general" disquisitions on imperialism, which ignore, or put into the background, the fundamental difference between socio-economic formations, inevitably turn into the most vapid banality or bragging. . . . Even the capitalist colonial policy of *previous* stages of capitalism is essentially different from the colonial policy of finance capital.

The principal feature of the latest stage of capitalism is the domination of monopolist associations of big employers. These monopolies are most firmly established when *all* the sources of raw materials are captured by one group, and we have seen with what zeal the international capitalist associations exert every effort to deprive their rivals of all opportunity of competing, to buy up, for example, iron fields, oil fields, etc. Colonial possession alone gives the monopolies complete guarantee against all contingencies in the struggle against competitors, including the case of the adversary wanting to be protected by a law establishing a state monopoly. The more capitalism is developed, the more strongly the shortage of raw materials is felt, the more intense the competition and the hunt for sources of raw materials throughout the whole world, the more desperate the struggle for the acquisition of colonies. . . .

Of course, the bourgeois reformists, and among them particularly the present-day adherents of Kautsky, try to belittle the importance of facts of this kind by arguing that raw materials "could be" obtained in the open market without a "costly and dangerous" colonial policy; and that the supply of raw materials "could be" increased enormously by "simply" improving conditions in agriculture in general. But such arguments become an apology for imperialism, an attempt to paint it in bright colors, because they ignore the principal feature of the latest stage of capitalism: monopolies. The free market is becoming more and more a thing of the past; monopolist syndicates and trusts are restricting it with every passing day, and "simply" improving conditions in agriculture means improving the conditions of the masses, raising wages, and reducing profits. Where, except in the imagination of sentimental reformists, are there any trusts capable of concerning themselves with the condition of the masses instead of the conquest of colonies?

Finance capital is interested not only in the already discovered sources of raw materials but also in potential sources, because present-day technical development is extremely rapid, and land which is useless today may be improved tomorrow if new methods are devised (to this end a big bank can equip a special expedition of engineers, agricultural experts, etc.), and if large amounts of capital are invested. This also applies to prospecting for minerals, to new methods of processing and utilizing raw materials, etc., etc. Hence, the inevitable striving of finance capital to enlarge its spheres of influence and even its actual territory. In the same way that the trusts capitalize their property at two or three times its value, taking into account its "potential" (and not actual) profits and the further results of monopoly, so finance capital in general strives to seize the largest possible amount of land of all kinds in all places, and by every means, taking into account potential sources of raw materials and fearing to be left behind in the fierce struggle for the last remnants of independent territory, or for the repartition of those territories that have been already divided. . . .

The interests pursued in exporting capital also give an impetus to the conquest of colonies, for in the colonial market it is easier to employ monopoly methods (and sometimes they are the only methods that can be employed) to eliminate competition, to ensure supplies, to secure the necessary "connections," etc.

The noneconomic superstructure which grows up on the basis of finance capital, its politics and its ideology, stimulates the striving for colonial conquest. "Finance capital does not want liberty; it wants domination," as Hilferding very truly says. And a French bourgeois writer, developing and supplementing, as it were, the ideas of Cecil Rhodes . . . writes that social causes should be added to the economic causes of modern colonial policy: "Owing to the growing complexities of life and the difficulties which weigh not only on the masses of the workers, but also on the middle classes, 'impatience, irritation, and hatred are accumulating in all the countries of the old civilization and are becoming a menace to public order; the energy which is being hurled out of the definite class channel must be given employment abroad in order to avert an explosion at home.' "

Since we are speaking of colonial policy in the epoch of capitalist imperialism, it must be observed that finance capital and its foreign policy, which is the struggle of the great powers for the economic and political division of the world, give rise to a number of *transitional* forms of state dependence. Not only are the two main groups of countries, those owning colonies and the colonies themselves, typical of this epoch but [the same is] also [true for] the diverse forms of dependent countries which, politically, are formally independent but in fact are enmeshed in the net of financial and diplomatic dependence. . . .

In order to finish with the question of the division of the world, I must make the following additional observation. This question was raised quite openly and definitely not only in American literature after the Spanish-American War and in English literature after the Anglo-Boer War, at the very end of the nineteenth century and the beginning of the twentieth; not only has German literature, which has "most jealously" watched "British imperialism," systematically given its appraisal of this fact. This question has also been raised in French bourgeois literature as definitely and broadly as is thinkable from the bourgeois point of view. Let me quote Driault . . . : "During the past few years, all the free territory of the globe, with the exception of China, has been occupied by the powers of Europe and North America. This has already brought about several conflicts and shifts of spheres of influence, and these foreshadow more terrible upheavals in the near future. For it is necessary to make haste. The nations which have not yet made provision for themselves run the risk of never receiving their share and never participating in the tremendous exploitation of the globe which will be one of the most essential features of the next century [that is, the twentieth]. That is why all Europe and America have lately been afflicted with the fever of colonial expansion, of 'imperialism,' that most noteworthy feature of the end of the nineteenth century." And the author added: "In this partition of the world, in this furious hunt for the treasures and the big markets of the globe, the relative strength of the empires founded in this nineteenth century is totally out of proportion to the place occupied in Europe by the nations which founded them. The dominant powers in Europe, the arbiters of her destiny, are *not* equally preponderant in the whole world. And, as colonial might, the hope of controlling as yet unassessed wealth, will evidently react upon the relative strength of the European powers, the colonial question—'imperialism,' if you will—which has already modified the political conditions of Europe itself, will modify them more and more."

7   Imperialism, as a Special Stage of Capitalism

We must now try to sum up, to draw together the threads of what has been said above on the subject of imperialism. Imperialism emerged as the development and direct continuation of the fundamental characteristics of capitalism in general. But capitalism only became capitalist imperialism at a definite and very high stage of its development, when certain of its fundamental characteristics began to change into their opposites, when the features of the epoch of transition from capitalism to a higher social and economic system had taken shape and revealed themselves in all spheres. Economically, the main thing in this process is the displacement of capitalist free competition by capitalist monopoly. Free competition is the basic feature of capitalism, and of commodity production generally; monopoly is the exact opposite of free competition, but we have seen the latter being transformed into monopoly before our eyes, creating large-scale industry and forcing out small industry, replacing large-scale by still larger-scale industry, and finally carrying concentration of production and capital to the point where monopoly has been and is the result: cartels, syndicates, and trusts, and merging with them, the capital of a dozen or so banks, which manipulate thousands of millions. At the same time the monopolies, which have grown out of free competition, do not eliminate the latter, but exist above it and alongside it, and thereby give rise to a number of very acute, intense antagonisms, frictions, and conflicts. Monopoly is the transition from capitalism to a higher system.

If it were necessary to give the briefest possible definition of imperialism we should have to say that imperialism is the monopoly stage of capitalism. Such a definition would include what is most important, for, on the one hand, finance capital is the bank capital of a few very big monopolist banks, merged with the capital of the monopolist associations of industrialists; and, on the other hand, the division of the world is the transition from a colonial policy which has extended without hindrance to territories unseized by any capitalist power, to a colonial policy of monopolist possession of the territory of the world, which has been completely divided up.

But very brief definitions, although convenient, for they sum up the main points, are nevertheless inadequate, since we have to deduce from them some especially important features of the phenomenon that has to be defined. And so, without forgetting the conditional and relative value of all definitions in general, which can never embrace all the concatenations of a phenomenon in its full development, we must give a definition of imperialism that will include the following five of its basic features:

(1) The concentration of production and capital has developed to such a high stage that it has created monopolies which play a decisive role in economic life; (2) the merging of bank capital with industrial capital, and the creation, on the basis of this "finance capital," of a financial oligarchy; (3) the export of capital as distinguished from the export of commodities acquires exceptional importance; (4) the formation of international monopolist capitalist associations which share the world among themselves; and (5) the territorial division of the whole world among the biggest capitalist

powers is completed. Imperialism is capitalism at that stage of development at which the dominance of monopolies and finance capital is established; in which the export of capital has acquired pronounced importance; in which the division of the world among the international trusts has begun; in which the division of all territories of the globe among the biggest capitalist powers has been completed.

We shall see later that imperialism can and must be defined differently if we bear in mind not only the basic, purely economic concepts—to which the above definition is limited—but also the historical place of this stage of capitalism in relation to capitalism in general, or the relation between imperialism and the two main trends in the working-class movement. The thing to be noted at this point is that imperialism, as interpreted above, undoubtedly represents a special stage in the development of capitalism. To enable the reader to obtain the most well-grounded idea of imperialism, I deliberately tried to quote as extensively as possible *bourgeois* economists who have to admit the particularly incontrovertible facts concerning the latest stage of capitalist economy. With the same object in view, I have quoted detailed statistics which reveal to what extent bank capital, etc., has grown, and which show precisely how the transformation of quantity into quality, of developed capitalism into imperialism, has expressed itself. Needless to say, of course, all boundaries in nature and in society are conventional and changeable, and it would be absurd to argue, for example, about the particular year or decade in which imperialism "definitely" became established. . . .

8   Parasitism and Decay of Capitalism

We now have to examine yet another significant aspect of imperialism to which most of the discussions on the subject usually attach insufficient importance. One of the shortcomings of the Marxist Hilferding is that on this point he has taken a step backward compared with the non-Marxist Hobson. I refer to parasitism, which is characteristic of imperialism.

As we have seen, the deepest economic foundation of imperialism is monopoly. This is capitalist monopoly, that is, monopoly which has grown out of capitalism and which exists in the general environment of capitalism, commodity production, and competition, in permanent and insoluble contradiction to this general environment. Nevertheless, like all monopoly, it inevitably engenders a tendency to stagnation and decay. Since monopoly prices are fixed, even temporarily, the motive cause of technical and, consequently, of all other progress disappears to a certain extent and, further, the *eco-*

nomic possibility arises of deliberately retarding technical progress. . . .

. . . Certainly, monopoly under capitalism can never completely . . . eliminate competition in the world market (and this, by the way, is one of the reasons why the theory of ultra-imperialism is so absurd). Certainly, the possibility of reducing the cost of production and increasing profits by introducing technical improvements operates in the direction of change. But the *tendency* to stagnation and decay, which is characteristic of monopoly, continues to operate, and in some branches of industry, in some countries, for certain periods of time, it gains the upper hand.

The monopoly ownership of very extensive, rich, or well-situated colonies operates in the same direction.

Further, imperialism is an immense accumulation of money capital in a few countries. . . . Hence the extraordinary growth of a class, or rather, of a stratum of *rentiers*, that is, people who live by "clipping coupons," who take no part in any enterprise whatever, whose profession is idleness. The export of capital, one of the most essential economic bases of imperialism, still more completely isolates the *rentiers* from production and sets the seal of parasitism on the whole country that lives by exploiting the labor of several overseas countries and colonies. . . .

The income of the *rentiers* [in Great Britain] is *five times greater* than the income obtained from the foreign trade of the biggest "trading" country in the world! This is the essence of imperialism and imperialist parasitism.

For that reason the term "*rentier* state" (*Rentnerstaat*), or usurer state, is coming into common use in the economic literature that deals with imperialism. The world has become divided into a handful of usurer states and a vast majority of debtor states. . . .

The *rentier* state is a state of parasitic, decaying capitalism, and this circumstance cannot fail to influence all the socio-political conditions of the countries concerned, in general, and the two fundamental trends in the working-class movement, in particular. To demonstrate this in the clearest possible manner let me quote Hobson, who is a most reliable witness, since he cannot be suspected of leaning towards Marxist orthodoxy; on the other hand, he is an Englishman who is very well acquainted with the situation in the country which is richest in colonies, in finance capital, and in imperialist experience.

With the Anglo-Boer War fresh in his mind, Hobson describes the connection between imperialism and the interests of the "financiers," their growing profits from contracts, supplies, etc., and writes: "While the directors of this definitely parasitic policy are capitalists, the same motives appeal to special classes of the workers. In many towns most important trades are dependent upon government employment or contracts; the imperialism of the metal and shipbuilding centers is attributable in no small degree to this fact." Two sets of circumstances, in this writer's opinion, have weakened the old empires: (1) "economic parasitism," and (2) the formation of armies recruited from subject peoples. "There is first the habit of economic parasitism, by which the ruling state has used its provinces, colonies, and dependencies in order to enrich its ruling class and to bribe its lower classes into acquiescence." And I shall add that the economic possibility of such bribery, whatever its form may be, requires high monopolist profits.

As for the second circumstance, Hobson writes: "One of the strangest symptoms of the blindness of imperialism is the reckless indifference with which Great Britain, France, and other imperial nations are embarking on this perilous dependence. Great Britain has gone farthest. Most of the fighting by which we have won our Indian Empire has been done by natives; in India, as more recently in Egypt, great standing armies are placed under British commanders; almost all the fighting associated with our African dominions, except in the southern part, has been done for us by natives."

Hobson gives the following economic appraisal of the prospect of the partitioning of China: "The greater part of Western Europe might then assume the appearance and character already exhibited by tracts of country in the South of England, in the Riviera and in the tourist-ridden or residential parts of Italy and Switzerland, little clusters of wealthy aristocrats drawing dividends and pensions from the Far East, with a somewhat larger group of professional retainers and tradesmen and a larger body of personal servants and workers in the transport trade and in the final stages of production of the more perishable goods; all the main arterial industries would have disappeared, the staple foods and manufactures flowing in as tribute from Asia and Africa. . . . We have foreshadowed the possibility of even a larger alliance of Western states, a European federation of great powers which, so far from forwarding the cause of world civilization, might introduce the gigantic peril of a Western parasitism, a group of advanced industrial nations, whose upper classes drew vast tribute from Asia and Africa, with which they supported great tame masses of retainers, no longer engaged in the staple industries of agriculture and manufacture, but kept in the performance of personal or minor industrial services under the control of a new financial aristocracy. Let those who would scout such a theory [it would be better to say: prospect] as undeserving of consideration examine the economic and social condition of districts in Southern England today which are already reduced to this condition, and reflect upon the vast extension of such a system which might be rendered feasible by the subjection of China to the economic control of similar groups of financiers, investors, and political and business officials, draining the greatest potential reservoir of profit the world has ever known, in order to consume it in Europe. The situation is far too complex, the play of world forces far too incalculable, to render this or any other single interpretation of the future very probable; but the influences which govern the imperialism of Western Europe today are moving in this direction, and, unless counteracted or diverted, make towards some such consummation."

The author is quite right: *if* the forces of imperialism had not been counteracted they would have led precisely to what he has described. The significance of a "United States of Europe" in the present imperialist situation is correctly appraised. He should have added, however, that, also *within* the working class movement, the opportunists, who are for the moment victorious in most countries, are "working" systematically and undeviatingly in this very direction. Imperialism, which means the partitioning of the world, and the exploitation of other countries besides China, which means high monopoly profits for a handful of very rich countries, makes it economically possible to bribe the upper strata of the proletariat and thereby fosters, gives shape to, and strengthens opportunism. We must not, however, lose sight of the forces which counteract imperialism in general, and opportunism in particular, and which, naturally, the social-liberal Hobson is unable to perceive.

The German opportunist, Gerhard Hildebrand, who was once expelled from the Party for defending imperialsm, and who could today be a leader of the so-called "Social-Democratic" Party of Germany, supplements Hobson well by his advocacy of a "United States of Western Europe" (without Russia) for the purpose of "joint" action . . . against the African Negroes, against the "great Islamic movement," for the maintenance of a "powerful army and navy," against a "Sino-Japanese coalition," etc. . . .

An increasing proportion of land in England is being taken out of cultivation and used for sport, for the diversion of the rich. As far as Scotland—the most aristocratic place for hunting and other sports—is concerned, it is said that "it lives on its past and on Mr. Carnegie" (the American multimillionaire). On horse racing and fox hunting alone England annually spends £14,000,000 (nearly 130 million rubles). The number of *rentiers* in England is about one million. The percentage of the productively employed population to the total population is declining:

	Population England and Wales (000,000)	Workers in basic industries (000,000)	Per cent of total population
1851	17.9	4.1	23
1901	32.5	4.9	15

And in speaking of the British working class the bourgeois student of "British imperialism at the beginning of the twentieth century" is obliged to distinguish systematically between the *"upper stratum"* of the workers and the *"lower stratum of the proletariat proper."* The upper stratum furnishes the bulk of the membership of cooperatives, of trade unions, of sporting clubs, and of numerous religious sects. To this level is adapted the electoral system, which in Great Britain is still *"sufficiently restricted to exclude the lower stratum of the proletariat proper"*![5] In order to present the condition of the British working class in a rosy light, only this upper stratum—which constitutes a *minority* of the proletariat—is usually spoken of. For instance, "the problem of unemployment is mainly a London problem and that of the lower proletarian stratum, *to which the politicians attach little importance. . . .*" He should have said: to which the bourgeois politicians and the "socialist" opportunists attach little importance.

One of the special features of imperialism connected with the facts I am describing is the decline in emigration from imperialist countries and the increase in immigration into these countries from the more backward countries where lower wages are paid. As Hobson observes, emigration from Great Britain has been declining since 1884. In that year the number of emigrants was 242,000, while in 1900, the number was 169,000. Emigration from Germany reached the highest point between 1881 and 1890, with a total of 1,453,000 emigrants. In the course of the following two decades, it fell to 544,000 and to 341,000. On the other hand, there was an increase in the number of workers entering Germany from Austria, Italy, Russia and other countries. According to the 1907 census, there were 1,342,294 foreigners in Germany, of whom 440,800 were industrial workers and 257,329 agricultural workers. In France, the workers employed in the mining industry are, "in great part," foreigners: Poles, Italians, and Spaniards. In the United States, immigrants from Eastern and Southern Europe are engaged in the most poorly paid jobs, while American workers provide the highest percentage of overseers or of the better-paid workers. Imperialism has the tendency to create privileged sections also among the workers and to detach them from the broad masses of the proletariat.

It must be observed that in Great Britain the tendency of imperialism to split the workers, to strengthen opportunism among them, and to cause temporary decay in the working-class movement revealed itself much earlier than the end of the nineteenth and the beginning of the twentieth centuries; for two important distinguishing features of

---

5 The electoral reform of 1918 in Great Britain altered this situation and granted nearly universal manhood suffrage. [*Ed.*]

imperialism were already observed in Great Britain in the middle of the nineteenth century—vast colonial possessions and a monopolist position in the world market. Marx and Engels traced this connection between opportunism in the working-class movement and the imperialist features of British capitalism systematically, during the course of several decades. For example, on October 7, 1858, Engels wrote to Marx: "The English proletariat is actually becoming more and more bourgeois, so that this most bourgeois of all nations is apparently aiming ultimately at the possession of a bourgeois aristocracy and a bourgeois proletariat *alongside* the bourgeoisie. For a nation which exploits the whole world this is of course to a certain extent justifiable." Almost a quarter of a century later . . . Engels speaks of the "worst English trade unions which allow themselves to be led by men sold to, or at least paid by, the middle class." In a letter to Kautsky . . . Engels wrote: "You ask me what the English workers think about colonial policy. Well, exactly the same as they think about politics in general. There is no workers' party here, there are only Conservatives and Liberal-Radicals, and the workers gaily share the feast of England's monopoly of the world market and the colonies." . . .

This clearly shows the causes and effects. The causes are : (1) exploitation of the whole world by this country; (2) its monopolist position in the world market; (3) its colonial monopoly. The effects are: (1) a section of the British proletariat becomes bourgeois; (2) a section of the proletariat allows itself to be led by men bought by, or at least paid by, the bourgeoisie. The imperialism of the beginning of the twentieth century completed the division of the world among a handful of states, each of which today exploits (in the sense of drawing superprofits from) a part of the "whole world" only a little smaller than that which England exploited in 1858; each of them occupies a monopolist position in the world market thanks to trusts, cartels, finance capital, and creditor and debtor relations; each of them enjoys to some degree a colonial monopoly. . . .

The distinctive feature of the present situation is the prevalence of such economic and political conditions that are bound to increase the irreconcilability between opportunism and the general and vital interests of the working-class movement: imperialism has grown from an embryo into the predominant system; capitalist monopolies occupy first place in economics and politics; the division of the world has been completed; on the other hand, instead of the undivided monopoly of Great Britain, we see a few imperialist powers contending for the right to share in this monopoly, and this struggle is characteristic of the whole period of the early twentieth century. Opportunism cannot now be completely triumphant in the working-class movement of one country for decades as it was in Britain in the second half of the nineteenth century; but in a number of countries it has grown ripe, overripe, and rotten, and has become completely merged with bourgeois policy in the form of "social-chauvinism." . . .

10   The Place of Imperialism in History

We have seen that in its economic essence imperialism is monopoly capitalism. This in itself determines its place in history, for monopoly that grows out of the soil of free competition, and precisely out of free competition, is the transition from the capitalist system to a higher socio-economic order. We must take special note of the four principal types of monopoly, or principal manifestations of monopoly capitalism, which are characteristic of the epoch we are examining.

First, monopoly arose out of the concentration of production at a very high stage. This refers to the monopolist capitalist associations, cartels, syndicates, and trusts. We have seen the important part these play in present-day economic life. At the beginning of the twentieth century, monopolies had acquired complete supremacy in the advanced countries, and although the first steps towards the formation of the cartels were taken by countries enjoying the protection of high tariffs (Germany, America), Great Britain, with her system of free trade, revealed the same basic phenomenon, only a little later, namely, the birth of monopoly out of the concentration of production.

Second, monopolies have stimulated the seizure of the most important sources of raw materials, especially for the basic and most highly cartelized industries in capitalist society: the coal and iron industries. The monopoly of the most important sources of raw materials has enormously increased the power of big capital and has sharpened the antagonism between cartelized and noncartelized industry.

Third, monopoly has sprung from the banks. The banks have developed from modest middleman enterprises into the monopolists of finance capital. Some three to five of the biggest banks in each of the foremost capitalist countries have achieved the "personal link-up" between industrial and bank capital and have concentrated in their hands the control of thousands upon thousands of millions which form the greater part of the capital and income of entire countries. A financial oligarchy, which throws a close network of dependence relationships over all the economic and political institutions of present-day bourgeois society without exception—such is the most striking manifestation of this monopoly.

Fourth, monopoly has grown out of colonial policy. To the numerous "old" motives of colonial policy, finance capital has added the struggle for the sources of raw materials, for the export of capital, for spheres of influence, that is, for spheres for profitable deals, concessions, monopoly profits and so on, economic territory in general. When the colonies of the European powers, for instance, comprised only one-tenth of the territory of Africa (as was the case in 1876), colonial policy was able to develop by methods other than those of monopoly—by the "free grabbing" of territories, so to speak. But when nine-tenths of Africa had been seized (by 1900), when the whole world had been divided up, there was inevitably ushered in the era of monopoly possession of colonies and, consequently, of particularly intense struggle for the division and the redivision of the world.

The extent to which monopolist capital has intensified all the contradictions of capitalism is generally known. It is sufficient to mention the high cost of living and the tyranny of the cartels. This intensification of contradictions constitutes the most powerful driving force of the transitional period of history, which began from the time of the final victory of world finance capital.

Monopolies, oligarchy, the striving for domination and not for freedom, the exploitation of an increasing number of small or weak nations by a handful of the richest or most powerful nations—all these have given birth to those distinctive characteristics of imperialism which compel us to define it as parasitic or decaying capitalism. More and more prominently there emerges, as one of the tendencies of imperialism, the creation of the "*rentier* state," the usurer state, in which the bourgeoisie to an ever-increasing degree lives on the proceeds of capital exports and by "clipping coupons." It would be a mistake to believe that this tendency to decay precludes the rapid growth of capitalism. It does not. In the epoch of imperialism, certain branches of industry, certain strata of the bourgeoisie, and certain countries betray, to a greater or lesser degree, now one and now another of these tendencies. On the whole, capitalism is growing far more rapidly than before; but this growth is not only becoming more and more uneven in general, its unevenness also manifests itself, in particular, in the decay of the countries which are richest in capital (Britain). . . .

The receipt of high monopoly profits by the capitalists in one of the numerous branches of industry, in one of the numerous countries, etc., makes it economically possible for them to bribe certain sections of the workers, and for a time a fairly considerable minority of them, and win them to the side of the bourgeoisie of a given industry or given nation against all the others. The intensification of antagonisms between imperialist nations for the division of the world increases this urge. And so there is created that bond between imperialism and opportunism, which revealed itself first and most clearly in Great Britain, owing to the fact that certain features of imperialist development were observable there much earlier than in other countries. Some writers . . . are prone to wave aside the connection between imperialism and opportunism in the working-class movement—a particularly glaring fact at the present time—by resorting to "official optimism" . . . like the following: the cause of the opponents of capitalism would be hopeless if it were progressive capitalism that led to the increase of opportunism, or, if it were the best-paid workers who were inclined towards opportunism, etc. We must have no illusions about "optimism" of this kind. It is optimism in respect of opportunism; it is optimism which serves to conceal opportunism. As a matter of fact the extraordinary rapidity and the particularly revolting character of the development of opportunism is by no means a guarantee that its victory will be durable: the rapid growth of a painful abscess on a healthy body can only cause it to burst more quickly and thus relieve the body of it. The most dangerous of all in this respect are those who do not wish to understand that the fight against imperialism is a sham and humbug unless it is inseparably bound up with the fight against opportunism.

II.

THE YEAR OF REVOLUTION: 1917

LETTERS FROM AFAR
(MARCH 1917)

The First Stage of the First Revolution

THE FIRST REVOLUTION engendered by the imperialist world war has broken out. The first revolution but certainly not the last.

Judging by the scanty information available in Switzerland, the first stage of this first revolution, namely, of the *Russian* revolution of March 1, 1917, has ended. This first stage of our revolution will certainly not be the last.

How could such a "miracle" have happened, that in only eight days . . . a monarchy collapsed that had maintained itself for centuries, and that in spite of everything had managed to maintain itself throughout the three years of the tremendous, nation-wide class battles of 1905–1907?

There are no miracles in nature or history, but every abrupt turn in history, and this applies to every revolution, presents such a wealth of content, unfolds such unexpected and specific combinations of forms of struggle and alignment of forces of the contestants, that to the lay mind there is much that must appear miraculous.

The combination of a number of factors of world-historic importance was required for the tsarist monarchy to have collapsed in a few days. We shall mention the chief of them.

Without the tremendous class battles and the revolutionary energy displayed by the Russian proletariat during the three years 1905–1907, the second revolution could not possibly have been so rapid in the sense that its *initial stage* was completed in a few days. The first revolution (1905) deeply ploughed the soil, uprooted age-old prejudices, awakened millions of workers and tens of millions of peasants to political life and political struggle and revealed to each other—and to the world—*all* classes (and all the principal parties) of Russian society in their true character and in the true alignment of their interests, their forces, their modes of action, and their immediate and ultimate aims. This first revolution, and the succeeding period

of counter-revolution (1907–1914), laid bare the very essence of the
tsarist monarchy, brought it to the "utmost limit," exposed all the
rottenness and infamy, the cynicism and corruption of the Tsar's
clique, dominated by that monster, Rasputin. It exposed all the
bestiality of the Romanov family—those pogrom-mongers who
drenched Russia in the blood of Jews, workers, and revolutionaries,
those *landlords*, "first among peers," *who own millions* of [acres] of
land and are prepared to stoop to any brutality, to any crime, to ruin
and strangle any number of citizens in order to preserve the "sacred
right of property" for themselves *and their class*.

Without the Revolution of 1905–1907 and the counter-revolution
of 1907–1914, there could not have been that clear "self-determina-
tion" of all classes of the Russian people and of the nations inhabit-
ing Russia, that determination of the relation of these classes to each
other and to the tsarist monarchy, which manifested itself during the
eight days of the February-March Revolution of 1917. This eight-
day revolution was "performed," if we may use a metaphorical expression, as though after a dozen major and minor rehearsals, the "actors"
knew each other, their parts, their places and their setting in every
detail, through and through, down to every more or less important
shade of political trend and mode of action.

For the first great Revolution of 1905 . . . led, after the lapse
of twelve years, to the "brilliant," the "glorious" Revolution of
1917. . . . But this required a great, mighty, and all-powerful "stage
manager," capable, on the one hand, of vastly accelerating the course
of world history, and, on the other, of engendering world-wide crises
of unparalleled intensity—economic, political, national, and international. Apart from an extraordinary acceleration of world history, it
was also necessary that history make particularly abrupt turns, in
order that at one such turn the filthy and blood-stained cart of the
Romanov monarchy should be overturned at *one stroke*.

This all-powerful "stage manager," this mighty accelerator was
the imperialist world war.

That it is a world war is now indisputable, for the United States
and China are already half involved today and will be fully involved
tomorrow.

That it is an imperialist war on *both* sides is now likewise indisputable. Only the capitalists and their hangers-on, the social-patriots
and social-chauvinists . . . can deny or gloss over this fact. *Both* the
German and the Anglo-French bourgeoisie are waging the war for the
plunder of foreign countries and the strangling of small nations, for
financial world supremacy and the division and redivision of colonies,
and in order to save the tottering capitalist regime by misleading and
dividing the workers of the various countries.

The imperialist war was bound, with objective inevitability, immensely to accelerate and intensify to an unprecedented degree the class struggle of the proletariat against the bourgeoisie; it was bound to turn into a civil war between the hostile classes.

This *transformation has been started* by the February-March Revolution of 1917, the first stage of which has been marked [initially] by a joint blow at tsarism struck by two forces: one, the whole of bourgeois and landlord Russia, with all her unconscious hangers-on and all her conscious leaders, the British and French ambassadors and capitalists, and the other, *the Soviet of Workers' Deputies*, which has begun to win over the soldiers' and peasants' deputies.

These three political camps, these three fundamental political forces—(1) the tsarist monarchy, the head of the feudal landlords, of the old bureaucracy and the military caste; (2) bourgeois and landlord Octobrist-Cadet Russia, behind which trailed the petty bourgeoisie . . .; (3) the Soviet of Workers' Deputies, which is seeking to make the entire proletariat and the entire mass of the poorest part of the population its allies—these three *fundamental* political forces fully and clearly revealed themselves even in the eight days of the "first stage" and even to an observer so remote from the scene of events as the present writer, who is obliged to content himself with the meager foreign press dispatches.[1]

But before dealing with this in greater detail, I must return to the part of my letter devoted to a factor of prime importance, namely, the imperialist world war.

The war shackled the belligerent powers, the belligerent groups of capitalists, the "bosses" of the capitalist system, the slave-owners of the capitalist slave system, to each other with *chains of iron. One bloody clot*—such is the social and political life of the present moment in history.

The socialists who deserted to the bourgeoisie on the outbreak of the war . . . clamored loud and long against the "illusions" of the revolutionaries . . . against the "farcical dream" of turning the imperialist war into a civil war. They sang praises in every key to the strength, tenacity, and adaptability allegedly revealed by capitalism— *they*, who had aided the capitalists to "adapt," tame, mislead, and divide the working classes of the various countries!

But "he who laughs last laughs best." The bourgeoisie has been unable to delay for long the revolutionary crisis engendered by the war. That crisis is growing with irresistible force in all countries, beginning with Germany, which, according to an observer who recently visited that country, is suffering "brilliantly organized famine," and ending with England and France, where *famine is also* looming,

---

1 Lenin was in political exile in Switzerland when the revolution against the Tsar broke out. [*Ed.*]

but where organization is far less "brilliant."

It was natural that the revolutionary crisis should have broken out *first of all* in tsarist Russia, where the disorganization was most appalling and the proletariat most revolutionary (not by virtue of any special qualities but because of the living traditions of 1905). This crisis was precipitated by the series of extremely severe defeats sustained by Russia and her allies. They shook up the old machinery of government and the old order and roused the anger of *all* classes of the population against them; they embittered the army, wiped out a very large part of the old commanding personnel, composed of die-hard aristocrats and exceptionally corrupt bureaucratic elements, and replaced it by young, fresh, mainly bourgeois, commoner, petty-bourgeois personnel. Those who, groveling to the bourgeoisie or simply lacking backbone, howled and wailed about "defeatism" are now faced by the fact of the historical connection between the defeat of the most backward and barbarous tsarist monarchy and the *beginning* of the revolutionary conflagration.

But while the defeats early in the war were a negative factor that precipitated the upheaval, the *connection* between Anglo-French finance capital, Anglo-French imperialism, and Russian Octobrist-Cadet capital was a factor that hastened this crisis by the direct *organization of a plot* again Nicholas Romanov.

This highly important aspect of the situation is, for obvious reasons, hushed up by the Anglo-French press and maliciously emphasized by the German. We Marxists must soberly face the truth and not allow ourselves to be confused either by the lies, the official sugary diplomatic and ministerial lies, of the first group of imperialist belligerents, or by the sniggering and smirking of their financial and military rivals of the other belligerent group. The whole course of events in the February-March Revolution clearly shows that the British and French embassies, with their agents and "connections," who had long been making the most desperate efforts to prevent "separate" agreements and a separate peace between Nicholas II (and last, we hope, and we will endeavor to make him that) and Wilhelm II, directly organized a plot in conjunction with the Octobrists and Cadets, in conjunction with a section of the generals and army and St. Petersburg garrison officers, with the express object of *deposing* Nicholas Romanov. . . .

That the revolution succeeded so quickly and—seemingly, at the first superficial glance—so radically, is only due to the fact that, as a result of an extremely unique historical situation, *absolutely dissimilar currents*, *absolutely heterogeneous* class interests, *absolutely contrary* political and social strivings have *merged*, and in a strikingly "harmonious" manner. Namely, the conspiracy of the Anglo-French imperialists, who impelled . . . [the bourgeoisie] to seize power *for the purpose of continuing the imperialist war,* for the purpose of conducting the war still more ferociously and obstinately, for the purpose of *slaughtering fresh millions* of Russian workers and peasants in order that the . . . [Russians] might obtain Constantinople, the French capitalists Syria, the British capitalists Mesopotamia, and so on. This on the one hand. On the other, there was a profound proletarian and mass popular movement of a revolutionary character (a movement of the entire poorest section of the population of town and country) for *bread*, for *peace*, for *real freedom*. . . .

Side by side with this government—which as regards the *present* war is but the agent of the billion-dollar "firm" "England and France"—there has arisen the chief, unofficial, as yet undeveloped and comparatively weak *workers' government*, which expresses the interests of the proletariat and of the entire poor section of the urban and rural population. This is the *Soviet of Workers' Deputies* in Petrograd, which is seeking connections with the soldiers and peasants, and also with the agricultural workers, with the latter particularly and primarily, of course, more than with the peasants.

Such is the *actual* political situation, which we must first endeavor to define with the greatest possible objective precision, in order that Marxist tactics may be based upon the only possible solid foundation —the foundation of *facts*.

The tsarist monarchy has been smashed, but not finally destroyed.

Ours is a bourgeois revolution, we Marxists say; *therefore* the workers must open the eyes of the people to the deception practiced by the bourgeois politicians, teach them to put no faith in words, to depend entirely on their *own* strength, their *own* organization, their *own* unity, and their *own* weapons.

The [present] government . . . *cannot,* even if it sincerely wanted to (only infants can think that . . . [its leaders] are sincere), *cannot* give the people *either peace, bread, or freedom.*

It cannot give peace because it is a war government, a government for the continuation of the imperialist slaughter, a government of *plunder*, out to plunder Armenia, Galicia, and Turkey, annex Constantinople, reconquer Poland, Courland, Lithuania, etc. It is a government bound hand and foot by Anglo-French imperialist capital. Russian capital is merely a branch of the world-wide "firm" which manipulates *hundreds of billions* of rubles and is called "England and France."

It cannot give bread because it is a bourgeois government. *At best*, it can give the people "brilliantly organized famine," as Germany has done. But the people will not accept famine. They will learn, and probably very soon, that there is bread and that it can be obtained, but only by methods that *do not respect the sanctity of capital and landownership.*

It cannot give freedom because it is a landlord and capitalist government which *fears* the people and has already begun to strike a bargain with the Romanov dynasty.

The tactical problems of our immediate attitude towards this government will be dealt with in another article. In it, we shall explain the peculiarity of the present situation, which is a *transition* from the first stage of the revolution to the second, and why the slogan, the "task of the day," at *this* moment must be: *Workers, you have performed miracles of proletarian heroism, the heroism of the people, in the civil war against tsarism. You must perform miracles of organization, organization of the proletariat and of the whole people, to prepare the way for your victory in the second stage of the revolution.*

Confining ourselves for the *present* to an analysis of the class struggle and the alignment of class forces at this stage of the revolution, we have still to put the question: who are the proletariat's *allies* in *this* revolution?

It has *two* allies: first, the broad mass of the semiproletarian and partly also of the small-peasant population, who number scores of millions and constitute the overwhelming majority of the population of Russia. For this mass, peace, bread, freedom, and land are *essential*. It is inevitable that to a certain extent this mass will be under the influence of the bourgeoisie, particularly of the petty bourgeoisie, to which it is most akin in its conditions of life, vacillating between the bourgeoisie and the proletariat. The cruel lessons of war, and they will be *the more* cruel the more vigorously the war is prosecuted . . . will *inevitably* push this mass towards the proletariat, compel it to follow the proletariat. We must now take advantage of the relative freedom of the new order and of the Soviets of Workers' Deputies to *enlighten* and *organize* this mass first of all and above all. Soviets of Peasants' Deputies and Soviets of Agriculture Workers—that is one of our most urgent tasks. In this connection we shall strive not only for the agricultural workers to establish their own separate Soviets, but also for the propertyless and poorest peasants to organize *separately* from the well-to-do peasants. The special tasks and special forms of organization urgently needed at the present time will be dealt with in the next letter.

Second, the ally of the Russian proletariat is the proletariat of all the belligerent countries and of all countries in general. At present this ally is to a large degree repressed by the war, and all too often the European social-chauvinists [who] speak in its name . . . have deserted to the bourgeoisie. But the liberation of the proletariat from their influence has progressed with every month of the imperialist war, and the Russian revolution will *inevitably* immensely hasten this process.

With these two allies, the proletariat, *utilizing the peculiarities* of the present transition situation, can and will proceed, first, to the achievement of a democratic republic and complete victory of the peasantry over the landlords . . . and then to *socialism*, which alone can give the war-weary people *peace*, *bread*, and *freedom*.

THE TASKS OF THE PROLETARIAT IN THE PRESENT REVOLUTION (APRIL 1917)

The April Theses

I DID NOT arrive in Petrograd until the night of April 3, and therefore at the meeting on April 4 I could, of course, deliver the report on the tasks of the revolutionary proletariat only on my own behalf, and with reservations as to insufficient preparation. . . .

I publish these personal theses of mine with only the briefest explanatory notes, which were developed in far greater detail in the report.

Theses

1) In our attitude towards the war, which under the new government . . . unquestionably remains on Russia's part a predatory imperialist war owing to the capitalist nature of that government, not the slightest concession to "revolutionary defensism" is permissible.

The class-conscious proletariat can give its consent to a revolutionary war, which would really justify revolutionary defensism, only on condition: (a) that power pass to the proletariat and the poorest sections of the peasants aligned with the proletariat; (b) that all annexations be renounced in deed and not in word; (c) that a complete break be effected in actual fact with all capitalist interests.

In view of the undoubted honesty of those broad sections of the mass believers in revolutionary defensism who accept the war only as a necessity, and not as a means of conquest, in view of the fact that they are being deceived by the bourgeoisie, it is necessary with particular thoroughness, persistence, and patience to explain their error to them, to explain the inseparable connection existing between capital and the imperialist war, and to prove that without overthrowing capital *it is impossible* to end the war by a truly democratic peace, a peace not imposed by violence.

The most widespread campaign for this view must be organized in the army at the front. Fraternization.

2) The specific feature of the present situation in Russia is that the country is *passing* from the first stage of the revolution—which, owing to the insufficient class-consciousness and organization of the proletariat, placed power in the hands of the bourgeoisie—to its *second* stage, which must place power in the hands of the proletariat and the poorest sections of the peasants.

This transition is characterized, on the one hand, by a maximum of legally recognized rights (Russia is *now* the freest of all the belligerent countries in the world); on the other, by the absence of violence towards the masses, and, finally, by their unreasoning trust in the government of capitalists, those worst enemies of peace and socialism.

This peculiar situation demands of us an ability to adapt ourselves to the *special* conditions of Party work among unprecedentedly large masses of proletarians who have just awakened to political life.

3) No support for the Provisional Government; the utter falsity of all its promises should be made clear, particularly of those relating to the renunciation of annexations. Exposure in place of the impermissible, illusion-breeding "demand" that *this* government, a government of capitalists, should *cease* to be an imperialist government.

4) Recognition of the fact that in most of the Soviets of Workers' Deputies our Party is in a minority, so far a small minority, as against *a bloc of all* the petty-bourgeois opportunist elements . . . who have yielded to the influence of the bourgeoisie and spread that influence among the proletariat.

The masses must be made to see that the Soviets of Workers' Deputies are the *only possible* form of revolutionary government, and that therefore our task is, as long as *this* government yields to the influence of the bourgeoisie, to present a patient, systematic, and persistent *explanation* of the errors of their tactics, an explanation especially adapted to the practical needs of the masses.

As long as we are in the minority we carry on the work of criticizing and exposing errors and at the same time we preach the necessity of transferring the entire state power to the Soviets of Workers' Deputies, so that the people may overcome their mistakes by experience.

5) Not a parliamentary republic—to return to a parliarmentary republic from the Soviets of Workers' Deputies would be a retrograde

step—but a Republic of Soviets of Workers', Agricultural Laborers' and Peasants' Deputies throughout the country, from top to bottom.

Abolition of the police, the army, and the bureaucracy.[1]

The salaries of all officials, all of whom are elective and displaceable at any time, not to exceed the average wage of a competent worker.

6) The weight of emphasis in the agrarian program to be shifted to the Soviets of Agricultural Laborers' Deputies.

Confiscation of all landed estates.

Nationalization of *all* lands in the country, the land to be disposed of by the local Soviets of Agricultural Laborers' and Peasants' Deputies. The organization of separate Soviets of Deputies of Poor Peasants. The setting up of a model farm on each of the large estates (ranging in size from 100 to 300 dessiatines [2] according to local and other conditions, and to the decisions of the local bodies) under the control of the Soviets of Agricultural Laborers' Deputies and for the public account.

7) The immediate amalgamation of all banks in the country into a single national bank, and the institution of control over it by the Soviet of Workers' Deputies.

8) It is not our *immediate* task to "introduce" socialism, but only to bring social production and the distribution of products at once under the *control* of the Soviets of Workers' Deputies.

9) Party tasks:

    (a) Immediate convocation of a Party congress;

    (b) Alteration of the Party Program, mainly:

        (1) On the question of imperialism and the imperialist war;

        (2) On our attitude towards the state and *our* demand for a "commune state"; [3]

        (3) Amendment of our out-of-date minimum program.

    (c) Change of the Party's name.

10) A new International. . . .

---

1   That is, the standing army to be replaced by the arming of the whole people. [*L.*]

2   One dessiatine equals approximately 2.7 acres. [Ed.]

3   That is, a state of which the Paris Commune was the prototype. [*L.*]

THE IMPENDING CATASTROPHE
AND HOW TO COMBAT IT
(OCTOBER 1917)

Famine Is Approaching

UNAVOIDABLE CATASTROPHE is threatening Russia. The railways are incredibly disorganized and the disorganization is progressing. The railways will come to a standstill. The delivery of raw materials and coal to the factories will cease. The delivery of grain will cease. The capitalists are deliberately and unremittingly sabotaging (damaging, stopping, disrupting, hampering) production, hoping that an unparalleled catastrophe will mean the collapse of the republic and democracy, and of the Soviets and proletarian and peasant associations generally, thus facilitating the return to a monarchy and the restoration of the unlimited power of the bourgeoisie and the landowners.

The danger of a great catastrophe and of famine is imminent. All the newspapers have written about this time and again. A tremendous number of resolutions have been adopted by the parties and by the Soviets of Workers', Soldiers' and Peasants' Deputies—resolutions which admit that a catastrophe is unavoidable, that it is very close, that extreme measures are necessary to combat it, that "heroic efforts" by the people are necessary to avert ruin, and so on.

Everybody says this. Everybody admits it. Everybody has decided it is so.

Yet nothing is being done.

Six months of revolution have elapsed. The catastrophe is even closer. Unemployment has assumed a mass scale. To think that there is a shortage of goods in the country, the country is perishing from a shortage of food and labor, although there is a sufficient quantity of grain and raw materials, and yet in such a country, at so critical a moment, there is mass unemployment! What better evidence is needed to show that after six months of revolution (which some call a great revolution, but which so far it would perhaps be fairer to call a rotten revolution), in a democratic republic, with an abundance of unions, organs, and institutions which proudly call themselves "revolutionary-democratic," absolutely *nothing* of any importance has actually been done to avert catastrophe, to avert famine? We are nearing ruin with increasing speed. The war will not wait and is causing increasing dislocation in every sphere of national life.

Yet the slightest attention and thought will suffice to satisfy anyone that the ways of combating catastrophe and famine are available, that the measures required to combat them are quite clear, simple, perfectly feasible, and fully within reach of the people's forces, and that these measures are *not* being adopted *only* because, *exclusively* because, their realization would affect the fabulous profits of a handful of landowners and capitalists.

And, indeed, it is safe to say that every single speech, every single article in a newspaper of any trend, every single resolution passed by any meeting or institution quite clearly and explicitly recognizes the chief and principal measure of combating, of averting, catastrophe and famine. This measure is control, supervision, accounting, regulation by the state, introduction of a proper distribution of labor-power in the production and distribution of goods, husbanding of the people's forces, the elimination of all wasteful effort, economy of effort. Control, supervision, and accounting are the prime requisites for combating catastrophe and famine. This is indisputable and universally recognized. And it is just what *is not being done* from fear of encroaching on the supremacy of the landowners and capitalists, on their immense, fantastic and scandalous profits, profits derived from high prices and war contracts (and, directly or indirectly, nearly everybody is now "working" for the war), profits about which everybody knows and which everybody sees, and over which everybody is sighing and groaning.

And absolutely nothing is being done to introduce such control, accounting, and supervision by the state as would be in the least effective.

Complete Government Inactivity

There is a universal, systematic, and persistent sabotage of every kind of control, supervision, and accounting and of all state attempts to institute them. And one must be incredibly naïve not to understand, one must be an utter hypocrite to pretend not to understand, where this sabotage comes from and by what means it is being carried on.

For this sabotage by the bankers and capitalists, their *frustration* of every kind of control, supervision, and accounting, is being adapted to the state forms of a democratic republic, to the existence of "revolutionary-democratic" institutions. The capitalist gentlemen have learned very well a fact which all supporters of scientific socialism profess to recognize but which the Mensheviks and Socialist-Revolutionaries tried to forget as soon as their friends had secured cushy jobs as ministers, deputy ministers, etc. That fact is that the economic substance of capitalist exploitation is in no wise affected by the substitution of republican-democratic forms of government for monarchist forms, and that, consequently, the reverse is also true—only the *form* of the struggle for the inviolability and sanctity of capitalist profits need be changed in order to uphold them under a democratic republic as effectively as under an absolute monarchy.

The present, modern republican-democratic sabotage of every kind of control, accounting, and supervision consists in the capitalists "eagerly" accepting in words the "principle" of control and the necessity for control (as, of course, do all Mensheviks and Socialist-Revolutionaries), insisting only that this control be introduced "gradually," methodically, and in a "state-regulated" way. In practice, however, these specious catchwords serve to conceal the *frustration* of control, its nullification, its reduction to a fiction, the mere playing at control, the delay of all businesslike and practically effective measures, the creation of extraordinarily complicated, cumbersome, and bureaucratically lifeless institutions of control which are hopelessly dependent on the capitalists, and which do absolutely nothing and cannot do anything. . . .

Control Measures Are Known to All and Easy to Take

One may ask: aren't methods and measures of control extremely complex, difficult, untried, and even unknown? Isn't the delay due to the fact that although the statesmen of the Cadet Party, the merchant and industrial class, and the Menshevik and Socialist-Revolutionary parties have for six months been toiling in the sweat of their brow, investigating, studying, and discovering measures and methods of control, still the problem is incredibly difficult and has not yet been solved?

Unfortunately, this is how they are trying to present matters to hoodwink the ignorant, illiterate, and downtrodden muzhiks and the Simple Simons who believe everything and never look into things. In reality, however, even tsarism, even the "old regime," when it set up the War Industries Committees, *knew* the principal measure, the chief method and way to introduce control, namely, by uniting the population according to profession, purpose of work, branch of labor, etc. But tsarism *feared* the union of the population and therefore did its best to restrict and artificially hinder this generally known, very easy, and quite practical method and way of control.

All the belligerent countries, suffering as they are from the extreme burdens and hardships of the war, suffering—in one degree or another—from economic chaos and famine, have long ago outlined, determined, applied, and tested a *whole series* of control measures, which consist almost invariably in uniting the population and in setting up or encouraging unions of various kinds, in which state representatives participate, which are under the supervision of the state, etc. All these measures of control are known to all, much has been said and written about them, and the laws passed by the advanced belligerent powers relating to control have been translated into Russian or expounded in detail in the Russian press.

If our state really *wanted* to exercise control in a businesslike and earnest fashion, if its institutions had not condemned themselves to "complete inactivity" by their servility to the capitalists, all the state would have to do would be to draw freely on the rich store of control measures which are already known and have been used in the past. The only obstacle to this . . . was, and still is, that control would bring to light the fabulous profits of the capitalists and would cut the ground from under these profits.

To explain this most important question more clearly (a question which is essentially equivalent to that of the program of *any* truly revolutionary government that would wish to save Russia from war and famine), let us enumerate these principal measures of control and examine each of them.

We shall see that all a government would have had to do, if its name of revolutionary-democratic government were not merely a joke, would have been to decree, in the very first week of its existence, the adoption of the principal measures of control, to provide for strict and severe punishment to be meted out to capitalists who fraudulently evaded control, and to call upon the population itself to exercise supervision over the capitalists and see to it that they scrupulously observed the regulations on control—and control would have been introduced in Russia long ago.

These principal measures are:

(1) Amalgamation of all banks into a single bank, and state control over its operations, or nationalization of the banks.

(2) Nationalization of the syndicates, that is, the largest, monopolistic capitalist associations (sugar, oil, coal, iron and steel, and other syndicates).

(3) Abolition of commercial secrecy.

(4) Compulsory syndication (that is, compulsory amalgamation into associations) of industrialists, merchants, and employers generally.

(5) Compulsory organization of the population into consumers' societies, or encouragement of such organization, and the exercise of control over it.

Let us see what the significance of each of these measures would be if carried out in a revolutionary-democratic way.

Nationalization of the Banks

The banks, as we know, are centers of modern economic life, the principal nerve centers of the whole capitalist economic system. To talk about "regulating economic life" and yet evade the question of the nationalization of the banks means either betraying the most profound ignorance or deceiving the "common people" by florid words and grandiloquent promises with the deliberate intention of not fulfilling these promises.

It is absurd to control and regulate deliveries of grain, or the production and distribution of goods generally, without controlling and regulating bank operations. It is like trying to snatch at odd kopeks and closing one's eyes to millions of rubles. Banks nowadays are so closely and intimately bound up with trade (in grain and everything else) and with industry that without "laying hands" on the banks nothing of any value, nothing "revolutionary-democratic," can be accomplished.

But perhaps for the state to "lay hands" on the banks is a very difficult and complicated operation? They usually try to scare philistines with this very idea—that is, the capitalists and their defenders try it—because it is to their advantage to do so.

In reality, however, nationalization of the banks, which would not deprive any "owner" of a single kopek, presents absolutely no technical or cultural difficulties, and is being delayed *exclusively* because of the vile greed of an insignificant handful of rich people. If nationalization of the banks is so often confused with the confiscation of private property, it is the bourgeois press, which has an interest in deceiving the public, that is to blame for this widespread confusion.

The ownership of the capital wielded by and concentrated in the banks is certified by printed and written certificates called shares, bonds, bills, receipts, etc. Not a single one of these certificates would be invalidated or altered if the banks were nationalized, that is, if all the banks were amalgamated into a single state bank. Whoever owned fifteen rubles on a savings account would continue to be the owner of fifteen rubles after the nationalization of the banks; and whoever had fifteen million rubles would continue after the nationalization of the banks to have fifteen million rubles in the form of shares, bonds, bills, commercial certificates and so on.

What, then, is the significance of nationalization of the banks?

It is that no effective control of any kind over the individual banks and their operations is possible (even if commercial secrecy, etc., were abolished) because it is impossible to keep track of the extremely complex, involved, and wily tricks that are used in drawing up balance-sheets, founding fictitious enterprises and subsidiaries, enlisting the services of figureheads, and so on, and so forth. Only the amalgamation of all banks into one, which in itself would imply no change whatever in respect of ownership, and which, we repeat, would not deprive any owner of a single kopek, would make it *possible* to exercise real control—provided, of course, all the other measures indicated above were carried out. Only by nationalizing the banks *can* the state *put itself in a position* to know where and how, whence and when, millions and billions of rubles flow. And only control over the banks, over the center, over the pivot and chief mechanism of capitalist circulation, would make it possible to organize real and not fictitious control over all economic life, over the production and distribution of staple goods, and organize that "regulation of economic life" which otherwise is inevitably doomed to remain a ministerial phrase designed to fool the common people. Only control over banking operations, provided they were concentrated in a single state bank, would make it possible, if certain other easily practicable measures were adopted, to organize the effective collection of income tax in such a way as to prevent the concealment of property and incomes; for at present the income tax is very largely a fiction.

Nationalization of the banks has only to be decreed, and it would be carried out by the directors and employees themselves. No special machinery, no special preparatory steps on the part of the state would be required, for this is a measure that can be effected by a single decree, "at a single stroke." It was made economically feasible by capitalism itself once it had developed to the stage of bills, shares, bonds, and so on. *All* that is required is to *unify accountancy*. And if the revolutionary-democratic government were to decide that immediately, by telegraph, meetings of managers and employees should be called in every city, and conferences in every region and in the country as a whole, for the immediate amalgamation of all banks into a single state bank, this reform would be carried out in a few weeks. Of course, it would be the managers and the higher bank officials who would offer resistance, who would try to deceive the state, delay matters, and so on, for these gentlemen would lose their highly remunerative posts and the opportunity of performing highly profitable fraudulent operations. *That is the heart of the matter.* But there is not the slightest technical difficulty in the way of the amalgamation of the banks; and if the state power were revolutionary not only in word (that is, if it did not fear to do away with inertia and routine), if it were democratic not only in word (that is, if it acted in the interests of the majority of the people and not of a handful of rich men), it would be enough to decree confiscation of property and imprisonment as the penalty for managers, board members, and big shareholders for the slightest delay or for attempting to conceal documents and accounts. It would be enough, for example, to organize the poorer employees *separately* and to reward them for detecting fraud and delay on the part of the rich for nationalization of the banks to be effected as smoothly and rapidly as can be.

The advantages accruing to the whole people from nationalization of the banks—*not* to the workers especially (for the workers have little to do with banks) but to the mass of peasants and small industrialists—would be enormous. The saving in labor would be gigantic, and, assuming that the state would retain the former number of bank employees, nationalization would be a highly important step towards making the use of the banks universal, towards increasing the number of their branches, putting their operations within easier reach, etc., etc. The availability of credit on easy terms for the *small* owners, for the peasants, would increase immensely. As to the state, it would for the first time be in a position first to *review* all the chief monetary operations, which would be unconcealed, then to *control* them, then to *regulate* economic life, and finally to *obtain* millions and billions for major state transactions, without paying the capitalist gentlemen sky-high "commissions" for their "services." That is the reason—and the only reason—why all the capitalists, all the bourgeois professors, all the bourgeoisie, and all the ["socialists"] . . . who serve them are prepared to fight tooth and nail against nationalization of the banks and invent thousands of excuses to prevent the adoption of this very easy and very pressing measure, although *even* from the standpoint of the "defense" of the country, that is, from the military standpoint, this measure would provide a gigantic advantage and would tremendously enhance the "military might" of the country. . . .

Nationalization of the banks would greatly facilitate the simultaneous nationalization of the insurance business, that is, the amalgamation of all the insurance companies into one, the centralization of their operations, and state control over them. Here, too, congresses of insurance company employees could carry out this amalgamation immediately and without any great effort, provided a revolutionary-democratic government decreed this and ordered directors and big shareholders to effect the amalgamation without the slightest delay and held every one of them strictly accountable for it. The capitalists have invested hundreds of millions of rubles in the insurance business;

the work is all done by the employees. The amalgamation of this business would lead to lower insurance premiums, would provide a host of facilities and conveniences for the insured, and would make it possible to increase their number without increasing expenditure of effort and funds. Absolutely nothing but the inertia, routine, and self-interest of a handful of holders of remunerative jobs are delaying this reform, which, among other things, would enhance the country's defense potential by economizing national labor and creating a number of highly important opportunities to "regulate economic life" not in word, but in deed.

Nationalization of the Syndicates

Capitalism differs from the old, precapitalistic systems of economy in having created the closest interconnection and interdependence of the various branches of the economy. Were this not so, incidentally, no steps towards socialism would be technically feasible. Modern capitalism, under which the banks dominate production, has carried this interdependence of the various branches of the economy to the utmost. The banks and the more important branches of industry and commerce have become inseparably merged. This means, on the one hand, that it is impossible to nationalize the banks alone, without proceeding to create a state monopoly of commercial and industrial syndicates (sugar, coal, iron, oil, etc.), and without nationalizing them. It means, on the other hand, that if carried out in earnest, the regulation of economic activity would demand the simultaneous nationalization of the banks and the syndicates.

Let us take the sugar syndicate as an example. It came into being under tsarism and at that time developed into a huge capitalist combine of splendidly equipped refineries. And, of course, this combine, thoroughly imbued with the most reactionary and bureaucratic spirit, secured scandalously high profits for the capitalists and reduced its employees to the status of humiliated and downtrodden slaves lacking any rights. Even at that time the state controlled and regulated production—in the interests of the rich, the magnates.

All that remains to be done here is to transform reactionary-bureaucratic regulation into revolutionary-democratic regulation by simple decrees providing for the summoning of a congress of employees, engineers, directors and shareholders, for the introduction of uniform accountancy, for control by the workers' unions, etc. This is an exceedingly simple thing, yet it has not been done! Under what is a democratic republic, the regulation of the sugar industry *actually* remains reactionary-bureaucratic; everything remains as of old—the dissipation of national labor, routine, and stagnation, and the enrichment of the [owners]. . . . Democrats and not bureaucrats, the workers and other employees and not the "sugar barons," should be called upon to exercise independent initiative—and this could and should be done in a few days, at a single stroke, if only the Socialist-Revolutionaries and Mensheviks did not befog the minds of the people by plans for "association" with these very sugar barons, for the very association with the wealthy from which the "complete inaction" of the government in the matter of regulating economic life follows with absolute inevitability, and of which it is a consequence.[1]

Abolition of Commercial Secrecy

Unless commercial secrecy is abolished, either control over production and distribution will remain an empty promise, only needed by the Cadets to fool the Socialist-Revolutionaries and Mensheviks, and by the Socialist-Revolutionaries and Mensheviks to fool the working classes, or control can be exercised only by reactionary-bureaucratic methods and means. Although this is obvious to every unprejudiced person, and although *Pravda* persistently demanded the abolition of commercial secrecy (and was suppressed largely for this reason by the Kerensky government which is subservient to capital), neither our republican government nor the "authorized bodies of revolutionary democracy" have even thought of this *first step* to real control.

This is the very key to all control. Here we have the most sensitive spot of capital, which is robbing the people and sabotaging production. And this is exactly why the Socialist-Revolutionaries and Mensheviks are afraid to do anything about it.

The usual argument of the capitalists, one reiterated by the petty bourgeoisie without reflection, is that in a capitalist economy the abolition of commercial secrecy is in general absolutely impossible, for private ownership of the means of production and the dependence of the individual undertakings on the market render essential the "sanctity" of commercial books and commercial operations, including, of course, banking operations.

Those who in one form or another repeat this or similar arguments allow themselves to be deceived and themselves deceive the people by shutting their eyes to two fundamental, highly important, and generally known facts of modern economic activity. The first

---

1 These lines had been written when I learned from the newspapers that the Kerensky government is introducing a sugar monopoly, and, of course, is introducing it in a reactionary-bureaucratic way, without congresses of workers and other employees, without publicity, and without curbing the capitalists! [L.]

fact is the existence of large-scale capitalism, that is, the peculiar features of the economic system of banks, syndicates, large factories, etc. The second fact is the war.

It is modern large-scale capitalism, which is everywhere becoming monopoly capitalism, that deprives commercial secrecy of every shadow of reasonableness, turns it into hypocrisy and into an instrument exclusively for concealing financial swindles and the fantastically high profits of big capital. Large-scale capitalist economy, by its very technical nature, is socialized economy, that is, it both operates for millions of people and, directly or indirectly, unites by its operations hundreds, thousands, and tens of thousands of families. It is not like the economy of the small handicraftsman or the middle peasant who keep no commercial books at all and who would therefore not be affected by the abolition of commercial secrecy!

As it is, the operations conducted in large-scale business are known to hundreds or more persons. Here the law protecting commercial secrecy does not serve the interests of production or exchange, but those of speculation and profit-seeking in their crudest form, and of direct fraud, which, as we know, in the case of joint-stock companies is particularly widespread and very skillfully concealed by reports and balance-sheets, so compiled as to deceive the public.

While commercial secrecy is unavoidable in small commodity production, that is, among the small peasants and handicraftsmen, where production itself is not socialized but scattered and disunited, in large-scale capitalist production, the protection of commercial secrecy means protection of the privileges and profits of literally a handful of people *against* the interest of the whole people. This has already been recognized by the law, inasmuch as provision is made for the publication of the accounts of joint-stock companies. But *this* control, which has already been introduced in all advanced countries, as well as in Russia, is a reactionary-bureaucratic control which does not open the eyes of the *people* and which *does not allow the whole truth* about the operations of joint-stock companies to become known.

To act in a revolutionary-democratic way, it would be necessary to immediately pass another law abolishing commercial secrecy, compelling the big undertakings and the wealthy to render the fullest possible accounts, and investing every group of citizens of substantial democratic numerical strength (1,000 or 10,000 voters, let us say) with the right to examine *all* the records of any large undertaking. Such a measure could be fully and easily effected by a simple decree. It *alone* would allow full scope for *popular* initiative in control, through the office employees' unions, the workers' unions, and all the political parties, and it alone would make control effective and democratic.

Add to this the war. The vast majority of commercial and industrial establishments are now working not for the "free market," but *for the government*, for the war. This is why I have already stated . . . that people who counter us with the argument that socialism cannot be introduced are liars, and barefaced liars at that, because it is not a question of introducing socialism now, directly, overnight, but of *exposing plunder of the state*.

Capitalist "war" economy (that is, economy directly or indirectly connected with war contracts) is systematic and legalized *plunder*, and the Cadet gentry, who, together with the Mensheviks and Socialist-Revolutionaries, are opposing the abolition of commercial secrecy, are nothing but *aiders and abettors of plunder*. . . .

Compulsory Association

Compulsory syndication, that is, compulsory association, of the industrialists, for example, is already being practiced in Germany. Nor is there anything new in it. . . .

Compulsory syndication is, on the one hand, a means whereby the state, as it were, expedites capitalist development, which everywhere leads to the organization of the class struggle and to a growth in the number, variety, and importance of unions. On the other hand, compulsory "unionization" is an indispensable precondition for any kind of effective control and for all economy of national labor.

The German law, for instance, binds the leather manufacturers of a given locality or of the whole country to form an association, on the board of which there is a representative of the state for the purpose of control. A law of this kind does not directly, that is, in itself, affect property relations in any way; it does not deprive any owner of a single kopek and does not predetermine whether the control is to be exercised in a reactionary-bureaucratic or a revolutionary-democratic form, direction, or spirit.

Such laws can and should be passed in our country immediately, without wasting a single week of precious time; it should be left to *social conditions themselves* to determine the more specific forms of enforcing the law, the speed with which it is to be enforced, the methods of supervision over its enforcement, etc. In this case, the state requires no special machinery, no special investigation, nor preliminary enquiries for the passing of such a law. All that is required is the determination to break with certain private interests of the capitalists, who are "not accustomed" to such interference and have no desire to forfeit the super-profits which are ensured by the old methods of management and the absence of control.

No machinery and no "statistics" (. . . to substitute for the revolutionary initiative of the peasants) are required to *pass* such a law, inasmuch as its implementation must be made the duty of the manufacturers or industrialists themselves, of the *available* public forces, under the control of the available public (that is, nongovernment, nonbureaucratic) forces too, which, however, must consist by all means of the so-called "lower estates," that is, of the oppressed and exploited classes, which in history have always proved to be immensely *superior* to the exploiters in their capacity for heroism, self-sacrifice, and comradely discipline.

Let us assume that we have a really revolutionary-democratic government and that it decides that the manufacturers and industrialists in every branch of production who employ, let us say, not less than two workers shall immediately amalgamate into . . . associations. Responsibility for the strict observance of the law is laid in the first place on the manufacturers, directors, board members, and big shareholders (for they are the real leaders of modern industry, its real masters). They shall be regarded as deserters from military service, and punished as such, if they do not work for the immediate implementation of the law, and shall bear mutual responsibility, one answering for all, and all for one, with the whole of their property. Responsibility shall next be laid on all office employees, who shall also form *one* union, and on all workers and their trade union. The purpose of "unionization" is to institute the fullest, strictest, and most detailed accountancy, but chiefly to *combine operations* in the purchase of raw materials, the sale of products, and the *economy* of national funds and forces. When the separate establishments are amalgamated into a single syndicate, this economy can attain tremendous proportions, as economic science teaches us and as is shown by the example of all syndicates, cartels, and trusts. And it must be repeated that this unionization will not in itself alter property relations one iota and will not deprive any owner of a single kopek. This circumstance must be strongly stressed, for the bourgeois press constantly "frightens" small and medium proprietors by asserting that socialists in general, and the Bolsheviks in particular, want to "expropriate" them—a deliberately false assertion, as socialists do not intend to, cannot, and will not expropriate the small peasant *even if there is a fully socialist* revolution. All the time we are speaking *only* of the immediate and urgent measures, which have already been introduced in Western Europe and which a democracy that is at all consistent ought to introduce immediately in our country to combat the impending and inevitable catastrophe.

Serious difficulties, both technical and cultural, would be encountered in amalgamating the small and very small proprietors into associations, owing to the extremely small proportions and technical primitiveness of their enterprises and the illiteracy or lack of education of the owners. But precisely such enterprises could be exempted from the law (as was pointed out above in our hypothetical example). Their non-amalgamation, let alone their belated amalgamation, could create no serious obstacle, for the part played by the huge number of small enterprises in the sum total of production and their importance to the economy as a whole are *negligible*, and, moreover, they are often in one way or another dependent on the big enterprises.

Only the big enterprises are of decisive importance; and here the technical and cultural means and forces for "unionization" *do exist*; what is lacking is the firm, determined initiative of a *revolutionary* government which should be ruthlessly severe towards the exploiters to set these forces and means in motion.

The poorer a country is in technically trained forces, and in intellectual forces generally, the more *urgent* it is to decree compulsory association as early and as resolutely as possible and to begin with the bigger and biggest enterprises when putting the decree into effect, for it is association that will *economize* intellectual forces and make it possible to use them *to the full* and to distribute them more correctly. If, after 1905, even the Russian peasants in their out-of-the-way districts, under the tsarist government, in face of the thousands of obstacles raised by that government, were able to make a tremendous forward stride in the creation of all kinds of associations, it is clear that the amalgamation of large- and medium-scale industry and trade could be effected in several months, if not earlier, provided compulsion to this end were exercised by a really revolutionary-democratic government relying on the support, participation, interest, and advantage of the "lower ranks," the democracy, the workers, and other employees, and calling upon *them* to exercise control.

Regulation of Consumption

The war has compelled all the belligerent and many of the neutral countries to resort to the regulation of consumption. Bread cards have been issued and have become customary, and this has led to the appearance of other ration cards. Russia is no exception and has also introduced bread cards.

Using this as an example, we can draw, perhaps, the most striking comparison of all between reactionary-bureaucratic methods of combating a catastrophe, which are confined to minimum reforms, and revolutionary-democratic methods, which, to justify their name, must directly aim at a violent rupture with the old, obsolete system and at the achievement of the speediest possible progress.

The bread card—this typical example of how consumption is regulated in modern capitalist countries—aims at, and achieves (at best), one thing only, namely, distributing available supplies of grain to give everybody his share. A maximum limit to consumption is established, not for all foodstuffs by far, but only for principal foodstuffs, those of "popular" consumption. And that is all. There is no intention of doing anything else. Available supplies of grain are calculated in a bureaucratic way, then divided on a per capita basis; a ration is fixed and introduced, and there the matter ends. Luxury articles are not affected, for they are "anyway" scarce and "anyway" so dear as to be beyond the reach of the "people." And so, in *all* the belligerent countries without exception, *even* in Germany, which evidently, without fear of contradiction, may be said to be a model of the most careful, pedantic, and strict regulation of consumption—*even* in Germany we find that the rich constantly *get around* all "rationing." This, too, "everybody" knows and "everybody" talks about with a smile; and in the German socialist papers, and sometimes even in the bourgeois papers, despite the fierce military stringency of the German censorship, we constantly find items and reports about the "menus" of the rich, saying how the wealthy can obtain white bread in any quantity at a certain health resort (visited, on the plea of illness, by everybody who has plenty of money), and how the wealthy substitute choice and rare articles of luxury for articles of popular consumption.

A reactionary capitalist state which *fears* to undermine the pillars of capitalism, of wage slavery, of the economic supremacy of the rich, which *fears* to encourage the initiative of the workers and the working people generally, which *fears* to provoke them to a more exacting attitude—*such* a state will be quite content with bread cards. Such a state does not for a moment, in any measure it adopts, lose sight of the *reactionary* aim of strengthening capitalism, preventing its being undermined, and confining the "regulation of economic life" in general, and the regulation of consumption in particular, to such measures as are absolutely essential to feed the people, *and makes no attempt* whatsoever at real regulation of consumption by exercising *control over the rich* and laying the *greater part* of the burden in wartime on those who are better off, who are privileged, well fed and overfed in peacetime.

The reactionary-bureaucratic solution to the problem with which the war has confronted the peoples confines itself to bread cards, to the equal distribution of "popular" foodstuffs, of those absolutely essential to feed the people, without retreating one little bit from bureaucratic and reactionary ideas, that is, from the aim of *not* encouraging the initiative of the poor, the proletariat, the mass of the people ("demos"), of *not* allowing *them* to exercise control over the rich, and of leaving *as many* loopholes *as possible* for the rich to compensate themselves with articles of luxury. And a great number of loopholes are left in *all* countries, we repeat, even in Germany— not to speak of Russia; the "common people" starve while the rich visit health resorts, supplement the meager official ration by all sorts of "extras" obtained on the side, and do *not* allow *themselves* to be controlled.

In Russia, which has only just made a revolution against the tsarist regime in the name of liberty and equality, in Russia, which, as far as its actual political institutions are concerned, has at once become a democratic republic, what particularly strikes the people, what particularly arouses popular discontent, irritation, anger, and indignation is that *everybody* sees the easy way in which the wealthy get around the bread cards. They do it very easily indeed. "From under the counter," and for a very high price, especially if one has "*pull*" (which only the rich have), one can obtain anything, and in large quantities, too. It is the people who are starving. The regulation of consumption is confined within the narrowest bureaucratic-reactionary limits. The government has not the slightest intention of putting regulation on a really revolutionary-democratic footing, is not in the least concerned about doing so.

"Everybody" is suffering from the queues but—but the rich send their servants to stand in the queues, and even engage special servants for the purpose! And that is "democracy"!

At a time when the country is suffering untold calamities, a revolutionary-democratic policy would not confine itself to bread cards to combat the impending catastrophe but would add, first, the compulsory organization of the whole population in consumers' societies, for otherwise control over consumption cannot be fully exercised; second, labor service for the rich, making them perform without pay secretarial and similar duties for these consumers' societies; third, the equal distribution among the population of absolutely all consumer goods, so as really to distribute the burdens of the war equitably; fourth, the organization of control in such a way as to have the poorer classes of the population exercise control over the consumption of the rich.

The establishment of real democracy in this sphere and the display of a real revolutionary spirit in the organization of control by the most needy classes of the people would be a very great stimulus to the employment of all available intellectual forces and to the development of the truly revolutionary energies of the entire people. Yet now the ministers of republican and revolutionary-democratic Russia, exactly like their colleagues in all other imperialist countries, make pompous speeches about "working in common for the good of the people" and about "exerting every effort," but the people see, feel, and sense the hypocrisy of this talk. . . .

Financial Collapse and Measures to Combat It

. . . There is no way of effectively combating financial disorganization and inevitable financial collapse except that of revolutionary rupture with the interests of capital and that of the organization of really democratic control, that is, control from "below," control by the workers and the poor peasants *over* the capitalists, a way to which we referred throughout the earlier part of this exposition.

Large issues of paper money encourage profiteering, enable the capitalists to make millions of rubles, and place tremendous difficulties in the way of a very necessary expansion of production, for the already high cost of materials, machinery, etc., is rising further by leaps and bounds. What can be done about it when the wealth acquired by the rich through profiteering is being concealed?

An income tax with progressive and very high rates for larger and very large incomes might be introduced. Our government has introduced one, following the example of other imperialist governments. But it is largely a fiction, a dead letter, for, first, the value of money is falling faster and faster, and, second, the more that incomes are derived from profiteering and the more securely that commercial secrecy is maintained, the greater their concealment.

Real and not nominal control is required to make the tax real and not fictitious. But control over the capitalists is impossible if it remains bureaucratic, for the bureaucracy is itself bound to and interwoven with the bourgeoisie by thousands of threads. That is why in the West-European imperialist states, monarchies and republics alike, financial order is obtained solely by the introduction of "labor service," which creates *wartime penal servitude* or *wartime slavery* for the workers.

Reactionary-bureaucratic control is the only method known to imperialist states—not excluding the democratic republics of France and America—of foisting the burdens of the war on to the proletariat and the working people.

The basic contradiction in the policy of our government is that, in order not to quarrel with the bourgeoisie, not to destroy the "coalition" with them, the government has to introduce reactionary-bureaucratic control, which it calls "revolutionary-democratic" control, deceiving the people at every step and irritating and angering the masses who have just overthrown tsarism.

Yet only revolutionary-democratic measures, only the organization of the oppressed classes, the workers and peasants, the masses, into unions would make it possible to establish a most effective control *over the rich* and wage a most successful fight against the concealment of incomes.

An attempt is being made to encourage the use of checks as a means of avoiding excessive issue of paper money. This measure is of no significance as far as the poor are concerned, for anyway they live from hand to mouth, complete their "economic cycle" in one week and return to the capitalists the few meager coppers they manage to earn. The use of checks might have great significance as far as the rich are concerned. It would enable the state, especially in conjunction with such measures as nationalization of the banks and abolition of commercial secrecy, *really to control* the incomes of the capitalists, really to impose taxation on them, and really to "democratize" (and at the same time bring order into) the financial system.

But this is hampered by the fear of infringing the privileges of the bourgeoisie and destroying the "coalition" with them. For unless truly revolutionary measures are adopted and compulsion is very seriously resorted to, the capitalists will not submit to any control, will not make known their budgets, and will not surrender their stocks of paper money for the democratic state to "keep account" of.

The workers and peasants, organized in unions, by nationalizing the banks, making the use of checks legally compulsory for all rich persons, abolishing commercial secrecy, imposing confiscation of property as a penalty for concealment of incomes, etc., might with extreme ease make control both effective and universal—control, that is, over the rich, and such control as would *secure the return* of paper money *from those* who have it, *from those* who conceal it, *to the treasury,* which issues it.

This requires a revolutionary dictatorship of the democracy, headed by the revolutionary proletariat; that is, it requires that the democracy should become revolutionary *in fact.* That is the crux of the matter. . . .

We usually do not even notice how thoroughly we are permeated by antidemocratic habits and prejudices regarding the "sanctity" of bourgeois property. When an engineer or banker publishes the income and expenditure of a worker, information about his wages and the productivity of his labor, this is regarded as absolutely legitimate and fair. Nobody thinks of seeing it as an intrusion into the "private life" of the worker, as "spying or informing" on the part of the engineer. Bourgeois society regards the labor and earnings of a wageworker as *its* open book, any bourgeois being entitled to peer into it at any moment, and at any moment to expose the "luxurious living" of the worker, his supposed "laziness," etc.

Well, and what about reverse control? What if the unions of employees, clerks, and *domestic servants* were invited by a *democratic* state to verify the income and expenditure of capitalists, to publish information on the subject, and to assist the government in combating concealment of incomes?

What a furious howl against "spying" and "informing" would be raised by the bourgeoisie! When "masters" control servants, or when capitalists control workers, this is considered to be in the nature of things; the private life of the working and exploited people is *not* considered inviolable. The bourgeoisie are entitled to call to account any "wage slave" and at any time to make public his income and expenditure. But if the oppressed attempt to control the oppressor, to show up *his* income and expenditure, to expose *his* luxurious living even in wartime, when his luxurious living is directly responsible for armies at the front starving and perishing—oh, no, the bourgeoisie will not tolerate "spying" and "informing"!

It all boils down to the same thing: the rule of the bourgeoisie *is irreconcilable* with truly revolutionary true democracy. We cannot be revolutionary democrats in the twentieth century and in a capitalist country *if we fear* to advance towards socialism.

Can We Go Forward if We Fear to Advance Toward Socialism?

What has been said so far may easily arouse the following objection on the part of a reader who has been brought up on the current opportunist ideas. . . . Most measures described here, he may say, are *already* in effect socialist and not democratic measures!

This current objection . . . is a reactionary defense of backward capitalism, a defense decked out in a Struvean [2] garb. It seems to say that we are not ripe for socialism, that it is too early to "introduce" socialism, that our revolution is a bourgeois revolution and therefore we must be the menials of the bourgeoisie (although the great bourgeois revolutionaries in France 125 years ago made their revolution a great revolution by exercising *terror* against all oppressors, landowners and capitalists alike!).

The pseudo-Marxist lackeys of the bourgeoisie . . . who argue in this way, do not understand . . . what imperialism is, what capitalist monopoly is, what the state is, and what revolutionary democracy is. For anyone who understands this is bound to admit that there can be no advance except towards socialism.

Everybody talks about imperialism. But imperialism is merely monopoly capitalism. . . .

And what is the state? It is an organization of the ruling class— in Germany, for instance, of the Junkers and capitalists. And there-

2   "Struvean" refers to Peter Struve, the Economist theoretician. [*Ed.*]

fore what . . . [is called] "wartime socialism" is in fact wartime state-monopoly capitalism, or, to put it more simply and clearly, wartime penal servitude for the workers and wartime protection for capitalist profits.

Now try to *substitute* for the Junker-capitalist state, for the landowner-capitalist state, a *revolutionary-democratic* state, that is, a state which in a revolutionary way abolishes *all* privileges and does not fear to introduce the fullest democracy in a revolutionary way. You will find that, given a really revolutionary-democratic state, state-monopoly capitalism inevitably and unavoidably implies a step, and more than one step, towards socialism!

For if a huge capitalist undertaking becomes a monopoly, it means that it serves the whole nation. If it has become a state monopoly, it means that the state (that is, the armed organization of the population, the workers and peasants above all, provided there is *revolutionary* democracy) directs the whole undertaking. In whose interest?

Either in the interest of the landowners and capitalists, in which case we have not a revolutionary-democratic, but a reactionary-bureaucratic state, an imperialist republic.

Or in the interest of revolutionary democracy—and then *it is a step towards socialism.*

For socialism is merely the next step forward from state-capitalist monopoly. Or, in other words, socialism is merely state-capitalist monopoly *which is made to serve the interests of the whole people* and has to that extent *ceased* to be capitalist monopoly.

There is no middle course here. The objective process of development is such that it is *impossible* to advance from *monopolies* (and the war has magnified their number, role, and importance tenfold) without advancing towards socialism.

Either we have to be revolutionary democrats in fact, in which case we must not fear to take steps towards socialism. Or we fear to take steps towards socialism, condemn them . . . by arguing that our revolution is a bourgeois revolution, that socialism cannot be "introduced," etc., in which case we inevitably sink to the level of . . . [the government and the right wing], that is, we in a *reactionary-bureaucratic* way suppress the "revolutionary-democratic" aspirations of the workers and peasants.

There is no middle course.

And therein lies the fundamental contradiction of our revolution.

It is impossible to stand still in history in general, and in wartime in particular. We must either advance or retreat. It is *impossible* in twentieth-century Russia, which has won a republic and democracy in a revolutionary way, to go forward without *advancing* towards socialism, without taking *steps* toward it (steps conditioned and determined by the level of technology and culture: large-scale machine production cannot be "introduced" in peasant agriculture nor abolished in the sugar industry).

But to fear to advance *means* retreating. . . .

The dialectics of history is such that the war, by extraordinarily expediting the transformation of monopoly capitalism into state-monopoly capitalism, has *thereby* extraordinarily advanced mankind towards socialism.

Imperialist war is the eve of socialist revolution. And this not only because the horrors of the war give rise to proletarian revolt —no revolt can bring about socialism unless the economic conditions for socialism are ripe—but because state-monopoly capitalism is a complete *material* preparation for socialism, the *threshold* of socialism, a rung on the ladder of history between which and the rung called socialism *there are no intermediate rungs.* . . .

The Struggle Against Economic Chaos —and the War

A consideration of the measures to avert the impending catastrophe brings us to another supremely important question, namely, the connection between home and foreign policy, or, in other words, the relation between a war of conquest, an imperialist war, and a revolutionary, proletarian war, between a criminal, predatory war and a just, democratic war.

All the measures to avert catastrophe we have described would, as we have already stated, greatly enhance the defense potential, or, in other words, the military might of the country. That, on the one hand. On the other hand, these measures cannot be put into effect without turning the war of conquest into a just war, turning the war waged by the capitalists in the interests of the capitalists into a war waged by the proletariat in the interests of all the working and exploited people.

And, indeed, nationalization of the banks and syndicates, taken in conjunction with the abolition of commercial secrecy and the establishment of workers' control over the capitalists, would not only imply a tremendous saving of national labor, the possibility of economizing forces and means, but would also imply an improvement in the conditions of the working *masses*, of the majority of the population. As everybody knows, economic organization is of decisive importance in modern warfare. Russia has enough grain, coal, oil, and iron; in this respect, we are in a better position than any of the belligerent European countries. And given a struggle against economic chaos by the measures indicated above, enlisting popular initiative in this struggle, improving the people's conditions, and nationalizing the banks and syndicates, Russia could use her revolution and her democracy to raise the whole country to an incomparably higher level of economic organization. . . .

The defense potential, the military might, of a country whose banks have been nationalized is *superior* to that of a country whose banks remain in private hands. The military might of a peasant country whose land is in the hands of peasant committees is *superior* to that of a country whose land is in the hands of landowners.

Reference is constantly being made to the heroic patriotism and the miracles of military valor performed by the French in 1792–1793. But the material, historical-economic conditions which alone made such miracles possible are forgotten. The suppression of obsolete feudalism in a really revolutionary way, and the introduction throughout the country of a superior mode of production and free peasant land tenure, effected, moreover, with truly revolutionary-democratic speed, determination, energy, and devotion—such were the material, economic conditions which with "miraculous" speed saved France by *regenerating and renovating* her economic foundation.

The example of France shows one thing, and one thing only, namely, that to render Russia capable of self-defense, to obtain in Russia, too, "miracles" of mass heroism, all that is obsolete must be swept away with "Jacobin" ruthlessness and Russia renovated and regenerated *economically*. And in the twentieth century this cannot be done merely by sweeping tsarism away (France did not confine herself to this 125 years ago). It cannot be done even by the mere revolutionary abolition of the landed estates . . . by the mere transfer of the land to the peasants. For we are living in the twentieth century, and mastery over the land *without mastery over the banks* cannot regenerate and renovate the life of the people.

The material, industrial renovation of France at the end of the eighteenth century was associated with a political and spiritual renovation, with the dictatorship of revolutionary democrats and the revolutionary proletariat (from which the democrats had not dissociated themselves and with which they were still almost fused), and with a ruthless war declared on everything reactionary. The whole people, and especially the masses, that is, the *oppressed* classes, were swept up by boundless revolutionary enthusiasm; *everybody* considered the war a just war of defense, as it *actually was*. Revolutionary France was defending herself against reactionary monarchist Europe. It was not in 1792–1793, but many years later, *after* the victory of reaction within the country, that the counter-revolutionary dictatorship of Napoleon turned France's wars from defensive wars into wars of conquest.

And what about Russia? We continue to wage an imperialist war in the interests of the capitalists, in alliance with the imperialists, and in accordance with the secret treaties the *Tsar* concluded with the capitalists of Britain and other countries, promising the Russian capitalists in these treaties the spoliation of foreign lands. . . .

The war will remain an unjust, reactionary, and predatory war on Russia's part as long as she does not propose a just peace and does not break with imperialism. The social character of the war, its true meaning, is not determined by the position of the enemy troops (as the Socialist-Revolutionaries and Mensheviks think, stooping to the vulgarity of an ignorant yokel). What determines this character is the *policy* of which the war is a continuation ("war is the continuation of politics"), the *class* that is waging the war, and the aims for which it is waging this war.

You cannot lead the people into a predatory war in accordance with secret treaties and expect them to be enthusiastic. The foremost class in revolutionary Russia, the proletariat, is becoming increasingly aware of the criminal character of the war, and not only have the bourgeoisie been unable to shatter this popular conviction, but, on the contrary, awareness of the criminal character of the war is growing. The proletariat *of both metropolitan cities* of Russia has definitely become internationalist!

How, then, can you expect mass enthusiasm for the war!

One is inseparable from the other—home policy is inseparable from foreign policy. The country cannot be made capable of self-defense without the supreme heroism of the people in boldly and resolutely carrying out great economic transformations. And it is impossible to arouse popular heroism without breaking with imperialism, without proposing a democratic peace to all nations, and without thus turning the war from a criminal war of conquest and plunder into a just, revolutionary war of defense.

Only a thorough and consistent break with the capitalists in both home and foreign policy can save our revolution and our country, which is gripped in the iron vice of imperialism.

The Revolutionary Democrats
and the Revolutionary Proletariat

To be really revolutionary, the democrats of Russia today must march in very close alliance with the proletariat, supporting it in its struggle as the only thoroughly revolutionary class.

Such is the conclusion prompted by an analysis of the means of combating an impending catastrophe of unparalleled dimensions.

The war has created such an immense crisis, has so strained the material and moral forces of the people, has dealt such blows at the entire modern social organization that humanity must now choose between perishing or entrusting its fate to the most revolutionary class for the swiftest and most radical transition to a superior mode of production.

Owing to a number of historical causes—the greater backwardness of Russia, the unusual hardships brought upon her by the war, the utter rottenness of tsarism, and the extreme tenacity of the traditions of 1905—the revolution broke out in Russia earlier than in other countries. The revolution has resulted in Russia catching up with the advanced countries in a few months, as far as her *political* system is concerned.

But that is not enough. The war is inexorable; it puts the alternative with ruthless severity: either perish or overtake and outstrip the advanced countries *economically as well.*

That is possible, for we have before us the experience of a large number of advanced countries, the fruits of their technology and culture. We are receiving moral support from the war protest that is growing in Europe, from the atmosphere of the mounting world-wide workers' revolution. We are being inspired and encouraged by a revolutionary-democratic freedom which is extremely rare in time of imperialist war.

Perish or forge full steam ahead. That is the alternative put by history.

And the attitude of the proletariat to the peasants in such a situation confirms the old Bolshevik concept, correspondingly modifying it, that the peasants must be wrested from the influence of the bourgeoisie. That is the sole guarantee of salvation for the revolution. . . .

STATE AND REVOLUTION (AUGUST–SEPTEMBER 1917)

The Marxist Theory of the State and the Tasks of the Proletariat in the Revolution

(UNFINISHED)

Chapter I   Class Society and the State

1   The State—A Product of the Irreconcilability of Class Antagonisms

WHAT is now happening to Marx's theory has, in the course of history, happened repeatedly to the theories of revolutionary thinkers and leaders of oppressed classes fighting for emancipation. During the lifetime of great revolutionaries, the oppressing classes constantly hounded them, received their theories with the most savage malice, the most furious hatred, and the most unscrupulous campaigns of lies and slander. After their death, attempts are made to convert them into harmless icons, to canonize them, so to say, and to hallow their *names* to a certain extent for the "consolation" of the oppressed classes and with the object of duping the latter, while at the same time robbing the revolutionary theory of its *substance*, blunting its revolutionary edge, and vulgarizing it. Today, the bourgeoisie and the opportunists within the labor movement concur in this doctoring of Marxism. They omit, obscure, or distort the revolutionary side of this theory, its revolutionary soul. They push to the foreground and extol what is or seems acceptable to the bourgeoisie. All the social-chauvinists are now "Marxists" (don't laugh!). And more and more frequently German bourgeois scholars, only yesterday specialists in the annihilation of Marxism, are speaking of the "national-German" Marx, who, they claim, educated the labor unions which are so splendidly organized for the purpose of waging a predatory war!

In these circumstances, in view of the unprecedentedly widespread distortion of Marxism, our prime task is to *re-establish* what Marx really taught on the subject of the state. This will necessitate a number of long quotations from the works of Marx and Engels themselves. Of course, long quotations will render the text cumbersome and not help at all to make it popular reading, but we cannot possibly dispense with them. All, or at any rate all the most essential, passages in the works of Marx and Engels on the subject of the state must by all means be quoted as fully as possible so that the reader may form an independent opinion of the totality of the views of the founders of scientific socialism, and of the evolution of those views, and so that their distortion by . . . [some socialists] may be documentarily proved and clearly demonstrated.

Let us begin with the most popular of Engels's works, *The Origin of the Family, Private Property, and the State.* . . .

Summing up his historical analysis, Engels says:

"The state is, therefore, by no means a power forced on society from without; just as little is it 'the reality of the ethical idea,' 'the image and reality of reason,' as Hegel maintains. Rather, it is a product of society at a certain stage of development; it is the admission that this society has become entangled in an insoluble contradiction with itself, that it has split into irreconcilable antagonisms which it is powerless to dispel. But in order that these antagonisms, these classes with conflicting economic interests might not consume themselves and society in fruitless struggle, it became necessary to have a power, seemingly standing above society, that would alleviate the conflict and keep it within the bounds of 'order'; and this power, arisen out of society but placing itself above it, and alienating itself more and more from it, is the state." [1]

This expresses with perfect clarity the basic idea of Marxism with regard to the historical role and the meaning of the state. The state is a product and a manifestation of the *irreconcilability* of class antagonisms. The state arises where, when, and insofar as class antagonisms objectively *cannot* be reconciled. And, conversely, the existence of the state proves that the class antagonisms are irreconcilable.

It is on this most important and fundamental point that the distortion of Marxism, proceeding along two main lines, begins.

On the one hand, the bourgeois, and particularly the petty-bourgeois, ideologists, compelled under the weight of indisputable historical facts to admit that the state only exists where there are class antagonisms and a class struggle, "correct" Marx in such a way as to make it appear that the state is an organ for the *reconciliation* of classes. According to Marx, the state could neither have arisen nor

1 The translations of Marx and Engels were done by Lenin himself from the German originals into Russian. They have been translated into English from Lenin's text by the Soviet translators. [*Ed.*]

maintained itself had it been possible to reconcile classes. From what the petty-bourgeois and philistine professors and publicists say, with quite frequent and benevolent references to Marx, it appears that the state does reconcile classes. According to Marx, the state is an organ of class *rule*, an organ for the *oppression* of one class by another; it is the creation of "order," which legalizes and perpetuates this oppression by moderating the conflict between the classes. In the opinion of the petty-bourgeois politicians, however, order means the reconciliation of classes, and not the oppression of one class by another; to alleviate the conflict means reconciling classes and not depriving the oppressed classes of definite means and methods of struggle to overthrow the oppressors.

For instance, when, in the revolution of 1917, the question of the significance and role of the state arose in all its magnitude as a practical question demanding immediate action, and, moreover, action on a mass scale, all the Socialist-Revolutionaries and Mensheviks descended at once to the petty-bourgeois theory that the "state" "reconciles" classes. Innumerable resolutions and articles by politicians of both these parties are thoroughly saturated with this petty-bourgeois and philistine "reconciliation" theory. That the state is an organ of the rule of a definite class which *cannot* be reconciled with its antipode (the class opposite to it) is something the petty-bourgeois democrats will never be able to understand. Their attitude to the state is one of the most striking manifestations of the fact that our Socialist-Revolutionaries and Mensheviks are not socialists at all (a point that we Bolsheviks have always maintained) but petty-bourgeois democrats using near-socialist phraseology.

On the other hand, the "Kautskyite" distortion of Marxism is far more subtle. "Theoretically," it is not denied that the state is an organ of class rule or that class antagonisms are irreconcilable. But what is overlooked or glossed over is this: if the state is the product of the irreconcilability of class antagonisms, if it is a power standing *above* society and "*alienating* itself *more and more* from it," it is clear that the liberation of the oppressed class is impossible not only without a violent revolution, *but also without the destruction* of the apparatus of state power which was created by the ruling class and which is the embodiment of this "alienation." As we shall see later, Marx very explicitly drew this theoretically self-evident conclusion on the strength of a concrete historical analysis of the tasks of the revolution. . . .

2 *Special Bodies of Armed Men, Prisons, etc.*

Engels continues:

"As distinct from the old gentile [tribal or clan] order, the state, first, divides its subjects *according to territory.* . . .

"This division seems 'natural' to us, but it cost a prolonged struggle against the old organization according to generations or tribes.

"The second distinguishing feature is the establishment of a *public power* which no longer directly coincides with the population organizing itself as an armed force. This special, public power is necessary because a self-acting armed organization of the population has become impossible since the split into classes. . . . This public power exists in every state; it consists not merely of armed men but also of material adjuncts, prisons, and institutions of coercion of all kinds, of which gentile [clan] society knew nothing. . . ."

Engels elucidates the concept of the "power" which is called the state, a power which arose from society but places itself above it and alienates itself more and more from it. What does this power mainly consist of? It consists of special bodies of armed men having prisons, etc., at their command.

We are justified in speaking of special bodies of armed men, because the public power which is an attribute of every state "does not directly coincide" with the armed population, with its "self-acting armed organization."

Like all great revolutionary thinkers, Engels tries to draw the attention of the class-conscious workers to what prevailing philistinism regards as least worthy of attention, as the most habitual thing, hallowed by prejudices that are not only deep-rooted but, one might say, petrified. A standing army and police are the chief instruments of state power. But how can it be otherwise?

From the viewpoint of the vast majority of Europeans of the end of the nineteenth century whom Engels was addressing, and who had not gone through or closely observed a single great revolution, it could not have been otherwise. They could not understand at all what a "self-acting armed organization of the population" was. When asked why it became necessary to have special bodies of armed men placed above society and alienating themselves from it (police and a standing army), the West-European and Russian philistines are inclined to utter a few phrases borrowed from Spencer . . . to refer to the growing complexity of social life, the differentiation of functions, and so on.

Such a reference seems "scientific" and effectively lulls the ordinary person to sleep by obscuring the important and basic fact, namely, the split of society into irreconcilably antagonistic classes.

Were it not for this split, the "self-acting armed organization of the population" would differ from the primitive organization of a stick-wielding herd of monkeys, or of primitive men, or of men united in clans, by its complexity, its high technical level, and so on. But such an organization would still be possible.

It is impossible because civilized society is split into antagonistic, and, moreover, irreconcilably antagonistic, classes, whose "self-acting" arming would lead to an armed struggle between them. A state arises, a special power is created, special bodies of armed men, and every revolution, by destroying the state apparatus, shows us the naked class struggle, clearly shows us how the ruling class strives to restore the special bodies of armed men which serve *it*, and how the oppressed class strives to create a new organization of this kind, capable of serving the exploited instead of the exploiters.

In the above argument, Engels raises theoretically the very same question which every great revolution raises before us in practice, palpably and, what is more, on a scale of mass action, namely, the question of the relationship between "special" bodies of armed men and the "self-acting armed organization of the population." We shall see how this question is specifically illustrated by the experience of the European and Russian revolutions.

But to return to Engels's exposition.

He points out that sometimes—in certain parts of North America, for example—this public power is weak (he has in mind a rare exception in capitalist society, and those parts of North America in its pre-imperialist days where the free colonist predominated), but that, generally speaking, it grows stronger:

"It [the public power] grows stronger, however, in proportion as class antagonisms within the state become more acute, and as adjacent states become larger and more populous. We have only to look at our present-day Europe, where class struggle and rivalry in conquest have tuned up the public power to such a pitch that it threatens to swallow the whole of society and even the state."

This was written not later than the early nineties of the last century. . . . The turn towards imperialism—meaning the complete domination of the trusts, the omnipotence of the big banks, a grand-scale colonial policy, and so forth—was only just beginning in France and was even weaker in North America and in Germany. Since then, "rivalry in conquest" has taken a gigantic stride, all the more because by the beginning of the second decade of the twentieth century the world had been completely divided up among these "rivals in conquest," that is, among the predatory Great Powers. Since then, military and naval armaments have grown fantastically and the predatory war of 1914–1917 for the domination of the world by Britain or Germany, for the division of the spoils, has brought the "swallowing" of all the forces of society by the rapacious state power close to complete catastrophe.

Engels could, as early as 1891, point to "rivalry in conquest" as one of the most important distinguishing features of the foreign policy of the Great Powers, while the social-chauvinist scoundrels ever since 1914, when this rivalry, many times intensified, gave rise to an imperialist war, have been covering up the defense of the predatory interests of "their own" bourgeoisie with phrases about "defense of the fatherland," "defense of the republic and the revolution," etc.!

3 The State—An Instrument for the Exploitation of the Oppressed Class

The maintenance of the special public power standing above society requires taxes and state loans.

"Having public power and the right to levy taxes," Engels writes, "the officials now stand, as organs of society, *above* society. The free, voluntary respect that was accorded to the organs of the gentile [clan] constitution does not satisfy them, even if they could gain it. . . ." Special laws are enacted proclaiming the sanctity and immunity of the officials. "The shabbiest police servant" has more "authority" than the representatives of the clan, but even the head of the military power of a civilized state may well envy the elder of a clan the "unstrained respect" of society.

The question of the privileged position of the officials as organs of state power is raised here. The main point indicated is: what is it that places them *above* society? We shall see how this theoretical question was answered in practice by the Paris Commune in 1871. . . .

"Because the state arose from the need to hold class antagonisms in check, but because it arose, at the same time, in the midst of the conflict of these classes, it is, as a rule, the state of the most powerful, economically dominant class, which, through the medium of the state, becomes also the politically dominant class, and thus acquires new means of holding down and exploiting the oppressed class. . . ." The ancient and feudal states were organs for the exploitation of the slaves and serfs; likewise, "the modern representative state is an instrument of exploitation of wage labor by capital. By way of exception, however, periods occur in which the warring classes balance each other so nearly that the state power as ostensible mediator acquires, for the moment, a certain degree of independence of both. . . ." Such were the absolute monarchies of the seventeenth and eighteenth centuries, the Bonapartism of the First and Second Empires in France, and the Bismarck regime in Germany.

Such, we may add, is the Kerensky government in republican Russia since it began to persecute the revolutionary proletariat at a moment when, owing to the leadership of the petty-bourgeois democrats, the Soviets have *already* become impotent, while the bourgeoisie are not *yet* strong enough simply to disperse them.

In a democratic republic, Engels continues, "wealth exercises its power indirectly, but all the more surely," first, by means of the "direct corruption of officials" (America); second, by means of an "alliance of the government and the Stock Exchange" (France and America).

At present, imperialism and the domination of the banks have "developed" into an exceptional art both these methods of defending and asserting the omnipotence of wealth in democratic republics of all descriptions. . . .

Another reason why the omnipotence of "wealth" is more *certain* in a democratic republic is that it does not depend on defects in the political machinery or on the faulty political shell of capitalism. A democratic republic is the best possible political shell for capitalism, and, therefore, once capital has gained possession of this very best shell . . . it establishes its power so securely, so firmly, that *no* change of persons, institutions, or parties in the bourgeois-democratic republic can shake it.

We must also note that Engels is most explicit in calling universal suffrage as well an instrument of bourgeois rule. Universal suffrage, he says, obviously taking account of the long experience of German Social-Democracy, is "the gauge of the maturity of the working class. It cannot and never will be anything more in the present-day state."

The petty-bourgeois democrats, such as our Socialist-Revolutionaries and Mensheviks, and also their twin brothers, all the social-chauvinists and opportunists of Western Europe, expect just this "more" from universal suffrage. They themselves share, and instill into the minds of the people, the false notion that universal suffrage "in the *present-day* state" is really capable of revealing the will of the majority of the working people and of securing its realization.

Here we can only indicate this false notion, only point out that Engels's perfectly clear, precise, and concrete statement is distorted at every step in the propaganda and agitation of the "official" (that is, opportunist) socialist parties. A detailed exposure of the utter falsity of this notion which Engels brushes aside here is given in our further account of the views of Marx and Engels on the "*present-day*" state.

Engels gives a general summary of his views . . . in the following words:

"The state, then, has not existed from all eternity. There have been societies that did without it, that had no idea of the state and state power. At a certain stage of economic development, which was necessarily bound up with the split of society into classes, the state became a necessity owing to this split. We are now rapidly approaching a stage in the development of production at which the existence of these classes not only will have ceased to be a necessity, but will become a positive hindrance to production. They will fall as inevitably as they arose at an earlier stage. Along with them the state will inevitably fall. Society, which will reorganize production on the basis of a free and equal association of the producers, will put the whole machinery of state where it will then belong: into a museum of antiquities, by the side of the spinning-wheel and the bronze axe."

We do not often come across this passage in the propaganda and agitation literature of the present-day Social-Democrats. Even when we do come across it, it is mostly quoted in the same manner as one bows before an icon, that is, it is done to show official respect for Engels, and no attempt is made to gauge the breadth and depth of the revolution that this relegating of "the whole machinery of state to a museum of antiquities" implies. In most cases we do not even find an understanding of what Engels calls the state machine.

4 The "Withering Away" of the State and Violent Revolution

Engels's words regarding the "withering away" of the state are so widely known, they are so often quoted, and so clearly reveal the essence of the customary adaptation of Marxism to opportunism that we must deal with them in detail. We shall quote the whole argument from which they are taken.

"The proletariat seizes state power and turns the means of production into state property to begin with. But thereby it abolishes itself as the proletariat, abolishes all class distinctions and class antagonisms, and abolishes also the state as state. Society thus far, operating amid class antagonisms, needed the state, that is, an organization of the particular exploiting class, for the maintenance of its external conditions of production, and, therefore, especially, for the purpose of forcibly keeping the exploited class in the conditions of oppression determined by the given mode of production (slavery, serfdom or bondage, wage-labor). The state was the official representative of society as a whole, its concentration in a visible corporation. But it was this only insofar as it was the state of that class which itself represented, for its own time, society as a whole: in ancient times, the state of slave-owning citizens; in the Middle Ages, of the feudal nobility; in our own time, of the bourgeoisie. When at last it becomes the real representative of the whole of society, it renders itself unnecessary. As soon as there is no longer any social class to be held in subjection, as soon as class rule, and the individual struggle for existence based upon the present anarchy in production, with the collisions and excesses arising from this struggle, are removed, nothing more remains to be held in subjection—nothing necessitating a special coercive force, a state. The first act by which the state really comes forward as the representative of the whole of society—the taking possession of the means of production in the name of society —is also its last independent act as a state. State interference in social relations becomes, in one domain after another, superfluous, and then

dies down of itself. The government of persons is replaced by the administration of things and by the conduct of processes of production. The state is not 'abolished.' *It withers away.* This gives the measure of the value of the phrase, 'a free people's state,' both as to its justifiable use for a time from an agitational point of view, and as to its ultimate scientific insufficiency; and also of the so-called anarchists' demand that the state be abolished overnight."

It is safe to say that of this argument of Engels's, which is so remarkably rich in ideas, only one point has become an integral part of socialist thought among modern socialist parties, namely, that according to Marx the state "withers away"—as distinct from the anarchist doctrine of the "abolition" of the state. To prune Marxism to such an extent means reducing it to opportunism, for this "interpretation" only leaves a vague notion of a slow, even, gradual change, of absence of leaps and storms, of absence of revolution. The current, widespread, popular, if one may say so, conception of the "withering away" of the state undoubtedly means obscuring, if not repudiating, revolution.

Such an "interpretation," however, is the crudest distortion of Marxism, advantageous only to the bourgeoisie. In point of theory, it is based on disregard for the most important circumstances and considerations indicated in, say, Engels's "summary" argument we have just quoted in full.

In the first place, at the very outset of his argument, Engels says that, in seizing state power, the proletariat thereby "abolishes the state as state." We are not accustomed to ponder the meaning of this. Generally, it is either ignored altogether or is considered to be something in the nature of "Hegelian weakness" on Engels's part. As a matter of fact, however, these words briefly express the experience of one of the greatest proletarian revolutions, the Paris Commune of 1871, of which we shall speak in greater detail in its proper place. As a matter of fact, Engels speaks here of the proletarian revolution "abolishing" the *bourgeois* state, while the words about the state withering away refer to the remnants of the *proletarian* state *after* the socialist revolution. According to Engels, the bourgeois state does not "wither away" but is "*abolished*" by the proletariat in the course of the revolution. What withers away after this revolution is the proletarian state or semi-state.

Second, the state is a "special coercive force." Engels gives this splendid and extremely profound definition here with the utmost lucidity. And from it follows that the "special coercive force" for the suppression of the proletariat by the bourgeoisie, of millions of working people by handfuls of the rich, must be replaced by a "special coercive force" for the suppression of the bourgeoisie by the proletariat (the dictatorship of the proletariat). This is precisely what is meant by "abolition of the state as state." This is precisely the "act" of taking possession of the means of production in the name of society. And it is self-evident that *such* a replacement of one (bourgeois) "special force" by another (proletarian) "special force" cannot possibly take place in the form of "withering away."

Third, in speaking of the state "withering away," and the even more graphic and colorful "dying down of itself," Engels refers quite clearly and definitely to the period *after* "the state has taken possession of the means of production in the name of the whole of society," that is, *after* the socialist revolution. We all know that the political form of the "state" at that time is the most complete democracy. But it never enters the head of any of the opportunists, who shamelessly distort Marxism, that Engels is consequently speaking here of *democracy* "dying down of itself," or "withering away." This seems very strange at first sight. But it is "incomprehensible" only to those who have not thought about democracy *also* being a state and, consequently, also disappearing when the state disappears. Revolution alone can "abolish" the bourgeois state. The state in general, that is, the most complete democracy, can only "wither away."

Fourth, after formulating his famous proposition that "the state withers away," Engels at once explains specifically that this proposition is directed against both the opportunists and the anarchists. In doing this, Engels puts in the forefront that conclusion, drawn from the proposition that "the state withers away," which is directed against the opportunists.

One can wager that out of every 10,000 persons who have read or heard about the "withering away" of the state, 9,990 are completely unaware, or do not remember, that Engels directed his conclusions from that proposition *not* against the anarchists *alone*. And of the remaining ten, probably nine do not know the meaning of a "free people's state" or why an attack on this slogan means an attack on the opportunists. This is how history is written! This is how a great revolutionary teaching is imperceptibly falsified and adapted to prevailing philistinism. The conclusion directed against the anarchists has been repeated thousands of times; it has been vulgarized, and rammed into people's heads in the shallowest form, and has acquired the strength of a prejudice, whereas the conclusion directed against the opportunists has been obscured and "forgotten"!

The "free people's state" was a program demand and a catchword current among the German Social-Democrats in the seventies. This catchword is devoid of all political content except that it describes the concept of democracy in a pompous philistine fashion. Insofar as it hinted in a legally permissible manner at a democratic republic, Engels was prepared to "justify" its use "for a time" from an agitational point of view. But it was an opportunist catchword, for it amounted to something more than prettifying bourgeois democracy; it was also a failure to understand the socialist criticism of the state in general. We are in favor of a democratic republic as the best form of state for the proletariat under capitalism. But we have no right to forget that wage slavery is the lot of the people even in the most democratic bourgeois republic. Furthermore, every state is a "special force" for the suppression of the oppressed class. Consequently, *every* state is *not* "free" and *not* a "people's state." Marx and Engels explained this repeatedly to their party comrades in the seventies.

Fifth, the same work of Engels's, whose argument about the withering away of the state everyone remembers, also contains an argument of the significance of violent revolution. Engels's historical analysis of its role becomes a veritable panegyric on violent revolution. This "no one remembers." It is not done in modern socialist parties to talk or even think about the significance of this idea, and it plays no part whatever in their daily propaganda and agitation among the people. And yet it is inseparably bound up with the "withering away" of the state into one harmonius whole.

Here is Engels's argument:

". . . That force, however, plays yet another role [other than that of a diabolical power] in history, a revolutionary role; that, in the words of Marx, it is the midwife of every old society which is pregnant with a new one, that it is the instrument with which social movement forces its way through and shatters the dead, fossilized political forms—of this there is not a word in Herr Dühring.[2] It is only with sighs and groans that he admits the possibility that force will perhaps be necessary for the overthrow of an economy based on exploitation—unfortunately, because all use of force demoralizes, he says, the person who uses it. And this in spite of the immense moral and spiritual impetus which has been given by every victorious revolution! And this in Germany, where a violent collision—which may, after all, be forced on the people—would at least have the advantage of wiping out the servility which has penetrated the nation's mentality following the humiliation of the Thirty Years' War. And this parson's mode of thought—dull, insipid, and impotent—presumes to impose itself on the most revolutionary party that history has known!"

How can this panegyric on violent revolution, which Engels insistently brought to the attention of the German Social-Democrats between 1878 and 1894, that is, right up to the time of his death, be combined with the theory of the "withering away" of the state to form a single theory?

2   Eugen Dühring (1833–1921), German philosopher who is remembered primarily because he was the target of Engels's virulent attack in the "anti-Dühring"(*Herr Eugen Dühring's Revolution in Science*). The section quoted above is from this work. [*Ed.*]

Usually the two are combined by means of eclecticism, by an unprincipled or sophistic selection made arbitrarily (or to please the powers that be) of first one, then another argument, and in ninety-nine cases out of a hundred, if not more, it is the idea of the "withering away" that is placed in the forefront. Dialectics are replaced by eclecticism—this is the most usual, the most widespread practice to be met with in present-day official Social-Democratic literature in relation to Marxism. This sort of substitution is, of course, nothing new; it was observed even in the history of classical Greek philosophy. In falsifying Marxism in opportunist fashion, the substitution of eclecticism for dialectics is the easiest way of deceiving the people. It gives an illusory satisfaction; it seems to take into account all sides of the process, all trends of development, all the conflicting influences, and so forth, whereas in reality it provides no integral and revolutionary conception of the process of social development at all.

We have already said above, and shall show more fully later, that the theory of Marx and Engels of the inevitability of a violent revolution refers to the bourgeois state. The latter *cannot* be superseded by the proletarian state (the dictatorship of the proletariat) through the process of "withering away," but, as a general rule, only through a violent revolution. The panegyric Engels sang in its honor, and which fully corresponds to Marx's repeated statements . . . —this panegyric is by no means a mere "impulse," a mere declamation, or a polemical [thrust]. The necessity of systematically imbuing the masses with *this* and precisely this view of violent revolution lies at the root of the *entire* theory of Marx and Engels. The betrayal of their theory by the now prevailing social-chauvinist and Kautskyite trends expresses itself strikingly in both these trends ignoring *such* propaganda and agitation.

The supersession of the bourgeois state by the proletarian state is impossible without a violent revolution. The abolition of the proletarian state, that is, of the state in general, is impossible except through the process of "withering away."

A detailed and concrete elaboration of these views was given by Marx and Engels when they studied each particular revolutionary situation, when they analyzed the lessons of the experience of each particular revolution. We shall now pass to this, undoubtedly the most important, part of their theory.

Chapter II   State and Revolution.
The Experience of 1848–1851

1   The Eve of the Revolution

The first works of mature Marxism—*The Poverty of Philosophy* and the *Communist Manifesto*—appeared just on the eve of the revolution of 1848. For this reason, in addition to presenting the general principles of Marxism, they reflect to a certain degree the concrete revolutionary situation of the time. It will, therefore, be more expedient, perhaps, to examine what the authors of these works said about the state immediately before they drew conclusions from the experience of the years 1848–1851.

In *The Poverty of Philosophy*, Marx wrote:

"The working class, in the course of development, will substitute for the old bourgeois society an association which will preclude classes and their antagonism, and there will be no more political power proper, since political power is precisely the official expression of class antagonism in bourgeois society."

It is instructive to compare this general exposition of the idea of the state disappearing after the abolition of classes with the exposition contained in the *Communist Manifesto*, written by Marx and Engels a few months later—in November 1847, to be exact:

". . . In depicting the most general phases of the development of the proletariat, we traced the more or less veiled civil war, raging within existing society up to the point where that war breaks out into open revolution, and where the violent overthrow of the bourgeoisie lays the foundation for the sway of the proletariat. . . .

". . . We have seen above that the first step in the revolution by the working class is to raise the proletariat to the position of ruling class, to win the battle of democracy.

"The proletariat will use its political supremacy to wrest, by degrees, all capital from the bourgeoisie, to centralize all instruments of production in the hands of the state, that is, of the proletariat organized as the ruling class, and to increase the total of productive forces as rapidly as possible."

Here we have a formulation of one of the most remarkable and most important ideas of Marxism on the subject of the state, namely, the idea of the "dictatorship of the proletariat" (as Marx and Engels began to call it after the Paris Commune); and also, a highly interesting definition of the state, which is also one of the "forgotten words" of Marxism: *"the state, that is, the proletariat organized as the ruling class."*

This definition of the state has never been explained in the prevailing propaganda and agitation literature of the official Social-Democratic parties. More than that, it has been deliberately ignored, for it is absolutely irreconcilable with reformism and is a slap in the face for the common opportunist prejudices and philistine illusions about the "peaceful development of democracy."

The proletariat needs the state—this is repeated by all the opportunists, social-chauvinists, and Kautskyites, who assure us that this is what Marx taught. But they "*forget*" to add that, in the first place, according to Marx, the proletariat needs only a state which is withering away, that is, a state so constituted that it begins to wither away immediately, and cannot but wither away. And, second, the working people need a "state, that is, the proletariat organized as the ruling class."

The state is a special organization of force: it is an organization of violence for the suppression of some class. What class must the proletariat suppress? Naturally, only the exploiting class, that is, the bourgeoisie. The working people need the state only to suppress the resistance of the exploiters, and only the proletariat can direct this suppression, can carry it out. For the proletariat is the only class that is consistently revolutionary, the only class that can unite all the working and exploited people in the struggle against the bourgeoisie, in completely removing it.

The exploiting classes need political rule to maintain exploitation, that is, in the selfish interests of an insignificant minority against the vast majority of the people. The exploited classes need political rule in order to completely abolish all exploitation, that is, in the interests of the vast majority of the people, and against the insignificant minority consisting of the modern slave-owners—the landowners and capitalists.

The petty-bourgeois democrats, those sham socialists who replaced the class struggle by dreams of class harmony, even pictured the socialist transformation in a dreamy fashion—not as the overthrow of the rule of the exploiting class, but as the peaceful submission of the minority to the majority which has become aware of its aims. This petty-bourgeois utopia, which is inseparable from the idea of the state being above classes, led in practice to the betrayal of the interests of the working classes, as was shown, for example, by the history of the French revolutions of 1848 and 1871, and by the experience of "socialist" participation in bourgeois cabinets in Britain, France, Italy, and other countries at the turn of the century.

All his life Marx fought against this petty-bourgeois socialism. . . . He developed his theory of the class struggle consistently, down to the theory of political power, of the state.

The overthrow of bourgeois rule can be accomplished only by the proletariat, the particular class whose economic conditions of existence prepare it for this task and provide it with the possibility and the power to perform it. While the bourgeoisie break up and disintegrate the peasantry and all the petty-bourgeois groups, they weld together, unite, and organize the proletariat. Only the proletariat—by virtue of the economic role it plays in large-scale production—is capable of being the leader of *all* the working and exploited people, whom the bourgeoisie exploit, oppress, and crush, often not less but more than they do the proletarians, but who are incapable of waging an *independent* struggle for their emancipation.

The theory of the class struggle, applied by Marx to the question of the state and the socialist revolution, leads as a matter of course to the recognition of the *political rule* of the proletariat, of its dictatorship, that is, of undivided power directly backed by the armed force of the people. The overthrow of the bourgeoisie can be achieved only by the proletariat becoming the *ruling class*, capable of crushing the inevitable and desperate resistance of the bourgeoisie, and of organizing *all* the working and exploited people for the new economic system.

The proletariat needs state power, a centralized organization of force, an organization of violence, both to crush the resistance of the exploiters and to *lead* the enormous mass of the population—the peasants, the petty bourgeoisie, and semiproletarians—in the work of organizing a socialist economy.

By educating the workers' party, Marxism educates the vanguard of the proletariat, capable of assuming power and *leading the whole people* to socialism, of directing and organizing the new system, of being the teacher, the guide, the leader of all the working and exploited people in organizing their social life without the bourgeoisie and against the bourgeoisie. By contrast, the opportunism now prevailing trains the members of the workers' party to be the representatives of the better-paid workers, who lose touch with the masses, "get along" fairly well under capitalism, and sell their birthright for a mess of pottage, that is, renounce their role as revolutionary leaders of the people against the bourgeoisie.

Marx's theory of "the state, that is, the proletariat organized as the ruling class," is inseparably bound up with the whole of his doctrine of the revolutionary role of the proletariat in history. The culmination of this role is the proletarian dictatorship, the political rule of the proletariat.

But since the proletariat needs the state as a *special* form of organization of violence *against* the bourgeoisie, the following conclusion suggests itself: is it conceivable that such an organization can be created without first abolishing, destroying the state machine created by the bourgeoisie *for themselves*? The *Communist Manifesto* leads straight to this conclusion, and it is of this conclusion that Marx speaks when summing up the experience of the revolution of 1848–1851.

2 *The Revolution Summed Up*

Marx sums up his conclusions from the revolution of 1848–1851, on the subject of the state we are concerned with, in the following argument:

"But the revolution is thoroughgoing. It is still journeying through purgatory. It does its work methodically. By December 2, 1851 [the day of Louis Bonaparte's coup d'état], it had completed one half of its preparatory work. It is now completing the other half. First it perfected the parliamentary power, in order to be able to overthrow it. Now that it has attained this, it is perfecting the *executive power*, reducing it to its purest expression, isolating it, setting it up against itself as the sole object, *in order to concentrate all its forces of destruction against it* [italics Lenin's]. And when it has done this second half of its preliminary work, Europe will leap from its seat and exultantly exclaim: well grubbed, old mole!

"This executive power with its enormous bureaucratic and military organization, with its vast and ingenious state machinery, with a host of officials numbering half a million, besides an army of another half million, this appalling parasitic body, which enmeshes the body of French society and chokes all its pores, sprang up in the days of the absolute monarchy, with the decay of the feudal system, which it helped to hasten." The first French Revolution developed centralization, "but at the same time" it increased "the extent, the attributes, and the number of agents of governmental power. Napoleon completed this state machinery." The legitimate monarchy and the July monarchy "added nothing but a greater division of labor.". . .

". . . Finally, in its struggle against the revolution, the parliamentary republic found itself compelled to strengthen, along with repressive measures, the resources and centralization of governmental power. *All revolutions perfected this machine instead of smashing it* [italics Lenin's]. The parties that contended in turn for domination regarded the possession of this huge state edifice as the principal spoils of the victor."

In this remarkable argument Marxism takes a tremendous step forward compared with the *Communist Manifesto*. In the latter the question of the state is still treated in an extremely abstract manner, in the most general terms and expressions. In the above-quoted passage, the question is treated in a concrete manner, and the conclusion is extremely precise, definite, practical, and palpable: all previous revolutions perfected the state machine, whereas it must be broken, smashed.

This conclusion is the chief and fundamental point in the Marxist theory of the state. . . .

The *Communist Manifesto* gives a general summary of history, which compels us to regard the state as the organ of class rule and leads us to the inevitable conclusion that the proletariat cannot overthrow the bourgeoisie without first winning political power, without attaining political supremacy, without transforming the state into the

"proletariat organized as the ruling class"; and that this proletarian
state will begin to wither away immediately after its victory because
the state is unnecessary and cannot exist in a society in which there
are no class antagonisms. The question as to how, from the point of
view of historical development, the replacement of the bourgeois by
the proletarian state is to take place is not raised here.

This is the question Marx raises and answers in 1852. True to
his philosophy of dialectical materialism, Marx takes as his basis
the historical experience of the great years of revolution, 1848 to
1851. Here, as everywhere else, his theory is a *summing up of experience*, illuminated by a profound philosophical conception of the
world and a rich knowledge of history.

The problem of the state is put specifically: How did the bourgeois state, the state machine necessary for the rule of the bourgeoisie,
come into being historically? What changes did it undergo, what
evolution did it perform in the course of bourgeois revolutions, in the
face of the independent actions of the oppressed classes? What are
the tasks of the proletariat in relation to this state machine?

The centralized state power that is peculiar to bourgeois society
came into being in the period of the fall of absolutism. Two institutions most characteristic of this state machine are the bureaucracy
and the standing army. In their works, Marx and Engels repeatedly
show that the bourgeoisie are connected with these institutions by
thousands of threads. Every worker's experience illustrates this connection in an extremely graphic and impressive manner. From its own
bitter experience, the working class learns to recognize this connection. That is why it so easily grasps and so firmly learns the doctrine
which shows the inevitability of this connection, a doctrine which
the petty-bourgeois democrats either ignorantly and flippantly deny, or
still more flippantly admit "in general," while forgetting to draw
appropriate practical conclusions.

The bureaucracy and the standing army are a "parasite" on the
body of bourgeois society—a parasite created by the internal antagonisms which rend that society, but a parasite which "chokes" all its
vital pores. . . .

The development, perfection, and strengthening of the bureaucratic
and military apparatus proceeded during all the numerous bourgeois
revolutions which Europe has witnessed since the fall of feudalism.
In particular, it is the petty bourgeoisie who are attracted to the side
of the big bourgeoisie and are largely subordinated to them through
this apparatus, which provides the upper sections of the peasants, small
artisans, tradesmen and the like with comparatively comfortable,
quiet, and respectable jobs raising their holders *above* the people. . . .

But the more the bureaucratic apparatus is "redistributed" among
the various bourgeois and petty-bourgeois parties . . . the more keenly

aware the oppressed classes, and the proletariat at their head, become of their irreconcilable hostility to the *whole* of bourgeois society. Hence the need for all bourgeois parties, even for the most democratic and "revolutionary-democratic" among them, to intensify repressive measures against the revolutionary proletariat, to strengthen the apparatus of coercion, that is the state machine. This course of events compels the revolution "*to concentrate all its forces of destruction*" against the state power, and to set itself the aim, not of improving the state machine, but of *smashing and destroying* it.

It was not logical reasoning, but actual developments, the actual experience of 1848–1851, that led to the matter being presented in this way. The extent to which Marx held strictly to the solid ground of historical experience can be seen from the fact that, in 1852, he did not yet specifically raise the question of *what* was to take the place of the state machine to be destroyed. Experience had not yet provided material for dealing with this question, which history placed on the agenda later on, in 1871. In 1852, all that could be established with the accuracy of scientific observation was that the proletarian revolution *had approached* the task of "concentrating all its forces of destruction" against the state power, of "smashing" the state machine.

Here the question may arise: is it correct to generalize the experience, observations, and conclusions of Marx, to apply them to a field that is wider than the history of France during the three years 1848–1851? Before proceeding to deal with this question, let us recall a remark made by Engels and then examine the facts. In his introduction to the third edition of *The Eighteenth Brumaire*, Engels wrote:

"France is the country where, more than anywhere else, the historical class struggles were each time fought out to a finish, and where, consequently, the changing political forms within which they move and in which their results are summarized have been stamped in the sharpest outlines. The center of feudalism in the Middle Ages, the model country, since the Renaissance, of a unified monarchy based on social estates, France demolished feudalism in the Great Revolution and established the rule of the bourgeoisie in a classical purity unequalled by any other European land. And the struggle of the upward-striving proletariat against the ruling bourgeoisie appeared here in an acute form unknown elsewhere."

The last remark is out of date inasmuch as since 1871 there has been a lull in the revolutionary struggle of the French proletariat, although, long as this lull may be, it does not at all preclude the possibility that in the coming proletarian revolution France may show herself to be the classic country of the class struggle to a finish.

Let us, however, cast a general glance over the history of the

advanced countries at the turn of the century. We shall see that the
same process went on more slowly, in more varied forms, in a much
wider field: on the one hand, the development of "parliamentary
power" both in the republican countries (France, America, Switzerland), and in the monarchies (Britain, Germany to a certain extent,
Italy, the Scandinavian countries, etc.); on the other hand, a struggle
for power among the various bourgeois and petty-bourgeois parties
which distributed and redistributed the "spoils" of office, with the
foundations of bourgeois society unchanged; and, lastly, the perfection and consolidation of the "executive power," of its bureaucratic
and military apparatus.

There is not the slightest doubt that these features are common
to the whole of the modern evolution of all capitalist states in general. In the three years 1848–1851 France displayed, in a swift,
sharp, concentrated form, the very same processes of development
which are peculiar to the whole capitalist world.

Imperialism—the era of bank capital, the era of gigantic capitalist
monopolies, of the development of monopoly capitalism into state-
monopoly capitalism—has clearly shown an extraordinary strengthening of the "state machine" and an unprecedented growth in its
bureaucratic and military apparatus in connection with the intensification of repressive measures against the proletariat both in the
monarchical and in the freest, republican countries.

World history is now undoubtedly leading, on an incomparably
larger scale than in 1852, to the "concentration of all the forces" of
the proletarian revolution on the "destruction" of the state machine.

What the proletariat will put in its place is suggested by the highly
instructive material furnished by the Paris Commune.

3   The Presentation of the Question by Marx in 1852 [3]

. . . Marx's letter to Weydemeyer dated March 5, 1852 . . . among
other things, contains the following remarkable observation:

"And now as to myself, no credit is due to me for discovering
the existence of classes in modern society or the struggle between
them. Long before me bourgeois historians had described the historical development of this class struggle and bourgeois economists,
the economic anatomy of the classes. What I did that was new was to
prove: (1) that the *existence of classes* is only bound up with *particular, historical phases in the development of production* (his-
torische Entwicklungsphasen der Produktion), (2) that the class
struggle necessarily leads to the *dictatorship of the proletariat*, (3)
that this dictatorship itself only constitutes the transition to the
abolition of all classes and to a *classless society*."

3   This section was added by Lenin in the second edition, December 1918.
[*Ed.*]

In these words, Marx succeeded in expressing with striking clarity, first, the chief and radical difference between his theory and that of the foremost and most profound thinkers of the bourgeoisie; and, second, the essence of his theory of the state.

It is often said and written that the main point in Marx's theory is the class struggle. But this is wrong. And this wrong notion very often results in an opportunist distortion of Marxism and its falsification in a spirit acceptable to the bourgeoisie. For the theory of the class struggle was created *not* by Marx, *but* by the bourgeoisie *before* Marx, and, generally speaking, it is *acceptable* to the bourgeoisie. Those who recognize *only* the class struggle are not yet Marxists; they may be found to be still within the bounds of bourgeois thinking and bourgeois politics. To confine Marxism to the theory of the class struggle means curtailing Marxism, distorting it, reducing it to something acceptable to the bourgeoisie. Only he is a Marxist who *extends* the recognition of the class struggle to the recognition of the *dictatorship of the proletariat*. This is what constitutes the most profound distinction between the Marxist and the ordinary petty (as well as big) bourgeois. This is the touchstone on which the *real* understanding and recognition of Marxism should be tested. . . .

Opportunism today, as represented by its principal spokesman, the ex-Marxist Karl Kautsky, fits in completely with Marx's characterization of the *bourgeois* position quoted above, for this opportunism limits recognition of the class struggle to the sphere of bourgeois relations. (Within this sphere, within its framework, not a single educated liberal will refuse to recognize the class struggle "in principle"!) Opportunism *does not extend* recognition of the class struggle to the cardinal point, to the period of *transition* from capitalism to communism, of the *overthrow* and the complete *abolition* of the bourgeoisie. In reality, this period inevitably is a period of an unprecedentedly violent class struggle in unprecedentedly acute forms, and, consequently, during this period the state must inevitably be a state that is democratic *in a new way* (for the proletariat and the propertyless in general) and dictatorial *in a new way* (against the bourgeoisie).

Further. The essence of Marx's theory of the state has been mastered only by those who realize that the dictatorship of a *single* class is necessary not only for every class society in general, not only for the *proletariat* which has overthrown the bourgeoisie, but also for the entire *historical period* which separates capitalism from "classless society," from communism. Bourgeois states are most varied in form, but their essence is the same: all these states, whatever their form, in the final analysis are inevitably the *dictatorship of the bourgeoisie*. The transition from capitalism to communism is certainly bound to yield a tremendous abundance and variety of political forms, but the essence will inevitably be the same: *the dictatorship of the proletariat.*

Chapter III State and Revolution. Experience of the Paris Commune of 1871. Marx's Analysis.

1 What Made the Communards' Attempt Heroic?

It is well known that in the autumn of 1870, a few months before the Commune, Marx warned the Paris workers that any attempt to overthrow the government would be the folly of despair. But when, in March 1871, a decisive battle was *forced* upon the workers and they accepted it, when the uprising had become a fact, Marx greeted the proletarian revolution with the greatest enthusiasm, in spite of unfavorable auguries. Marx did not persist in the pedantic attitude of condemning an "untimely" movement. . . .

Marx, however, was not only enthusiastic about the heroism of the Communards, who, as he expressed it, "stormed heaven." Although the mass revolutionary movement did not achieve its aim, he regarded it as a historic experience of enormous importance, as a certain advance of the world proletarian revolution, as a practical step that was more important than hundreds of programs and arguments. Marx endeavored to analyze this experiment, to draw tactical lessons from it and re-examine his theory in the light of it.

The only "correction" Marx thought it necessary to make to the *Communist Manifesto* he made on the basis of the revolutionary experience of the Paris Communards.

The last preface to the new German edition of the *Communist Manifesto*, signed by both its authors, is dated June 24, 1872. In this preface the authors, Karl Marx and Frederick Engels, say that the program of the *Communist Manifesto* "has in some details become out-of-date," and they go on to say:

". . . *One thing especially was proved by the Commune, namely, that 'the working class cannot simply lay hold of the ready-made state machinery and wield it for its own purposes.'. . .*"

The authors took the words that are in single quotation marks in this passage from Marx's book, *The Civil War in France*.

Thus, Marx and Engels regarded one principal and fundamental lesson of the Paris Commune as being of such enormous importance that they introduced it as an important correction into the *Communist Manifesto*.

Most characteristically, it is this important correction that has been distorted by the opportunists, and its meaning probably is not known to nine-tenths, if not ninety-nine-hundredths, of the readers of the *Communist Manifesto*. We shall deal with this distortion more fully farther on, in a chapter devoted specially to distortions. Here it will be sufficient to note that the current, vulgar "interpretation" of Marx's famous statement just quoted is that Marx here allegedly emphasizes the idea of slow development in contradistinction to the seizure of power, and so on.

As a matter of fact, *the exact opposite is the case*. Marx's idea is that the working class must *break up*, *smash* the "ready-made state machinery," and not confine itself merely to laying hold of it.

On April 12, 1871, that is, just at the time of the Commune, Marx wrote . . . :

"If you look up the last chapter of my *Eighteenth Brumaire*, you will find that I declare that the next attempt of the French Revolution will be no longer, as before, to transfer the bureaucratic-military machine from one hand to another, but to *smash* it, and this is the precondition for every real people's revolution on the Continent. And this is what our heroic Party comrades in Paris are attempting.". . .

The words, "to smash the bureaucratic-military machine," briefly express the principal lesson of Marxism regarding the tasks of the proletariat during a revolution in relation to the state. . . .

As for Marx's reference to *The Eighteenth Brumaire*, we have quoted the relevant passage in full above.

It is interesting to note, in particular, two points in the above-quoted argument of Marx. First, he restricts his conclusion to the Continent. This was understandable in 1871, when Britain was still the model of a purely capitalist country, but without a militarist clique and, to a considerable degree, without a bureaucracy. Marx therefore excluded Britain, where a revolution, even a people's revolution, then seemed possible, and indeed was possible, *without* the precondition of destroying the "ready-made state machinery."

Today, in 1917, at the time of the first great imperialist war, this restriction made by Marx is no longer valid. Both Britain and America, the biggest and the last representatives—in the whole world—of Anglo-Saxon "liberty," in the sense that they had no militarist cliques and bureaucracy, have completely sunk into the all-European filthy, bloody morass of bureaucratic-military institutions which subordinate everything to themselves, and suppress everything. Today, in Britain and America, too, "the precondition for every real people's revolution" is the *smashing*, the *destruction* of the "ready-made state machinery" (made and brought up to "European," general imperialist, perfection in those countries in the years 1914–1917).

Second, particular attention should be paid to Marx's extremely profound remark that the destruction of the bureaucratic-military state machine is "the precondition for every real *people's* revolution.". . .

If we take the revolutions of the twentieth century as examples, we shall, of course, have to admit that the Portuguese and the Turkish revolutions are both bourgeois revolutions. Neither of them, however, is a "people's" revolution, since in neither does the mass of the people, their vast majority, come out actively, independently, with their own economic and political demands to any noticeable degree. By contrast, although the Russian bourgeois revolution of 1905–1907 displayed no such "brilliant" successes as at times fell to the Portuguese and Turkish revolutions, it was undoubtedly a "real people's" revolution, since the mass of the people, their majority, the very lowest social groups, crushed by oppression and exploitation, rose independently and stamped on the entire course of the revolution the imprint of *their* own demands, *their* attempts to build in their own way a new society in place of the old society that was being destroyed.

In Europe, in 1871, the proletariat did not constitute the majority of the people in any country on the Continent. A "people's" revolution, one actually sweeping the majority into its stream, could be such only if it embraced both the proletariat and the peasants. These two classes then constituted the "people." These two classes are united by the fact that the "bureaucratic-military state machine" oppresses, crushes, exploits them. To *smash* this machine, *to break it up*, is truly in the interest of the "people," of their majority, of the workers and most of the peasants, is "the precondition" for a free alliance of the poor peasants and the proletarians, whereas without such an alliance democracy is unstable and socialist transformation is impossible.

As is well known, the Paris Commune was actually working its way toward such an alliance, although it did not reach its goal owing to a number of circumstances, internal and external.

Consequently, in speaking of a "real people's revolution," Marx, without in the least discounting the special features of the petty bourgeoisie (he spoke a great deal about them and often), took strict account of the actual balance of class forces in most of the continental countries of Europe in 1871. On the other hand, he stated that the "smashing" of the state machine was required by the interests of both the workers and the peasants, that it united them, that it placed before them the common task of removing the "parasite" and of replacing it by something new.

By what exactly?

2   *What Is to Replace the Smashed Machine?*

In 1847, in the *Communist Manifesto*, Marx's answer to this question was as yet a purely abstract one; to be exact, it was an answer that indicated the tasks but not the ways of accomplishing them. The answer given in the *Communist Manifesto* was that this machine was to be replaced by "the proletariat organized as the ruling class," by the "winning of the battle of democracy."

Marx did not indulge in utopias; he expected the *experience* of the mass movement to provide the reply to the question as to the specific forms this organization of the proletariat as the ruling class would assume and as to the exact manner in which this organization would be combined with the most complete, most consistent "winning of the battle of democracy."

Marx subjected the experience of the Commune, meager as it was, to the most careful analysis in *The Civil War in France*. Let us quote the most important passages of this work:

Originating from the Middle Ages, there developed in the nineteenth century "the centralized state power, with its ubiquitous organs of standing army, police, bureaucracy, clergy, and judicature." With the development of class antagonisms between capital and labor, "state power assumed more and more the character of a public force for the suppression of the working class, of a machine of class rule. After every revolution, which marks an advance in the class struggle, the purely coercive character of the state power stands out in bolder and bolder relief." After the revolution of 1848–1849, state power became "the national war instrument of capital against labor." The Second Empire consolidated this.

"The direct antithesis to the empire was the Commune." It was the "specific form" of "a republic that was not only to remove the monarchical form of class rule, but class rule itself. . . ."

What was this "specific" form of the proletarian, socialist republic? What was the state it began to create?

". . . The first decree of the Commune . . . was the suppression of the standing army and its replacement by the armed people. . . ."

This demand now figures in the program of every party calling itself socialist. The real worth of their programs, however, is best shown by the behavior of our Socialist-Revolutionaries and Mensheviks, who, right after the revolution of February 27, actually refused to carry out this demand!

"The Commune was formed of the municipal councillors, chosen by universal suffrage in the various wards of Paris, responsible and revocable at any time. The majority of its members were naturally working men, or acknowledged representatives of the working class.

. . . The police, which until then had been the instrument of the Government, was at once stripped of its political attributes and turned into the responsible and at all times revocable instrument of the Commune. So were the officials of all other branches of the administration. From the members of the Commune downwards, public service had to be done at *workmen's wages*. The privileges and the representation allowances of the high dignitaries of state disappeared along with the dignitaries themselves. . . . Having once got rid of the standing army and the police, the instruments of the physical force of the old Government, the Commune proceeded at once to break the instrument of spiritual suppression, the power of the priests. . . . The judicial functionaries lost that sham independence . . . they were thenceforward to be elective, responsible, and revocable. . . ."

The Commune, therefore, appears to have replaced the smashed state machine "only" by fuller democracy: abolition of the standing army; all officials to be elected and subject to recall. But as a matter of fact this "only" signifies a gigantic replacement of certain institutions by other institutions of a fundamentally different type. This is exactly a case of "quantity being transformed into quality": democracy, introduced as fully and consistently as is at all conceivable, is transformed from bourgeois into proletarian democracy; from the state ($=$ a special force for the suppression of a particular class) into something which is no longer the state proper.

It is still necessary to suppress the bourgeoisie and crush their resistance. This was particularly necessary for the Commune; and one of the reasons for its defeat was that it did not do this with sufficient determination. The organ of suppression, however, is here the majority of the population, and not a minority, as was always the case under slavery, serfdom, and wage slavery. And since the majority of the people *itself* suppresses its oppressors, a "special force" for suppression *is no longer necessary*! In this sense, the state *begins to wither away*. Instead of the special institutions of a privileged minority (privileged officialdom, the chiefs of the standing army), the majority itself can directly fulfill all these functions, and the more the functions of state power are performed by the people as a whole, the less need there is for the existence of this power.

In this connection, the following measures of the Commune, emphasized by Marx, are particularly noteworthy: the abolition of all representation allowances and of all monetary privileges to officials, the reduction of the remuneration of *all* servants of the state to the level of "*workmen's wages.*" This shows more clearly than anything else the *turn* from bourgeois to proletarian democracy, from the democracy of the oppressors to that of the oppressed classes, from the state as a "*special force*" for the suppression of a particular class to the suppression of the oppressors by the *general force* of the majority of the people—the workers and the peasants. And it is on this particularly striking point, perhaps the most important as far as the problem of the state is concerned, that the ideas of Marx have been most completely ignored! In popular commentaries, the number of which is legion, this is not mentioned. The thing done is to keep silent about it as if it were a piece of old-fashioned "naïveté," just as Christians, after their religion had been given the status of a state religion, "forgot" the "naïveté" of primitive Christianity with its democratic revolutionary spirit.

The reduction of the remuneration of high state officials seems to be "simply" a demand of naïve, primitive democracy. One of the "founders" of modern opportunism, the ex-Social-Democrat Eduard Bernstein, has more than once repeated the vulgar bourgeois jeers at "primitive" democracy. Like all opportunists . . . he did not understand at all that, first of all, the transition from capitalism to socialism is *impossible* without a certain "reversion" to "primitive" democracy (for how else can the majority, and then the whole population without exception, proceed to discharge state functions?); and that, second, "primitive democracy" based on capitalism and capitalist culture is not the same as primitive democracy in prehistoric or pre-capitalist times. Capitalist culture has *created* large-scale production, factories, railways, the postal service, telephones, etc., and *on this basis* the great majority of the functions of the old "state power" have become so simplified and can be reduced to such exceedingly simple operations of registration, filing and checking that they can be easily performed by every literate person, can quite easily be performed for ordinary "workmen's wages," and that these functions can (and must) be stripped of every shadow of privilege, of every semblance of "official grandeur."

All officials, without exception, elected and subject to recall *at any time*, their salaries reduced to the level of ordinary "workmen's wages"—these simple and "self-evident" democratic measures, while completely uniting the interests of the workers and the majority of the peasants, at the same time serve as a bridge leading from capitalism to socialism. These measures concern the reorganization of the state, the purely political reorganization of society; but, of course, they acquire their full meaning and significance only in connection with the "expropriation of the expropriators" either being accomplished or in preparation, that is, with the transformation of capitalist private ownership of the means of production into social ownership.

"The Commune," Marx wrote, "made that catchword of all bourgeois revolutions, cheap government, a reality, by abolishing the two greatest sources of expenditure—the army and the officialdom."

From the peasants, as from other sections of the petty bourgeoisie, only an insignificant few "rise to the top," "get on in the world" in the bourgeois sense, that is, become either well-to-do, bourgeois, or officials in secure and privileged positions. In every capitalist country where there are peasants (as there are in most capitalist countries), the vast majority of them are oppressed by the government and long for its overthrow, long for "cheap" government. This can be achieved *only* by the proletariat; and by achieving it, the proletariat at the same time takes a step towards the socialist reorganization of the state.

3 Abolition of Parliamentarism

"The Commune," Marx wrote, "was to be a working, not a parliamentary, body, executive and legislative at the same time. . . .

"Instead of deciding once in three or six years which member of the ruling class was to represent and repress [*verund zertreten*] the people in parliament, universal suffrage was to serve the people constituted in communes, as individual suffrage serves every other employer in the search for workers, foremen, and accountants for his business."

Owing to the prevalence of social-chauvinism and opportunism, this remarkable criticism of parliamentarism, made in 1871, also belongs now to the "forgotten words" of Marxism. The professional Cabinet Ministers and parliamentarians, the traitors to the proletariat and the "practical" socialists of our day, have left all criticism of parliamentarism to the anarchists, and, on this wonderfully reasonable ground, they denounce *all* criticism of parliamentarism as "anarchism"!! . . .

For Marx, however, revolutionary dialectics was never the empty fashionable phrase, the toy rattle, which . . . others have made of it. Marx knew how to break with anarchism ruthlessly for its inability to make use even of the "pigsty" of bourgeois parliamentarism, especially when the situation was obviously not revolutionary; but at the same time he knew how to subject parliamentarism to genuinely revolutionary proletarian criticism.

To decide once every few years which member of the ruling class is to repress and crush the people through parliament—this is the real essence of bourgeois parliamentarism, not only in parliamentary-constitutional monarchies, but also in the most democratic republics.

But if we deal with the question of the state, and if we consider parliamentarism as one of the institutions of the state, from the point of view of the tasks of the proletariat in *this* field, what is the way out of parliamentarism? How can it be dispensed with?

Once again we must say: the lessons of Marx, based on the study of the Commune, have been so completely forgotten that the present-day "Social-Democrat" (that is, present-day traitor to socialism) really cannot understand any criticism of parliamentarism other than anarchist or reactionary criticism.

The way out of parliamentarism is not, of course, the abolition of representative institutions and the elective principle, but the conversion of the representative institutions from talking shops into "working" bodies. "The Commune was to be a working, not a parliamentary, body, executive and legislative at the same time."

"A working, not a parliamentary, body"—this is a blow straight from the shoulder at the present-day parliamentarians and parliamentary "lap dogs" of Social-Democracy! Take any parliamentary country, from America to Switzerland, from France to Britain, Norway and so forth—in these countries the real business of "state" is performed behind the scenes and is carried on by the departments, chancelleries, and General Staffs. Parliament is given up to talk for the special purpose of fooling the "common people." This is so true that even in the Russian republic, a bourgeois-democratic republic, all these sins of parliamentarism came out at once, even before it managed to set up a real parliament. . . .

The Commune substitutes for the venal and rotten parliamentarism of bourgeois society institutions in which freedom of opinion and discussion does not degenerate into deception, for the parliamentarians themselves have to work, have to execute their own laws, have themselves to test the results achieved in reality, and to account directly to their constituents. Representative institutions remain, but there is *no* parliamentarism here as a special system, as the division of labor between the legislative and the executive, as a privileged position for the deputies. We cannot imagine democracy, even proletarian democracy, without representative institutions, but we can and *must* imagine democracy without parliamentarism, if criticism of bourgeois society is not mere words for us, if the desire to overthrow the rule of the bourgeoisie is our earnest and sincere desire, and not a mere "election" cry for catching workers' votes. . . .

It is extremely instructive to note that, in speaking of the functions of *those* officials who are necessary for the Commune and for proletarian democracy, Marx compares them to the workers of "every other employer," that is, of the ordinary capitalist enterprise, with its "workers, foremen, and accountants."

There is no trace of utopianism in Marx, in the sense that he made up or invented a "new" society. No, he studied the *birth* of the new society *out of* the old, and the forms of transition from the latter to the former, as a natural-historical process. He examined the actual experience of a mass proletarian movement and tried to draw practical lessons from it. He "learned" from the Commune, just as all the great revolutionary thinkers learned unhesitatingly from the experience of great movements of the oppressed classes, and never addressed them with pedantic "homilies". . . .

Abolishing the bureaucracy at once, everywhere and completely, is out of the question. It is a utopia. But to *smash* the old bureaucratic machine at once and to begin immediately to construct a new one that will make possible the gradual abolition of all bureaucracy—this is *not* a utopia, it is the experience of the Commune, the direct and immediate task of the revolutionary proletariat.

Capitalism simplifies the functions of "state" administration; it makes it possible to cast "bossing" aside and to confine the whole matter to the organization of the proletarians (as the ruling class), which will hire "workers, foremen, and accountants" in the name of the whole of society.

We are not utopians, we do not "dream" of dispensing *at once* with all administration, with all subordination. These anarchist dreams, based upon incomprehension of the tasks of the proletarian dictatorship, are totally alien to Marxism, and, as a matter of fact, serve only to postpone the socialist revolution until people are different. No, we want the socialist revolution with people as they are now, with people who cannot dispense with subordination, control, and "foremen and accountants."

The subordination, however, must be to the armed vanguard of all the exploited and working people, that is, to the proletariat. A beginning can and must be made at once, overnight, to replace the specific "bossing" of state officials by the simple functions of "foremen and accountants," functions which are already fully within the ability of the average town dweller and can well be performed for "workmen's wages."

We, the workers, shall organize large-scale production on the basis of what capitalism has already created, relying on our own experience as workers, establishing strict, iron discipline backed up by the state power of the armed workers. We shall reduce the role of state officials to that of simply carrying out our instructions as responsible, revocable, modestly paid "foremen and accountants" (of course, with the aid of technicians of all sorts, types, and degrees). This is *our* proletarian task, this is what we can and must *start* with in accomplishing the proletarian revolution. Such a beginning, on the basis of large-scale production, will of itself lead to the gradual "withering away" of all bureaucracy, to the gradual creation of an order— an order without inverted commas, an order bearing no similarity to wage slavery—and order under which the functions of control and accounting, becoming more and more simple, will be performed by each in turn, will then become a habit, and will finally die out as the *special* functions of a special section of the population.

A witty German Social-Democrat of the seventies of the last century called the *postal service* an example of the socialist economic system. This is very true. At present the postal service is a business organized on the lines of a state-*capitalist* monopoly. Imperialism is gradually transforming all trusts into organizations of a similar type, in which, standing over the "common" people, who are overworked and starved, one has the same bourgeois bureaucracy. But the mechanism of social management is here already to hand. Once we have overthrown the capitalists, crushed the resistance of these exploiters with the iron hand of the armed workers, and smashed the bureaucratic machine of the modern state, we shall have a splendidly equipped mechanism, freed from the "parasite," a mechanism which can very well be set going by the united workers themselves, who will hire technicians, foremen, and accountants, and pay them *all*, as indeed *all* "state" officials in general, workmen's wages. Here is a concrete, practical task which can immediately be fulfilled in relation to all trusts, a task whose fulfilment will rid the working people of exploitation, a task which takes account of what the Commune had already begun to practice (particularly in building up the state).

To organize the *whole* economy on the lines of the postal service so that the technicians, foremen, and accountants, as well as *all* officials, shall receive salaries no higher than "a workman's wage," all under the control and leadership of the armed proletariat—this is our immediate aim. This is the state, and this is the economic foundation we need. This is what will bring about the abolition of parliamentarism and the preservation of representative institutions. This is what will rid the laboring classes of the bourgeoisie's prostitution of these institutions. . . .

5 Abolition of the Parasite State

We have already quoted Marx's words on this subject, and we must now supplement them.

". . . It is generally the fate of new historical creations," he wrote, "to be mistaken for the counterpart of older and even defunct forms of social life, to which they may bear a certain likeness. Thus, this new Commune, which breaks [*bricht*, smashes] the modern state power, has been regarded as a revival of the medieval communes . . . as a federation of small states (as Montesquieu and the Girondins visualized it) . . . as an exaggerated form of the old struggle against overcentralization. . . .

". . . The Communal Constitution would have restored to the social body all the forces hitherto absorbed by that parasitic excrescence, the 'state,' feeding upon and hampering the free movement of society. By this one act it would have initiated the regeneration of France. . . .

". . . The Communal Constitution would have brought the rural producers under the intellectual lead of the central towns of their districts, and there secured to them, in the town working men, the natural trustees of their interests. The very existence of the Commune involved, as a matter of course, local self-government, but no longer as a counterpoise to state power, now become superfluous."

"Breaking state power," which was a "parasitic excrescence"; its "amputation," its "smashing"; "state power, now become superfluous"—these are the expressions Marx used in regard to the state when appraising and analyzing the experience of the Commune.

All this was written a little less than half a century ago; and now one has to engage in excavations, as it were, in order to bring undistorted Marxism to the knowledge of the mass of the people. The conclusions drawn from the observation of the last great revolution which Marx lived through were forgotten just when the time for the next great proletarian revolutions had arrived.

". . . The multiplicity of interpretations to which the Commune has been subjected, and the multiplicity of interests which expressed themselves in it show that it was a thoroughly flexible political form, while all previous forms of government had been essentially repressive. Its true secret was this: it was essentially *a working-class government,* the result of the struggle of the producing against the appropriating class, the political form at last discovered under which the economic emancipation of labor could be accomplished. . . .

"Except on this last condition, the Communal Constitution would have been an impossibility and a delusion. . . ."

The utopians busied themselves with "discovering" political forms under which the socialist transformation of society was to take place. The anarchists dismissed the question of political forms altogether. The opportunists of present-day Social-Democracy accepted the bourgeois political forms of the parliamentary democratic state as the limit which should not be overstepped; they battered their foreheads praying before this "model," and denounced as anarchism every desire to *break* these forms.

Marx deduced from the whole history of socialism and the political struggle that the state was bound to disappear, and that the transitional form of its disappearance (the transition from state to non-state) would be the "proletariat organized as the ruling class." Marx, however, did not set out to *discover* the political *forms* of this future stage. He limited himself to carefully observing French history, to analyzing it, and to drawing the conclusion to which the year 1851 had led, namely, that matters were moving towards the *destruction* of the bourgeois state machine.

And when the mass revolutionary movement of the proletariat burst forth, Marx, in spite of its failure, in spite of its short life and patent weakness, began to study the forms it had *discovered.*

The Commune is the form "at last discovered" by the proletarian revolution, under which the economic emancipation of labor can take place.

The Commune is the first attempt by a proletarian revolution to *smash* the bourgeois state machine; and it is the political form "at last discovered" by which the smashed state machine can and must be *replaced.*

6 Engels on the Overcoming of Democracy

. . . In the usual arguments about the state, the mistake is constantly made against which Engels warned . . . namely, it is constantly forgotten that the abolition of the state means also the abolition of democracy: that the withering away of the state means the withering away of democracy.

At first sight this assertion seems exceedingly strange and incomprehensible; indeed, someone may even suspect us of expecting the advent of a system of society in which the principle of subordination of the minority to the majority will not be observed—for democracy means the recognition of this very principle.

No, democracy is *not* identical with the subordination of the minority to the majority. Democracy is a *state* which recognizes the subordination of the minority to the majority, that is, an organization for the systematic use of *force* by one class against another, by one section of the population against another.

We set ourselves the ultimate aim of abolishing the state, that is, all organized and systematic violence, all use of violence against people in general. We do not expect the advent of a system of society in which the principle of subordination of the minority to the majority will not be observed. In striving for socialism, however, we are convinced that it will develop into communism and, therefore, that the need for violence against people in general, for the *subordination* of one man to another, and of one section of the population to another, will vanish altogether since people will *become accustomed* to observing the elementary conditions of social life *without violence* and *without subordination.*

In order to emphasize this element of habit, Engels speaks of a new *generation,* "reared in new, free social conditions," which will "be able to discard the entire lumber of the state"—of any state, including the democratic-republican state.

In order to explain this, it is necessary to analyze the economic basis of the withering away of the state.

Chapter V   The Economic Basis of the Withering Away of the State

1   Presentation of the Question by Marx

From a superficial comparison of Marx's [and] . . . Engels's [views] . . . it might appear that Marx was much more of a "champion of the state" than Engels, and that the difference of opinion between the two writers on the question of the state was very considerable.

Engels suggested . . . that all chatter about the state be dropped altogether, that the word "state" be eliminated from the program altogether and the word "community" substituted for it. Engels even declared that the Commune was no longer a state in the proper sense of the word. Yet Marx even spoke of the "future state in communist society," that is, he would seem to recognize the need for the state even under communism.

But such a view would be fundamentally wrong. A closer examination shows that Marx's and Engels's views on the state and its withering away were completely identical, and that Marx's expression quoted above refers to the state in the process of *withering away*.

Clearly there can be no question of specifying the moment of the *future* "withering away," the more so since it will obviously be a lengthy process. The apparent difference between Marx and Engels is due to the fact that they dealt with different subjects and pursued different aims. Engels set out to show . . . graphically, sharply, and in broad outline the utter absurdity of the current prejudices concerning the state . . . Marx only touched upon *this* question in passing, being interested in another subject, namely, the *development* of communist society.

The whole theory of Marx is the application of the theory of development—in its most consistent, complete, considered, and pithy form—to modern capitalism. Naturally, Marx was faced with the problem of applying this theory both to the *forthcoming* collapse of capitalism and to the *future* development of *future* communism.

On the basis of what *facts*, then, can the question of the future development of future communism be dealt with?

On the basis of the fact that it *has its origin* in capitalism, that it develops historically from capitalism, that it is the result of the action of a social force to which capitalism *gave birth*. There is no trace of an attempt on Marx's part to make up a utopia, to indulge in idle guess-work about what cannot be known. Marx treated the question of communism in the same way as a naturalist would treat the question of the development of, say, a new biological variety, once he knew that it had originated in such and such a way and was changing in such and such a definite direction.

To begin with, Marx brushed aside the confusion the Gotha Program brought into the question of the relationship between state and society. He wrote:

" 'Present-day society' is capitalist society, which exists in all civilized countries, being more or less free from medieval admixture, more or less modified by the particular historical development of each country, more or less developed. On the other hand, the 'present-day state' changes with a country's frontier. It is different in the Prusso-German Empire from what it is in Switzerland, and different in England from what it is in the United States. '*The* present-day state' is, therefore, a fiction.

"Nevertheless, the different states of the different civilized countries, in spite of their motley diversity of form, all have this in common, that they are based on modern bourgeois society, only one more or less capitalistically developed. They have, therefore, also certain essential characteristics in common. In this sense it is possible to speak of the 'present-day state,' in contrast with the future, in which its present root, bourgeois society, will have died off.

"The question then arises: what transformation will the state undergo in communist society? In other words, what social functions will remain in existence there that are analogous to present state functions? This question can only be answered scientifically, and one does not get a flea-hop nearer to the problem by a thousandfold combination of the word people with the word state."

After thus ridiculing all talk about a "people's state," Marx formulated the question and gave warning, as it were, that those seeking a scientific answer to it should use only firmly established scientific data.

The first fact that has been established most accurately by the whole theory of development, by science as a whole—a fact that was ignored by the utopians, and is ignored by the present-day opportunists, who are afraid of the socialist revolution—is that, historically, there must undoubtedly be a special stage, or a special phase, of *transition* from capitalism to communism.

2   *The Transition from Capitalism to Communism*

Marx continued:

"Between capitalist and communist society lies the period of the revolutionary transformation of the one into the other. Corresponding to this is also a political transition period in which the state can be nothing but *the revolutionary dictatorship of the proletariat*."

Marx bases this conclusion on an analysis of the role played by the proletariat in modern capitalist society, on the data concerning the development of this society, and on the irreconcilability of the antagonistic interests of the proletariat and the bourgeoisie.

Previously the question was put as follows: to achieve its emancipation, the proletariat must overthrow the bourgeoisie, win political power and establish its revolutionary dictatorship.

Now the question is put somewhat differently: the transition from capitalist society—which is developing towards communism—to communist society is impossible without a "political transition period," and the state in this period can only be the revolutionary dictatorship of the proletariat.

What, then, is the relation of this dictatorship to democracy?

We have seen that the *Communist Manifesto* simply places side by side the two concepts: "to raise the proletariat to the position of the ruling class" and "to win the battle of democracy." On the basis of all that has been said above, it is possible to determine more precisely how democracy changes in the transition from capitalism to communism.

In capitalist society, providing it develops under the most favorable conditions, we have a more or less complete democracy in the democratic republic. But this democracy is always hemmed in by the narrow limits set by capitalist exploitation, and consequently always remains, in effect, a democracy for the minority, only for the propertied classes, only for the rich. Freedom in capitalist society always remains about the same as it was in the ancient Greek republics: freedom for the slave-owners. Owing to the conditions of capitalist exploitation, the modern wage slaves are so crushed by want and poverty that "they cannot be bothered with democracy," "cannot be bothered with politics"; in the ordinary, peaceful course of events, the majority of the population is debarred from participation in public and political life.

The correctness of this statement is perhaps most clearly confirmed by Germany, because constitutional legality steadily endured there for a remarkably long time—nearly half a century (1871–1914)—and during this period the Social-Democrats were able to achieve far more than in other countries in the way of "utilizing legality," and organized a larger proportion of the workers into a political party than anywhere else in the world.

What is this largest proportion of politically conscious and active wage slaves that has so far been recorded in capitalist society? One million members of the Social-Democratic Party—out of fifteen million wage-workers! Three million organized in trade unions—out of fifteen million!

Democracy for an insignificant minority, democracy for the rich— that is the democracy of capitalist society. If we look more closely into the machinery of capitalist democracy, we see everywhere, in the "petty"—supposedly petty—details of the suffrage (residential qualification, exclusion of women, etc.), in the technique of the representative institutions, in the actual obstacles to the right of assembly (public buildings are not for "paupers"!), in the purely capitalist organization of the daily press, etc., etc.—we see restriction after restriction upon democracy. These restrictions, exceptions, exclusions, obstacles for the poor seem slight, especially in the eyes of one who has never known want himself and has never been in close contact with the oppressed classes in their mass life (and nine out of ten, if not ninety-nine out of a hundred, bourgeois publicists and politicians come under this category); but in their sum total these restrictions exclude and squeeze out the poor from politics, from active participation in democracy.

Marx grasped this *essence* of capitalist democracy splendidly when, in analysing the experience of the Commune, he said that the oppressed are allowed once every few years to decide which particular representatives of the oppressing class shall represent and repress them in parliament!

But from this capitalist democracy—that is inevitably narrow and stealthily pushes aside the poor and is therefore hypocritical and false through and through—forward development does not proceed simply, directly, and smoothly towards "greater and greater democracy," as the liberal professors and petty-bourgeois opportunists would have us believe. No, forward development, that is, development towards communism, proceeds through the dictatorship of the proletariat, and cannot do otherwise, for the *resistance* of the capitalist exploiters cannot be *broken* by anyone else or in any other way.

And the dictatorship of the proletariat, that is, the organization of the vanguard of the oppressed as the ruling class for the purpose of suppressing the oppressors, cannot result merely in an expansion of democracy. *Simultaneously* with an immense expansion of democracy, which *for the first time* becomes democracy for the poor, democracy for the people, and not democracy for the money-bags, the dictatorship of the proletariat imposes a series of restrictions on the freedom of the oppressors, the exploiters, the capitalists. We must suppress them in order to free humanity from wage slavery; their resistance must be crushed by force; it is clear that there is no freedom and no democracy where there is suppression and where there is violence.

Engels expressed this splendidly . . . when he said . . . that "the proletariat needs the state, not in the interests of freedom but in order to hold down its adversaries, and as soon as it becomes possible to speak of freedom the state as such ceases to exist."

Democracy for the vast majority of the people, and suppression by force, that is, exclusion from democracy, of the exploiters and oppressors of the people—this is the change democracy undergoes during the *transition* from capitalism to communism.

Only in communist society, when the resistance of the capitalists has been completely crushed, when the capitalists have disappeared, when there are no classes (that is, when there is no distinction between the members of society as regards their relation to the social means of production), *only* then "the state . . . ceases to exist," and "*it becomes possible to speak of freedom.*" Only then will a truly complete democracy become possible and be realized, a democracy without any exceptions whatever. And only then will democracy begin to *wither away,* owing to the simple fact that, freed from capitalist slavery, from the untold horrors, savagery, absurdities, and infamies of capitalist exploitation, people will gradually *become accustomed* to observing the elementary rules of social intercourse that have been known for centuries and repeated for thousands of years in all copy-book maxims. They will become accustomed to observing them without force, without coercion, without subordination, *without the special apparatus* for coercion called the state.

The expression "the state *withers away*" is very well chosen, for it indicates both the gradual and the spontaneous nature of the process. Only habit can, and undoubtedly will, have such an effect; for we see around us on millions of occasions how readily people become accustomed to observing the necessary rules of social intercourse when there is no exploitation, when there is nothing that arouses indignation, evokes protest and revolts, and creates the need for *suppression.*

And so in capitalist society we have a democracy that is curtailed, wretched, false, a democracy only for the rich, for the minority. The dictatorship of the proletariat, the period of transition to communism, will for the first time create democracy for the people, for the majority, along with the necessary suppression of the exploiters, of the minority. Communism alone is capable of providing really complete democracy, and the more complete it is, the sooner it will become unnecessary and wither away of its own accord.

In other words, under capitalism we have the state in the proper sense of the word, that is, a special machine for the suppression of one class by another, and, what is more, of the majority by the minority. Naturally, to be successful, such an undertaking as the systematic suppression of the exploited majority by the exploiting minority calls for the utmost ferocity and savagery in the matter of suppressing; it calls for seas of blood, through which mankind is actually wading its way in slavery, serfdom, and wage labor.

Furthermore, during the *transition* from capitalism to communism suppression is *still* necessary, but it is now the suppression of the exploiting minority by the exploited majority. A special apparatus, a special machine for suppression, the "state," is *still* necessary, but this is now a transitional state. It is no longer a state in the proper sense of the word; for the suppression of the minority of exploiters by the majority of the wage slaves of *yesterday* is comparatively so easy, simple, and natural a task that it will entail far less bloodshed than the suppression of the risings of slaves, serfs, or wage-laborers, and it will cost mankind far less. And it is compatible with the extension of democracy to such an overwhelming majority of the population that the need for a *special machine* of suppression will begin to disappear. Naturally, the exploiters are unable to suppress the people without a highly complex machine for performing this task, but *the people* can suppress the exploiters even with a very simple "machine," almost without a "machine," without a special apparatus, by the simple *organization of the armed people* (such as the Soviets of Workers' and Soldiers' Deputies, we would remark, running ahead).

Last, only communism makes the state absolutely unnecessary, for there is *nobody* to be suppressed—"nobody" in the sense of a *class*, of a systematic struggle against a definite section of the population. We are not utopians and do not in the least deny the possibility and inevitability of excesses on the part of *individual persons*, or the need to stop *such* excesses. In the first place, however, no special machine, no special apparatus of suppression, is needed for this; this will be done by the armed people themselves, as simply and as readily as any crowd of civilized people, even in modern society, interferes to put a stop to a scuffle or to prevent a woman from being assaulted. And, second, we know that the fundamental social cause of excesses, which consist in the violation of the rules of social intercourse, is the exploitation of the people, their want, and their poverty. With the removal of this chief cause, excesses will inevitably begin to "*wither away*." We do not know how quickly and in what succession, but we do know they will wither away. With their withering away the state will also *wither away*.

Without building utopias, Marx defined more fully what can be defined *now* regarding this future, namely, the difference between the lower and higher phases (levels, stages) of communist society.

3 The First Phase of Communist Society

In the *Critique of the Gotha Program*, Marx goes into detail to disprove Lassalle's idea that under socialism the worker will receive the "undiminished" or "full product of his labor." Marx shows that from the whole of the social labor of society there must be deducted a reserve fund, a fund for the expansion of production, a fund for the replacement of the "wear and tear" of machinery, and so on. Then, from the means of consumption must be deducted a fund for administrative expenses, for schools, hospitals, old people's homes, and so on.

. . . Marx makes a sober estimate of exactly how socialist society will have to manage its affairs. Marx proceeds to make a *concrete* analysis of the conditions of life of a society in which there will be no capitalism, and says:

"What we have to deal with here . . . is a communist society, not as it has *developed* on its own foundations, but, on the contrary, just as it *emerges* from capitalist society; which is, therefore, in every respect, economically, morally, and intellectually still stamped with the birthmarks of the old society from whose womb it comes."

It is this communist society, which has just emerged into the light of day out of the womb of capitalism and which is in every respect stamped with the birthmarks of the old society, that Marx terms the "first," or lower, phase of communist society.

The means of production are no longer the private property of individuals. The means of production belong to the whole of society. Every member of society, performing a certain part of the socially necessary work, receives a certificate from society to the effect that he has done a certain amount of work. And with this certificate he receives from the public store of consumer goods a corresponding quantity of products. After a deduction is made of the amount of labor which goes to the public fund, every worker, therefore, receives from society as much as he has given to it.

"Equality" apparently reigns supreme. . . .

"Equal right," says Marx, we certainly do have here; but it is *still* a "bourgeois right," which, like every right, *implies inequality*. Every right is an application of an *equal* measure to *different* people who in fact are not alike, are not equal to one another. That is why "equal right" is a violation of equality and an injustice. In fact, everyone, having performed as much social labor as another, receives an equal share of the social product (after the above-mentioned deductions).

But people are not alike: one is strong, another is weak; one is married, another is not; one has more children, another has less, and so on. And the conclusion Marx draws is:

"With an equal performance of labor, and hence an equal share in the social consumption fund, one will in fact receive more than another, one will be richer than another, and so on. To avoid all these defects, right would have to be unequal rather than equal."

The first phase of communism, therefore, cannot yet provide justice and equality: differences, and unjust differences, in wealth will still persist, but the *exploitation* of man by man will have become impossible because it will be impossible to seize the *means of production*—the factories, machines, land, etc.—and to make them private property. . . . Marx shows the *course of development* of communist society, which is *compelled* to abolish at first *only* the "injustice" of the means of production seized by individuals, and which is *unable* at once to eliminate the other injustice, which consists in the distribution of consumer goods "according to the amount of labor performed" (and not according to needs).

The vulgar economists . . . constantly reproach the socialists with forgetting the inequality of people and with "dreaming" of eliminating this inequality. Such a reproach, as we see, only proves the extreme ignorance of the bourgeois ideologists.

Marx not only most scrupulously takes account of the inevitable inequality of men, but he also takes into account the fact that the mere conversion of the means of production into the common property of the whole of society (commonly called "socialism") *does not remove* the defects of distribution and the inequality of "bourgeois right," which *continues to prevail* so long as products are divided "according to the amount of labor performed." Continuing, Marx says:

"But these defects are inevitable in the first phase of communist society as it is when it has just emerged, after prolonged birth pangs, from capitalist society. Right can never be higher than the economic structure of society and its cultural development conditioned thereby."

And so, in the first phase of communist society (usually called socialism) "bourgeois right" is *not* abolished in its entirety, but only in part, only in proportion to the economic revolution so far attained, that is, only in respect of the means of production. "Bourgeois right" recognizes them as the private property of individuals. Socialism converts them into *common* property. *To that extent*—and to that extent alone—"bourgeois right" disappears.

However, it persists as far as its other part is concerned; it persists in the capacity of regulator (determining factor) in the distribution of products and the allotment of labor among the members of society. The socialist principle, "He who does not work shall not eat," is *already* realized; the other socialist principle, "An equal amount of products for an equal amount of labor," is also *already* realized. But this is not yet communism, and it does not yet abolish "bourgeois right," which gives unequal individuals, in return for unequal (really unequal) amounts of labor, equal amounts of products.

This is a "defect," says Marx, but it is unavoidable in the first phase of communism; for if we are not to indulge in utopianism, we must not think that having overthrown capitalism people will at once learn to work for society *without any standard of right*. Besides, the abolition of capitalism *does not immediately create* the economic prerequisites for *such* a change.

Now, there is no other standard than that of "bourgeois right." To this extent, therefore, there still remains the need for a state, which, while safeguarding the common ownership of the means of production, would safeguard equality in labor and in the distribution of products.

The state withers away insofar as there are no longer any capitalists, any classes, and, consequently, no *class* can be *suppressed*.

But the state has not yet completely withered away, since there still remains the safeguarding of "bourgeois right," which sanctifies actual inequality. For the state to wither away completely, complete communism is necessary.

4   *The Higher Phase of Communist Society*

Marx continues:

"In a higher phase of communist society, after the enslaving subordination of the individual to the division of labor and with it also the antithesis between mental and physical labor has vanished, after labor has become not only a livelihood but life's prime want, after the productive forces have increased with the all-round development of the individual, and all the springs of cooperative wealth flow more abundantly—only then can the narrow horizon of bourgeois right be crossed in its entirety and society inscribe on its banners: From each according to his ability, to each according to his needs!"

Only now can we fully appreciate the correctness of Engels's remarks mercilessly ridiculing the absurdity of combining the words "freedom" and "state." So long as the state exists there is no freedom. When there is freedom, there will be no state.

The economic basis for the complete withering away of the state is such a high stage of development of communism at which the antithesis between mental and physical labor disappears, at which there consequently disappears one of the principal sources of modern *social* inequality—a source, moreover, which cannot on any account be removed immediately by the mere conversion of the means of production into public property, by the mere expropriation of the capitalists.

This expropriation will make it *possible* for the productive forces to develop to a tremendous extent. And when we see how incredibly capitalism is already *retarding* this development, when we see how much progress could be achieved on the basis of the level of technique already attained, we are entitled to say with the fullest confidence that the expropriation of the capitalists will inevitably result in an enormous development of the productive forces of human society. But how rapidly this development will proceed, how soon it will reach the point of breaking away from the division of labor, of doing away with the antithesis between mental and physical labor, of transforming labor into "life's prime want"—we do not and *cannot* know.

That is why we are entitled to speak only of the inevitable withering away of the state, emphasizing the protracted nature of this process and its dependence upon the rapidity of development of the *higher phase* of communism, and leaving the question of the time required for, or the concrete forms of, the withering away quite open, because there is *no* material for answering these questions.

The state will be able to wither away completely when society adopts the rule: "From each according to his ability, to each according to his needs," that is, when people have become so accustomed to observing the fundamental rules of social intercourse and when their labor has become so productive that they will voluntarily work *according to their ability*. "The narrow horizon of bourgeois right," which compels one to calculate with the heartlessness of a Shylock whether one has not worked half an hour more than somebody else, whether one is not getting less pay than somebody else—this narrow horizon will then be crossed. There will then be no need for society, in distributing products, to regulate the quantity to be received by each; each will take freely "according to his needs."

From the bourgeois point of view, it is easy to declare that such a social order is "sheer utopia" and to sneer at the socialists for promising everyone the right to receive from society, without any control over the labor of the individual citizen, any quantity of truffles, cars, pianos, etc. Even to this day, most bourgeois "savants" confine themselves to sneering in this way, thereby betraying both their ignorance and their selfish defense of capitalism.

Ignorance—for it has never entered the head of any socialist to "promise" that the higher phase of the development of communism will arrive; as for the great socialists' *forecast* that it will arrive, it presupposes not the present productivity of labor and *not the present* ordinary run of people, who . . . are capable of damaging the stocks of public wealth "just for fun" and of demanding the impossible.

Until the "higher" phase of communism arrives, the socialists demand the *strictest* control by society *and by the state* over the measure of labor and the measure of consumption; but this control must *start* with the expropriation of the capitalists, with the establishment of workers' control over the capitalists, and must be exercised not by a state of bureaucrats, but by a state of *armed workers*.

The selfish defense of capitalism by the bourgeois ideologists . . .

consists in that they *substitute* arguing and talk about the distant
future for the vital and burning question of *present-day* politics,
namely, the expropriation of the capitalists, the conversion of *all*
citizens into workers and other employees of *one* huge "syndicate"—
the whole state—and the complete subordination of the entire work
of this syndicate to a genuinely democratic state, *the state of the
Soviets of Workers' and Soldiers' Deputies. . . .*

And this brings us to the question of the scientific distinction between socialism and communism which Engels touched on in his
above-quoted argument about the incorrectness of the name "Social-
Democrat." Politically, the distinction between the first, or lower,
and the higher phase of communism will in time, probably, be tremendous. But it would be ridiculous to recognize this distinction now,
under capitalism, and only individual anarchists, perhaps, could invest it with primary importance. . . .

But the scientific distinction between socialism and communism
is clear. What is usually called socialism was termed by Marx the
"first," or lower, phase of communist society. Insofar as the means
of production become *common* property, the word "communism" is
also applicable here, providing we do not forget that this is *not* complete communism. The great significance of Marx's explanations is
that here, too, he consistently applies materialist dialectics, the theory
of development, and regards communism as something which develops
out of capitalism. Instead of scholastically invented, "concocted" definitions and fruitless disputes over words (What is socialism? What is
communism?), Marx gives an analysis of what might be called the
stages of the economic maturity of communism.

In its first phase, or first stage, communism *cannot* as yet be
fully mature economically and entirely free from traditions or vestiges
of capitalism. Hence the interesting phenomenon that communism in
its first phase retains "the narrow horizon of *bourgeois* right." Of
course, bourgeois right in regard to the distribution of *consumer* goods
inevitably presupposes the existence of the *bourgeois state*, for right
is nothing without an apparatus capable of *enforcing* the observance
of the standards of right.

It follows that under communism there remains for a time not
only bourgeois right, but even the bourgeois state, without the bourgeoisie!

This may sound like a paradox or simply a dialectical conundrum
of which Marxism is often accused by people who have not taken
the slightest trouble to study its extraordinarily profound content.

But in fact, remnants of the old, surviving in the new, confront
us in life at every step, both in nature and in society. And Marx
did not arbitrarily insert a scrap of "bourgeois" right into communism,

but indicated what is economically and politically inevitable in a society emerging *out of the womb* of capitalism.

Democracy is of enormous importance to the working class in its struggle against the capitalists for its emancipation. But democracy is by no means a boundary not to be overstepped; it is only one of the stages on the road from feudalism to capitalism, and from capitalism to communism.

Democracy means equality. The great significance of the proletariat's struggle for equality and of equality as a slogan will be clear if we correctly interpret it as meaning the abolition of *classes*. But democracy means only *formal* equality. And as soon as equality is achieved for all members of society *in relation* to ownership of the means of production, that is, equality of labor and wages, humanity will inevitably be confronted with the question of advancing farther, from formal equality to actual equality, that is, to the operation of the rule "from each according to his ability, to each according to his needs." By what stages, by means of what practical measures humanity will proceed to this supreme aim we do not and cannot know. But it is important to realize how infinitely mendacious is the ordinary bourgeois conception of socialism as something lifeless, rigid, fixed once and for all, whereas in reality *only* socialism will be the beginning of a rapid, genuine, truly mass forward movement, embracing first the *majority* and then the whole of the population, in all spheres of public and private life.

Democracy is a form of the state, one of its varieties. Consequently, it, like every state, represents, on the one hand, the organized, systematic use of force against persons; but, on the other hand, it signifies the formal recognition of equality of citizens, the equal right of all to determine the structure of, and to administer, the state. This, in turn, results in the fact that, at a certain stage in the development of democracy, it first welds together the class that wages a revolutionary struggle against capitalism—the proletariat—and enables it to crush, smash to atoms, wipe off the face of the earth the bourgeois, even the republican-bourgeois, state machine, the standing army, the police, and the bureaucracy and to substitute for them a *more* democratic state machine, but a state machine nevertheless, in the shape of armed workers who proceed to form a militia involving the entire population.

Here "quantity turns into quality": *such* a degree of democracy implies overstepping the boundaries of bourgeois society and beginning its socialist reorganization. If really *all* take part in the administration of the state, capitalism cannot retain its hold. The development of capitalism, in turn, creates the *preconditions* that *enable* really "all" to take part in the administration of the state.

Some of these preconditions are: universal literacy, which has already been achieved in a number of the most advanced capitalist countries, then the "training and disciplining" of millions of workers by the huge, complex, socialized apparatus of the postal service, railways, big factories, large-scale commerce, banking, etc., etc.

Given these *economic* preconditions, it is quite possible, after the overthrow of the capitalists and the bureaucrats, to proceed immediately, overnight, to replace them in the *control* over production and distribution, in the work of *keeping account* of labor and products, by the armed workers, by the whole of the armed population. (The question of control and accounting should not be confused with the question of the scientifically trained staff of engineers, agronomists, and so on. These gentlemen are working today in obedience to the wishes of the capitalists and will work even better tomorrow in obedience to the wishes of the armed workers.)

Accounting and control—that is *mainly* what is needed for the "smooth working," for the proper functioning, of the *first phase* of communist society. *All* citizens are transformed into hired employees of the state, which consists of the armed workers. All citizens become employees and workers of a *single* countrywide state "syndicate." All that is required is that they should work equally, do their proper share of work, and get equal pay. The accounting and control necessary for this have been *simplified* by capitalism to the utmost and reduced to the extraordinarily simple operations—which any literate person can perform—of supervising and recording, knowledge of the four rules of arithmetic, and issuing appropriate receipts.[4]

When the *majority* of the people begin independently and everywhere to keep such accounts and exercise such control over the capitalists (now converted into employees) and over the intellectual gentry who preserve their capitalist habits, this control will really become universal, general, and popular; and there will be no getting away from it, there will be "nowhere to go."

The whole of society will have become a single office and a single factory, with equality of labor and pay.

But this "factory" discipline, which the proletariat, after defeating the capitalists, after overthrowing the exploiters, will extend to the whole of society, is by no means our ideal, or our ultimate goal. It is only a necessary *step* for thoroughly cleaning society of all the infamies and abominations of capitalist exploitation, *and for further progress.*

4 When the more important functions of the state are reduced to such accounting and control by the workers themselves, it will cease to be a "political state" and "public functions will lose their political character and become mere administrative functions." . . . [L.]

From the moment all members of society, or at least the vast majority, have learned to administer the state *themselves*, have taken this work into their own hands, have organized control over the insignificant capitalist minority, over the gentry who wish to preserve their capitalist habits, and over the workers who have been thoroughly corrupted by capitalism—from this moment the need for government of any kind begins to disappear altogether. The more complete the democracy, the nearer the moment when it becomes unnecessary. The more democratic the "state" which consists of the armed workers, and which is "no longer a state in the proper sense of the word," the more rapidly *every form* of state begins to wither away.

For when *all* have learned to administer and actually do independently administer social production, independently keep accounts and exercise control over the parasites, the sons of the wealthy, the swindlers, and other "guardians of capitalist traditions," the escape from this popular accounting and control will inevitably become so incredibly difficult, such a rare exception, and will probably be accompanied by such swift and severe punishment (for the armed workers are practical men and not sentimental intellectuals, and they will scarcely allow anyone to trifle with them) that the *necessity* of observing the simple, fundamental rules of the community will very soon become a *habit*.

Then the door will be thrown wide open for the transition from the first phase of communist society to its higher phase, and with it to the complete withering away of the state. . . .

Chapter VII   The Experience of the Russian Revolutions of 1905 and 1917

The subject indicated in the title of this chapter is so vast that volumes could and should be written about it. In the present pamphlet we shall have to confine ourselves, naturally, to the most important lessons provided by experience, those bearing directly upon the tasks of the proletariat in the revolution with regard to state power.[5]

Postscript to the First Edition

This pamphlet was written in August and September 1917. I had already drawn up the plan for the next, the seventh, chapter, "The

5 The manuscript breaks off at this point. [*Ed.*]

Experience of the Russian Revolutions of 1905 and 1917." Apart from the title, however, I had no time to write a single line of the chapter; I was "interrupted" by a political crisis—the eve of the October revolution of 1917. Such an "interruption" can only be welcomed; but the writing of the second part of the pamphlet ("The Experience of the Russian Revolutions of 1905 and 1917") will probably have to be put off for a long time.[6] It is more pleasant and useful to go through the "experience of the revolution" than to write about it.

The Author

Petrograd
November 30, 1917

---

6   Lenin, in fact, never completed the work. [*Ed.*]

LETTER TO CENTRAL COMMIT-TEE MEMBERS (OCTOBER 24 [NOVEMBER 6] 1917)

COMRADES,

I am writing these lines on the evening of the 24th.[1] The situation is critical in the extreme. In fact it is now absolutely clear that to delay the uprising would be fatal.

With all my might I urge comrades to realize that everything now hangs by a thread; that we are confronted by problems which are not to be solved by conferences or congresses (even congresses of Soviets,) but exclusively by peoples, by the masses, by the struggle of the armed people.

The bourgeois onslaught . . . show[s] that we must not wait. We must at all costs, this very evening, this very night, arrest the government, having first disarmed the officer cadets (defeating them, if they resist), and so on.

We must not wait! We may lose everything!

The value of the immediate seizure of power will be the defense of the *people* (not of the congress, but of the people, the army and the peasants in the first place) from the Kornilovite government, which has . . . hatched a second Kornilov [2] plot.

Who must take power?

That is not important at present. Let the Revolutionary Military Committee do it, or "some other institution" which will declare that it will relinquish power only to the true representatives of the interests of the people, the interests of the army (the immediate proposal of peace), the interests of the peasants (the land to be taken immediately and private property abolished), the interests of the starving.

All districts, all regiments, all forces must be mobilized at once and must immediately send their delegations to the Revolutionary

1 November 6 in the New Style Calendar. [*Ed.*]

2 L. G. Kornilov, tsarist general who attempted a coup against the Provisional Government in the summer of 1917. [*Ed.*]

Military Committee and to the Central Committee of the Bolsheviks with the insistent demand that under no circumstances should power be left in the hands of . . . [the Provisional Government] until the 25th—not under any circumstances; the matter must be decided without fail this very evening, or this very night.

History will not forgive revolutionaries for procrastinating when they could be victorious today (and they certainly will be victorious today), while they risk losing much tomorrow, in fact, they risk losing everything.

If we seize power today, we seize it not in opposition to the Soviets but on their behalf.

The seizure of power is the business of the uprising; its political purpose will become clear after the seizure.

It would be a disaster, or a sheer formality, to await the wavering vote of October 25. The people have the right and are in duty bound to decide such questions not by a vote, but by force; in critical moments of revolution, the people have the right and are in duty bound to give directions to their representatives, even their best representatives, and not to wait for them.

This is proved by the history of all revolutions; and it would be an infinite crime on the part of the revolutionaries were they to let the chance slip, knowing that the *salvation of the revolution*, the offer of peace, the salvation of Petrograd, salvation from famine, the transfer of the land to the peasants depend upon them.

The government is tottering. It must be *given the deathblow* at all costs.

To delay action is fatal.

III.

CIVIL WAR AND
CONSOLIDATION OF POWER:
1918–1920

SPEECH TO THE EXTRAORDI-
NARY SEVENTH CONGRESS OF
THE RUSSIAN COMMUNIST
PARTY (BOLSHEVIKS),
MARCH 7, 1918

1 Political Report of the Central Committee, March 7

A POLITICAL REPORT might consist of an enumeration of measures taken by the Central Committee; but the essential thing at the present moment is not a report of this kind, but a review of our revolution as a whole; that is the only thing that can provide a truly Marxist substantiation of all our decisions. We must examine the whole preceding course of development of the revolution and ascertain why the course of its further development has changed. There have been turning-points in our revolution that will have enormous significance for the world revolution. One such turning-point was the *October Revolution.*[1]

. . . The policy we adopted, the slogan of "Power to the Soviets," which we instilled into the minds of the majority of the people, enabled us, in October, to achieve victory very easily in St. Petersburg and transformed the last months of the Russian revolution into one continuous triumphal march.

Civil war became a fact. The transformation of the imperialist war into civil war, which we had predicted at the beginning of the revolution, and even at the beginning of the war, and which considerable sections of socialist circles treated sceptically and even with ridicule, actually took place on October 25, 1917, in one of the largest and

1 Lenin goes on to argue that the period between the February and October Revolutions was one of easy victories for the Bolsheviks. Success was achieved with relatively little effort because of the failure of the Provisional government to deal with the critical question of land reform and its inability to extricate itself from the war. By the autumn of 1917 the Provisional government was thoroughly discredited and the Bolsheviks, who had alone remained aloof from the new regime, were able to reap the benefits of their strategy. [*Ed.*]

most backward of the belligerent countries. In this civil war the overwhelming majority of the population proved to be on our side, and that is why victory was achieved with such extraordinary ease.

The troops who abandoned the front carried with them wherever they went the maximum of revolutionary determination to put an end to collaboration; and the collaborationist elements, the white guards and the landowners' sons, found themselves without support among the population. The war against them gradually turned into a victorious triumphal march of the revolution as the masses of the people and the military units that were sent against us came over to the side of the Bolsheviks. . . .

. . . A wave of civil war swept over the whole of Russia, and everywhere we achieved victory with extraordinary ease precisely because the fruit had ripened, because the masses had already gone through the experience of collaboration with the bourgeoisie. Our slogan, "All Power to the Soviets," which the masses had tested in practice by long historical experience, had become part of their flesh and blood.

That is why the Russian revolution was a continuous triumphal march in the first months after October 25, 1917. As a result of this the difficulties which the socialist revolution immediately encountered, and could not but encounter, were forgotten, were pushed into the background. One of the fundamental differences between bourgeois revolution and socialist revolution is that for the bourgeois revolution, which arises out of feudalism, the new economic organizations are gradually created in the womb of the old order, gradually changing all the aspects of feudal society. The bourgeois revolution faced only one task—to sweep away, to cast aside, to destroy all the fetters of the preceding social order. By fulfilling this task every bourgeois revolution fulfills all that is required of it; it accelerates the growth of capitalism.

The socialist revolution is in an altogether different position. The more backward the country which, owing to the zigzags of history, has proved to be the one to start the socialist revolution, the more difficult is it for that country to pass from the old capitalist relations to socialist relations. New, incredibly difficult tasks, organizational tasks, are added to the tasks of destruction. Had not the popular creative spirit of the Russian revolution, which had gone through the great experience of the year 1905, given rise to the Soviets as early as February 1917, they could not under any circumstances have assumed power in October, because success depended entirely upon the existence of available organizational forms of a movement embracing millions. The Soviets were the available form, and that is why in the political sphere the future held out to us those brilliant successes, the continuous triumphal march, that we had; for the new form of political power was already available, and all we had to do was to pass a few decrees, and transform the power of the Soviets from the embryonic state in which it existed in the first months of the revolution into the legally recognized form which had become established in the Russian state—that is, into the Russian Soviet Republic. The Republic was born at one stroke; it was born so easily because in February 1917 the masses had created the Soviets even before any party had managed to proclaim this slogan. It was the great creative spirit of the people, which had passed through the bitter experience of 1905 and had been made wise by it, that gave rise to this form of proletarian power. The task of achieving victory over the internal enemy was an extremely easy one. The task of creating the political power was an extremely easy one because the masses had created the skeleton, the basis of this power. The Republic of Soviets was born at one stroke. But two exceedingly difficult problems still remained, the solution of which could not possibly be the triumphal march we experienced in the first months of our revolution—we did not doubt, we could not doubt, that the socialist revolution would be later confronted with enormously difficult tasks.

First, there was the problem of internal organization, which confronts every socialist revolution. The difference between a socialist revolution and a bourgeois revolution is that in the latter case there are ready-made forms of capitalist relationships; Soviet power—the proletarian power—does not inherit such ready-made relationships, if we leave out of account the most developed forms of capitalism, which, strictly speaking, extended to but a small top layer of industry and hardly touched agriculture. The organization of accounting, the control of large enterprises, the transformation of the whole of the state economic mechanism into a single huge machine, into an economic organism that will work in such a way as to enable hundreds of millions of people to be guided by a single plan—such was the enormous organizational problem that rested on our shoulders. Under the present conditions of labor this problem could not possibly be solved by the "hurrah" methods by which we were able to solve the problems of the Civil War. The very nature of the task prevented a solution by these methods. We achieved [some] easy victories . . . and created the Soviet Republic in face of a resistance that was not even worth serious consideration; the course of events was predetermined by the whole of the preceding objective development, so that all we had to do was say the last word and change the signboard, that is, take down the sign, "The Soviet exists as a trade union organization," and put up instead the sign, "The Soviet is the sole form of state power"; the situation, however, was altogether different in regard to organizational problems. In this field we encountered enormous difficulties. It immediately became clear to everyone who cared to ponder over the tasks of our revolution that only by the hard and long path of self-discipline would it be possible to overcome the disintegration that the war had caused in capitalist society, that only by extraordinarily hard, long, and persistent effort could we cope with this disintegration and defeat those elements aggravating it, elements which regarded the revolution as a means of discarding old fetters and getting as much out of it for themselves as they possible could. The emergence of a large number of such elements was inevitable in a small-peasant country at a time of incredible economic chaos, and the fight against these elements that is ahead of us, that we have only just started, will be a hundred times more difficult; it will be a fight which promises no spectacular opportunities. We are only in the first stage of this fight. Severe trials await us. The objective situation precludes any idea of limiting ourselves to a triumphal march with flying banners. . . . Anyone who attempted to apply these methods of struggle to the organizational tasks that confront the revolution would only prove his bankruptcy as a politician, as a socialist, as an active worker in the socialist revolution.

The same thing awaited some of our young comrades who were carried away by the initial triumphal march of the revolution, when it came up against the second enormous difficulty—the international question. The reason we achieved such an easy victory . . . the reason we so easily set up our government and without the slightest difficulty passed decrees on the socialization of the land and on workers' control, the reason we achieved all this so easily was a fortunate combination of circumstances that protected us for a short time from international imperialism. International imperialism, with the entire might of its capital, with its highly organized war machine, which is a real force, a real stronghold of international capital, could not, under any circumstances, under any conditions, live side by side with the Soviet Republic, both because of its objective position and because of the economic interests of the capitalist class embodied in it, because of commercial connections, of international financial relations. In this sphere a conflict is inevitable. This is the greatest difficulty of the Russian revolution, its greatest historical problem—the need to solve, international problems, the need to evoke a world revolution, to effect the transition from our strictly national revolution to the world revolution. This problem confronts us in all its incredible difficulty. I repeat, very many of our young friends who regard themselves as Lefts have begun to forget the most important thing: why in the course of the weeks and months of the enormous triumph after October we were able so easily to pass from victory to victory. And yet this was due only to a special combination of international circumstances that temporarily shielded us from imperialism. Imperialism had other things to bother about besides us. And it seemed to us that we, too, had other things to bother about besides imperialism. Individual imperialists had no time to bother with us, solely because the whole of the great social, political, and military might of modern world imperialism was split by internecine war into two groups. The imperialist plunderers involved in this struggle had gone to such incredible lengths, were locked in mortal combat to such a degree, that neither of the groups was able to concentrate any effective forces against the Russian revolution. These were the circumstances in which we found ourselves in October. It is paradoxical but true that our revolution broke out at so fortunate a moment when unprecedented disasters involving the destruction of millions of human beings had overtaken most of the imperialist countries, when the unprecedented calamities attending the war had exhausted the nations, when in the fourth year of the war the belligerent countries had reached an impasse, a parting of the ways, when the question arose objectively—could nations reduced to such a state continue fighting? It was only because our revolution broke out at so fortunate a moment as this, when neither of the two gigantic groups of plunderers was in a position immediately either to hurl itself at the other or to unite with the other against us; our revolution could (and did) take advantage only of a situation such as this in international political and economic relations to accomplish its brilliant triumphal march in European Russia. . . . This alone explains the appearance of Party functionaries, intellectual supermen, in the leading circles of our Party who allowed themselves to be carried away by this triumphal march and who said we could cope with international imperialism; over there, there will also be a triumphal march, over there, there will be no real difficulties. This was at variance with the objective position of the Russian revolution which had merely taken advantage of the setback of international imperialism; the engine that was supposed to bear down on us with the force of a railway train bearing down on a wheelbarrow and smashing it to splinters was temporarily stalled—and the engine was stalled because the two groups of predators had clashed. Here and there the revolutionary movement was growing, but in all the imperialist countries without exception it was still mainly in the initial stage. Its rate of development was entirely different from ours. Anyone who has given careful thought to the economic prerequisites of the socialist revolution in Europe must be clear on the point that in Europe it will be immeasurably more difficult to start, whereas it was immeasurably more easy for us to start; but it will be more difficult for us to continue the revolution than it will be over there. This objective situation caused us to experience an extraordinarily sharp and difficult turn in history. From the continuous triumphal march on our internal front, against our counter-revolution, against the enemies of Soviet power in October, November, and December, we had to pass to a collision with real international imperialism, in its real hostility towards us. From the period of the triumphal march we had to pass to a period in which we were in an extraordinary difficult and painful situation, one which certainly could not be brushed aside with words, with brilliant slogans—however pleasant that would have been—because in our disorganized country we had to deal with incredibly weary masses, who had reached a state in which they could not possibly go on fighting, who were so shattered by three years of agonizing war that they were absolutely useless from the military point of view. Even before the October Revolution we saw representatives of the masses of the soldiers, not members of the Bolshevik Party, who did not hesitate to tell the bourgeoisie the truth that the Russian army would not fight. This state of the army has brought about a gigantic crisis. A small-peasant country, disorganized by war, reduced to an incredible state, has been placed in an extremely difficult position. We have no army, but we have to go on living side by side with a predator who is armed to the teeth, a predator who still remains and will continue to remain a plunderer and is not, of course, affected by agitation in favor of peace without annexations and indemnities. A tame, domestic animal has been lying side by side with a tiger and trying to persuade the latter to conclude a peace without annexations and indemnities, although the only way such a peace could be attained was by attacking the tiger. The top layer of our Party—intellectuals and some of the workers' organizations—has been trying in the main to brush this prospect aside with phrases and such excuses as "that is not the way it should be." This peace was too incredible a prospect for them to believe that we, who up to now had marched in open battle with colors flying and had stormed the enemy's positions with "hurrahs," could yield and accept these humiliating terms. Never! We are exceedingly proud revolutionaries; we declare above all: "The Germans cannot attack."

This was the first argument with which these people consoled themselves. History has now placed us in an extraordinarily difficult position; in the midst of organizational work of unparalleled difficulty we shall have to experience a number of painful defeats. Regarded from the world-historical point of view, there would doubtlessly be no hope of the ultimate victory of our revolution if it were to remain alone, if there were no revolutionary movements in other countries. When the Bolshevik Party tackled the job alone, it did so in the firm conviction that the revolution was maturing in all countries and that in the end—but not at the very beginning—no matter what difficulties we experienced, no matter what defeats were in store for us, the world socialist revolution would come—because it is coming; would mature—because it is maturing and will reach full maturity. I repeat, our salvation from all these difficulties is an all-Europe revolution.

Taking this truth, this absolutely abstract truth, as our starting-point, and being guided by it, we must see to it that it does not in time become a mere phrase, because every abstract truth, if it is accepted without analysis, becomes a mere phrase. If you say that every strike conceals the hydra of revolution, and he who fails to understand this is no socialist, you are right. Yes, the socialist revolution looms behind every strike. But if you say that every single strike is an immediate step towards the socialist revolution, you will be uttering perfectly empty phrases. We have heard these phrases "every blessed time in the same place" and have got so sick and tired of them that the workers have rejected these anarchist phrases, because undoubtedly, clear as it is that behind every strike there looms the hydra of socialist revolution, it is equally clear that the assertion that every strike can develop into revolution is utter nonsense. Just as it is indisputable that all the difficulties in our revolution will be overcome only when the world socialist revolution matures—and it is maturing now everywhere—it is absolutely absurd to declare that we must conceal every real difficulty of our revolution today and say: "I bank on the international socialist movement—I can commit any piece of folly I please." "Liebknecht [2] will help us out, because he is going to win, anyhow." He will create such an excellent organization, he will plan everything beforehand so well that we shall be able to take ready-made forms in the same way as we took the ready-made Marxist doctrine from Western Europe—and maybe that is why it triumphed in our country in a few months, whereas it has been taking decades to triumph in Western Europe. Thus it would have been reckless gambling to apply the old method of solving the problem of the struggle by a triumphal march to the new historical period which has set in, and which has confronted us, not with feeble [enemies] . . . , but with an international predator—the imperialism of Germany, where the revolution has been maturing but has obviously not yet reached maturity. The assertion that the enemy would not dare attack the revolution was such a gamble. The situation at the time of the Brest [3] negotiations was not yet such as to compel us to accept any peace

2   Karl Liebknecht (1871–1919), left-wing German socialist and one of the founders of the German Communist Party. The reference here is to the faith of many Russian Communists in an imminent German Revolution which would save the Russian Revolution. Their reasoning was based on the Marxist principle that revolution would occur at the end of capitalist development. Since Germany was considered the most highly developed capitalist country, and the one with the strongest socialist movement, it was logical to assume that the German Revolution would signal the triumph of socialism. [*Ed.*]

3   Brest-Litovsk, the site of the truce negotiation and the eventual signing of the peace treaty between Russia and Germany on March 3, 1918 which took Russia unilaterally out of World War I. [*Ed.*]

terms. The objective alignment of forces was such that a respite would not have been enough. It took the Brest negotiations to show that the Germans would attack, that German society was not so pregnant with revolution that it could give birth to it at once; and we cannot blame the German imperialists for not having prepared that outbreak by their conduct, or, as our young friends who regard themselves as Lefts say, for not having created a situation in which the Germans could not attack. When we tell them that we have no army, that we were compelled to demobilize—we were compelled to do so, although we never forgot that a tiger was lying beside our tame, domestic animal—they refuse to understand. Although we were compelled to demobilize we did not for a moment forget that it was impossible to end the war unilaterally by issuing an order to stick the bayonets in the ground.

Generally speaking, how is it that not a single trend, not a single tendency, not a single organization in our Party opposed this demobilization? Had we gone mad? Not in the least. Officers, not Bolsheviks, had stated even before October that the army could not fight, that it could not be kept at the front even for a few weeks longer. After October this became obvious to everybody who was willing to recognize the facts, willing to see the unpleasant, bitter reality and not hide, or pull his cap over his eyes, and make shift with proud phrases. We have no army; we cannot hold it. The best thing we can do is to demobilize it as quickly as possible. This is the sick part of the organism, which has suffered incredible torture, has been ravaged by the privations of a war into which it entered technically unprepared, and from which it has emerged in such a state that it succumbs to panic at every attack. We cannot blame these people who have experienced incredible suffering. In hundreds of resolutions, even in the first period of the Russian revolution, the soldiers have said quite frankly: "We are drowning in blood, we cannot go on fighting." One could have delayed the end of the war artificially . . . one could have postponed the end for a few weeks, but objective reality broke its own road. This is the sick part of the Russian state organism which can no longer bear the burden of the war. The quicker we demobilize the army, the sooner it will become absorbed by those parts that are not so sick and the sooner will the country be prepared for new severe trials. That is what we felt when we unanimously, without the slightest protest, adopted the decision—which was absurd from the point of view of foreign events—to demobilize the army. It was the proper step to take. We said that it was a frivolous illusion to believe that we could hold the army. The sooner we demobilized the army, the sooner would the social organism as a whole recover. That is why the revolutionary phrase, "The Germans cannot attack," from which the other phrase ("We can declare the state of war terminated. Neither war nor the signing of peace." [4]) derived, was such a profound mistake, such a bitter overestimation of events. But suppose the Germans do attack? "No, they cannot attack." But have you the right to risk the world revolution? What about the concrete question of whether you may not prove to be accomplices of German imperialism when that moment comes? But we, who since October 1917 have all become defensists, who have recognized the principle of defense of the fatherland, we all know that we have broken with imperialism, not merely in word but in deed; we have destroyed the secret treaties, vanquished the bourgeoisie in our own country, and proposed an open and honest peace so that all the nations may see what our intentions really are. How could people who seriously uphold the position of defending the Soviet Republic agree to this gamble, which has already produced results? And this is a fact, because the severe crisis which our Party is now experiencing, owing to the formation of a "Left" opposition within it, is one of the gravest crises the Russian revolution has experienced.

This crisis will be overcome. Under no circumstances will it break the neck of our Party, or of our revolution, although at the present moment it has come very near to doing so; there was a possibility of it. The guarantee that we shall not break our neck on this question is this: instead of applying the old method of settling factional differences, the old method of issuing an enormous quantity of literature, of having many discussions and plenty of splits, instead of this old method, events have provided our people with a new method of learning things. This method is to put everything to the test of facts, events, the lessons of world history. You said that the Germans could not attack. The logic of your tactics was that we could declare the state of war to be terminated. History has taught you a lesson; it has shattered this illusion. Yes, the German revolution is growing, but not in the way we should like it, not as fast as Russian intellectuals would have it, not at the rate our history developed in October— when we entered any town we liked, proclaimed Soviet power, and within a few days nine-tenths of the workers came over to our side. The German revolution has the misfortune of not moving so fast. What do you think? Must we reckon with the revolution, or must the revolution reckon with us? You wanted the revolution to reckon with you. But history has taught you a lesson. It is a lesson, because it is the absolute truth that without a German revolution we are doomed—perhaps not in Petrograd, not in Moscow, but in Vladivostok, in more remote places to which perhaps we shall have to retreat, and the distance to which is perhaps greater than the distance from Petrograd to Moscow. At all events, under all conceivable circum-

4 The phrase is Trotsky's. [*Ed.*]

stances, if the German revolution does not come, we are doomed. Nevertheless, this does not in the least shake our conviction that we must be able to bear the most difficult position without [wavering].

The revolution will not come as quickly as we expected. History has proved this, and we must be able to take this as a fact, to reckon with the fact that the world socialist revolution cannot begin so easily in the advanced countries as the revolution began in Russia—in the land of Nicholas and Rasputin, the land in which an enormous part of the population was absolutely indifferent as to what peoples were living in the outlying regions, or what was happening there. In such a country it was quite easy to start a revolution, as easy as lifting a feather.

But to start without preparation a revolution in a country in which capitalism is developed and has given democratic culture and organization to everybody, down to the last man—to do so would be wrong, absurd. There we are only just approaching the painful period of the beginning of socialist revolutions. This is a fact. We do not know, no one knows; perhaps—it is quite possible—it will triumph within a few weeks, even within a few days, but we cannot stake everything on that. We must be prepared for extraordinary difficulties, for extraordinarily severe defeats, which are inevitable because the revolution in Europe has not yet begun, although it may begin tomorrow; and when it does begin, then, of course, we shall not be tortured by doubts; there will be no question about a revolutionary war, but just one continuous triumphal march. That is to come, it will inevitably be so, but it is not so yet. This is the simple fact that history has taught us, with which it has hit us very painfully—and it is said a man who has been thrashed is worth two who haven't. That is why I think that now history has given us a very painful thrashing, because of our hope that the Germans could not attack and that we could get everything by shouting "hurrah!"; this lesson, with the help of our Soviet organizations, will be very quickly brought home to the masses all over Soviet Russia. They are all up and doing, gathering, preparing for the Congress, passing resolutions, thinking over what has happened. What is taking place at the present time does not resemble the old pre-revolutionary controversies, which remained within narrow Party circles; now all decisions are submitted for discussion to the masses, who demand that they be tested by experience, by deeds, who never allow themselves to be carried away by frivolous speeches and never allow themselves to be diverted from the path prescribed by the objective progress of events. Of course, an intellectual, or a Left Bolshevik, can try to talk his way out of difficulties. He can try to talk his way out of such facts as the absence of an army and the failure of the revolution to begin in Germany. The millions-strong masses—and politics begin where millions of men and women are; where there are not thousands, but millions, that is where serious politics begin—the masses know what the army is like; they have seen soldiers returning from the front. They know—that is, if you take, not individual persons, but real masses—that we cannot fight, that every man at the front has endured everything imaginable. The masses have realized the truth that if we have no army, and a predator is lying beside us, we shall have to sign a most harsh, humiliating peace treaty. That is inevitable until the birth of the revolution, until you cure your army, until you allow the men to return home. Until then the patient will not recover. And we shall not be able to cope with the German predator by shouting "hurrah!"; we shall not be able to throw him off as easily as we threw off . . . [the Provisional Government]. This is the lesson the masses have learned without the excuses that certain of those who desire to evade bitter reality have tried to present them with. . . .

. . . [One] must know how to retreat. We cannot hide the incredibly bitter, deplorable reality from ourselves with empty phrases; we must say: God grant that we retreat in what is half-way good order. We cannot retreat in good order; but God grant that our retreat is [in] half-way good order, that we gain a little time in which the sick part of our organism can be absorbed at least to some extent. On the whole the organism is sound; it will overcome its sickness. But you cannot expect it to overcome it all at once, instantaneously; you cannot stop an army in flight. . . .

. . . If the European revolution is late in coming, gravest defeats await us because we have no army, because we lack organization, because, at the moment, these are two problems we cannot solve. If you are unable to adapt yourself, if you are not inclined to crawl on your belly in the mud, you are not a revolutionary but a chatterbox; and I propose this, not because I like it, but because we have no other road, because history has not been kind enough to bring the revolution to maturity everywhere simultaneously.

The way things are turning out is that the civil war has begun as an attempt at a clash with imperialism, and this has shown that imperialism is rotten to the core, and that proletarian elements are rising in every army. Yes, we shall see the world revolution, but for the time being it is a very good fairy-tale, a very beautiful fairy-tale— I quite understand children liking beautiful fairy-tales. But I ask, is it proper for a serious revolutionary to believe in fairy-tales? There is an element of reality in every fairy-tale. If you told children fairy-tales in which the cock and the cat did not converse in human language they would not be interested. In the same way, if you tell the people that civil war will break out in Germany and also guarantee that instead of a clash with imperialism we shall have a field revolution on a world-wide scale, the people will say you are deceiving them. In doing this you will be overcoming the difficulties with which history has confronted us only in your own minds, by your own wishes. It will be a good thing if the German proletariat is able to take action. But have you measured it, have you discovered an instrument that will show that the German revolution will break out on such-and-such a day? No, you do not know that, and neither do we. You are staking everything on this card. If the revolution breaks out, everything is saved. Of course! But if it does not turn out as we desire, if it does not achieve victory tomorrow—what then? Then the masses will say to you, you acted like gamblers—you staked everything on a fortunate turn of events that did not take place, you proved unfit for the situation that actually arose instead of the world revolution, which will inevitably come, but which has not yet reached maturity.

One may dream about the field revolution on a world-wide scale, for it will come. Everything will come in due time; but for the time being, set to work to establish self-discipline, subordination before all else, so that we can have exemplary order, so that the workers for at least one hour in twenty-four may train to fight. This is a little more difficult than relating beautiful fairytales. This is what we can do today; in this way you will help the German revolution, the world revolution. We do not know how many days the respite will last, but we have got it. . . .

Yes, of course, we are violating the treaty; [5] we have violated it thirty of forty times. Only children can fail to understand that in an epoch like the present, when a long painful period of emancipation is setting in, which has only just created and raised the Soviet power three stages in its development—only children can fail to understand that in this case there must be a long, circumspect struggle. . . .

The last war has been a bitter, painful, but serious lesson for the Russian people. It has taught them to organize, to become disciplined, to obey, to establish a discipline that will be exemplary. Learn discipline from the Germans; for, if we do not, we, as a people, are doomed; we shall live in eternal slavery.

This way, and no other, has been the way of history. History tells us that peace is a respite for war; war is a means of obtaining a somewhat better or somewhat worse peace. . . .

We do not know how long the respite will last—we will try to take advantage of the situation. Perhaps the respite will last longer; perhaps it will last only a few days. Anything may happen, no one knows, or can know, because all the major powers are bound, restricted, compelled to fight on several fronts. . . .

We must learn to work in a new way. That is immensely more

5   The Treaty of Brest-Litovsk. [Ed.]

difficult, but it is by no means hopeless. It will not break Soviet power if we do not break it ourselves by utterly senseless adventurism. The time will come when the people will say, we will not permit ourselves to be tortured any longer. But this will take place only if we do not agree to this adventure but prove able to work under harsh conditions and under the unprecedentedly humiliating treaty we signed the other day, because a war, or a peace treaty, cannot solve such a historical crisis. . . .

We should have but one slogan—to learn the art of war properly and put the railways in order. To wage a socialist revolutionary war without railways would be rank treachery. We must produce order, and we must produce all the energy and all the strength that will produce the best that is in the revolution.

Grasp even an hour's respite if it is given you, in order to maintain contact with the remote rear and there create new armies. Abandon illusions for which real events have punished you and will punish you more severely in the future. An epoch of most grievous defeats is ahead of us; it is with us now; we must be able to reckon with it; we must be prepared for persistent work in conditions of illegality, in conditions of downright slavery to the Germans; it is no use painting it in bright colors. . . . If we are able to act in this way, then, in spite of defeats, we shall be able to say with absolute certainty—victory will be ours.

THE IMMEDIATE TASKS OF THE SOVIET GOVERNMENT (APRIL 1918)

The International Position of the Russian Soviet Republic and the Fundamental Tasks of the Socialist Revolution

THANKS to the peace which has been achieved—despite its extremely onerous character and extreme instability—the Russian Soviet Republic has gained an opportunity to concentrate its efforts for a while on the most important and most difficult aspect of the socialist revolution, namely, the task of organization. . . .

A fundamental condition for the successful accomplishment of the primary task of organization confronting us is that the people's political leaders, that is, the members of the Russian Communist Party (Bolsheviks), and following them all the class-conscious representatives of the mass of the working people, shall fully appreciate the radical distinction in this respect between previous bourgeois revolutions and the present socialist revolution.

In bourgeois revolutions, the principal task of the mass of working people was to fulfill the negative or destructive work of abolishing feudalism, monarchy, and medievalism. The positive or constructive work of organizing the new society was carried out by the property-owning bourgeois minority of the population. And the latter carried out this task with relative ease, despite the resistance of the workers and the poor peasants, not only because the resistance of the people exploited by capital was then extremely weak, since they were scattered and uneducated, but also because the chief organizing force of anarchically built capitalist society is the spontaneously growing and expanding national and international market.

In every socialist revolution, however—and consequently in the socialist revolution in Russia which we began on October 25, 1917—

the principal task of the proletariat, and of the poor peasants which it leads, is the positive or constructive work of setting up an extremely intricate and delicate system of new organizational relationships extending to the planned production and distribution of the goods required for the existence of tens of millions of people. Such a revolution can be successfully carried out only if the majority of the population, and primarily the majority of the working people, engage in independent creative work as makers of history. Only if the proletariat and the poor peasants display sufficient class-consciousness, devotion to principle, self-sacrifice and perseverance, will the victory of the socialist revolution be assured. By creating a new, Soviet type of state, which gives the working and oppressed people the chance to take an active part in the independent building up of a new society, we solved only a small part of this difficult problem. The principal difficulty lies in the economic sphere, namely, the introduction of the strictest and universal accounting and control of the production and distribution of goods, raising the productivity of labor and *socializing* production *in practice*.

The development of the Bolshevik Party, which today is the governing party in Russia, very strikingly indicates the nature of the turning-point in history we have now reached, which is the peculiar feature of the present political situation, and which calls for a new orientation of Soviet power, that is, for a new presentation of new tasks.

The first task of every party of the future is to convince the majority of the people that its program and tactics are correct. . . . This task has now been fulfilled in the main, for . . . the majority of the workers and peasants of Russia are obviously on the side of the Bolsheviks; but of course, it is far from being completely fulfilled (and it can never be completely fulfilled).

The second task that confronted our Party was to capture political power and to suppress the resistance of the exploiters. This task has not been completely fulfilled either, and it cannot be ignored because the monarchists and Constitutional-Democrats on the one hand, and their henchmen and hangers-on, the Mensheviks and Right Socialist-Revolutionaries, on the other, are continuing their efforts to unite for the purpose of overthrowing Soviet power. In the main, however, the task of suppressing the resistance of the exploiters was fulfilled in the period from October 25, 1917 to (approximately) February 1918. . . .

A third task is now coming to the fore as the immediate task and one which constitutes the peculiar feature of the present situation, namely, the task of organizing [the] *administration* of Russia. Of course, we advanced and tackled this task on the very day following October 25, 1917. Up to now, however, since the resistance of the exploiters still took the form of open civil war, up to now the task of administration *could not* become the *main*, the *central* task.

Now it has become the main and central task. We, the Bolshevik Party, have *convinced* Russia. We have *won* Russia from the rich for the poor, from the exploiters for the working people. Now we must *administer* Russia. And the whole peculiarity of the present situation, the whole difficulty, lies in understanding *the specific features of the transition* from the principal task of convincing the people and of suppressing the exploiters by armed force to the principal task of *administration*.

For the first time in human history a socialist party has managed to complete in the main the conquest of power and the suppression of the exploiters, and has managed to *approach directly* the task of *administration*. We must prove worthy executors of this most difficult (and most gratifying) task of the socialist revolution. We must *fully realize* that in order to administer successfully, *besides* being able to convince people, besides being able to win a civil war, we must be able to do *practical organizational work*. This is the most difficult task, because it is a matter of organizing in a new way the most deep-rooted, the economic, foundations of life of scores of millions of people. And it is the most gratifying task, because only *after* it has been fulfilled (in the principal and main outlines) will it be possible to say that Russia *has become* not only a Soviet, but also a socialist, republic.

The General Slogan of the Moment

The objective situation reviewed above, which has been created by the extremely onerous and unstable peace, the terrible state of ruin, the unemployment, and famine we inherited from the war and the rule of the bourgeoisie . . . , all this has inevitably caused extreme weariness and even exhaustion of wide sections of the working people. These people insistently demand—and cannot but demand—a respite. The task of the day is to restore the productive forces destroyed by the war and by bourgeois rule; to heal the wounds inflicted by the war, by the defeat in the war, by profiteering and the attempts of the bourgeoisie to restore the overthrown rule of the exploiters; to achieve economic revival; to provide reliable protection of elementary order. It may sound paradoxical, but in fact, considering the objective conditions indicated above, it is absolutely certain that at the present moment the Soviet system can secure Russia's transition to socialism only if these very elementary, extremely elementary problems of maintaining public life are practically solved in spite of the resistance of the bourgeoisie, the Mensheviks, and the Right Socialist-Revolutionaries. In view of the specific features of the present situation, and in view of the existence of Soviet power with its land socialization law, workers' control law, etc., the practical solution of these extremely elementary problems and the overcoming of the organizational difficulties of the first stages of progress towards socialism are now two aspects of the same picture.

Keep regular and honest accounts of money, manage economically, do not be lazy, do not steal, observe the strictest labor discipline— it is these slogans, justly scorned by the revolutionary proletariat when the bourgeoisie used them to conceal its rule as an exploiting class, that are now, since the overthrow of the bourgeoisie, becoming the immediate and the principal slogans of the moment. On the one hand, the practical application of these slogans by *the mass* of working people is the *sole* condition for the salvation of a country which has been tortured almost to death by the imperialist war and by the imperialist robbers . . . ; on the other hand, the practical application of these slogans by the *Soviet* state, by *its* methods, on the basis of *its* laws, is a necessary and *sufficient* condition for the final victory of socialism. This is precisely what those who contemptuously brush aside the idea of putting such "hackneyed" and "trivial" slogans in the forefront fail to understand. In a small-peasant country, which overthrew tsarism only a year ago, and which liberated itself from the Kerenskys less than six months ago, there has naturally remained not a little of spontaneous anarchy, intensified by the brutality and savagery that accompany every protracted and reactionary war, and there has arisen a good deal of despair and aimless bitterness. And if we add to this the provocative policy of the lackeys of the bourgeoisie . . . it will become perfectly clear what prolonged and persistent efforts must be exerted by the best and the most class-conscious workers and peasants in order to bring about a complete change in the mood of the people and to bring them on to the proper path of steady and disciplined labor. Only such a transition brought about by the mass of the poor (the proletarians and semiproletarians) can consummate the victory over the bourgeoisie and particularly over the peasant bourgeoisie, more stubborn and numerous.

The New Phase of the Struggle Against the Bourgeoisie

The bourgeoisie in our country has been conquered, but it has not yet been uprooted, not yet destroyed, and not even utterly broken. That is why we are faced with a new and higher form of struggle against the bourgeoisie, the transition from the very simple task of further expropriating the capitalists to the much more complicated and difficult task of creating conditions in which it will be impossible for the bourgeoisie to exist, or for a new bourgeoisie to arise. Clearly, this task is immeasurably more significant than the previous one; and until it is fulfilled there will be no socialism.

If we measure our revolution by the scale of West-European revolutions we shall find that at the present moment we are approximately at the level reached in 1793 and 1871. We can be legitimately proud of having risen to this level, and of having certainly, in one respect, advanced somewhat further, namely: we have decreed and introduced throughout Russia the highest *type* of state— Soviet power. Under no circumstances, however, can we rest content with what we have achieved, because we have only just started the transition to socialism, we have *not yet* done the decisive thing in *this* respect.

The decisive thing is the organization of the strictest and country-wide accounting and control of production and distribution of goods. And yet, we have *not yet* introduced accounting and control in those enterprises and in those branches and fields of economy which we have taken away from the bourgeoisie; and without this there can be no thought of achieving the second and equally essential material condition for introducing socialism, namely, raising the productivity of labor on a national scale.

That is why the present task could not be defined by the simple formula: continue the offensive against capital. Although we have certainly not finished off capital and although it is certainly necessary to continue the offensive against this enemy of the working people, such a formula would be inexact, would not be concrete, would not take into account the *peculiarity* of the present situation in which, in order to go on advancing successfully *in the future*, we must "suspend" our offensive *now*.

This can be explained by comparing our position in the war against capital with the position of a victorious army that has captured, say, a half or two-thirds of the enemy's territory and is compelled to halt in order to muster its forces, to replenish its supplies of munitions, repair and reinforce the lines of communication, build new store-houses, bring up new reserves, etc. To suspend the offensive of a victorious army under such conditions is necessary precisely in order to gain the rest of the enemy's territory, in order to achieve complete victory. Those who have failed to understand that the objective state of affairs at the present moment dictates to us precisely such a "suspension" of the offensive against capital have failed to understand anything at all about the present political situation.

It goes without saying that we can speak about the "suspension" of the offensive against capital only in quotation marks, that is, only metaphorically. In ordinary war, a general order can be issued to stop the offensive; the advance can actually be stopped. In the war against capital, however, the advance cannot be stopped, and there can be no thought of our abandoning the further expropriation of capital. What we are discussing is the shifting of the *center of gravity* of our economic and political work. Up to now measures for the direct expropriation of the expropriators were *in the forefront.* Now the organization of accounting and control in those enterprises in which the capitalists have already been expropriated, and in all other enterprises, advances *to the forefront.*

If we decided to continue to expropriate capital at the same rate at which we have been doing it up to now, we should certainly suffer defeat, because our work of organizing proletarian accounting and control has obviously—obviously to every thinking person—*fallen behind* the work of *directly* "expropriating the expropriators." If we now concentrate all our efforts on the organization of accounting and control, we shall be able to solve this problem, we shall be able to make up for lost time, we shall *completely* win our "campaign" against capital.

But is not the admission that we must make up for lost time tantamount to admission of some kind of an error? Not in the least. Take another military example. If it is possible to defeat and push back the enemy merely with detachments of light cavalry, it should be done. But if this can be done successfully only up to a certain point, then it is quite conceivable that when this point has been reached, it will be necessary to bring up heavy artillery. By admitting that it is now necessary to make up for lost time in bringing up heavy artillery, we do not admit that the successful cavalry attack was a mistake.

Frequently, the lackeys of the bourgeoisie reproached us for having launched a "Red Guard" attack on capital. The reproach is absurd and is worthy only of the lackeys of the money-bags, because *at one time* the "Red Guard" attack on capital was absolutely dictated by circumstances. First, *at that time* capital put up military resistance through the medium of Kerensky and [others]. . . . Military resistance cannot be broken except by military means, and the Red Guards fought in the noble and supreme historical cause of liberating the working and exploited people from the yoke of the exploiters.

Second, we could not at that time put methods of administration in the forefront in place of methods of suppression, because the art of administration is not innate, but is acquired by experience. At that time we lacked this experience; now we have it. Third, at that time we could not have specialists in the various fields of knowledge and technology at our disposal because those specialists were either fighting in the ranks of the . . . [counter-revolutionaries] or were still able to put up systematic and stubborn passive resistance by way of *sabotage*. Now we have broken the sabotage. The "Red Guard" attack on capital was successful, was victorious, because we broke capital's military resistance and its resistance by sabotage.

Does that mean that a "Red Guard" attack on capital is *always* appropriate, under *all* circumstances, that we have *no* other means of fighting capital? It would be childish to think so. We achieved victory with the aid of light cavalry, but we also have heavy artillery. We achieved victory by methods of suppression; we shall be able to achieve victory also by methods of administration. We must know how to change our methods of fighting the enemy to suit changes in the situation. We shall not for a moment renounce "Red Guard" suppression of the . . . landowner and bourgeois counter-revolution-aries. We shall not be so foolish, however, as to put "Red Guard" methods in the forefront at a time when the period in which "Red Guard" attacks were necessary has, in the main, drawn to a close (and to a victorious close), and when the period of utilizing bourgeois specialists by the proletarian state power for the purpose of reploughing the soil in order to prevent the growth of any bour-geoisie whatever is knocking at the door.

This is a peculiar epoch, or rather stage of development, and in order to defeat capital completely, we must be able to adapt the forms of our struggle to the peculiar conditions of this stage.

Without the guidance of experts in the various fields of knowledge, technology, and experience, the transition to socialism will be im-possible, because socialism calls for a conscious mass advance to greater productivity of labor compared with capitalism, and on the basis achieved by capitalism. Socialism must achieve this advance *in its own way*, by its own methods—or, to put it more concretely, by *Soviet* methods. And the specialists, because of the whole social environment which made them specialists, are, in the main, inevitably bourgeois. Had our proletariat, after capturing power, quickly solved the problem of accounting, control, and organization on a national scale (which was impossible owing to the war and Russia's backward-ness), then we, after breaking the sabotage, would also have com-pletely subordinated these bourgeois experts to ourselves by means of universal accounting and control. Owing to the considerable "delay" in introducing accounting and control generally, we, although we have managed to conquer sabotage, have *not yet* created the conditions which would place the bourgeois specialists at our disposal. The mass of saboteurs are "going to work," but the best organizers and the top experts can be utilized by the state either in the old way, in the bourgeois way (that is, for high salaries), or in the new way, in the proletarian way (that is, creating the conditions of national accounting and control from below, which would inevitably and of themselves subordinate the experts and enlist them for our work).

Now we have to resort to the old bourgeois method and to agree to pay a very high price for the "services" of the top bourgeois experts. All those who are familiar with the subject appreciate this, but not all ponder over the significance of this measure being adopted by the proletarian state. Clearly, this measure is a compromise, a departure from the principles of the Paris Commune and of every proletarian power, which call for the reduction of all salaries to the level of the wages of the average worker, which urge that careerism be fought not merely in words, but in deeds.

Moreover, it is clear that this measure not only implies the cessation—in a certain field and to a certain degree—of the offensive against capital (for capital is not a sum of money, but a definite social relation); it is also *a step backward* on the part of our socialist Soviet state power, which from the very outset proclaimed and pursued the policy of reducing high salaries to the level of the wages of the average worker.

Of course, the lackeys of the bourgeoisie, particularly the small fry, such as the Mensheviks . . . will giggle over our confession that we are taking a step backward. But we need not mind their giggling. We must study the specific features of the extremely difficult and new path to socialism without concealing our mistakes and weaknesses, and try to be prompt in doing what has been left undone. To conceal from the people the fact that the enlistment of bourgeois experts by means of extremely high salaries is a retreat from the principles of the Paris Commune would be sinking to the level of bourgeois politicians and deceiving the people. Frankly explaining how and why we took this step backward, and then publicly discussing what means are available for making up for lost time, means educating the people and learning from experience, learning together with the people how to build socialism. There is hardly a single victorious military campaign in history in which the victor did not commit certain mistakes, suffer partial reverses, temporarily yield something, and in some places retreat. The "campaign" which we have undertaken against capitalism is a million times more difficult than the most difficult military campaign, and it would be silly and disgraceful to give way to despondency because of a particular and partial retreat.

We shall now discuss the question from the practical point of view. Let us assume that the Russian Soviet Republic requires one thousand first-class scientists and experts in various fields of knowledge, technology, and practical experience to direct the labor of the people towards securing the speediest possible economic revival. Let us assume also that we shall have to pay these "stars of the first magnitude"—of course the majority of those who shout loudest about the corruption of the workers are themselves utterly corrupted by bourgeois morals—25,000 rubles per annum each. Let us assume that this sum (25,000,000 rubles) will have to be doubled (assuming that we have to pay bonuses for particularly successful and rapid fulfillment of the most important organizational and technical tasks), or even quadrupled (assuming that we have to enlist several hundred foreign specialists, who are more demanding). The question is, would the annual expenditure of fifty or a hundred million rubles by the Soviet Republic for the purpose of reorganizing the labor of the people on modern scientific and technological lines be excessive or too heavy? Of course not. The overwhelming majority of the class-conscious workers and peasants will approve of this expenditure because they know from practical experience that our backwardness causes us to lose thousands of millions, and that we have *not yet* reached that degree of organization, accounting, and control which would induce all the "stars" of the bourgeois intelligentsia to participate voluntarily in *our* work.

It goes without saying that this question has another side to it. The corrupting influence of high salaries—both upon the Soviet authorities (especially since the revolution occurred so rapidly that it was impossible to prevent a certain number of adventurers and rogues from getting into positions of authority, and they, together with a number of inept or dishonest commissars, would not be averse to becoming "star" embezzlers of state funds) and upon the mass of the workers—is indisputable. Every thinking and honest worker and poor peasant, however, will agree with us, will admit, that we cannot immediately rid ourselves of the evil legacy of capitalism, and that we can liberate the Soviet Republic from the duty of paying an annual "tribute" of fifty million or one hundred million rubles (a tribute for our own backwardness in organizing *country-wide* accounting and control *from below*) only by organizing ourselves, by tightening up discipline in our own ranks, by purging our ranks of all those who are "preserving the legacy of capitalism," who "follow the traditions of capitalism," that is, of idlers, parasites, and embezzlers of state funds (now all the land, all the factories, and all the railways are the "state funds" of the Soviet Republic). If the class-conscious advanced workers and poor peasants manage with the aid of the Soviet institutions to organize, become disciplined, pull themselves together, create powerful labor discipline in the course of one year, then in a year's time we shall throw off this "tribute," which can be reduced even before that . . . in exact proportion to the successes we achieve in our workers' and peasants' labor discipline and organization. The sooner we ourselves, workers and peasants, learn the best labor discipline and the most modern technique of labor, using the bourgeois experts to teach us, the sooner we shall liberate ourselves from any "tribute" to these specialists.

Our work of organizing country-wide accounting and control of production and distribution under the supervision of the proletariat has lagged very much behind our work of directly expropriating the expropriators. This proposition is of fundamental importance for understanding the specific features of the present situation and the tasks of the Soviet government that follow from it. The center of gravity of our struggle against the bourgeoisie is shifting to the organization of such accounting and control. Only with this as our starting-point will it be possible to determine correctly the immediate tasks of economic and financial policy in the sphere of nationalization of the banks, monopolization of foreign trade, the state control of money circulation, the introduction of a property and income tax satisfactory from the proletarian point of view, and the introduction of compulsory labor service.

We have been lagging very far behind in introducing socialist reforms in these spheres (very, very important spheres), and this is because accounting and control are insufficiently organized in general. It goes without saying that this is one of the most difficult tasks, and in view of the ruin caused by the war, it can be fulfilled only over a long period of time; but we must not forget that it is precisely here that the bourgeoisie—and particularly the numerous petty and peasant bourgeoisie—are putting up the most serious fight, disrupting the control that is already being organized, disrupting the grain monopoly, for example, and gaining positions for profiteering and speculative trade. We have far from adequately carried out the things we have decreed, and the principal task of the moment is to concentrate all efforts on the businesslike, practical *realization* of the principles of the reforms which have already become law (but not yet reality). . . .

The Significance of the Struggle for Country-Wide Accounting and Control

The state, which for centuries has been an organ for oppression and robbery of the people, has left us a legacy of the people's supreme hatred and suspicion of everything that is connected with the state. It is very difficult to overcome this, and only a Soviet government can do it. Even a Soviet government, however, will require plenty of time and enormous perseverance to accomplish it. This "legacy" is especially apparent in the problem of accounting and control—the fundamental problem facing the socialist revolution on the morrow of the overthrow of the bourgeoisie. A certain amount of time will inevitably pass before the people, who feel free for the first time now that the landowners and the bourgeoisie have been overthrown, will understand—not from books, but from their own, *Soviet* experience—will understand and *feel* that without comprehensive state accounting and control of the production and distribution of goods, the power of the working people, the freedom of the working people, *cannot* be maintained, and that a return to the yoke of capitalism is *inevitable*.

All the habits and traditions of the bourgeoisie, and of the petty bourgeoisie in particular, also oppose *state* control, and uphold the inviolability of "sacred private property," of "sacred" private enterprise. It is now particularly clear to us how correct is the Marxist thesis that anarchism and anarcho-syndicalism are *bourgeois* trends, how irreconcilably opposed they are to socialism, proletarian dictatorship, and communism. The fight to instill into the people's minds the idea of *Soviet* state control and accounting, and to carry out this idea in practice; the fight to break with the rotten past—which taught the people to regard the procurement of bread and clothes as a "private" affair, and buying and selling as a transaction "which concerns only myself"—is a great fight of world-historic significance, a fight between socialist consciousness and bourgeois-anarchist spontaneity.

We have introduced workers' control as a law, but this law is only just beginning to operate and is only just beginning to penetrate the minds of broad sections of the proletariat. In our agitation we do not sufficiently explain that lack of accounting and control in the production and distribution of goods means the death of the rudiments of socialism, means the embezzlement of state funds (for all property belongs to the state and the state is the Soviet state in which power belongs to the majority of the working people). . . . Until workers' control has become a fact, until the advanced workers have organized and carried out a victorious and ruthless crusade against the violators of this control, or against those who are careless in matters of control, it will be impossible to pass from the first step (from workers' control) to the second step towards socialism, that is, to pass on to workers' regulation of production.

The socialist state can arise only as a network of producers' and consumers' communes, which conscientiously keep account of their production and consumption, economize on labor, and steadily raise the productivity of labor, thus making it possible to reduce the working day to seven, six, and even fewer hours. Nothing will be achieved unless the strictest, country-wide, comprehensive accounting and control of *grain* and the *production of grain* (and later of all other essential goods) are set going.

Raising the Productivity of Labor

In every socialist revolution, after the proletariat has solved the problem of capturing power, and to the extent that the task of expropriating the expropriators and suppressing their resistance has been carried out in the main, there necessarily comes to the forefront the fundamental task of creating a social system superior to capitalism, namely, raising the productivity of labor, and in this connection (and for this purpose) securing better organization of labor. Our Soviet state is precisely in the position where, thanks to the victories over the exploiters . . . it is able to approach this task directly, to tackle it in earnest. And here it becomes immediately clear that while it is possible to take over the central government in a few days, while it is possible to suppress the military resistance (and sabotage) of the exploiters even in different parts of a great country in a few weeks, the capital solution of the problem of raising the productivity of labor requires, at all events (particularly after a most terrible and devastating war), several years. The protracted nature of the work is certainly dictated by objective circumstances.

The raising of the productivity of labor first of all requires that the material basis of large-scale industry shall be assured, namely, the development of the production of fuel, iron, the engineering, and chemical industries. The Russian Soviet Republic enjoys the favorable position of having at its command, even after the Brest peace, enormous reserves of ore . . . fuel . . . enormous timber reserves, water power, raw materials for the chemical industry, etc. The development of these natural resources by methods of modern technology will provide the basis for the unprecedented progress of the productive forces.

Another condition for raising the productivity of labor is, first, the raising of the educational and cultural level of the mass of the population. This is now taking place extremely rapidly, a fact which those who are blinded by bourgeois routine are unable to see; they are unable to understand what an urge towards enlightenment and initiative is now developing among the "lower ranks" of the people thanks to the Soviet form of organization. Second, a condition for economic revival is the raising of the working people's discipline, their skill, the effectiveness, the intensity of labor and its better organization.

In this respect the situation is particularly bad and even hopeless if we are to believe those who have allowed themselves to be intimidated by the bourgeoisie or by those who are serving the bourgeoisie for their own ends. These people do not understand that there has not been, nor could there be, a revolution in which the supporters of the old system did not raise a howl about chaos, anarchy, etc. Naturally, among the people who have only just thrown off an unprecedentedly savage yoke there is deep and widespread seething and ferment; the working out of new principles of labor discipline by the people is a very protracted process, and this process could not even start until complete victory had been achieved over the land-owners and the bourgeoisie.

We, however, without in the least yielding to the despair (it is often false despair) which is spread by the bourgeoisie and the bourgeois intellectuals (who have despaired of retaining their old privileges), must under no circumstances conceal an obvious evil. On the contrary, we shall expose it and intensify the Soviet methods of combating it, because the victory of socialism is inconceivable without the victory of proletarian conscious discipline over spontaneous petty-bourgeois anarchy. . . .

The more class-conscious vanguard of the Russian proletariat has already set itself the task of raising labor discipline. . . . This work must be supported and pushed ahead with all speed. We must raise the question of piece-work and apply and test it in practice; we must raise the question of applying much of what is scientific and progressive in the Taylor[1] system; we must make wages correspond to the total amount of goods turned out, or to the amount of work done by the railways, the water transport system, etc., etc.

The Russian is a bad worker compared with people in advanced countries. It could not be otherwise under the tsarist regime and in view of the persistence of the hangover from serfdom. The task that Soviet government must set the people in all its scope is—learn to work. The Taylor system, the last word of capitalism in this respect, like all capitalist progress, is a combination of the refined brutality of bourgeois exploitation and a number of the greatest scientific achievements in the field of analyzing mechanical motions during work, the elimination of superfluous and awkward motions, the elaboration of correct methods of work, the introduction of the best system of accounting and control, etc. The Soviet Republic must at all costs adopt all that is valuable in the achievements of science and technology in this field. The possibility of building socialism depends exactly upon our success in combining the Soviet power and the Soviet organization of administration with the up-to-date achievements of capitalism. We must organize in Russia the study and teaching of the Taylor system and systematically try it out and adapt it to our own ends. At the same time, in working to raise the productivity of labor, we must take into account the specific features of the transition period from capitalism to socialism, which, on the one hand, require that the foundations be laid of the socialist organiza-

1 Frederick Winslow Taylor (1856–1915), an American engineer and the originator of time-motion studies of industrial activities. [*Ed.*]

tion of competition, and, on the other hand, require the use of compulsion, so that the slogan of the dictatorship of the proletariat shall not be desecrated by the practice of a lily-livered proletarian government.

The Organization of Competition

Among the absurdities which the bourgeoisie are fond of spreading about socialism is the allegation that socialists deny the importance of competition. In fact, it is only socialism which, by abolishing classes, and, consequently, by abolishing the enslavement of the people, for the first time opens the way for competition on a really mass scale. And it is precisely the Soviet form of organization, by ensuring transition from the formal democracy of the bourgeois republic to real participation of the mass of working people in *administration,* that for the first time puts competition on a broad basis. It is much easier to organize this in the political field than in the economic field; but for the success of socialism, it is the economic field that matters.

Take, for example, a means of organizing competition such as publicity. The bourgeois republic ensures publicity only formally; in practice, it subordinates the press to capital, entertains the "mob" with sensationalist political trash, and conceals what takes place in the workshops, in commercial transactions, contracts, etc., behind a veil of "trade secrets," which protect "the sacred right of property." The Soviet government has abolished trade secrets; it has taken a new path; but we have done hardly anything to utilize publicity for the purpose of encouraging economic competition. While ruthlessly suppressing the thoroughly mendacious and insolently slanderous bourgeois press, we must set to work systematically to create a press that will not entertain and fool the people with political sensation and trivialities, but which will submit the questions of everyday economic life to the people's judgment and assist in the serious study of these questions. Every factory, every village is a producers' and consumers' commune, whose right and duty it is to apply the general Soviet laws in their own way ("in their own way," not in the sense of violating them, but in the sense that they can apply them in various forms) and in their own way to solve the problem of accounting in the production and distribution of goods. Under capitalism, this was the "private affair" of the individual capitalist [or] landowner. . . . Under the Soviet system, it is not a private affair, but a most important affair of state.

We have scarcely yet started on the enormous, difficult, but rewarding task of organizing competition between communes, of introducing accounting and publicity in the process of the production of grain, clothes, and other things, of transforming dry, dead, bureaucratic accounts into living examples, some repulsive, others attractive. Under the capitalist mode of production, the significance of individual example, say the example of a co-operative workshop, was inevitably very much restricted, and only those imbued with petty-bourgeois illusions could dream of "correcting" capitalism through the example of virtuous institutions. After political power has passed to the proletariat, after the expropriators have been expropriated, the situation radically changes and—as prominent socialists have repeatedly pointed out—force of example for the first time is able to influence the people. Model communes must and will serve as educators, teachers, helping to raise the backward communes. The press must serve as an instrument of socialist construction, give publicity to the successes achieved by the model communes in all their details, must study the causes of these successes, the methods of management these communes employ, and, on the other hand, must put on the "black list" those communes which persist in the "traditions of capitalism," that is, anarchy, laziness, disorder, and profiteering. In capitalist society, statistics were entirely a matter for "government servants" or for narrow specialists; we must carry statistics to the people and make them popular so that the working people themselves may gradually learn to understand and see how long and in what way it is necessary to work, how much time and in what way one may rest, so that *the comparison of the business results* of the various communes may become a matter of general interest and study, and that the most outstanding communes may be rewarded immediately (by reducing the working day, raising remuneration, placing a larger amount of cultural or aesthetic facilities or values at their disposal, etc.).

When a new class comes on to the historical scene as the leader and guide of society, a period of violent "rocking," shocks, struggle, and storm, on the one hand, and a period of uncertain steps, experiments, wavering, hesitation in regard to the selection of new methods corresponding to new objective circumstances, on the other, are inevitable. The moribund feudal nobility avenged themselves on the bourgeoisie which vanquished them and took their place, not only by conspiracies and attempts at rebellion and restoration, but also by pouring ridicule over the lack of skill, the clumsiness, and the mistakes of the "upstarts" and the "insolent" who dared to take over the "sacred helm" of state without the centuries of training which the princes, barons, nobles, and dignitaries had had; in exactly the same way . . . the whole of that fraternity of heroes of bourgeois swindling or bourgeois scepticism avenge themselves on the working class of Russia for having had the "audacity" to take power.

Of course, not weeks, but long months and years are required for a new social class, especially a class which up to now has been oppressed and crushed by poverty and ignorance, to get used to its new position, look around, organize its work, and promote its *own* organizers. It is understandable that the Party which leads the revolutionary proletariat has not been able to acquire the experience and habits of large organizational undertakings embracing millions and tens of millions of citizens; the remolding of the old, almost exclusively agitators' habits is a very lengthy process. But there is nothing impossible in this, and as soon as the necessity for a change is clearly appreciated, as soon as there is firm determination to effect the change and perseverance in pursuing a great and difficult aim, we shall achieve it. There is an enormous amount of organizing talent among the "people," that is, among the workers and the peasants who do not exploit the labor of others. Capital crushed these talented people in thousands; it killed their talent and threw them on to the scrapheap. We are not yet able to find them, encourage them, put them on their feet, promote them. But we shall learn to do so if we set about it with all-out revolutionary enthusiasm, without which there can be no victorious revolutions.

No profound and mighty popular movement has ever occurred in history without dirty scum rising to the top, without adventurers and rogues, boasters and ranters attaching themselves to the inexperienced innovators, without absurd muddle and fuss, without individual "leaders" trying to deal with twenty matters at once and not finishing any of them. Let the lap-dogs of bourgeois society . . . squeal and yelp about every extra chip that is sent flying in cutting down the big, old wood. What else are lap-dogs for if not to yelp at the proletarian elephant? Let them yelp. We shall go our way and try as carefully and as patiently as possible to test and discover real organizers, people with sober and practical minds, people who combine loyalty to socialism with ability without fuss (and in spite of muddle and fuss), to get a large number of people working together steadily and concertedly within the framework of Soviet organization. *Only* such people, after they have been tested a dozen times, by being transferred from the simplest to the more difficult tasks, should be promoted to the responsible posts of leaders of the people's labor, leaders of administration. We have not yet learned to do this, but we shall learn.

"Harmonious Organization" and Dictatorship

[A recent] resolution . . . advanced as the primary task of the moment the establishment of a "harmonious organization" and the tightening of discipline. Everyone now readily "votes for" and "subscribes to" resolutions of this kind; but usually people do not think over the fact that the application of such resolutions calls for coercion—coercion precisely in the form of dictatorship. And yet it would be extremely stupid and absurdly utopian to assume that the transition from capitalism to socialism is possible without coercion and without dictatorship. Marx's theory very definitely opposed this petty-bourgeois-democratic and anarchist absurdity long ago. And Russia of 1917–1918 confirms the correctness of Marx's theory in this respect so strikingly, palpably, and imposingly that only those who are hopelessly dull or who have obstinately decided to turn their backs on the truth can be under any misapprehension concerning this. Either the dictatorship of [militarists] . . . or the dictatorship of the proletariat —any other choice is *out of the question* for a country which is developing at an extremely rapid rate with extremely sharp turns and amidst desperate ruin created by one of the most horrible wars in history. Every solution that offers a middle path is either a deception of the people by the bourgeoisie . . . or an expression of the dull-wittedness of the petty-bourgeois democrats . . . who chatter about the unity of democracy, the dictatorship of democracy, the general democratic front, and similar nonsense. Those whom even the progress of the Russian Revolution of 1917–1918 has not taught that a middle course is impossible must be given up for lost.

On the other hand, it is not difficult to see that during every transition from capitalism to socialism, dictatorship is necessary for two main reasons, or along two main channels. First, capitalism cannot be defeated and eradicated without the ruthless suppression of the resistance of the exploiters, who cannot at once be deprived of their wealth, of their advantages of organization and knowledge, and consequently for a fairly long period will inevitably try to overthrow the hated rule of the poor; second, every great revolution, and a socialist revolution in particular, even if there is no external war, is inconceivable without internal war, that is, civil war, which is even more devastating than external war, and involves thousands and millions of cases of wavering and desertion from one side to another, implies a state of extreme indefiniteness, lack of equilibrium and chaos. And of course, all the elements of disintegration of the old society, which are inevitably very numerous and connected mainly with the petty bourgeoisie (because it is the petty bourgeoisie that every war and every crisis ruins and destroys first), are bound to "reveal themselves" during such a profound revolution. And these elements of disintegration *cannot* "reveal themselves" otherwise than in an increase of crime, hooliganism, corruption, profiteering, and outrages of every kind. To put these down requires time and *requires an iron hand*.

There has not been a single great revolution in history in which the people did not instinctively realize this and did not show salutary firmness by shooting thieves on the spot. The misfortune of previous revolutions was that the revolutionary enthusiasm of the people, which sustained them in their state of tension and gave them the strength to suppress ruthlessly the elements of disintegration, did not last long. The social, that is, the class, reason for this instability of the revolutionary enthusiasm of the people was the weakness of the proletariat, which *alone* is able (if it is sufficiently numerous, class-conscious, and disciplined) to win over to its side *the majority* of the working and exploited people (the majority of the poor, to speak more simply and popularly) and retain power sufficiently long to suppress completely all the exploiters as well as all the elements of disintegration.

It was this historical experience of all revolutions, it was this world-historic—economic and political—lesson that Marx summed up when he gave his short, sharp, concise, and expressive formula: dictatorship of the proletariat. And the fact that the Russian revolution has been correct in its approach to this world-historic task *has been proved* by the victorious progress of the Soviet form of organization among all the peoples and tongues of Russia. For Soviet power is nothing but an organizational form of the dictatorship of the proletariat, the dictatorship of the advanced class, which raises to a new democracy and to independent participation in the administration of the state tens upon tens of millions of working and exploited people, who by their own experience learn to regard the disciplined and class-conscious vanguard of the proletariat as their most reliable leader.

Dictatorship, however, is a big word, and big words should not be thrown about carelessly. Dictatorship is iron rule, government that is revolutionarily bold, swift, and ruthless in suppressing both exploiters and hooligans. But our government is excessively mild; very often it resembles jelly more than iron. We must not forget for a moment that the bourgeois and petty-bourgeois element is fighting against the Soviet system . . . in two ways; on the one hand, it is operating from without . . . by conspiracies and rebellions, and by . . . filthy "ideological" reflection, the flood of lies and slander in the Constitutional-Democratic, Right Socialist-Revolutionary and Menshevik press; on the other hand, this element operates from within and takes advantage of every manifestation of disintegration, of every weakness, in order to bribe, to increase indiscipline, laxity, and chaos. The nearer we approach the complete military suppression of the bourgeoisie, the more dangerous does the element of petty-bourgeois anarchy become. And the fight against this element cannot be waged solely with the aid of propaganda and agitation, solely by organizing competition and by selecting organizers. The struggle must also be waged by means of coercion.

As the fundamental task of the government becomes, not military suppression, but administration, the typical manifestation of suppression and compulsion will be, not shooting on the spot, but trial by court. In this respect also the revolutionary people after October 25, 1917 took the right path and demonstrated the viability of the revolution by setting up their own workers' and peasants' courts, even before the decrees dissolving the bourgeois bureaucratic judiciary were passed. But our revolutionary and people's courts are extremely, incredibly weak. One feels that we have not yet done away with the people's attitude towards the courts as towards something official and alien, an attitude inherited from the yoke of the landowners and of the bourgeoisie. It is not yet sufficiently realized that the courts are an organ which enlists precisely the poor, every one of them, in the work of state administration (for the work of the courts is one of the functions of state administration), that the courts are an *organ of the power* of the proletariat and of the poor peasants, that the courts are an instrument *for inculcating discipline*. There is not yet sufficient appreciation of the simple and obvious fact that if the principal misfortunes of Russia at the present time are hunger and unemployment, these misfortunes cannot be overcome by spurts, but only by comprehensive, all-embracing, country-wide organization, and discipline in order to increase the output of bread for the people and bread for industry (fuel), to transport these in good time to the places where they are required, and to distribute them properly; and it is not fully appreciated that, consequently, it is *those* who violate labor discipline at any factory, in any undertaking, in any matter, who are *responsible* for the sufferings caused by the famine and unemployment, that we must know how to find the guilty ones, to bring them to trial and ruthlessly punish them. Where the petty-bourgeois anarchy against which we must now wage a most persistent struggle makes itself felt is in the failure to appreciate the economic and political connection between famine and unemployment, on the one hand, and general laxity in matters of organization and discipline, on the other—in the tenacity of the *small-proprietor* outlook, namely, I'll grab all I can for myself; the rest can go hang.

In the rail transport service, which perhaps most strikingly embodies the economic ties of an organism created by large-scale capitalism, the struggle between the element of petty-bourgeois laxity and proletarian organization is particularly evident. The "administrative" elements provide a host of saboteurs and bribe-takers; the best part of the proletarian elements fight for discipline; but among both elements there are, of course, many waverers and "weak" characters who are unable to withstand the "temptation" of profiteering, bribery, personal gain obtained by spoiling the whole apparatus, upon the proper working of which the victory over famine and unemployment depends.

The struggle that has been developing around the recent decree on the management of the railways, the decree which grants individual executives dictatorial powers (or "unlimited" powers), is characteristic. The conscious (and to a large extent, probably, unconscious) representatives of petty-bourgeois laxity would like to see in this granting of "unlimited" (that is, dictatorial) powers to individuals a departure from the collegiate principle, from democracy and from the principles of Soviet government. Here and there . . . a positively hooligan agitation, that is, agitation appealing to the base instincts and to the small proprietor's urge to "grab all he can," has been developed against the dictatorship decree. The question has become one of really enormous significance. First, the question of principle, namely, is the appointment of individuals, dictators with unlimited powers, in general compatible with the fundamental principles of Soviet government? Second, what relation has this case—this precedent, if you will—to the special tasks of government in the present concrete situation? We must deal very thoroughly with both these questions.

That in the history of revolutionary movements the dictatorship of individuals was very often the expression, the vehicle, the channel of the dictatorship of the revolutionary classes has been shown by the irrefutable experience of history. Undoubtedly, the dictatorship of individuals was compatible with bourgeois democracy. On this point, however, the bourgeois denigrators of the Soviet system, as well as their petty-bourgeois henchmen, always display sleight of hand: on the one hand, they declare the Soviet system to be something absurd, anarchistic, and savage, and carefully pass over in silence all our historical examples and theoretical arguments which prove that the Soviets are a higher form of democracy, and what is more, the beginning of a *socialist* form of democracy; on the other hand, they demand of us a higher democracy than bourgeois democracy and say: personal dictatorship is absolutely incompatible with your, Bolshevik (that is, not bourgeois, *but socialist*), Soviet democracy.

These are exceedingly poor arguments. If we are not anarchists, we must admit that the state, *that is, coercion*, is necessary for the transition from capitalism to socialism. The form of coercion is determined by the degree of development of the given revolutionary class, and also by special circumstances, such as, for example, the legacy of a long and reactionary war and the forms of resistance put up by the bourgeoisie and the petty bourgeoisie. There is, therefore, absolutely *no* contradiction in principle between Soviet (*that is*, socialist) democracy and the exercise of dictatorial powers by individuals. The difference between proletarian dictatorship and bourgeois dictatorship is that the former strikes at the exploiting minority in the interests of the exploited majority, and that it is exercised—*also through individuals*—not only by the working and exploited people, but also by organizations which are built in such a way as to rouse these people to history-making activity. (The Soviet organizations are organizations of this kind.)

In regard to the second question, concerning the significance of individual dictatorial powers from the point of view of the specific tasks of the present moment, it must be said that large-scale machine industry—which is precisely the material source, the productive source, the foundation of socialism—calls for absolute and strict *unity of will*, which directs the joint labors of hundreds, thousands, and tens of thousands of people. The technical, economic, and historical necessity of this is obvious, and all those who have thought about socialism have always regarded it as one of the conditions of socialism. But how can strict unity of will be ensured? By thousands subordinating their will to the will of one.

Given ideal class-consciousness and discipline on the part of those participating in the common work, this subordination would be something like the mild leadership of a conductor of an orchestra. It may assume the sharp forms of a dictatorship if ideal discipline and class-consciousness are lacking. But be that as it may, *unquestioning subordination* to a single will is absolutely necessary for the success of processes organized on the pattern of large-scale machine industry. On the railways it is twice and three times as necessary. In this transition from one political task to another, which *on the surface* is totally dissimilar to the first, lies the whole originality of the present situation. The revolution has only just smashed the oldest, strongest, and heaviest of fetters, to which the people submitted under duress. That was yesterday. Today, however, the same revolution demands—precisely in the interests of its development and consolidation, precisely in the interests of socialism—that the people *unquestioningly obey the single will* of the leaders of labor. Of course, such a transition cannot be made at one step. Clearly, it can be achieved only as a result of tremendous jolts, shocks, reversions to old ways, the enormous exertion of effort on the part of the proletarian vanguard, which is leading the people to the new ways. Those who drop into . . . philistine hysterics . . . do not stop to think about this.

Take the psychology of the average, ordinary representative of the toiling and exploited masses; compare it with the objective, material conditions of his life in society. Before the October Revolution he did *not* see a single instance of the propertied, exploiting classes making any real sacrifice for him, giving up anything for his benefit. He did *not* see them giving him the land and liberty that had been repeatedly promised him, giving him peace, sacrificing "Great Power" interests and the interests of Great Power secret treaties, sacrificing capital and profits. He saw this only *after* October 25, 1917, when he took it himself by force, and had to defend by force what he had taken. . . . Naturally, for a certain time, all his attention, all his thoughts, all his spiritual strength, were concentrated on taking a breath, on unbending his back, on straightening his shoulders, on taking the blessings of life that were there for the taking, and that had always been denied him by the now overthrown exploiters. Of course, a certain amount of time is required to enable the ordinary working man not only to see for himself, not only to become convinced, but also to feel that he cannot simply "take," snatch, grab things, that this leads to increased disruption, to ruin. . . . The corresponding change in the conditions of life (and consequently in the psychology) of the ordinary working men is only just beginning. And our whole task, the task of the Communist Party (Bolsheviks), which is the class-conscious spokesman for the strivings of the exploited for emancipation, is to appreciate this change, to understand that it is necessary, to stand at the head of the exhausted people who are wearily seeking a way out and lead them along the true path, along the path of labor discipline, along the path of coordinating the task of arguing at mass meetings *about* the conditions of work with the task of unquestioningly obeying the will of the Soviet leader, of the dictator, *during* the work.

The "mania for meetings" is an object of the ridicule, and still more often of the spiteful hissing of the bourgeoisie, the Mensheviks . . . [and those] who see only the chaos, the confusion, and the outbursts of small-proprietor egoism. But without the discussions at public meetings the mass of the oppressed could never have changed from the discipline forced upon them by the exploiters to conscious, voluntary discipline. The airing of questions at public meetings is the genuine democracy of the working people, their way of unbending their backs, their awakening to a new life, their first steps along the road which they themselves have cleared of vipers (the exploiters, the imperialists, the landowners, and capitalists) and which they want to learn to build themselves, in their own way, for themselves, on the principles of their own *Soviet*, and not alien, not aristocratic, not bourgeois rule. It required precisely the October victory of the working people over the exploiters; it required a whole historical period in which the working people themselves could first of all discuss the new conditions of life and the new tasks, in order to make possible the durable transition to superior forms of labor discipline, to the conscious appreciation of the necessity for the dictatorship of the proletariat, to unquestioning obedience to the orders of individual representatives of the Soviet government during the work.

This transition has now begun.

We have successfully fulfilled the first task of the revolution; we have seen how the mass of working people evolved in themselves the fundamental condition for its success: they united their efforts against the exploiters in order to overthrow them. Stages like that of October 1905, February and October 1917 are of world-historic significance.

We have successfully fulfilled the second task of the revolution: to awaken, to raise those very "lower ranks" of society whom the exploiters had pushed down, and who only after October 25, 1917 obtained complete freedom to overthrow the exploiters and to begin to take stock of things and arrange life in their own way. The airing of questions at public meetings by the most oppressed and downtrodden, by the least educated mass of working people, their coming over to the side of the Bolsheviks, their setting up everywhere of their own Soviet organizations—this was the second great stage of the revolution.

The third stage is now beginning. We must consolidate what we ourselves have won, what we ourselves have decreed, made law, discussed, planned—consolidate all this in stable forms of *everyday labor discipline*. This is the most difficult, but the most gratifying task, because only its fulfillment will give us a socialist system. We must learn to combine the "public meeting" democracy of the working people—turbulent, surging, overflowing its banks like a spring flood—with *iron* discipline while at work, with *unquestioning obedience* to the will of a single person, the Soviet leader, while at work.

We have not yet learned to do this.

We shall learn it.

Yesterday we were menaced by the restoration of bourgeois exploitation. . . . We . . . [were victorious]. This restoration, this very same restoration menaces us today in another form, in the form of the element of petty-bourgeois laxity and anarchism, or small-proprietor "it's not my business" psychology, in the form of the daily, petty, but numerous sorties and attacks of this element against proletarian discipline. We must, and we shall, vanquish this element of petty-bourgeois anarchy.

The Development of Soviet Organization

The socialist character of Soviet, that is, *proletarian*, democracy, as concretely applied today, lies first in the fact that the electors are the working and exploited people; the bourgeoisie is excluded. Second, it lies in the fact that all bureaucratic formalities and restrictions of elections are abolished; the people themselves determine the order and time of elections and are completely free to recall any elected person. Third, it lies in the creation of the best mass organization of the vanguard of the working people, that is, the proletariat engaged in large-scale industry, which enables it to lead the vast mass of the exploited, to draw them into independent political life, to educate them politically by their own experience; therefore for the first time a start is made by the *entire* population in learning the art of administration and in beginning to administer.

These are the principal distinguishing features of the democracy now applied in Russia, which is a higher *type* of democracy, a break with the bourgeois distortion of democracy, transition to socialist democracy and to the conditions in which the state can begin to wither away.

It goes without saying that the element of petty-bourgeois disorganization (which must *inevitably* be apparent to some extent in *every* proletarian revolution, and which is especially apparent in our revolution, owing to the petty-bourgeois character of our country, its backwardness, and the consequences of a reactionary war) cannot but leave its impress upon the Soviets as well.

We must work unremittingly to develop the organization of the Soviets and of the Soviet government. There is a petty-bourgeois tendency to transform the members of the Soviets into "parliamentarians" or else into bureaucrats. We must combat this by drawing *all* the members of the Soviets into the practical work of administration. In many places the departments of the Soviets are gradually merging with the Commissariats. Our aim is to draw *the whole of the poor* into the practical work of administration, and all steps that are taken in this direction—the more varied they are, the better—should be carefully recorded, studied, systematized, tested by wider experience, and embodied in law. Our aim is to ensure that *every* toiler, having finished his eight hours' "task" in productive labor, shall perform state duties *without pay*; the transition to this is particularly difficult, but this transition alone can guarantee the final consolidation of socialism. Naturally, the novelty and difficulty of the change lead to an abundance of steps being taken, as it were, gropingly, to an abundance of mistakes, vacillation—without this, any marked progress is impossible. The reason why the present position seems peculiar to many of those who would like to be regarded as socialists is that they have been accustomed to contrasting capitalism with socialism abstractly and that they profoundly put between the two the word "leap" (some of them, recalling fragments of what they have read of Engels's writings, still more profoundly add the phrase "leap from the realm of necessity into the realm of freedom"). The majority of these so-called socialists, who have "read in books" about socialism but who have never seriously thought over the matter, are unable to consider that by "leap" the teachers of socialism meant turning-points on a world-historical scale, and that leaps of this kind extend over decades and even longer periods. Naturally, in such times, the notorious "intelligentsia" provides an infinite number of mourners of the dead. Some mourn over the Constituent Assembly, others mourn over bourgeois discipline, others again mourn over the capitalist system, still others mourn over the cultured landowner, and still others again mourn over imperialist Great Power policy, etc., etc.

The real interest of the epoch of great leaps lies in the fact that the abundance of fragments of the old, which sometimes accumulate more rapidly than the rudiments (not always immediately discernible) of the new, calls for the ability to discern what is most important in the line or chain of development. History knows moments when the most important thing for the success of the revolution is to heap up as large a quantity of the fragments as possible, that is, to blow up as many of the old institutions as possible; moments arise when enough has been blown up and the next task is to perform the "prosaic" (for the petty-bourgeois revolutionary, the "boring") task of clearing away the fragments; and moments arise when the careful nursing of the rudiments of the new system, which are growing amidst the wreckage on a soil which as yet has been badly cleared of rubble, is the most important thing.

It is not enough to be a revolutionary and an adherent of socialism or a Communist in general. You must be able at each particular moment to find the particular link in the chain which you must grasp with all your might in order to hold the whole chain and to prepare firmly for the transition to the next link; the order of the links, their form, the manner in which they are linked together, the way they differ from each other in the historical chain of events, are not as simple and not as meaningless as those in an ordinary chain made by a smith.

The fight against the bureaucratic distortion of the Soviet form of organization is assured by the firmness of the connection between the Soviets and the "people," meaning by that the working and exploited people, and by the flexibility and elasticity of this connection. Even in the most democratic capitalist republics in the world, the poor never regard the bourgeois parliament as "their" institution. But the Soviets are "theirs" and not alien institutions to the mass of workers and peasants. . . .

It is the closeness of the Soviets to the "people," to the working people, that creates the special forms of recall and other means of control from below which must be most zealously developed now. . . . Nothing could be sillier than to transform the Soviets into something congealed and self-contained. The more resolutely we now have to stand for a ruthlessly firm government, for the dictatorship of individuals *in definite processes of work*, in definite aspects of *purely executive* functions, the more varied must be the forms and methods of control from below in order to counteract every shadow of a possibility of distorting the principles of Soviet government, in order repeatedly and tirelessly to weed out bureaucracy.

Conclusion

An extraordinarily difficult, complex, and dangerous situation in international affairs; the necessity of maneuvering and retreating; a period of waiting for new outbreaks of the revolution which is maturing in the West at a painfully slow pace; within the country a period of slow construction and ruthless "tightening up," of prolonged and persistent struggle waged by stern, proletarian discipline against the menacing element of petty-bourgeois laxity and anarchy—these in brief are the distinguishing features of the special stage of the socialist revolution in which we are now living. This is the link in the historical chain of events which we must at present grasp with all our might in order to prove equal to the tasks that confront us before passing to the next link to which we are drawn by a special brightness, the brightness of the victories of the international proletarian revolution.

Try to compare with the ordinary everyday concept, "revolutionary," the slogans that follow from the specific conditions of the present stage, namely, maneuver, retreat, wait, build slowly, ruthlessly tighten up, rigorously discipline, smash laxity. . . . Is it surprising that when certain "revolutionaries" hear this they are seized with noble indignation and begin to "thunder" abuse at us for forgetting the traditions of the October Revolution, for compromising with the bourgeois experts, for compromising with the bourgeoisie, for being petty bourgeois, reformists, and so on and so forth?

The misfortune of these sorry "revolutionaries" is that even those of them who are prompted by the best motives in the world and are absolutely loyal to the cause of socialism fail to understand the particular, and particularly "unpleasant," condition that a backward country, which has been lacerated by a reactionary and disastrous war and which began the socialist revolution long before the more advanced countries, inevitably has to pass through; they lack stamina in the difficult moments of a difficult transition. Naturally, it is the "Left Socialist-Revolutionaries" who are acting as an "official" opposition of *this* kind against our Party. Of course, there are and always will be individual exceptions from group and class types. But social types remain. In the land in which the small-proprietor population greatly predominates over the purely proletarian population, the difference between the proletarian revolutionary and petty-bourgeois revolutionary will inevitably make itself felt, and from time to time will make itself felt very sharply. The petty-bourgeois revolutionary wavers and vacillates at every turn of events; he is an ardent revolutionary in March 1917 and praises "coalition" in May, hates the Bolsheviks (or laments over their "adventurism") in July and apprehensively turns away from them at the end of October, supports them in December, and, finally, in March and April 1918 such types, more often than not, turn up their noses contemptuously and say: "I am not one of those who sing hymns to 'organic' work, to practicalness and gradualism."

The social origin of such types is the small proprietor, who has been driven to frenzy by the horrors of war, by sudden ruin, by unprecedented torments of famine and devastation, who hysterically rushes about seeking a way out, seeking salvation, places his confidence in the proletariat and supports it one moment and the next gives way to fits of despair. We must clearly understand and firmly remember the fact that socialism cannot be built on such a social basis. The only class that can lead the working and exploited people is the class that unswervingly follows its path without losing courage and without giving way to despair even at the most difficult, arduous, and dangerous stages. Hysterical impulses are of no use to us. What we need is the steady advance of the iron battalions of the proletariat.

ECONOMICS AND POLITICS IN THE ERA OF THE DICTATORSHIP OF THE PROLETARIAT (OCTOBER 1919)

I HAD INTENDED to write a short pamphlet on the subject indicated in the title on the occasion of the second anniversary of Soviet power. But owing to the rush of everyday work I have so far been unable to get beyond preliminary preparations for some of the sections. I have therefore decided to essay a brief, summarized exposition of what, in my opinion, are the most essential ideas on the subject. A summarized exposition, of course, possesses many disadvantages and shortcomings. Nevertheless, a short magazine article may perhaps achieve the modest aim in view, which is to present the problem and the groundwork for its discussion by the Communists of various countries.

1

Theoretically, there can be no doubt that between capitalism and communism there lies a definite transition period. It cannot but combine the features and properties of both these forms of social economy. This transition period has to be a period of struggle between dying capitalism and nascent communism—or, in other words, between capitalism which has been defeated but not destroyed and communism which has been born but which is still very feeble.

The necessity for a whole historical era distinguished by these transitional features should be obvious not only to Marxists, but to every educated person who is in any degree acquainted with the theory of development. Yet all the talk on the subject of the transition to socialism which we hear from present-day petty-bourgeois democrats (and such, in spite of their spurious socialist label, are all the leaders of the Second International . . .) is marked by complete disregard of this obvious truth. Petty-bourgeois democrats are distinguished by an aversion to class struggle, by their dreams of avoiding it, by their efforts to smooth over and reconcile, to take the edge off sharp corners. Such democrats, therefore, either avoid recognizing any necessity for a whole historical period of transition from capitalism to communism or regard it as their duty to concoct schemes for reconciling the two contending forces, instead of leading the struggle of one of these forces.

2

In Russia, the dictatorship of the proletariat must inevitably differ in certain particulars from what it would be in the advanced countries, owing to the very great backwardness and petty-bourgeois character of our country. But the basic forces—and the basic forms of social economy—are the same in Russia as in any capitalist country, so that these peculiarities can apply only to what is of lesser importance.

These basic forms of social economy are capitalism, petty commodity production, and communism. The basic forces are the bourgeoisie, the petty bourgeoisie (the peasantry in particular), and the proletariat.

The economic system of Russia in the era of the dictatorship of the proletariat represents the struggle of labor, united on communist principles on the scale of a single vast state and making its first steps—the struggle against petty commodity production and against the capitalism which still persists and that which is newly arising on the basis of petty commodity production.

In Russia, labor is united communistically insofar as, first, private ownership of the means of production has been abolished, and, second, the proletarian state power is organizing large-scale production on state-owned land and in state-owned enterprises on a national scale, is distributing labor-power among the various branches of production and the various enterprises, and is distributing among the working people large quantities of articles of consumption belonging to the state.

We speak of "the first steps" of communism in Russia (it is also put that way in the Program of our Party adopted in March 1919), because all these conditions have been only partially achieved in our country, or, to put it differently, the achievement of these conditions is only in its early stages. We accomplished instantly, at one revolutionary blow, all that can be instantly accomplished in general: for instance, on the first day of the dictatorship of the proletariat, October 26 (November 8), 1917, the private ownership of land was abolished without compensation to the big landowners; the big landowners were expropriated. Within the space of a few months practically all the big capitalists, owners of mills and factories, joint-stock companies, banks, railways, and so forth, were also expropriated without compensation. The state organization of large-scale production in industry and the transition from "workers' control" to "workers' administration" of factories and railways—this has, by and large, already been accomplished; but in relation to agriculture it has only just begun ("state farms," that is, large farms organized by the workers' state on state-owned land). Similarly, we have only just begun the organization of various forms of co-operative societies of small farmers as a transition from petty commodity agriculture to communist agriculture. The same must be said of the state-organized distribution of products in place of private trade, that is, the state procurement and delivery of grain to the cities and of industrial products to the countryside. . . .

Peasant farming continues to be petty commodity production. Here we have an extremely broad and very sound, deep-rooted basis for capitalism. On this basis capitalism persists and arises anew in a bitter struggle against communism. The forms of this struggle are private speculation and profiteering, as against state procurement of grain (and other products) and state distribution of products in general.

3

. . . The [available] figures speak clearly of a slow but steady improvement in the state of affairs from the point of view of the victory of communism over capitalism. This improvement is being achieved in spite of the difficulties without world parallel, caused by the Civil War organized by Russian and foreign capitalists who are harnessing all the forces of the world's strongest powers.

Therefore, in spite of the lies and slanders of the bourgeoisie of all countries and of their open or masked henchmen (the "socialists" of the Second International), one thing remains beyond dispute—from the point of view of the basic economic problem of the dictatorship of the proletariat, the victory of communism over capitalism in our country is assured. Throughout the world the bourgeoisie is raging and fuming against Bolshevism and is organizing military expeditions, plots, etc., against the Bolsheviks, because it realizes full well that our success in reconstructing the social economy is inevitable, provided we are not crushed by military force. And its attempts to crush us in this way are not succeeding. . . .

4

. . . The working people have been emancipated from their age-old oppressors and exploiters, the landowners and capitalists. This step in the direction of real freedom and real equality, a step which for its extent, dimensions, and rapidity is without parallel in the world, is ignored by the followers of the bourgeoisie (including the petty-bourgeois democrats), who, when they talk of freedom and equality, mean parliamentary bourgeois democracy, which they falsely declare to be "democracy" in general, or "pure democracy" (Kautsky).

But the working people are concerned only with real equality and real freedom (freedom from the landowners and capitalists), and that is why they give the Soviet government such firm support.

In this peasant country, those who were the first to gain, to gain most, and gain immediately from the dictatorship of the proletariat, were the peasantry as a whole. The peasant in Russia starved under the landowners and capitalists. Throughout the long centuries of our history, the peasant never had an opportunity to work for himself; he starved while handing over hundreds of millions of poods[1] of grain to the capitalists, for the cities and for export. The peasant *for the first time* has been working for himself and *feeding better than the city dweller* under the dictatorship of the proletariat. For the first time the peasant has seen real freedom—freedom to eat his bread, freedom from starvation. In the distribution of the land, as we know, the maximum equality has been established; in the vast majority of cases the peasants are dividing the land according to the number of "mouths to feed."

Socialism means the abolition of classes.

In order to abolish classes it is necessary, first, to overthrow the landowners and capitalists. This part of our task has been accomplished, but it is only a part, and moreover, *not* the most difficult part. In order to abolish classes it is necessary, second, to abolish the difference between factory worker and peasant, to make them *all workers*. This cannot be done all at once. This task is incomparably more difficult and will of necessity be a protracted one. It is not a problem that can be solved by overthrowing a class. It can be solved only by the organizational reconstruction of the whole social economy, by a transition from individual, disunited, petty commodity production to large-scale social production. This transition must of necessity be extremely protracted. It may only be delayed and complicated by hasty and incautious administrative and legislative measures. It can be accelerated only by affording such assistance to the peasant as will enable him to effect an immense improvement in his whole agricultural technique, to reform it radically.

In order to solve the second and most difficult part of the problem, the proletariat, after having defeated the bourgeoisie, must unswervingly conduct its policy towards the peasantry along the following fundamental lines. The proletariat must separate, demarcate the working peasant from the peasant owner, the peasant worker from

1 One pood equals about 36 pounds. [*Ed.*]

the peasant huckster, the peasant who labors from the peasant who profiteers.

In this demarcation lies the *whole essence* of socialism. . . .

The demarcation we here refer to is extremely difficult, for in real life all the features of the "peasant," however diverse they may be, however contradictory they may be, are fused into one whole. Nevertheless, demarcation is possible; and not only is it possible, it inevitably follows from the conditions of peasant farming and peasant life. The working peasant has for ages been oppressed by the landowners, the capitalists, the hucksters and profiteers, and by *their* state, including even the most democratic bourgeois republics. Throughout the ages the working peasant has trained himself to hate and loathe these oppressors and exploiters, and this "training," engendered by the conditions of life, *compels* the peasant to seek for an alliance with the worker against the capitalist and against the profiteer and huckster. Yet at the same time, economic conditions, the conditions of commodity production, inevitably turn the peasant (not always, but in the vast majority of cases) into a huckster and profiteer.

The [available] statistics . . . reveal a striking difference between the working peasant and the peasant profiteer. That peasant who during 1918–1919 delivered to the hungry workers of the cities 40,000,000 poods of grain at fixed state prices, who delivered this grain to the state agencies in spite of all the shortcomings of the latter, shortcomings fully realized by the workers' government, but which were unavoidable in the first period of the transition to socialism—that peasant is a working peasant, a comrade on an equal footing with the socialist worker, his most faithful ally, his blood brother in the fight against the yoke of capital. Whereas that peasant who clandestinely sold 40,000,000 poods of grain at ten times the state price, taking advantage of the need and hunger of the city worker, deceiving the state, and everywhere increasing and creating deceit, robbery, and fraud—that peasant is a profiteer, an ally of the capitalist, a class enemy of the worker, an exploiter. For whoever possesses surplus of grain gathered from land belonging to the whole state with the help of implements in which in one way or another is embodied the labor not only of the peasant but also of the worker and so on, whoever possesses a surplus of grain and profiteers in that grain is an exploiter of the hungry worker.

You are violators of freedom, equality, and democracy—they shout at us on all sides, pointing to the inequality of the worker and the peasant under our Constitution, to the dissolution of the Constituent Assembly, to the forcible confiscation of surplus grain, and so forth. We reply—never in the world has there been a state which has done so much to remove the actual inequality, the actual lack of freedom from which the working peasant has suffered for centuries.

But we shall never recognize equality with the peasant profiteer, just as we do not recognize "equality" between the exploiter and the exploited, between the sated and the hungry, nor the "freedom" for the former to rob the latter. And those educated people who refuse to recognize this difference we shall treat as whiteguards, even though they may call themselves democrats, socialists, internationalists, Kautskys. . . .

5

Socialism means the abolition of classes. The dictatorship of the proletariat has done all it could to abolish classes. But classes cannot be abolished at one stroke.

And classes still *remain* and *will remain* in the era of the dictatorship of the proletariat. The dictatorship will become unnecessary when classes disappear. Without the dictatorship of the proletariat they will not disappear.

Classes have remained, but in the era of the dictatorship of the proletariat *every* class has undergone a change, and the relations between the classes have also changed. The class struggle does not disappear under the dictatorship of the proletariat; it merely assumes different forms.

Under capitalism the proletariat was an oppressed class, a class bereft of all ownership in the means of production, the only class which stood directly and completely opposed to the bourgeoisie, and therefore the only one capable of being revolutionary to the very end. Having overthrown the bourgeoisie and conquered political power, the proletariat has become the *ruling* class; it wields state power, it disposes of means of production already socialized; it guides the wavering and intermediary elements and classes; it crushes the increasingly stubborn resistance of the exploiters. All these are *specific* tasks of the class struggle, tasks which the proletariat formerly did not and could not have set itself.

The class of exploiters, the landowners and capitalists, has not disappeared and cannot disappear all at once under the dictatorship of the proletariat. The exploiters have been smashed, but not destroyed. They still have an international base in the form of international capital, of which they are a branch. They still retain certain means of production in part, they still have money, they still have vast social connections. Because they have been defeated, the energy of their resistance has increased a hundred- and a thousandfold. The "art" of state, military, and economic administration gives them a superiority, and a very great superiority, so that their importance is incomparably greater than their numerical proportion of the population. The class struggle waged by the overthrown exploiters against the victorious vanguard of the exploited, that is, the proletariat, has become incomparably more bitter. And it cannot be otherwise in the case of a revolution, if this concept is not replaced . . . by reformist illusions.

Last, the peasants, like the petty bourgeoisie in general, occupy a half-way, intermediate position even under the dictatorship of the proletariat: on the one hand, they are a fairly large (and in backward Russia, a vast) mass of working people, united by the common interest of all working people to emancipate themselves from the landowner and the capitalist; on the other hand, they are disunited small proprietors, property-owners, and traders. Such an economic position inevitably causes them to vacillate between the proletariat and the bourgeoisie. And in view of the acute form which the struggle between these latter has assumed, in view of the incredibly severe breakup of all social relations, and in view of the great attachment of the peasants and the petty bourgeoisie generally to the old, the routine, and the unchangeable, it is only natural that we should inevitably find them swinging from one side to the other, that we should find them wavering, changeable, uncertain, and so on.

The task of the proletariat in relation to this class—or to these social elements—is to strive to establish its influence over it, to guide it. The proletariat must take the leadership over the vacillating and unstable.

If we compare all the basic forces or classes and their interrelations, as modified by the dictatorship of the proletariat, we shall realize how unutterably nonsensical and theoretically stupid is the common petty-bourgeois idea shared by all representatives of the Second International, that the transition to socialism is possible "by means of democracy" in general. The fundamental source of this error lies in the prejudice inherited from the bourgeoisie that "democracy" is something absolute and not concerned with classes. As a matter of fact, democracy itself passes into an entirely new phase under the dictatorship of the proletariat, and the class struggle rises to a higher level, dominating over each and every form.

General talk about freedom, equality, and democracy is in fact but a blind repetition of concepts shaped by the relations of commodity production. To attempt to solve the concrete problems of the dictatorship of the proletariat by such generalities means accepting the theories and principles of the bourgeoisie in their entirety. From the point of view of the proletariat, the question can be put only in the following way: freedom from oppression by which class? equality of which class with which? democracy based on private property, or on a struggle for the abolition of private property?—and so forth.

Long ago Engels in his *Anti-Dühring* explained that the concept [of] equality is molded from the relations of commodity production;

equality becomes a prejudice if it is not understood to mean the *abolition of classes.* This elementary truth regarding the distinction between the bourgeois-democratic and the socialist conception of equality is constantly being forgotten. But if it is not forgotten, it becomes obvious that by overthrowing the bourgeoisie the proletariat takes the most decisive step towards the abolition of classes, and that in order to complete the process the proletariat must continue its class struggle, making use of the apparatus of state power and employing various methods of combating, influencing, and bringing pressure to bear on the overthrown bourgeoisie and the vacillating petty bourgeoisie.

(To be continued)[2]

"LEFT-WING" COMMUNISM, AN INFANTILE DISORDER (APRIL–MAY 1920)

1 In What Sense Can We Speak of the International Significance of the Russian Revolution?

IN THE FIRST MONTHS after the proletariat in Russia had gained political power (October 25 [November 7], 1917),[1] it might have seemed that the tremendous difference between backward Russia and the advanced countries of Western Europe would cause the proletarian revolution in these latter countries to have very little resemblance to ours. Now we already have very considerable international experience which most definitely shows that certain fundamental features of our revolution have a significance which is not local, not peculiarly national, not Russian only, but international. I speak here of international significance not in the broad sense of the term—not a few but all the fundamental and many of the secondary features of our revolution are of international significance in the sense that our revolution influences all countries. Taking it in the narrowest sense, however, taking international significance to mean the international validity or the historical inevitability of a repetition on an international scale of what has taken place in our country, it must be admitted that certain fundamental features of our revolution do possess this significance.

Of course, it would be a very great mistake to exaggerate this truth and to extend it beyond certain fundamental features of our revolution. It would also be a mistake to lose sight of the fact that after the victory of the proletarian revolution in at least one of the advanced countries things will in all probability take a sharp turn—

---

1 The two dates refer to the "old" and "new" style calendars respectively. Before 1918 Russia followed the Julian calendar which, in the twentieth century, was thirteen days behind the Gregorian or Western European calendar. Thus, the "October" and "February" revolutions actually occurred in November and March according to the present calendar. [*Ed.*]

Russia will soon after cease to be the model country and once again become a backward country (in the "Soviet" and the socialist sense).

But as matters stand at the present moment in history, the Russian model reveals to *all* countries something, and something very essential, of their near and inevitable future. Advanced workers in every land have long understood this; and more often they have not so much understood it as grasped it, sensed it by revolutionary class instinct. Herein lies the international "significance" (in the narrow sense of the term) of Soviet power, and of the fundamentals of Bolshevik theory and tactics. . . .

2 One of the Fundamental Conditions for the Bolsheviks' Success

Almost everyone today probably realizes that the Bolsheviks could not have maintained power for two and a half months, let alone two and a half years, unless the strictest, truly iron discipline had prevailed in our Party, and unless the latter had been rendered the fullest and unreserved support of the whole mass of the working class, that is, of all its thinking, honest, self-sacrificing, and influential elements who are capable of leading or carrying with them the backward strata.

The dictatorship of the proletariat is a most determined and most ruthless war waged by the new class against a *more powerful* enemy, the bourgeoisie, whose resistance is increased *tenfold* by their overthrow (even if only in one country), and whose power lies not only in the strength of international capital, in the strength and durability of their international connections, but also in the *force of habit*, in the strength of *small production*. For, unfortunately, small production is still very, very widespread in the world, and small production *engenders* capitalism and the bourgeoisie continuously, daily, hourly, spontaneously, and on a mass scale. For all these reasons the dictatorship of the proletariat is essential, and victory over the bourgeoisie is impossible without a long, stubborn, desperate, life-and-death struggle, demanding perseverance, discipline, firmness, implacability, and unity of will.

I repeat, the experience of the victorious dictatorship of the proletariat in Russia has clearly shown even to those who are unable to think, or who have not had occasion to give thought to this question, that absolute centralization and the strictest discipline of the proletariat constitute one of the fundamental conditions for victory over the bourgeoisie.

This is often discussed. But not nearly enough thought is given to what it means, and under what conditions it is possible. Would it not be better if greetings in honor of Soviet power and the Bolsheviks were *more frequently* attended by a *profound analysis* of the reasons *why* the Bolsheviks were able to build up the discipline needed by the revolutionary proletariat?

As a trend of political thought and as a political party, Bolshevism has existed since 1903. Only the history of Bolshevism during the *whole* period of its existence can satisfactorily explain why it was able to build up and to maintain under most difficult conditions the iron discipline needed for the victory of the proletariat.

And first of all the question arises—how is the discipline of the revolutionary party of the proletariat maintained? How is it tested? How is it reinforced? First, by the class-consciousness of the proletarian vanguard and by its devotion to the revolution, by its perseverance, self-sacrifice, and heroism. Second, by its ability to link itself with, to keep in close touch with, and to a certain extent, if you like, to merge with the broadest masses of the working people—primarily with the proletariat, *but also with the nonproletarian* laboring masses. Third, by the correctness of the political leadership exercised by this vanguard, by the correctness of its political strategy and tactics, provided that the broadest masses have been convinced *by their own experience* that they are correct. Without these conditions, discipline in a revolutionary party that is really capable of being the party of the advanced class, whose mission it is to overthrow the bourgeoisie and transform the whole of society, cannot be achieved. Without these conditions, all attempts to establish discipline inevitably fall flat and end up in phrase-mongering and clowning. On the other hand, these conditions cannot emerge at once. They are created only by prolonged effort and hard-won experience. Their creation is facilitated by correct revolutionary theory, which, in its turn, is not a dogma, but assumes final shape only in close connection with the practical activity of a truly mass and truly revolutionary movement.

The fact that Bolshevism was able, in 1917–1920, under unprecedentedly difficult conditions, to build up and successfully maintain the strictest centralization and iron discipline was simply due to a number of historical peculiarities of Russia.

On the one hand, Bolshevism arose in 1903 on the very firm foundation of the theory of Marxism. And the correctness of this, and only this, revolutionary theory has been proved not only by world experience throughout the nineteenth century, but particularly by the experience of the wanderings and vacillations, the mistakes and disappointments of revolutionary thought in Russia. For nearly half a century—approximately from the forties to the nineties of the last century—advanced thought in Russia, oppressed by an unprecedentedly savage and reactionary tsarism, sought eagerly for a correct revolutionary theory and followed with astonishing diligence and thoroughness each and every "last word" in this sphere in Europe and America. Russia reached Marxism, the only correct revolutionary theory, through veritable *suffering*, through half a century of unprecedented torment and sacrifice, of unprecedented revolutionary heroism, incredible energy, devoted searching, study, practical trial, disappointment, verification and comparison with European experience. Thanks to the enforced emigration caused by tsarism, revolutionary Russia in the second half of the nineteenth century acquired a wealth of international connections and excellent information on world forms and theories of the revolutionary movement such as no other country in the world possessed.

On the other hand, having been built on this granite theoretical foundation, Bolshevism passed through fifteen years (1903–1917) of practical history which in wealth of experience has no equal anywhere else in the world. For no other country during these fifteen years had anything even approximating this revolutionary experience, this rapid and varied succession of different forms of the movement—legal and illegal, peaceful and stormy, underground and open, narrow circles and mass movements, parliamentary and terrorist forms. In no other country has there been concentrated during so short a period such a wealth of forms, shades, and methods of struggle of *all* classes of modern society, and moreover, a struggle which, owing to the backwardness of the country and the severity of the tsarist yoke, matured with exceptional rapidity and assimilated most eagerly and successfully the appropriate "last word" of American and European political experience. . . .

4 In the Struggle Against What Enemies Within the Working-Class Movement Did Bolshevism Grow Up and Become Strong and Steeled?

. . . Today, when I hear our tactics at the time of the conclusion of the Brest-Litovsk Treaty assailed by the Socialist-Revolutionaries, for instance, or when I hear Comrade Lansbury [2] say in conversation with me—"Our British trade union leaders say that if it was permissible for the Bolsheviks to compromise, it is permissible for them to compromise too,"—I usually reply by first of all giving a simple and "popular" example:

Imagine that your car is held up by armed bandits. You hand them over your money, passport, revolver, and car. In return you are relieved of the pleasant company of the bandits. That is unquestionably a compromise. *"Do ut des"* ("I give" you money, fire-arms,

2 George Lansbury (1859–1940), British Labour Party official and Member of Parliament. [*Ed.*]

a car "so that you give" me the opportunity to depart in peace). But it would be difficult to find a sane man who would declare such a compromise to be "inadmissible on principle," or who would proclaim the compromiser an accomplice of the bandits (even though the bandits might use the car and the fire-arms for further robberies). Our compromise with the bandits of German imperialism was a compromise of such a kind.

But when . . . [right-wing socialists in Russia, Germany, Austria, France, and England] entered into *compromises* with the bandits of their own, and sometimes of the "Allied," bourgeoisie *against* the revolutionary proletariat of their own country, all these gentlemen did act as *accomplices in banditry*.

The conclusion is clear: to reject compromises "on principle," to reject the admissibility of compromises in general, no matter of what kind, is childishness, which it is difficult even to take seriously. A political leader who desires to be useful to the revolutionary proletariat must know how to distinguish *concrete* cases when compromises are inadmissible, when they are an expression of opportunism and *treachery*, and direct all the force of criticism, the full intensity of merciless exposure and relentless war, against *those concrete* compromises, and not allow the past masters at "practical" socialism and the parliamentary Jesuits to dodge and wriggle out of responsibility by disquisitions on "compromises in general." It is precisely in this way that the "leaders" of the British trade unions, as well as the Fabian society and the "Independent" Labour Party, dodge responsibility *for the treachery they have perpetrated*, for having made a compromise that is really tantamount to the worst kind of opportunism, treachery, and betrayal.

There are compromises and compromises. One must be able to analyze the situation and the concrete conditions of each compromise, or of each variety of compromise. One must learn to distinguish between a man who gave the bandits money and fire-arms in order to lessen the damage they can do and facilitate their capture and execution, and a man who gives bandits money and fire-arms in order to share in the loot. In politics this is by no means always as easy as it is in this childishly simple example. But anyone who set out to invent a recipe for the workers that would provide in advance ready-made solutions for all cases in life, or who promised that the policy of the revolutionary proletariat would never encounter difficult or intricate situations, would simply be a charlatan. . . .

5   "Left-Wing" Communism in Germany. Leaders—Party—Class—Masses

The German Communists of whom we must now speak do not

call themselves "Lefts" but, if I am not mistaken, the "opposition on principle." But that they reveal all the symptoms of the "infantile disorder of Leftism" will be seen from what follows.

A pamphlet supporting the point of view of this opposition, and entitled *The Split in the Communist Party of Germany* . . . sets forth the substance of the views of this opposition most saliently, precisely, clearly, and briefly. A few quotations will suffice to acquaint the reader with the substance of their views:

"The Communist Party is the party of the most determined class struggle. . . ."

". . . Politically, the transition period [between capitalism and socialism] is the period of the proletarian dictatorship. . . ."

". . . The question arises: Who should be the vehicle of this dictatorship: *the Communist Party or the proletarian class*? . . . *Fundamentally*, should we strive for the dictatorship of the Communist Party, or for the dictatorship of the proletarian class? . . ."

(All italics as in the original.)

Further, the author of the pamphlet accuses the Central Committee of the Communist Party of Germany of seeking to reach a *coalition with the Independent Social-Democratic Party of Germany*,[3] of raising "*the question of recognizing in principle all political means*" of struggle, including parliamentarism, only in order to conceal its real and main efforts to form a coalition with the Independents. And the pamphlet goes on to say:

"The opposition has chosen another road. It is of the opinion that the question of the rule of the Communist Party and of the dictatorship of the party is only a question of tactics. In any case, the rule of the Communist Party is the final form of all party rule. *Fundamentally*, we must strive for the dictatorship of the proletarian class. And all the measures of the party, its organization, its methods of struggle, its strategy and tactics should be directed to this end. Accordingly, one must emphatically reject all compromise with other parties, all reversion to parliamentary forms of struggle, which have become historically and politically obsolete, all policy of maneuvering and agreement. . . . Specifically proletarian methods of revolutionary struggle must be strongly emphasized. New forms of organization must be created upon the widest basis and with the widest scope in order to enlist the broadest proletarian circles and strata, which are to take part in the revolutionary struggle under the leadership of the Communist Party. The rallying point for all revolutionary elements should be . . . based on factory organizations. It should embrace all the

3 The Independent Social-Democratic Party was formed in April, 1917, from left-wing elements in the German Social-Democratic Party. Its leaders included both Bernstein and Kautsky. Its aims were generally radical and pacifist rather than revolutionary. [*Ed.*]

workers who follow the slogan: 'Leave the trade unions!' Here they will organize the fighting proletariat in the broadest battle ranks. Recognition of the class struggle, the Soviet system, and the dictatorship should be sufficient for admittance. All subsequent political training of the fighting masses and their political orientation in the struggle is the task of the Communist Party. . . .

". . . Consequently, two Communist parties are now arrayed one against the other:

"*One is a party of leaders,* which strives to organize the revolutionary struggle and to direct it from *above,* resorting to compromises and parliamentarism in order to create a situation which would enable it to enter a coalition government in whose hands the dictatorship would rest.

"*The other is a mass party,* which expects an upsurge of the revolutionary struggle from *below,* knowing and applying only one method in the struggle, a method which clearly leads to the goal, and rejecting all parliamentary and opportunist methods; this one method is the unconditional *overthrow of the bourgeoisie* with the object of then establishing the proletarian class dictatorship for the accomplishment of socialism. . . .

". . . There, the dictatorship of leaders; here, the dictatorship of the masses! That is our slogan."

Such are the most essential points characterizing the views of the opposition in the German Communist Party.

Any Bolshevik who has consciously participated in, or has closely observed, the development of Bolshevism since 1903 will at once say after reading these arguments, "What old and familiar rubbish! What 'Left' childishness!"

But let us examine these arguments a little more closely.

The mere presentation of the question—"dictatorship of the party *or* dictatorship of the class, dictatorship (party) of the leaders, *or* dictatorship (party) of the masses?"—testifies to the most incredibly and hopelessly confused thinking. These people are striving to *invent* something quite out of the ordinary, and, in their effort to be clever, make themselves ridiculous. Everyone knows that the masses are divided into classes; that the masses can be contrasted to classes only by contrasting the vast majority in general, regardless of division according to status in the social system of production, to categories holding a definite status in the social system of production; that usually, and in the majority of cases, at least in modern civilized countries, classes are led by political parties; that political parties, as a general rule, are directed by more or less stable groups composed of the most authoritative, influential, and experienced members, who are elected to the most responsible positions and are called leaders. All this is elementary. All this is simple and clear. Why replace this by some rigmarole. . . . On the one hand, these people apparently got confused when they found themselves in difficult straits, when the party's abrupt change-over from legality to illegality disturbed the customary, normal, and simple relations between leaders, parties, and classes. In Germany, as in other European countries, people had become too accustomed to legality, to the free and proper election of "leaders" at regular party congresses, to the convenient method of testing the class composition of parties through parliamentary elections, mass meetings, the press, the sentiments of the trade unions and other associations, etc. When, instead of this customary procedure, it became necessary, owing to the stormy development of the revolution and the development of the civil war, to pass quickly from legality to illegality, to combine the two, and to adopt the "inconvenient" and "undemocratic" methods of selecting, or forming, or preserving "groups of leaders"—people lost their heads and began to think up some supernatural nonsense. . . .

On the other hand, we see a simply thoughtless and incoherent use of the now "fashionable" terms "masses" and "leaders." These people have heard and committed to memory a great many attacks on "leaders" in which they were contrasted to the "masses" but were unable to think matters out and gain a clear understanding of what it was all about.

The divergence between "leaders" and "masses" was brought out with particular clarity and sharpness in all countries at the end of and after the imperialist war. The principal reason for this phenomenon was explained many times by Marx and Engels between the years 1852 and 1892 by the example of England. That country's monopoly position led to the separation from the "masses" of a semi-petty-bourgeois, opportunist "labor aristocracy." The leaders of this labor aristocracy constantly deserted to the bourgeoisie and were directly or indirectly in its pay. Marx earned the honor of incurring the hatred of these scoundrels by openly branding them as traitors. Modern (twentieth century) imperialism created a privileged, monopoly position for a few advanced countries, and this gave rise everywhere in the Second International to a certain type of traitor, opportunist, social-chauvinist leaders, who champion the interests of their own craft, their own section of the labor aristocracy. This separated the opportunist parties from the "masses," that is, from the broadest strata of the working people, from their majority, from the lowest-paid workers. The victory of the revolutionary proletariat is impossible unless this evil is combated, unless the opportunist, social-traitor leaders are exposed, discredited, and expelled. And this is the policy on which the Third International embarked.

To go so far in this connection as to contrast, *in general*, dictatorship of the masses to dictatorship of the leaders is ridiculously absurd and stupid. What is particularly curious is that actually, in place of the old leaders, who hold the common human views on ordinary matters, *new leaders* are put forth (under cover of the slogan "Down with the leaders!") who talk unnatural stuff and nonsense. . . .

Repudiation of the party principle and of party discipline—such is the opposition's *net result*. And this is tantamount to completely disarming the proletariat *in the interests of the bourgeoisie*. It is tantamount to that petty-bourgeois diffuseness, instability, incapacity for sustained effort, unity, and organized action, which, if indulged in, must inevitably destroy every proletarian revolutionary movement. From the standpoint of communism, the repudiation of the party principle means trying to leap from the eve of the collapse of capitalism (in Germany), not to the lower, or the intermediate, but to the higher phase of communism. We in Russia (in the third year since the overthrow of the bourgeoisie) are going through the first steps in the transition from capitalism to socialism, or the lower stage of communism. Classes still remain, and will remain everywhere *for years after* the conquest of power by the proletariat. Perhaps in England, where there is no peasantry (but where there are small owners!), this period may be shorter. The abolition of classes means not only driving out the landowners and capitalists—that we accomplished with comparative ease—it also means *abolishing the small commodity producers*, and they *cannot be driven out*, or crushed; we *must* learn to live with them, they can (and must) be remolded and re-educated only by very prolonged, slow, cautious organizational work. They encircle the proletariat on every side with a petty-bourgeois atmosphere, which permeates and corrupts the proletariat and causes constant relapses among the proletariat into petty-bourgeois spinelessness, disunity, individualism, and alternate moods of exaltation and dejection. The strictest centralization and discipline are required within the political party of the proletariat in order to counteract this, in order that the *organizational* role of the proletariat (and that is its *principal* role) may be exercised correctly, successfully, victoriously. The dictatorship of the proletariat is a persistent struggle—bloody and bloodless, violent and peaceful, military and economic, educational and administrative—against the forces and traditions of the old society. The force of habit of millions and tens of millions is a most terrible force. Without an iron party tempered in the struggle, without a party enjoying the confidence of all that is honest in the given class, without a party capable of watching and influencing the mood of the masses, it is impossible to conduct such a struggle successfully. It is a thousand times easier to vanquish the centralized big bourgeoisie than to "vanquish" the millions upon millions of small owners; yet they, by their ordinary, everyday, imperceptible, elusive, demoralizing activity, achieve the *very* results which the bourgeoisie need and which tend to *restore* the bourgeoisie. Who-

ever effects even the slightest weakening of the iron discipline of the
party of the proletariat (especially during the time of its dictatorship),
actually aids the bourgeoisie against the proletariat. . . .

6 Should Revolutionaries Work in Reactionary Trade Unions?

. . . In its work, the [Communist] Party relies directly on the
trade unions, which, at present, according to the data of the last
congress (April 1920), have over 4,000,000 members, and which
are formally *non-Party*. Actually, all the directing bodies of the vast
majority of the unions, and primarily, of course, of the all-Russian
general trade union center or bureau (the All-Russian Central Coun-
cil of Trade Unions), consist of Communists and carry out all the
directives of the Party. Thus, on the whole, we have a formally non-
communist, flexible, and relatively wide and very powerful proletarian
apparatus, by means of which the Party is closely linked up with the
class and with the *masses*, and by means of which, under the leadership of the Party, the *dictatorship of the class* is exercised. Without
close contact with the trade unions, without their hearty support and
self-sacrificing work, not only in economic, *but also in military* affairs,
it would, of course, have been impossible for us to govern the country and to maintain the dictatorship for two and a half months, let
alone two and a half years. Naturally, in practice, this close contact
calls for very complicated and diversified work in the form of propaganda, agitation, timely and frequent conferences, not only with
the leading trade union workers, but with influential trade union
workers generally; it calls for a determined struggle against the
Mensheviks, who still have a certain, though very small, number of
adherents to whom they teach all possible counter-revolutionary
tricks, from ideologically defending democracy (*bourgeois*) and
preaching "independence" of the trade unions (independence of the
proletarian state power!) to sabotaging proletarian discipline, etc., etc.

We consider that contact with the "masses" through trade unions
is not enough. In the course of the revolution, practical activities
have given rise to *non-Party workers' and peasants' conferences*, and
we strive by every means to support, develop, and extend this institution in order to be able to follow the sentiments of the masses, to
come closer to them, to respond to their requirements, to promote
the best among them to state posts, etc.

Then, of course, all the work of the Party is carried on through
the Soviets, which embrace the working masses irrespective of occu-
pation. The district congresses of Soviets are *democratic* institutions
the like of which even the best of the democratic republics of the

bourgeois world have never known; and through these congresses (whose proceedings the Party endeavors to follow with the closest attention), as well as by continually appointing class-conscious workers to various posts in the rural districts, the proletariat exercises its role of leader of the peasantry, realizes the dictatorship of the urban proletariat, wages a systematic struggle against the rich, bourgeois, exploiting, and profiteering peasantry, etc.

Such is the general mechanism of the proletarian state power viewed "from above," from the standpoint of the practical realization of the dictatorship. It can be hoped that the reader will understand why the Russian Bolshevik, who has known this mechanism for twenty-five years and has watched it grow out of small, illegal, underground circles, cannot help regarding all this talk about "from above" or "from below," about the dictatorship of leaders or the dictatorship of the masses, etc., as ridiculous and childish nonsense, something like discussing whether a man's left leg or right arm is the more useful to him.

And we cannot but regard as equally ridiculous and childish nonsense the pompous, very learned, and frightfully revolutionary disquisitions of the German Lefts to the effect that Communists cannot and should not work in reactionary trade unions, that it is permissible to turn down such work, that it is necessary to leave the trade unions and to create an absolutely brand-new, immaculate "Workers' Union" invented by very nice (and, probably, for the most part very youthful) Communists, etc., etc.

Capitalism inevitably leaves socialism the legacy, on the one hand, of old trade and craft distinctions among the workers, distinctions evolved in the course of centuries; and, on the other hand, trade unions, which only very slowly, in the course of years and years, can and will develop into broader industrial unions with less of the craft union about them (embracing whole industries, and not only crafts, trades, and occupations), and later proceed, through these industrial unions, to eliminate the division of labor among people, to educate and school people, give *them all-round development and an all-round* training, so that they *know how to do everything*. Communism is advancing and must advance towards this goal, and *will reach* it, but only after very many years. To attempt in practice today to anticipate this future result of a fully developed, fully stabilized and formed, fully expanded and mature communism would be like trying to teach higher mathematics to a four-year-old child.

We can (and must) begin to build socialism, not with abstract human material, not with human material specially prepared by us, but with the human material bequeathed to us by capitalism. True, that is very "difficult," but no other approach to this task is serious enough to warrant discussion.

The trade unions were a tremendous step forward for the working class in the early days of capitalist development, inasmuch as they represented a transition from the disunity and helplessness of the workers to the *rudiments* of the class organization. When the *highest* form of proletarian class organization, the *revolutionary party of the proletariat*, began to take shape (and the party will not deserve the name until it learns to weld the leaders into one indivisible whole with the class and the masses), the trade unions inevitably began to reveal *certain* reactionary features, a certain craft narrowness, a certain tendency to be nonpolitical, a certain inertness, etc. But the development of the proletariat did not, and could not, proceed anywhere in the world otherwise than through the trade unions, through reciprocal action between them and the party of the working class. The conquest of political power by the proletariat is a gigantic forward step for the proletariat as a class, and the party must more than ever and in a new way, not only in the old way, educate and guide the trade unions, at the same time bearing in mind that they are and will long remain an indispensable "school of communism" and a preparatory school that trains proletarians to exercise their dictatorship, an indispensable organization of the workers for the gradual transfer of the management of the whole economic life of the country to the working *class* (and not to the separate trades), and later to all the working people.

A *certain* amount of "reactionariness" in the trade unions, in the sense mentioned, is *inevitable* under the dictatorship of the proletariat. Failure to understand this signifies complete failure to understand the fundamental conditions of the *transition* from capitalism to socialism. To fear *this* "reactionariness," to try to *avoid* it, to leap over it, would be the greatest folly, for it would be fearing that function of the proletarian vanguard which consists in training, educating, enlightening, and drawing into the new life the most backward strata and masses of the working class and the peasantry. On the other hand, to postpone the achievement of the dictatorship of the proletariat until a time comes when not a single worker is left with a narrow craft outlook, or with craft and craft-union prejudices, would be a still greater mistake. The art of politics (and the Communist's correct understanding of his tasks) is in correctly gauging the conditions and the moment when the vanguard of the proletariat can successfully seize power, when it is able, during and after the seizure of power, to obtain adequate support from sufficiently broad strata of the working class and of the nonproletarian working masses, and when it is able thereafter to maintain, consolidate, and extend its rule by educating, training, and attracting ever broader masses of the working people.

Further. In countries more advanced than Russia, a certain re-

actionism in the trade unions has been and was bound to be manifested to a much stronger degree than in our country. Our Mensheviks
found support in the trade unions (and to some extent still find
in a small number of unions), because of craft narrowness, craft
egoism, and opportunism. The Mensheviks of the West have acquired a much firmer footing in the trade unions; there the *craft-
union, narrow-minded, selfish, case-hardened, covetous, petty-bourgeois* "labor aristocracy," *imperialist-minded, imperialist-bribed, and
imperialist-corrupted*, developed into a much stronger section than in
our country. That is incontestable. The struggle against . . . [such
unionists] in Western Europe is much more difficult than the struggle
against our Mensheviks, who represent an *absolutely homogeneous*
social and political type. This struggle must be waged ruthlessly, and
it must unfailingly be brought—as we brought it—to a point when
all the incorrigible leaders of opportunism and social-chauvinism are
completely discredited and driven out of the trade unions. Political
power cannot be captured (and the attempt to capture it should not
be made) until the struggle has reached a *certain* stage. This "certain
stage" will be *different* in different countries and in different circumstances; it can be correctly gauged only by thoughtful, experienced,
and knowledgeable political leaders of the proletariat in each particular country. . . .

7 Should We Participate in Bourgeois Parliaments?

The German "Left" Communists, with the greatest contempt—and
with the greatest frivolity—reply to this question in the negative.
Their arguments? In the passage quoted above we read:

". . . One must emphatically reject . . . all reversion to parliamentary forms of struggle, which have become historically and
politically obsolete. . . ."

This is said with absurd pretentiousness and is obviously incorrect. "Reversion" to parliamentarism! Perhaps there is already a
Soviet republic in Germany? It seems not! How, then, can one speak
of "reversion"? Is this not an empty phrase?

Parliamentarism has become "historically obsolete." That is true
in the propaganda sense. But everyone knows that it is still a long
way from propaganda to overcoming it *practically*. Capitalism could
have been declared, and with full justice, to be "historically obsolete" many decades ago, but that does not at all remove the need for
a very long and very persistent struggle *on the soil* of capitalism.
Parliamentarism is "historically obsolete" from the standpoint of

world history, that is to say, the *era* of bourgeois parliamentarism has come to an end and the *era* of the proletarian dictatorship has *begun*. That is incontestable. But world history reckons in decades. Ten or twenty years sooner or later makes no difference when measured by the scale of world history; from the standpoint of world history it is a trifle that cannot be calculated even approximately. But for that very reason it is a glaring theoretical blunder to apply the scale of world history to practical politics.

Is parliamentarism "politically obsolete"? That is quite another matter. Were that true, the position of the "Lefts" would be a strong one. But it has to be proved by a most searching analysis, and the "Lefts" do not even know how to approach it. . . .

In the first place, contrary to the opinion of such outstanding political leaders as Rosa Luxemburg [4] and Karl Liebknecht, the German "Lefts," as we know, considered parliamentarism to be "politically obsolete" even in January 1919. We know that the "Lefts" were mistaken. This fact alone utterly destroys, at a single stroke, the proposition that parliamentarism is "politically obsolete." The obligation falls upon the "Lefts" of proving why their error, indisputable at that time, has now ceased to be an error. They do not, and cannot, produce even a shadow of proof. The attitude of a political party towards its own mistakes is one of the most important and surest ways of judging how earnest the party is and how it *in practice* fulfills its obligations towards its *class* and the *working people*. Frankly admitting a mistake, ascertaining the reasons for it, analyzing the conditions which led to it, and thoroughly discussing the means of correcting it— that is the hallmark of a serious party; that is the way it should perform its duties, that is the way it should educate and train the *class*, and then the *masses*. By failing to fulfill this duty, by failing to give the utmost attention, care, and consideration to the study of their obvious mistake, the "Lefts" . . . have proved that they are not a *party of the class*, but a circle, not a *party of the masses*, but a group of intellectuals and of a few workers who imitate the worst features of intellectualism.

Second, in the same pamphlet . . . we read:

". . . The millions of workers who still follow the policy of the Center [the Catholic "Center" Party] are counter-revolutionary. The rural proletarians provide the legions of counter-revolutionary troops." . . .

Everything goes to show that this statement is much too sweeping and exaggerated. But the basic fact set forth here is incontrovert-

4   Rosa Luxemburg (1871–1919), left-wing Polish and German socialist, co-founder of the German Communist Party. She was assassinated in 1919 by German rightists. [*Ed.*]

ible, and its acknowledgement by the "Lefts" is particularly clear evidence of their mistake. How can one say that "parliamentarism is politically obsolete" when "millions" and "legions" of *proletarians* are not only still in favor of parliamentarism in general, but are downright "counter-revolutionary"!? Clearly, parliamentarism in Germany is *not yet* politically obsolete. Clearly, the "Lefts" in Germany have mistaken *their desire*, their politico-ideological attitude, for objective reality. That is a most dangerous mistake for revolutionaries to make. In Russia—where, over a particularly long period and in particularly varied forms, the extremely fierce and savage yoke of tsarism produced revolutionaries of diverse shades, revolutionaries who displayed astonishing devotion, enthusiasm, heroism and strength of will—in Russia we have observed this mistake of the revolutionaries very closely, we have studied it very attentively and have first-hand knowledge of it; and we can therefore see it especially clearly in others. Parliamentarism, of course, is "politically obsolete" for the Communists in Germany; but—and that is the whole point—we must *not* regard what is obsolete *for us* as being obsolete *for the class*, as being obsolete *for the masses*. Here again we find that the "Lefts" do not know how to reason, do not know how to act as the party of the *class*, as the party of the *masses*. You must not sink to the level of the masses, to the level of the backward strata of the class. That is incontestable. You must tell them the bitter truth. You must call their bourgeois-democratic and parliamentary prejudices—prejudices. But at the same time you must *soberly* follow the *actual* state of class-consciousness and preparedness of the whole class (not only of its communist vanguard), of all the *working people* (not only of their advanced elements).

Even if not "millions" and "legions," but only a fairly large *minority* of industrial workers follow the Catholic priests—and a similar minority of rural workers follow the landowners and . . . [rich peasants]—it *undoubtedly* follows that parliamentarism in Germany is *not yet* politically obsolete, that participation in parliamentary elections and in the struggle on the parliamentary rostrum is *obligatory* for the party of the revolutionary proletariat *specifically* for the purpose of educating the backward strata of *its own class*, for the purpose of awakening and enlightening the undeveloped, downtrodden, ignorant rural *masses*. As long as you are unable to disperse the bourgeois parliament and every other type of reactionary institution, you *must* work inside them because *it is there* you will still find workers who are doped by the priests and stultified by the conditions of rural life; otherwise you risk becoming mere babblers.

Third, the "Left" Communists have a great deal to say in praise of us Bolsheviks. One sometimes feels like telling them to praise us less and try to understand the tactics of the Bolsheviks more, to become more familiar with them! We took part in the elections to the Russian bourgeois parliament, the Constituent Assembly, in September-November 1917. Were our tactics correct or not? If not, then this should be clearly stated and proved, for it is essential in working out correct tactics for international communism. If they were correct, then you must draw certain conclusions. Of course, there can be no question of placing conditions in Russia on a par with conditions in Western Europe. But as regards the special question of the meaning of the concept that "parliamentarism has become politically obsolete," it is essential to take careful account of our experience, for unless concrete experience is taken into account such concepts very easily turn into empty phrases. In September-November 1917, did not we, the Russian Bolsheviks, have *more* right than any Western Communists to consider that parliamentarism was politically obsolete in Russia? Of course we did, for the point is not whether bourgeois parliaments have existed for a long time or a short time, but how far the broad masses of the working people are *prepared* (ideologically, politically, and practically) to accept the Soviet system and to disperse the bourgeois-democratic parliament (or allow it to be dispersed). It is an absolutely incontestable and fully established historical fact that, owing to a number of special conditions, the urban working class and the soldiers and peasants of Russia were in September-November 1917 exceptionally well prepared to accept the Soviet system and to disperse the most democratic of bourgeois parliaments. Nevertheless, the Bolsheviks did *not* boycott the Constituent Assembly but took part in the elections both before the proletariat conquered political power *and after.* . . . [These] elections yielded exceedingly valuable (and for the proletariat, highly useful) political results. . . .

The conclusion which follows from this is absolutely incontrovertible; it has been proved that participation in a bourgeois-democratic parliament even a few weeks before the victory of a Soviet republic, and even *after* such a victory, not only does not harm the revolutionary proletariat, but actually helps it to *prove* to the backward masses why such parliaments deserve to be dispersed; it *helps* their successful dispersal, and *helps* to make bourgeois parliamentarism "politically obsolete." To refuse to heed this experience, and at the same time to claim affiliation to the Communist *International*, which must work out its tactics internationally (not as narrow or one-sided national tactics, but as international tactics), is to commit the gravest blunder and actually to retreat from internationalism while recognizing it in words. . . .

In Western Europe and America parliament has become especially abhorrent to the advanced revolutionary members of the working class. That is incontestable. It is quite comprehensible, for it is difficult to imagine anything more vile, abominable, and treacherous than the behavior of the vast majority of the socialist and Social-Democratic parliamentary deputies during and after the war. But it would be not only unreasonable, but actually criminal, to yield to this mood when deciding *how* this generally recognized evil should be fought. In many countries of Western Europe the revolutionary mood, we might say, is at present a "novelty," or a "rarity," which had all too long been vainly and impatiently awaited; and perhaps that is why people so easily give way to it. Certainly, without a revolutionary mood among the masses, and without conditions facilitating the growth of this mood, revolutionary tactics would never be converted into action; but we in Russia have become convinced by very long, painful, and bloody experience of the truth that revolutionary tactics cannot be built on revolutionary moods alone. Tactics must be based on a sober and strictly objective appraisal of *all* the class forces of the particular state (and of the states that surround it, and of all states the world over) as well as of the experience of revolutionary movements. To show how "revolutionary" one is solely by hurling abuse at parliamentary opportunism, solely by repudiating participation in parliaments, is very easy; but just because it is too easy, it is not the solution for a difficult, a very difficult problem. It is much more difficult to create a really revolutionary parliamentary group in a European parliament than it was in Russia. That stands to reason. But it is only a particular expression of the general truth that it was easy for Russia, in the specific, historically very unique situation of 1917, to *start* the socialist revolution, but it will be more difficult for Russia than for the European countries to *continue* the revolution and bring it to its consummation. I had occasion to point this out already at the beginning of 1918, and our experience of the past two years has entirely confirmed the correctness of this view. Certain specific conditions—(1) the possibility of linking up the Soviet revolution with the ending, as a consequence of this revolution, of the imperialist war, which has exhausted the workers and peasants to an incredible degree; (2) the possibility of taking advantage for a certain time of the mortal conflict between the world's two most powerful groups of imperialist robbers, who were unable to unite against their Soviet enemy; (3) the possibility of enduring a comparatively lengthy civil war, partly owing to the enormous size of the country and to the poor means of communication; (4) the existence of such a profound bourgeois-democratic revolutionary movement among the peasantry that the party of the proletariat was able to adopt the revolutionary demands of the peasant party . . . and realize them at once, thanks to the conquest of political power by the proletariat—these specific conditions do not exist in Western Europe at present; and a repetition of such or similar conditions will not occur so easily.

That, by the way, apart from a number of other causes, is why it will be more difficult for Western Europe to *start* a socialist revolution than it was for us. To attempt to "circumvent" this difficulty by "skipping" the arduous job of utilizing reactionary parliaments for revolutionary purposes is absolutely childish. You want to create a new society; yet you fear the difficulties involved in forming a good parliamentary group, made up of convinced, devoted, heroic Communists, in a reactionary parliament! Is that not childish? . . .

The German "Lefts" complain about bad "leaders" in their party, give way to despair, and go to the absurd length of "repudiating" "leaders." But when conditions are such that it is often necessary to hide "leaders" underground, the *development* of good, reliable, tested, and authoritative "leaders" is a very difficult matter, and these difficulties *cannot* be successfully overcome without combining legal and illegal work, and *without testing the "leaders," among other ways*, in the parliamentary arena. Criticism—the keenest, most ruthless, and uncompromising criticism—must be directed, not against parliamentarism or parliamentary activities, but against those leaders who are unable—and still more against those who are *unwilling*—to utilize parliamentary elections and the parliamentary rostrum in a revolutionary, communist manner. Only such criticism—combined, of course, with the expulsion of incapable leaders and their replacement by capable ones—will constitute useful and fruitful revolutionary work that will simultaneously train the "leaders" to be worthy of the working class and of all working people, and train the masses to be able properly to understand the political situation and the often very complicated and intricate tasks that spring from that situation.

8 No Compromises?

In the quotation from the . . . pamphlet we saw how emphatically the "Lefts" advance this slogan. It is sad to see that people who without doubt consider themselves Marxists and want to be Marxists forget the fundamental truths of Marxism. This is what Engels—who, like Marx, was one of those rarest of authors whose every sentence in every one of their great works contains remarkably profound meaning—wrote in 1874 in opposition to the manifesto of the thirty-three Blanquist Communards: [5]

" 'We are Communists [wrote the Blanquist Communards in their manifesto] because we want to attain our goal without stopping at intermediate stations, without any compromises, which only postpone the day of victory and prolong the period of slavery.'

[5] Followers of Louis Blanqui (1805–1881), French Revolutionary theorist and leader who advocated conspiratorial seizure of power. [*Ed.*]

"The German Communists are Communists because through all the intermediate stations and all compromises, created not by them, but by the course of historical development, they clearly perceive and constantly pursue the final aim—the abolition of classes and the creation of a society in which there will no longer be private ownership of land or of the means of production. The thirty-three Blanquists are Communists because they imagine that merely because *they* want to skip the intermediate stations and compromises, that settles the matter, and if 'it begins' in the next few days—which they take for granted—and they come to the helm, 'communism will be introduced' the day after tomorrow. If that is not immediately possible, they are not Communists.

"What childish innocence it is to present just impatience as a theoretically convincing argument!"

. . . Of course, to very young and inexperienced revolutionaries, as well as to petty-bourgeois revolutionaries of even a very respectable age and very experienced, it seems exceedingly "dangerous," incomprehensible, and incorrect to "allow compromises." And many sophists (being unusually or excessively "experienced" politicians) reason exactly in the same way. . . . "If the Bolsheviks may make a certain compromise, why may we not make any kind of compromise?" But proletarians schooled in numerous strikes (to take only this manifestation of the class struggle) usually understand quite well the very profound (philosophical, historical, political, and psychological) truth expounded by Engels. Every proletarian has been through strikes and has experienced "compromises" with the hated oppressors and exploiters, when the workers had to go back to work either without having achieved anything or agreeing to only a partial satisfaction of their demands. Every proletarian—owing to the conditions of the mass struggle and the sharp intensification of class antagonisms in which he lives—notices the difference between a compromise enforced by objective conditions (such as lack of strike funds, no outside support, extreme hunger, and exhaustion), a compromise which in no way diminishes the revolutionary devotion and readiness for further struggle on the part of the workers who have agreed to such a compromise, and a compromise by traitors who try to ascribe to outside causes their own selfishness (strike-breakers also enter into "compromises"!), cowardice, desire to toady to the capitalists, and readiness to yield to intimidation, sometimes to persuasion, sometimes to sops, and sometimes to flattery on the part of the capitalists. (The history of the British labor movement provides an especially large number of cases of such treacherous compromises by British trade union leaders, but, in one form or another, nearly all workers in all countries have witnessed the same sort of thing.)

Naturally, there are individual cases of exceptional difficulty and intricacy when the real character of this or that "compromise" can be correctly determined only with the greatest difficulty; just as there are cases of homicide where it is by no means easy to decide whether the homicide was fully justified and even necessary (as, for example, legitimate self-defense), or due to unpardonable negligence, or even to a cunningly executed perfidious plan. Of course, in politics, where it is sometimes a matter of extremely complicated—national and international—relations between classes and parties, very many cases will arise that will be much more difficult than the questions of a legitimate "compromise" in a strike or the treacherous "compromise" of a strike-breaker, traitor leader, etc. It would be absurd to formulate a recipe or general rule ("No compromises!") to serve all cases. One must use one's own brains and be able to find one's bearings in each particular case. It is, in fact, one of the functions of a party organization, and of party leaders worthy of the title, to acquire, through the prolonged, persistent, variegated, and comprehensive efforts of all thinking representatives of the given class,[6] the knowledge, the experience and—in addition to knowledge and experience—the political instinct necessary for the speedy and correct solution of intricate political problems.

Naïve and utterly inexperienced people imagine that it is sufficient to admit the permissibility of compromises *in general* in order to obliterate the dividing line between opportunism, against which we wage and must wage an irreconcilable struggle, and revolutionary Marxism, or communism. But if such people do not yet know that *all* dividing lines in nature and in society are constantly shifting and are to a certain extent conventional, they cannot be assisted otherwise than by a long process of training, education, enlightenment, and by political and everyday experience. It is important to single out from the practical questions of the politics of each separate or specific historical moment those which reveal the principal type of impermissible, treacherous compromises, compromises embodying the opportunism that is fatal to the revolutionary class, and to exert all efforts to explain them and combat them. During the imperialist war of 1914–1918 between two groups of equally predatory and rapacious countries, the principal, fundamental type of opportunism was social-chauvinism, that is, support of "defense of the fatherland," which, in *such* a war, was really equivalent to defense of the predatory interests

6   Within every class, even in the conditions prevailing in the most enlightened countries, even within the most advanced class, and even when the circumstances of the moment have roused all its spiritual forces to an exceptional degree, there always are—and inevitably *will be* as long as classes exist, as long as classless society has not fully entrenched and consolidated itself, and has not developed on its own foundations—representatives of the class who do *not* think and are incapable of thinking. Were this not so, capitalism would not be the oppressor of the masses it is. [*L.*]

of one's "own" bourgeoisie. After the war, the defense of the robber League of Nations, the defense of direct or indirect alliances with the bourgeoisie of one's own country against the revolutionary proletariat and the "Soviet" movement, and the defense of bourgeois democracy and bourgeois parliamentarism against "Soviet power" became the principal manifestations of those impermissible and treacherous compromises, the sum-total of which constituted the opportunism that is fatal to the revolutionary proletariat and its cause.

". . . One must emphatically reject all compromise with other parties . . . all policy of maneuvering and agreement."

[Thus] write the German Lefts. . . .

It is a wonder that, holding such views, these Lefts do not emphatically condemn Bolshevism! For the German Lefts must know that the whole history of Bolshevism, both before and after the October Revolution, is *full* of instances of maneuvering, making agreements and compromising with other parties, bourgeois parties included!

To carry on a war for the overthrow of the international bourgeoisie, a war which is a hundred times more difficult, protracted, and complicated than the most stubborn of ordinary wars between states, and to refuse beforehand to maneuver, to utilize the conflict of interests (even though temporary) among one's enemies, to refuse to agree and compromise with possible (even though temporary, unstable, vacillating, and conditional) allies—is not this ridiculous in the extreme? Is it not like making a difficult ascent of an unexplored and hitherto inaccessible mountain and refusing beforehand ever to move in zigzags, ever to retrace our steps, ever to abandon the course once selected and to try others? And yet people so immature and inexperienced (if youth were the explanation, it would not be so bad; young people are ordained by God himself to talk such nonsense for a period) meet with the support—whether direct or indirect, open or covert, whole or partial, does not matter—of some . . . [Communists]!

After the first socialist revolution of the proletariat, after the overthrow of the bourgeoisie in one country, the proletariat of that country *for a long time* remains *weaker* than the bourgeoisie, simply because of the latter's extensive international connections, and also because of the spontaneous and continuous restoration and regeneration of capitalism and the bourgeoisie by the small commodity producers of the country which has overthrown the bourgeoisie. The more powerful enemy can be vanquished only by exerting the utmost effort, and by the most thorough, careful, attentive and skillful *obligatory* use of every, even the smallest, "rift" among the enemies, every antagonism of interests among the bourgeoisie of the various countries and among the various groups or types of bourgeoisie within the various countries, and also by taking advantage of every, even the smallest, opportunity of gaining a mass ally, even though this ally be temporary, vacillating, unstable, unreliable, and conditional. Those who fail to understand this, fail to understand even a particle of Marxism, or of scientific, modern socialism *in general*. Those who have not proved by *deeds* over a fairly considerable period of time, and in fairly varied political situations, their ability to apply this truth in practice have not yet learned to assist the revolutionary class in its struggle to emancipate all toiling humanity from the exploiters. And this applies equally to the period *before* and *after* the proletariat has conquered political power.

Our theory is not a dogma, but a *guide to action*, said Marx and Engels; and it is the greatest mistake, the greatest crime on the part of such "patented" Marxists as Karl Kautsky, Otto Bauer, etc., that they have not understood this, have been unable to apply it at crucial moments of the proletarian revolution. "Political activity is not the pavement of the Nevsky Prospekt" (the clean, broad, smooth pavement of the perfectly straight principal street of St. Petersburg), N. G. Chernyshevsky, the great Russian socialist of the pre-Marxian period, used to say. Since Chernyshevsky's time, ignoring or forgetting this truth has cost Russian revolutionaries innumerable sacrifices. We must strive at all costs to *prevent* the Left Communists and the West-European and American revolutionaries who are devoted to the working class paying *as dearly* for the assimilation of this truth as the backward Russians did. . . .

Capitalism would not be capitalism if the "pure" proletariat were not surrounded by a large number of exceedingly motley types intermediate between the proletarian and the semiproletarian (who earns his livelihood in part by the sale of his labor-power), between the semiproletarian and the small peasant (and petty artisan, handicraft worker, and small master in general), between the small peasant and the middle peasant, and so on, and if the proletariat itself were not divided into more developed and less developed strata, if it were not divided according to territorial origin, trade, sometimes according to religion, and so on. And from all this follows the necessity, the absolute necessity, for the vanguard of the proletariat, its class-conscious section, the Communist Party, to resort to maneuvers, agreements, and compromises with the various groups of proletarians, with the various parties of the workers and small masters. It is entirely a case of *knowing how* to apply these tactics in order to *raise*, and not lower, the *general* level of proletarian class-consciousness, revolutionary spirit, and ability to fight and win. . . .

10   Some Conclusions

The Russian bourgeois revolution of 1905 revealed a very peculiar turn in world history: in one of the most backward capitalist countries the strike movement attained a breadth and power without precedent anywhere in the world. In the *first month* of 1905 *alone* the number of strikers was ten times the *annual* average for the previous ten years (1895–1904); and from January to October 1905 strikes grew continuously and reached enormous dimensions. Under the influence of a number of entirely unique historical conditions, backward Russia was the first to show the world not only the growth, by leaps and bounds, of the independent activity of the oppressed masses in time of revolution (this had occurred in all great revolutions), but also that the significance of the proletariat is infinitely greater than its proportion of the total population; it showed a combination of the economic strike and the political strike, the transformation of the latter into armed uprising, and the birth of the Soviets, a new form of mass struggle and mass organization of the classes oppressed by capitalism.

The revolutions of February and October 1917 led to the all-round development of the Soviets on a national scale, and to their victory in the proletarian, socialist revolution. And in less than two years the international character of the Soviets, the spread of this form of struggle and organization to the world working-class movement, and the historical mission of the Soviets as the grave-digger, heir, and successor of bourgeois parliamentarism, and the bourgeois democracy in general, had all become clear.

And this is not all. The history of the working-class movement now shows that in all countries it is about to experience (and has already begun to experience) a struggle between communism, which is emerging, gaining strength, and marching towards victory, and, first and foremost, its *own* (in each country) "Menshevism," that is, opportunism and social-chauvinism, and, second—as a supplement, so to say—"Left-wing" communism. The former struggle has developed in all countries, apparently without a single exception, as a struggle between the Second International (already virtually killed) and the Third International. The latter struggle can be observed in Germany, Great Britain, Italy, America (at any rate, a certain *section* of the Industrial Workers of the World and of the anarcho-syndicalist trends uphold the errors of Left-wing communism side by side with an almost universal and undivided acceptance of the Soviet system) and France (the attitude of a section of the former syndicalists towards the political party and parliamentarism, again side by side with the acceptance of the Soviet system), in other words, the struggle is undoubtedly being waged not only on an international but even on a world-wide scale.

But while the working-class movement is everywhere passing through what is actually the same kind of preparatory school for

victory over the bourgeoisie, it is in each country achieving this development in its *own way*. The big, advanced capitalist countries
are marching along this road *much more rapidly* than did Bolshevism,
which history granted fifteen years to prepare itself, as an organized
political trend, for victory. In the short space of one year, the Third
International has already scored a decisive victory; it has defeated the
Second, yellow, social-chauvinist International, which only a few
months ago was incomparably stronger than the Third International,
seemed to be stable and powerful and enjoyed the all-round support—
direct and indirect, material (Cabinet posts, passports, the press) and
ideological—of the world bourgeoisie.

The whole point now is that the Communists of every country
should quite consciously take into account both the main fundamental
tasks of the struggle against opportunism and "Left" doctrinairism
and the *specific features* which this struggle assumes and inevitably
must assume in each separate country in conformity with the peculiar features of its economics, politics, culture, national composition
(Ireland, etc.), its colonies, religious divisions, and so on and so
forth. Dissatisfaction with the Second International is felt everywhere and is spreading and growing, both because of its opportunism
and because of its inability, or incapacity, to create a really centralized,
a really leading center that would be capable of directing the international tactics of the revolutionary proletariat in its struggle for a
world Soviet republic. We must clearly realize that such a leading
center cannot under any circumstances be built up on stereotyped,
mechanically equalized, and identical tactical rules of struggle. As
long as national and state differences exist among peoples and countries—and these differences will continue to exist for a very long time
even after the dictatorship of the proletariat has been established on
a world scale—the unity of international tactics of the communist
working-class movement of all countries demands, not the elimination
of variety, not the abolition of national differences (that is a foolish
dream at the present moment), but an application of the *fundamental*
principles of communism (Soviet power and the dictatorship of the
proletariat) such as will *correctly modify* these principles in certain
particulars, correctly adapt and apply them to national and national-
state differences. The main task of the historical period through which
all the advanced (and not only the advanced) countries are now passing is to investigate, study, seek, divine, grasp that which is peculiarly
national, specifically national, in the *concrete* manner in which each
country is to approach the fulfillment of the tasks *common* to all—
the victory over opportunism and Left doctrinairism within the working-class movement, the overthrow of the bourgeoisie, and the establishment of a Soviet republic and a proletarian dictatorship. The main
thing—not everything by a very long way, of course, but the main

thing—has already been achieved: the vanguard of the working class has been won over; it has ranged itself on the side of Soviet government against parliamentarism, on the side of the dictatorship of the proletariat against bourgeois democracy. Now all efforts, all attention must be concentrated on the *next* step, namely, seeking the forms of *transition* or *approach* to the proletarian revolution, which seems—and from a certain standpoint really is—less fundamental, but which, on the other hand, is actually closer to the practical carrying out of the task.

The proletarian vanguard has been won over ideologically. That is the main thing. Without this not even the first step towards victory can be made. But it is still a fairly long way from victory. Victory cannot be won with the vanguard alone. To throw the vanguard alone into the decisive battle, before the whole class, before the broad masses have taken up a position either of direct support of the vanguard, or at least of sympathetic neutrality towards it, and one in which they cannot possibly support the enemy, would be not merely folly but a crime. And in order that really the whole class, that really the broad masses of the working people, those oppressed by capital, may take up such a position, propaganda and agitation alone are not enough. For this the masses must have their own political experience. Such is the fundamental law of all great revolutions, now confirmed with astonishing force and vividness not only in Russia but also in Germany. In order to turn resolutely towards communism, not only the uncultured, often illiterate masses of Russia, but the highly cultured masses of Germany, who are all literate, had to realize through their own painful experience the absolute impotence and spinelessness, the absolute helplessness and servility to the bourgeoisie, the utter vileness of the government of the knights of the Second International, to realize that a dictatorship of the extreme reactionaries . . . is inevitably the only alternative to a dictatorship of the proletariat.

The immediate task that confronts the class-conscious vanguard of the international working-class movement, that is, the Communist parties, groups, and trends, is to be able *to lead* the broad masses (now, for the most part, slumbering, apathetic, bound by routine, inert, and dormant) to their new position, or, rather, to be able to lead *not only* their own party, but also these masses in their approach, their transition to the new position. While the first historic task (that of winning over the class-conscious vanguard of the proletariat to Soviet power and the dictatorship of the working class) could not be accomplished without a complete ideological and political victory over opportunism and social-chauvinism, the second task, which now becomes the immediate task, and which consists in being able to lead the *masses* to the new position that can ensure the victory of the vanguard in the revolution—this immediate task cannot be accomplished without eliminating Left doctrinairism, without completely overcoming and eliminating its mistakes.

Propaganda was in the forefront so long as and to the extent that the question was (and insofar as it still is) one of winning over the vanguard of the proletariat to communism; even propaganda circles, with all the defects of the circle spirit, are useful under these conditions and produce fruitful results. But when it is a question of practical action by the masses, of the disposition, if one may so express it, of vast armies, of the alignment of *all* the class forces of the given society *for the final and decisive battle*, then propaganda habits alone, the mere repetition of the truths of "pure" communism, are of no avail. In these circumstances one must not count in thousands, as the propagandist does who belongs to a small group that has not yet given leadership to the masses; in these circumstances one must count in millions and tens of millions. In these circumstances we must not only ask ourselves whether we have convinced the vanguard of the revolutionary class, but also whether the historically effective forces of *all* classes—positively of all the classes of the given society without exception—are aligned in such a way that everything has fully matured for the decisive battle; in such a way that (1) all the class forces hostile to us have become sufficiently entangled, are sufficiently at loggerheads with each other, have sufficiently weakened themselves in a struggle which is beyond their strength; (2) all the vacillating, wavering, unstable, intermediate elements—the petty bourgeoisie and the petty-bourgeois democrats as distinct from the bourgeoisie—have sufficiently exposed themselves in the eyes of the people, have sufficiently disgraced themselves through their practical bankruptcy; and (3) among the proletariat a mass sentiment in favor of supporting the most determined, supremely bold, revolutionary action against the bourgeoisie has emerged and begun to grow vigorously. Then revolution is indeed ripe; then, indeed, if we have correctly gauged all the conditions indicated and briefly outlined above, and if we have chosen the moment rightly, our victory is assured.

The differences that exist between the Churchills and the Lloyd Georges—with insignificant national distinctions these political types exist in *all* countries—on the one hand, and between the Hendersons [7] and the Lloyd Georges on the other, are quite minor and unimportant from the standpoint of pure (that is, abstract) communism, that is, communism that has not yet matured to the stage of practical, mass, political action. But from the standpoint of this practical action by the masses, these differences are very, very important. To take account of these differences, to determine the moment when the inevitable con-

7 Arthur Henderson (1863–1935), one of the leaders of the British Labour Party. [*Ed.*]

flicts between these "friends" which weaken and enfeeble *all the "friends" taken together* will have completely matured—that is the whole concern, the whole task of the Communist who wants to be not merely a class-conscious and convinced propagandist of ideas, but a practical leader of the *masses* in the revolution. The strictest devotion to the ideas of communism must be combined with the ability to effect all the necessary practical compromises, maneuvers, agreements, zigzags, retreats and so on, in order to accelerate the coming to, and loss of, political power by the Hendersons . . . ; to accelerate their inevitable bankruptcy in practice, which will enlighten the masses precisely in the spirit of our ideas, in the direction of communism; to accelerate the inevitable friction, quarrels, conflicts, and discord between the Hendersons, the Lloyd Georges, and Churchills . . . and to select the proper moment when the discord among these "pillars of sacred private property" is at its height, in order, by a determined offensive of the proletariat, to defeat them all and capture political power.

History generally, and the history of revolutions in particular, is always richer in content, more varied, more versatile, more lively and "subtle" than even the best parties and the most class-conscious vanguards of the most advanced classes imagine. This is understandable, because even the best vanguards express the class-consciousness, will, passion, and imagination of tens of thousands; whereas revolutions are made, at moments of particular upsurge and the exertion of all human capacities, by the class-consciousness, will, passion, and imagination of tens of millions, spurred on by a most acute struggle of classes. From this follow two very important practical conclusions: first, that in order to fulfill its task the revolutionary class must be able to master *all* forms, or aspects, of social activity without any exception (completing, after the capture of political power, sometimes at great risk and very great danger, what it did not complete before the capture of power); second, that the revolutionary class must be ready to pass from one form to another in the quickest and most unexpected manner.

Everyone will agree that an army which does not train itself to wield all arms, all the means and methods of warfare that the enemy possesses or may possess, behaves in an unwise or even in a criminal manner. But this applies to politics even more than it does to war. In politics it is even harder to forecast what methods of struggle will be applicable and advantageous to us under specific future conditions. Unless we master all means of struggle, we may suffer grave, often even decisive, defeat if changes beyond our control in the position of the other classes bring to the forefront forms of activity in which we are particularly weak. If, however, we master all means of struggle, victory will be certain, because we represent the interests of the really foremost and really revolutionary class, even if circumstances do not permit us to bring into play the weapons that are most dangerous to the enemy, weapons that deal the swiftest mortal blows. Inexperienced revolutionaries often think that legal methods of struggle are opportunist because in this field the bourgeoisie has with the greatest frequency (particularly in "peaceful," nonrevolutionary times) deceived and fooled the workers, and that illegal methods of struggle are revolutionary. But that is not true. What is true is that those parties and leaders are opportunists and traitors to the working class who are unable or unwilling (don't say I can't, say I shan't) to apply illegal methods of struggle in conditions such as those which prevailed, for example, during the imperialist war of 1914–1918, when the bourgeoisie of the freest democratic countries deceived the workers in the most insolent and brutal manner, forbidding the truth to be told about the predatory character of the war. But revolutionaries who are unable to combine illegal forms of struggle with *every* form of legal struggle are poor revolutionaries indeed. It is not difficult to be a revolutionary when revolution has already broken out and is at its height, when everybody is joining the revolution just because they are carried away, because it is the fashion, and sometimes even out of careerist motives. After its victory, the proletariat has to make the most strenuous efforts, to suffer the pains of martyrdom, one might say, to "liberate" itself from such pseudo-revolutionaries. It is far more difficult—and of far greater value—to be a revolutionary when the conditions for direct, open, really mass and really revolutionary struggle *do not yet exist,* to be able to champion the interests of the revolution (by propaganda, agitation, and organization) in nonrevolutionary bodies and often enough in downright reactionary bodies, in a nonrevolutionary situation, among masses who are incapable of immediately appreciating the need for revolutionary methods of action. To be able to find, to probe for, to correctly determine the specific path or the particular turn of events that will *lead* the masses to the real, last, decisive, and great revolutionary struggle—such is the main task of communism in Western Europe and America today.

. . . The Communists in Western Europe and America must learn to create a new, unusual, nonopportunist, noncareerist parliamentarism; the Communist parties must issue their slogans; real proletarians, with the help of the unorganized and downtrodden poor, should scatter and distribute leaflets, canvass workers' houses and the cottages of the rural proletarians and peasants in the remote villages (fortunately there are many times less remote villages in Europe than in Russia, and in England the number is very small); they should go into the most common taverns, penetrate into the unions, societies, and casual meetings where the common people gather and talk to the people, not in learned (and not in very parliamentary) language; they should not at all strive to "get seats" in parliament but should everywhere strive to make people think and draw the masses into the struggle, to hold the bourgeoisie to its word and utilize the apparatus it has set up, the elections it has appointed, the appeals it has made to the whole people; they should try to explain to the people what Bolshevism is in a way that was never possible (under bourgeois rule) outside of election times (not counting, of course, times of big strikes, when in Russia a *similar* apparatus for widespread popular agitation worked even more intensively). It is very difficult to do this in Western Europe and America, very, very difficult; but it can and must be done, for the task of communism cannot be fulfilled without effort; and our efforts must be devoted to fulfilling *practical* tasks, ever more varied, ever more closely connected with all branches of social life, *winning* branch after branch and sphere after sphere *from the bourgeoisie.*

. . . Because in the era of imperialism generally, and especially now, after the war, which was a torment to the peoples and quickly opened their eyes to the truth (that is, that tens of millions were killed and maimed for the sole purpose of deciding whether the British or the German pirates should plunder the largest number of countries), all spheres of social life are being especially charged with inflammable material and are creating numerous causes of conflicts, crises, and the accentuation of the class struggle. We do not and cannot know which spark—of the innumerable sparks that are flying around in all countries as a result of the economic and political world crisis—will kindle the conflagration, in the sense of specially rousing the masses; we must, therefore, with the aid of our new, communist principles set to work to "stir up" all and sundry, even the oldest, mustiest, and seemingly hopeless spheres, for otherwise we shall not be able to cope with our tasks, we shall not be comprehensively prepared, we shall not master all arms, and we shall not prepare ourselves to achieve either the victory over the bourgeoisie (which arranged all sides of social life—and has now disarranged them—in its bourgeois way) or the impending communist reorganization of every sphere of life after that victory.

Since the proletarian revolution in Russia and its victories on an international scale, which came unexpected to the bourgeoisie and the philistines, the whole world has changed, and the bourgeoisie has changed everywhere too. It is terrified of "Bolshevism," incensed with it almost to the point of frenzy, and, for that very reason, it is, on the one hand, accelerating the progress of events and, on the other, concentrating attention on the suppression of Bolshevism by force, thereby weakening its own position in a number of other fields. In their tactics the Communists in all advanced countries must take both these circumstances into account.

. . . The bourgeoisie sees practically only one side of Bolshevism —insurrection, violence, terror; it therefore strives to prepare itself for resistance and opposition particularly in *this* field. It is possible that in certain instances, in certain countries, and for certain brief periods, it will succeed in this. We must reckon with such a possibility, and there will be absolutely nothing terrible for us if it does succeed. Communism "springs" from positively every sphere of public life; its shoots are to be seen literally everywhere. The "contagion" (to use the favorite metaphor of the bourgeoisie and the bourgeois police, the one most to their liking) has very thoroughly penetrated the organism and has completely impregnated it. If special efforts are made to "stop up" one of the channels, the "contagion" will find another, sometimes a very unexpected channel. Life will assert itself. Let the bourgeoisie rave, work itself into a frenzy, go to extremes, commit follies, take vengeance on the Bolsheviks in advance, and endeavor to kill off . . . more hundreds, thousands, and hundreds of thousands of yesterday's and tomorrow's Bolsheviks. In acting thus, the bourgeoisie is acting as all classes doomed by history have acted. Communists should know that the future in any case belongs to them; therefore, we can (and must) combine the most intense passion in the great revolutionary struggle with the coolest and most sober estimation of the frenzied ravings of the bourgeoisie. . . .

. . . Only one thing is lacking to enable us to march forward more confidently and firmly to victory, namely, the universal and thoroughly well thought-out appreciation by all Communists in all countries of the necessity of displaying the utmost *flexibility* in their tactics. The communist movement, which is developing magnificently, especially in the advanced countries, now lacks this appreciation and the ability to apply it in practice.

What happened to such leaders of the Second International, such highly erudite Marxists devoted to socialism as Kautsky, Otto Bauer, and others, could (and should) serve as a useful lesson. They fully appreciated the need for flexible tactics; they learned themselves and taught others Marxist dialectics (and much of what they have done in this respect will forever remain a valuable contribution to socialist literature); but *in the application* of these dialectics they committed such a mistake, or proved in practice to be so *un*dialectical, so incapable of taking into account the rapid change of forms and the rapid acquiring of new content by the old forms, that their fate is not . . . [very] enviable. . . . The principal reason for their bankruptcy was that they were "enchanted" by one definite form of growth of the working-class movement and socialism; they forgot all about the one-sidedness of this form; they were afraid of seeing the sharp break-up which objective conditions made inevitable and continued to repeat simple and, at first glance, incontestable axioms that had been learned by rote, such as: "three is more than two." But politics is more like algebra than arithmetic and still more like higher than elementary mathematics. In reality, all the old forms of the socialist movement have acquired a new content, and, consequently, a new sign, the "minus" sign, has appeared in front of all the figures; but our wise-acres stubbornly continued (and still continue) to persuade themselves and others that "minus three" is more than "minus two."

We must see to it that Communists do not make the same mistake, only the other way round; or, rather, we must see to it that the *same mistake*, only the other way round, made by the "Left" Communists, is corrected as soon as possible and overcome as quickly and pain-lessly as possible. It is not only Right doctrinairism that is a mis-take; Left doctrinairism is also a mistake. Of course, mistake of Left doctrinairism in communism is at present a thousand times less dan-gerous and less significant than the mistake of Right doctrinairism (that is, social-chauvinism and Kautskyism); but, after all, that is only due to the fact that Left communism is a very young trend, is only just coming into being. It is only for this reason that, under cer-tain conditions, the disease can be easily cured; and we must set to work to cure it with the utmost energy.

The old forms burst asunder, for it turned out that their new —antiproletarian and reactionary—content had attained an inordinate development. From the standpoint of the development of inter-national communism, our work today has such a durable, strong, and powerful content (for Soviet power, for the dictatorship of the proletariat) that it can *and must* manifest itself in any form, both new and old; it can and must, regenerate, conquer, and subjugate all forms, not only the new, but also the old—not for the purpose of reconciling itself with the old, but the purpose of making all and every form—new and old—a weapon for the complete, final, decisive, and irrevocable victory of communism.

Communists must exert every effort to direct the working-class movement and social development in general along the straightest and shortest road to the universal victory of Soviet power and the dictatorship of the proletariat. That is an incontestable truth. But it is enough to take one little step further—a step that might seem to be in the same direction—and truth becomes error. We have only to say, as the German and British Left Communists say, that we recog-nize only one road, only the direct road, that we will not permit maneuvering, making agreements, compromising—and it will be a mistake which may cause, and in part has already caused, and is caus-ing, very serious harm to communism. Right doctrinairism persisted in recognizing only the old forms and became utterly bankrupt, for it did not perceive the new content. Left doctrinairism persists in the unconditional repudiation of certain old forms, failing to see that the new content is forcing its way through all and sundry forms, that it is our duty as Communists to master all forms, to learn how, with the maximum rapidity, to supplement one form with another, to substitute one for another, and to adapt our tactics to every such change not called forth by our class, or by our efforts.

World revolution has received such a powerful impetus and acceleration from the horrors, vileness, and abominations of the world imperialist war and from the hopelessness of the situation it created—this revolution is developing in breadth and depth with such magnificent rapidity, with such a splendid variety of changing forms, with such an instructive practical refutation of all doctrinairism, that there is every reason to hope for a rapid and complete recovery of the international communist movement from the infantile disorder of "Left-wing" communism.

PRELIMINARY DRAFT OF THESES ON THE NATIONAL AND COLONIAL QUESTIONS

For the Second Congress of the Communist International

. . . 1) THE ABSTRACT or formal treatment of equality in general, and national equality in particular, is in the very nature of bourgeois democracy. Under the guise of the equality of individuals in general, bourgeois democracy proclaims the formal or legal equality of the property-owner and the proletarian, the exploiter and the exploited, thereby grossly deceiving the oppressed classes. On the plea that all men are absolutely equal, the bourgeoisie is transforming the idea of equality, which is itself a reflection of the relations of commodity production, into a weapon in its struggle against the abolition of classes. The demand for equality has real meaning only as a demand for the abolition of classes.

2) In conformity with its fundamental task of combating bourgeois democracy and exposing its falsity and hypocrisy, the Communist Party, as the conscious champion of the proletarian struggle to overthrow the bourgeois yoke, must base its policy in the national question too, not on abstract and formal principles, but, first, on an exact appraisal of the specific historical situation and, primarily, of economic conditions; second, on a clear distinction between the interests of the oppressed classes, of the working and exploited people, and the general concept of national interests as a whole, which implies the interests of the ruling class; third, on an equally clear distinction between the oppressed, dependent, and subject nations and the oppressing, exploiting, and sovereign nations, in order to counter the bourgeois-democratic lies obscuring the colonial and financial enslavement of the vast majority of the world's population by an insignificant minority of the richest and advanced capitalist countries, which is characteristic of the era of finance capital and imperialism.

3) The imperialist war of 1914–1918 has very clearly revealed to all nations and to the oppressed classes of the whole world the falsity of the bourgeois-democratic phrase-mongering by practically

demonstrating that the Treaty of Versailles of the celebrated "Western democracies" is an even more brutal and despicable act of violence against weak nations than was the Treaty of Brest-Litovsk of the German Junkers and the Kaiser. The League of Nations and the whole post-war policy of the Entente reveal this truth with even greater clarity and distinctness; they are everywhere intensifying the revolutionary struggle, both of the proletariat in the advanced countries and of the laboring masses in the colonial and dependent countries. They are hastening the collapse of the petty-bourgeois nationalist illusion that under capitalism nations can live together in peace and equality.

4) From these fundamental premises it follows that the whole policy of the Communist International on the national and colonial questions should rest on closer union of the proletarians and working masses generally of all nations and countries for a joint revolutionary struggle to overthrow the landowners and the bourgeoisie. For this alone will guarantee victory over capitalism, without which the abolition of national oppression and inequality is impossible.

5) The world political situation has now placed the dictatorship of the proletariat on the order of the day. World political developments inevitably revolve around one central point—the struggle of the world bourgeoisie against the Soviet Russian Republic, around which are inevitably grouping, on the one hand, the Soviet movements of the advanced workers of all countries, and, on the other, all the national-liberation movements in the colonies and among the oppressed nationalities, who are being taught by bitter experience that their only salvation lies in the victory of the Soviet system over world imperialism.

6) Consequently, one cannot confine oneself at the present time to the bare recognition or proclamation of the need for closer union between the working people of the various nations; it is necessary to pursue a policy that will achieve the closest alliance of all the national and colonial liberation movements with Soviet Russia, the form of this alliance to be determined by the degree of development of the communist movement among the proletariat of each country, or of the bourgeois-democratic liberation movement of the workers and peasants in backward countries or among backward nationalities.

7) Federation is a transitional form to the complete unity of the working people of different nations. . . .

8) The task of the Communist International in this respect is further to develop and also to study and to test by experience these new federations which are arising on the basis of the Soviet system and the Soviet movement. In recognizing that federation is a transitional form to complete unity, it is necessary to strive for ever closer federal unity, bearing in mind, first, that the Soviet republics, sur-

rounded as they are by the imperialist powers of the whole world—which from the military standpoint are immeasurably stronger—cannot possibly continue to exist without the closest alliance; second, that close economic alliance between the Soviet republics is necessary; otherwise it will be impossible to restore the productive forces ruined by imperialism and ensure the well-being of the working people; and third, that there is a tendency towards the creation of a single world economy, regulated by the proletariat of all nations as an integral whole and according to a common plan. This tendency is already quite clearly revealed under capitalism and is bound to be further developed and fully consummated under socialism.

9) As far as interstate relations are concerned, the national policy of the Communist International cannot be limited to the bare, formal, purely declaratory, and in reality noncommittal recognition of the equality of nations to which the bourgeois democrats confine themselves—both those who frankly admit themselves to be such and those who assume the name of socialists (the socialists of the Second International, for example).

In all their propaganda and agitation—both inside and outside parliament—the Communist parties must consistently expose the constant violation of the equality of nations and of the guaranteed rights of national minorities that takes place in all capitalist countries, despite their "democratic" constitutions. But in addition it is necessary, first, constantly to explain that only the Soviet system is capable of securing real equality of nations, by uniting at first the proletarians and then the whole mass of the working population in the struggle against the bourgeoisie; and, second, all Communist parties should render direct aid to the revolutionary movements among the dependent and underprivileged nations (for example, Ireland, the Negroes in America, etc.) and in the colonies.

Without the latter condition, which is particularly important, the struggle against the oppression of dependent nations and colonies as well as recognition of their right to secede are but a mendacious signboard. . . .

10) Recognition of internationalism in word, and its replacement by petty-bourgeois nationalism and pacifism in deed, in all propaganda, agitation and practical work, is very common not only among the parties of the Second International, but also among those which have withdrawn from it, and often even among parties which now call themselves communist. The struggle against this evil, against the most deep-rooted petty bourgeois national prejudices, becomes more necessary, the more the task of transforming the dictatorship of the proletariat from a national one (that is, existing in one country and incapable of determining world politics) into an international one (that is, a dictatorship of the proletariat covering at least

several advanced countries and capable of exercising decisive influence upon the whole of world politics) becomes a pressing question of the day. Petty-bourgeois nationalism proclaims as internationalism the bare recognition of the equality of nations, and nothing more. Quite apart from the fact that this recognition is purely verbal, petty-bourgeois nationalism preserves national egoism intact, whereas proletarian internationalism demands, first, that the interests of the proletarian struggle in one country be subordinated to the interests of that struggle on a world scale, and, second, that a nation which is achieving victory over the bourgeoisie be able and willing to make the greatest national sacrifices for the sake of overthrowing international capital.

Thus, in countries that are already fully capitalist and have workers' parties that really act as the vanguard of the proletariat, the struggle against opportunist and petty-bourgeois pacifist distortions of the concept and policy of internationalism is a primary and cardinal task.

11) With regard to the more backward states and nations, in which feudal or patriarchal and patriarchal-peasant relations predominate, it is particularly important to bear in mind:

first, that all Communist parties must assist the bourgeois-democratic liberation movement in these countries, and that the duty of rendering the most active assistance rests primarily with the workers of the country upon which the backward nation is dependent colonially or financially;

second, the need for struggle against the clergy and other influential reactionary and medieval elements in backward countries;

third, the need to combat the Pan-Islamic and similar trends which strive to combine the liberation movement against European and American imperialism with an attempt to strengthen the positions of the khans, landowners, mullahs, etc.;

fourth, the need, in backward countries, to give special support to the peasant movement against the landowners, against landed proprietorship, and against all manifestations or survivals of feudalism, and to strive to lend the peasant movement the most revolutionary character by establishing the closest possible alliance between the West-European communist proletariat and the revolutionary peasant movement in the East, in the colonies, and in the backward countries generally. It is particularly necessary to exert every effort to apply the basic principles of the Soviet system in countries where precapitalist relations predominate—by setting up "working people's Soviets," etc.;

fifth, the need for determined struggle against attempts to give a communist coloring to bourgeois-democratic liberation trends in the backward countries; the Communist International should support bourgeois-democratic national movements in colonial and backward countries only on condition that, in these countries, the elements of future proletarian parties, which will be communist not only in name, are brought together and trained to understand their special tasks, that is, to fight the bourgeois-democratic movements within their own nations. The Communist International must enter into a temporary alliance with bourgeois democracy in colonial and backward countries but must not merge with it and must under all circumstances uphold the independence of the proletarian movement even if it is in its earliest embryonic form;

sixth, the need constantly to explain and expose among the broadest working masses of all countries, and particularly of the backward countries, the deception systematically practiced by the imperialist powers, which, under the guise of politically independent states, set up states that are wholly dependent upon them economically, financially, and militarily. Under modern international conditions there is no salvation for dependent and weak nations except in a union of Soviet republics.

12) The age-old oppression of colonial and weak nationalities by the imperialist powers has not only fired the working masses of the oppressed countries with animosity towards the oppressor nations but also aroused the distrust of these nations in general, even of their proletariat. The despicable betrayal of socialism by the majority of the official leaders of this proletariat in 1914–1919, when "defense of the fatherland" was used as a social-chauvinist cloak to conceal the defense of the "right" of "their own" bourgeoisie to oppress colonies and rob financially dependent countries, was certain to enhance this perfectly legitimate distrust. On the other hand, the more backward the country, the stronger is the hold of small agricultural production, patriarchalism, and isolation, which inevitably lend particular strength and tenacity to the deepest of petty-bourgeois prejudices, to national egoism and national narrowness. These prejudices are bound to die out very slowly, for they can disappear only after imperialism and capitalism have disappeared in the advanced countries, and after the whole foundation of the economic life of the backward countries has radically changed. It is therefore the duty of the class-conscious communist proletariat of all countries to treat with particular caution and attention the survivals of national sentiments among the countries and nationalities which have been longest oppressed, and it is equally necessary to make certain concessions with a view to more rapidly overcoming this distrust and these prejudices. Unless the proletariat and, following it, the mass of working people of all countries and nations all over the world voluntarily strive for alliance and unity, the victory over capitalism cannot be successfully accomplished.

IV.

THE LAST YEARS: 1921–1923

THE TAX IN KIND (JUNE 1921)

The Significance of the New Policy and Its Conditions

In Lieu of an Introduction

THE QUESTION of the tax in kind is at present attracting very great attention and is giving rise to much discussion and argument. This is quite natural, because under present conditions it is indeed one of the principal questions of policy.

The discussion bears a rather disjointed character, a sin from which all of us suffer for reasons that are quite understandable. All the more useful would it be, therefore, to try to approach the question, not from its "topical" aspect, but from the aspect of general principle. In other words, to examine the general, fundamental background of the picture on which we are now tracing the pattern of definite practical measures of present-day policy.

In order to make this attempt I will take the liberty of quoting a long passage from my pamphlet, *The Chief Task of Our Day*. *"Left-Wing" Childishness and Petty-Bourgeois Mentality*. This pamphlet was published . . . in 1918 and contains, first a newspaper article . . . on the Brest peace, and, second, my polemic against the then existing group of Left Communists. . . . The polemic is superfluous now and so I delete it. I leave what appertains to the discussion about "state capitalism" and the main elements of our contemporary economy, the transitional economy from capitalism to socialism.

This is what I wrote at that time:

The Contemporary Economy of Russia
Excerpt from the 1918 Pamphlet [1]

State capitalism would be a step forward as compared with the present state of affairs in our Soviet Republic. If in approximately

---

1 In quoting the 1918 pamphlet for this article Lenin introduced a large number of editorial changes. [*Note in Soviet edition—Ed.*]

six months' time state capitalism were to be established in our Republic, that would be a great success and a sure guarantee that within a year socialism will have gained a permanently firm hold and will have become invincible in our country.

I can imagine with what noble indignation some people will recoil from these words. . . . What! The transition to state *capitalism* in the Soviet Socialist Republic would be a step forward? . . . Isn't this the betrayal of socialism?

It is this point that we must deal with in greater detail.

In the first place, we must examine the nature of the *transition* from capitalism to socialism which gives us the right and the reason for calling our country the Socialist Republic of Soviets.

Second, we must expose the error of those who fail to recognize the petty-bourgeois economic conditions and the petty-bourgeois element as the *principal* enemy of socialism in our country.

Third, we must fully understand the significance of the difference between the *Soviet* state and the bourgeois state from the point of view of economics.

Let us examine these three points.

No one, I think, in studying the question of the economics of Russia, has denied its transitional character. Nor, I think, has any Communist denied that the term Socialist Soviet Republic implies the determination of Soviet power to achieve the transition to socialism, and not that the existing economic system is recognized as socialist.

But what does the word "transition" mean? Does it not mean, as applied to economics, that the present system contains elements, particles, pieces of both capitalism and socialism? Everyone will admit that it does. But not all who admit this take the trouble to consider the precise elements of the various socio-economic formations which exist in Russia at the present time. And this is the crux of the question.

Let us enumerate these elements:

(1) patriarchal, that is, to a considerable extent natural, peasant farming;

(2) small commodity production (this includes the majority of those peasants who sell their grain);

(3) private capitalism;

(4) state capitalism;

(5) socialism.

Russia is so vast and so varied that all these different types of socio-economic formation are intermingled. This is what constitutes the specific feature of the situation.

The question arises: what elements predominate? Clearly, in a small-peasant country, the petty-bourgeois element predominates and it must predominate, for the majority, and the overwhelming majority at that, of those working the soil are small commodity producers. The shell of state capitalism (grain monopoly, state-controlled entrepreneurs and traders, bourgeois cooperators) is pierced in one place or another by *profiteers*, the chief object of profiteering being *grain*.

It is precisely in this field that the struggle is mainly proceeding. Between what elements is this struggle being waged if we are to speak in terms of economic categories such as "state capitalism"? Between the fourth and the fifth in the order in which I have just enumerated them? Of course not. It is not state capitalism that is at war with socialism, but the petty bourgeoisie plus private capitalism fighting together against both state capitalism and socialism. The petty bourgeoisie oppose *every kind* of state interference, accounting, and control, whether it be state-capitalist or state-socialist. This is an absolutely unquestionable fact of reality, the failure to understand which lies at the root of many economic mistakes. The profiteer, the trade marauder, the disrupter of monopoly—these are our principal "internal" enemies, the enemies of the economic measures of Soviet power. A hundred and twenty-five years ago it might have been excusable for the French petty bourgeoisie, the most ardent and sincere revolutionaries, to endeavour to crush the profiteer by executing a few of the "chosen" and by the thunder of their declarations. Today, however, the purely French attitude to this question assumed by some Left Socialist-Revolutionaries can rouse nothing but disgust and revulsion in every politically conscious revolutionary. We know perfectly well that the economic basis of profiteering is both the small proprietors, who are exceptionally widespread in Russia, and private capitalism, of which every petty bourgeois is an agent. We know that the million tentacles of this petty-bourgeois monster encircle first one and then another section of the workers, that it is not state monopoly but profiteering that forces its way through all the pores of our social and economic organism.

Those who fail to see this show by their blindness that they are slaves to petty-bourgeois prejudices. . . .

The petty bourgeois has a bit of money put away, several thousands gained during the war by "honest" and especially by dishonest means. He is the economic type, the typical character who serves as the basis of profiteering and private capitalism. Money is a certificate entitling the possessor to receive social wealth; and a vast section of small proprietors, numbering millions, cling to this certificate and conceal it from the "state." They do not believe in socialism or communism and "mark time" until the proletarian storm blows over. Either we subordinate the petty bourgeoisie to our control and accounting (we can do this if we organize the poor, that is, the majority of the population or semiproletarians, around the politically

conscious proletarian vanguard), or they will overthrow our workers'
power as surely and as inevitably as the revolution was overthrown
by the Napoleons and Cavaignacs who sprang from this very soil of
petty proprietorship. This, and this alone, is the way the matter stands.

The petty bourgeois who hoards his thousands is an enemy of
state capitalism. He wants to employ his thousands just for himself,
against the poor, in opposition to any kind of state control. And the
sum total of these thousands, amounting to many thousands of millions, forms the base for profiteering, which undermines our socialist
construction. Let us assume that a certain number of workers produce in a few days values equal to 1,000. Let us then assume that
200 of this total is lost to us, vanishes owing to petty profiteering, all
kinds of embezzlement, and the "evading" by the small proprietors of
Soviet decrees and regulations. Every politically conscious worker
will say that if better order and organization could be obtained at the
price of 300 out of the 1,000 he would willingly give 300 instead of
200, for it will be quite easy under Soviet power to reduce this "tribute" later on to, say, 100 or 50, once order and organization are established and once the petty-bourgeois disruption of state monopoly
is completely overcome.

This simple illustration in figures, which I have deliberately simplified to the utmost in order to make it absolutely clear, explains the
present correlation of state capitalism and socialism. The workers
hold state power and have every legal opportunity of "taking" the
whole thousand, that is, without giving up a single kopek, except
for socialist purposes. This legal opportunity, which rests upon the
actual transition of power to the workers, is an element of socialism.
But in many ways, the small-proprietor and private-capitalist element
undermines this legal position, drags in profiteering, hinders the execution of Soviet decrees. State capitalism would be a gigantic step
forward *even if* we paid *more* than we are paying at present (I took
this numerical example deliberately to bring this out more sharply),
because it is worthwhile paying for "tuition," because it is useful for
the workers, because victory over disorder, economic ruin, and lack
of organization is the most important thing; because the continuation
of small proprietary anarchy is the greatest, the most serious danger
which will *certainly* be our ruin (unless we overcome it), whereas
not only will the payment of a heavier tribute to state capitalism not
ruin us, it will lead us to socialism by the surest road. When the
working class has learned how to defend law and order against the
anarchy of small proprietors, when it has learned to organize large-
scale production on a national scale and along state-capitalist lines,
it will hold, if I may use the expression, all the trump cards, and the
consolidation of socialism will be assured.

In the first place, *economically*, state capitalism is immeasurably superior to our present economic system.

In the second place, there is nothing terrible in it for Soviet power, for the Soviet state is a state in which the power of the workers and the poor is assured. . . .

To elucidate the question still more, let us first of all take the most concrete example of state capitalism. Everybody knows what this example is. It is Germany. Here we have "the last word" in modern, large-scale capitalist engineering and planned organization, *subordinated to Junker-bourgeois imperialism.* Cross out the words in italics, and in place of the militarist, Junker, bourgeois, imperialist state put also a state, but of a different social type, of a different class content—a Soviet state, that is, a proletarian state—and you will have the totality of conditions that is socialism.

Socialism is inconceivable without large-scale capitalist engineering based on the last word in modern science. It is inconceivable without planned state organization by means of which tens of millions of people are made strictly to observe a single standard in production and distribution. We Marxists have always spoken of this, and it is not worth while wasting two seconds talking to people who do not understand even this (anarchists and a good half of the Left Socialist-Revolutionaries).

At the same time socialism is inconceivable unless the proletariat is the ruler of the state. This also is ABC. And history (which nobody, except Menshevik blockheads of the first order, ever expected to bring about "complete" socialism smoothly, gently, easily, and simply) took such a peculiar course that it gave birth in 1918 to two unconnected halves of socialism existing side by side like two chicks in the single shell of international imperialism. In 1918 Germany and Russia were the embodiment of the most striking material realization of the economic, the productive, and the socio-economic conditions for socialism, on the one hand, and the political conditions, on the other.

A successful proletarian revolution in Germany would immediately and very easily have shattered any shell of imperialism (which unfortunately is made of the best steel and hence cannot be broken by the efforts of any chick) and would have brought about the victory of world socialism for certain, without any difficulty, or with slight difficulty—if, of course, by "difficulty" we mean difficult on a world-historical scale, and not in the very narrow sense.

While the revolution in Germany is still slow in "coming forth," our task is *to learn* state capitalism from the Germans, *to spare no effort* in copying it and not shrink from adopting dictatorial methods to hasten the copying of Western practices by barbarian Russia, without hesitating to use barbarous methods in fighting barbarism. If there are anarchists and Left Socialist-Revolutionaries . . . who indulge in . . . reflections that it is unbecoming for us revolutionaries to "take lessons" from German imperialism, there is only one thing we can say in reply—a revolution would perish irrevocably (and deservedly) if it took these people seriously.

At present, petty-bourgeois capitalism prevails in Russia, and it is *one and the same road* that leads from it to both large-scale state capitalism and to socialism, *through one and the same* intermediary station called "national accounting and control of production and distribution." Those who fail to understand this are making an unpardonable mistake in economics. Either they do not know the facts of life, do not see what actually exists, and are unable to look the truth in the face; or they confine themselves to abstractly comparing "capitalism" and "socialism" and fail to study the concrete forms and stages of the transition that is taking place in our country.

Let it be said in parenthesis that this is the very theoretical mistake which misled the best people in the . . . [Menshevik] camp. The worst and the mediocre of these, owing to their stupidity and spinelessness, drag at the tail of the bourgeoisie, of whom they stand in awe. The best of them failed to understand that it was not without reason that the teachers of socialism spoke of a whole period of transition from capitalism to socialism and emphasized the prolonged pangs attending the birth of new society. And this new society is again an abstraction which can come into being only by passing through a series of varied, imperfect, concrete attempts to create this or that socialist state.

It is precisely because Russia cannot advance from the economic situation now existing here without traversing the ground *that is common* to state capitalism and to socialism (national accounting and control) that the attempt to frighten others as well as themselves with "evolution *towards* state capitalism" is sheer theoretical nonsense. It means that one's thoughts are wandering away from the true road of "evolution," and one fails to understand what this road is. In practice it is equivalent to *dragging back* to small-proprietor capitalism.

In order to convince the reader that this is not the first time I have given this "high" appreciation of state capitalism and that I gave it *before* the Bolsheviks seized power, I take the liberty of quoting the following passage from my pamphlet, *The Impending Catastrophe and How To Combat It*, written in September 1917.

"Try to substitute for the Junker-capitalist state, for the landlord-capitalist state, a revolutionary-democratic state, that is, a state which in a revolutionary way destroys all privileges and does not fear to introduce the fullest democracy in a revolutionary way, and you will find that, given a really revolutionary-democratic state, state-monopoly capitalism inevitably and unavoidably implies a step towards social-ism. . . .

"For socialism is nothing but the next step forward from state-capitalist monopoly. . . .

"State-monopoly capitalism is a complete material preparation for socialism, the threshold of socialism, a rung in the ladder of history between which and the rung called socialism there are no intermedi-ate rungs." . . .

Please note that this was written when Kerensky was in power, that we are discussing, *not* the dictatorship of the proletariat, *not* the socialist state, but the "revolutionary-democratic" state. Is it not clear that *the higher* we stand on this political ladder, *the more completely* we incorporate the socialist state and the dictatorship of the prole-tariat in the Soviets, *the less* ought we to fear "state capitalism"? Is is not clear that from the *material*, economic, and productive point of view, we are not yet "on the threshold" of socialism? And how other-wise than by way of this "threshold," which we have not yet reached, shall we pass through the door of socialism? . . .

The following is also extremely instructive.

In our controversy with Comrade Bukharin . . . ,[2] he declared, among other things, that on the question of high salaries for specialists "we" were "more to the right than Lenin," for in this case we see no deviation from principle, bearing in mind Marx's words that under certain conditions it is more expedient for the working class to "buy off the whole lot of them" (namely, the whole lot of capitalists, that is, *to buy* from the bourgeoisie the land, factories, and other means of production).

This is an extremely interesting statement. . . .

Let us consider Marx's idea carefully.

Marx was talking about Britain of the seventies of the last cen-tury, about the culminating point in the development of premonopoly capitalism. At that time Britain was a country in which militarism and bureaucracy were less pronounced than in any other, a country in which there was the greatest possibility of a "peaceful" victory for socialism in the sense of the workers "buying off" the bourgeoisie. And Marx said that under certain conditions the workers would certainly

2   Nikolai Bukharin (1888–1938) one of the major theoreticians of Bol-shevism and, despite doctrinal squabbles, Lenin's favorite among the heirs apparent. Originally Bukharin's "deviation" was of the "left" variety but in the twenties he emerged as one of the most articulate spokesmen for the New Economic Policy (NEP). From 1925 to 1928 Bukharin shared power with Stalin. They broke, however, over Stalin's proposals for agricultural collectivi-zation and forced industrialization. Bukharin was identified as the leader of the Right Opposition and lost most of his political power. He was the main de-fendant in the 1938 Moscow Purge trial, was condemned to death and executed. [*Ed.*]

not refuse to buy off the bourgeoisie. Marx did not commit himself, or the future leaders of the socialist revolution, to matters of form, to ways and means of bringing about the revolution. He understood perfectly well that a vast number of new problems would arise, that the whole situation would change in the course of the revolution, would change radically and often in the course of the revolution.

Well, and what about Soviet Russia? Is it not clear that *after* the seizure of power by the proletariat and *after* the crushing of the exploiters' armed resistance and sabotage, *certain* conditions prevail which correspond to those which might have existed in Britain half a century ago had a peaceful transition to socialism begun there? The subordination of the capitalists to the workers in Britain would have been assured at that time under the following circumstances: (1) the absolute preponderance of workers, of proletarians in the population owing to the absence of a peasantry (in Britain in the seventies there was every hope of an extremely rapid spread of socialism among agricultural laborers); (2) the excellent organization of the proletariat in trade unions (Britain was at that time the leading country in the world in this respect); (3) the comparatively high level of culture of the proletariat which had been trained as political liberties developed in the course of centuries; (4) the old habit of the well-organized British capitalists of settling political and economic questions by compromise—at that time the British capitalists were better organized than the capitalists of any country in the world (this superiority has now passed to Germany). These were the circumstances which at that time gave rise to the idea that the *peaceful* subjugation of the British capitalists by the workers was possible.

In our country, at the present time, this subjugation is assured by certain concrete premises (the victory in October and the suppression, from October to February, of the capitalists' armed resistance and sabotage). But *instead of* the absolute preponderance of workers, of proletarians in the population, and *instead of* a high degree of organization among them, the important factor of victory in Russia was the support the proletarians received from the poor peasants who had rapidly become ruined. Finally, we have neither a high degree of culture nor the habit of compromise. If these concrete conditions are considered, it will become clear that we can and ought to employ two methods *simultaneously*. On the one hand we must ruthlessly suppress the uncultured capitalists who refuse to have anything to do with "state capitalism" or to consider any form of compromise, and who continue by means of profiteering, by bribing the poor peasants, etc., to hinder the realization of the measures taken by the Soviets. On the other hand we must use the *method of compromise*, or of buying off the cultured capitalists who consent to "state capitalism," who are capable of putting it into practice, and who are useful to the proletariat as the clever and experienced organizers of the largest types of enterprises which actually supply products to tens of millions of people.

Bukharin is a well-educated Marxist economist. He therefore remembered that Marx was profoundly right when he taught the workers the importance of preserving the organization of large-scale production, precisely for the purpose of facilitating the transition to socialism. Marx taught that (as an exception, and Britain was then an exception) the idea was conceivable of *paying the capitalists well*, of buying them off, if the circumstances were such as to compel the capitalists to submit peacefully and to come over to socialism in a cultured and organized fashion, provided they were bought off.

But Bukharin went astray because he did not sufficiently study the specific features of the situation in Russia at the present time—an exceptional situation when we, the Russian proletariat, are *in advance* of any Britain or any Germany as regards our political order, as regards the strength of the workers' political power, but we are *behind* the most backward West-European country as regards well-organized state capitalism, as regards our level of culture and the degree of material and productive preparedness for the "introduction" of socialism. Is it not clear that the specific nature of the present situation creates the need for a specific type of "buying off" which the workers must offer to the most cultured, the most skilled, the most capable organizers among the capitalists who are ready to enter the service of Soviet power and to help honestly in organizing "state" production on the largest possible scale? Is it not clear that in this specific situation we must make every effort to avoid two mistakes, both of which are of a petty-bourgeois nature? On the one hand, it would be a fatal mistake to declare that since there is a discrepancy between our economic "forces" and our political strength, it "follows" that we should not have seized power. Such an argument can be advanced only by "men who live in shells" and who forget that there will always be such a "discrepancy," that it always exists in the development of nature as well as in the development of society, that only by a series of attempts—each of which, taken by itself, will be one-sided and will suffer from certain inconsistencies—will full-scale socialism be created by the revolutionary cooperation of the proletarians of *all* countries.

On the other hand, it would be an obvious mistake to give free rein to bawlers and phrase-mongers who allow themselves to be carried away by the "dazzling" revolutionary spirit but who are incapable of sustained, thoughtful, and deliberate revolutionary work which takes into account the most difficult stages of transition.

Fortunately, the history of the development of the revolutionary parties and of the struggle that Bolshevism waged against them has left us a heritage of sharply defined types, of which the Left Socialist-

Revolutionaries and anarchists are striking examples of sorry revolutionaries. They are now shouting, shouting hysterically, choking and shouting themselves hoarse, against the "compromise" of the "Right Bolsheviks." But they are incapable of thinking *what* is bad in "compromise," and *why* "compromise" has been justly condemned by history and the course of the revolution.

Compromise in [1917] . . . meant the surrender of power to the imperialist bourgeoisie, and the question of power is the fundamental question of every revolution. The compromise of a section of the Bolsheviks in October-November 1917 either meant that they feared the proletariat seizing power or wished to *share* power equally, not only with "unreliable fellow-travelers" like the Left Socialist-Revolutionaries, but also with the enemies. . . . The latter would inevitably have hindered us in fundamental matters, such as the dissolution of the Constituent Assembly, the ruthless suppression of [counter-revolutionaries] . . . , the complete implementation of measures of Soviet institutions, and in every act of confiscation.

Now power has been seized, retained, and consolidated in the hands of a single party, the party of the proletariat, even without the "unreliable fellow-travelers." To speak of compromise at the present time when there is no question, and can be none, of sharing *power*, of renouncing the dictatorship of the proletariat over the bourgeoisie, is merely to repeat, parrot-fashion, words which have been learned by heart, but not understood. To describe as "compromise" the fact that, having arrived at a situation when we can and must rule the country, we try to win over to our side, not grudging the cost, the most skilled people capitalism has trained and to take them into our service against small-proprietor disintegration, reveals a total incapacity to think about the economic tasks of socialist construction.

The Tax in Kind, Free Trade and Concessions

In the arguments of 1918 quoted above there are a number of mistakes as regards the periods of time involved. The periods turned out to be longer than was anticipated at that time. That is not surprising. But the basic elements of our economy have remained the same. In a very large number of cases the peasant "poor" (proletarians and semiproletarians) have become middle peasants. This has caused an increase in the small-proprietor, petty-bourgeois "element." The Civil War of 1918–1920 aggravated the devastation of the country, retarded the restoration of its productive forces, and bled the proletariat more than any other class. To this was added the crop failure of 1920, fodder shortage and the dying off of cattle, which still further retarded the rehabilitation of transport and industry, because, among other things, it interfered with the employment of peasants' horses for carting wood, our main fuel.

As a result, the political situation in the spring of 1921 was such that immediate, very resolute, and urgent measures had to be taken to improve the condition of the peasants and to increase their productive forces.

Why the peasants and not the workers?

Because in order to improve the conditions of the workers, grain and fuel are required. This is the biggest "hitch" at the present time, from the point of view of the economy as a whole. And it is impossible to increase the production and collection of grain and the storage and delivery of fuel except by improving the condition of the peasantry, by raising their productive forces. We must start with the peasantry. Those who fail to understand this, those who are inclined to regard this putting the peasantry in the forefront as the "renunciation," or something similar to the renunciation, of the dictatorship of the proletariat, simply do not stop to think, and yield to the power of words. The dictatorship of the proletariat is the direction of policy by the proletariat. The proletariat, as the leading, ruling class, must be able to direct policy in such a way as to solve first the most urgent, the most "vexed" problem. The most urgent thing at the present time is to take measures that will immediately increase the productive forces of peasant farming. Only *in this way* will it be possible to improve the condition of the workers and strengthen the alliance between the workers and peasants, strengthen the dictatorship of the proletariat. The proletarian or representative of the proletariat who *refused* to improve the conditions of the workers *in this way* would *in fact* prove himself to be an accomplice of the whiteguards and the capitalists; to refuse to do it in this way would mean putting the craft interests of the workers above their class interests, would mean sacrificing the interests of the whole of the working class, of its dictatorship, its alliance with the peasantry against the landowners and capitalists, its leading role in the struggle for the emancipation of labor from the yoke of capital, for the sake of the immediate, momentary, and partial gain of the workers.

Thus, the first thing required is immediate and serious measures to raise the productive forces of the peasantry.

This cannot be done without making important changes in our food policy. The replacement of the surplus-appropriation system by the tax in kind, which implies free trade, at least in local economic exchange, after the tax has been paid, was such a change.

What, in essence, is the replacement of the surplus-appropriation system by the tax in kind?

Wrong ideas are widespread concerning this point. These wrong ideas are due mainly to the fact that people make no attempt to study the meaning of the change; they do not ask from what and to what the change is being made. They imagine that the change is from communism in general to the bourgeois system in general. To counteract this mistake, one has to refer to what was said in May 1918.

The tax in kind is one of the forms of transition from that peculiar War Communism,[3] which we were forced to resort to by extreme want, ruin, and war, to the proper socialist exchange of products. The latter, in its turn, is one of the forms of transition from socialism to communism with the peculiar features due to the population being predominantly one of small peasants.

The essence of this peculiar War Communism was that we actually took from the peasant all surpluses—and sometimes even not only surpluses, but part of what the peasant needed for food—to meet the requirements of the army and sustain the workers. Most of it we took on loan, for paper money. Had we not done that we would have been unable to vanquish the landowners and capitalists in a ruined small-peasant country. And the fact that we were victorious (in spite of the assistance our exploiters obtained from the most powerful countries of the world) not only shows what miracles of heroism the workers and peasants are capable of in the struggle for their emancipation; it also shows that [many "Socialists"] . . . acted as lackeys of the bourgeoisie when they *blamed* us for this War Communism. It should be put to our credit.

And everyone should know the real extent of the service that stands to our credit. We were forced to resort to War Communism by war and ruin. It was not, nor could it be, a policy that corresponded to the economic tasks of the proletariat. It was a temporary measure. The correct policy of the proletariat which is exercising its dictatorship in a small-peasant country is to obtain grain in exchange for the manufactured goods the peasant needs. Only such a food policy corresponds to the tasks of the proletariat; only such a policy can strengthen the foundations of socialism and lead to its complete victory.

The tax in kind is a transition to this policy. We are still so ruined, so crushed by the burden of war (the war of yesterday and the war which, owing to the rapacity and malice of the capitalists, may break out tomorrow) that we cannot give the peasant manufactured goods for *all* the grain we need. Knowing this, we are introducing the tax in kind, that is, we shall take the minimum of grain we require

3 "War Communism," the name given to the period of civil war after the Bolshevik seizure of power (1918–1920). The economic breakdown induced by the war led to the use of a number of seemingly "communist" methods such as barter. One of the chief characteristics of the period was forced grain requisition in order to feed the cities under Bolshevik control. [*Ed.*]

(for the army and the workers) in the form of a tax and will obtain the rest in exchange for manufactured goods.

Moreover, we must not forget the following. Our poverty and ruin are so great that we cannot *at one stroke* restore large-scale socialist state industry. This can be done if we have large stocks of grain and fuel in the big industrial centers, if we replace the worn-out machines with new ones, and so on. Experience has convinced us that this cannot be done at one stroke, and we know that after the ruinous imperialist war even the wealthiest and most advanced countries will be able to solve this problem only over a fairly long period of years. Hence, it is necessary, to a certain extent, to help to restore *small* industry, which does not need machines, does not demand large stocks of raw material, fuel, and food from the state, and which can immediately render some assistance to peasant farming and increase its productive forces.

What will be the effect of this?

The effect will be the revival of the petty bourgeoisie and of capitalism on the basis of a certain amount of free trade (if only local). This is beyond doubt. It would be ridiculous to shut our eyes to it.

The questions arise: Is it necessary? Can it be justified? Is it not dangerous?

Many questions like this are being asked, and in the majority of cases they merely reveal the simplicity, to put it mildly, of those who ask them.

Examine the way I defined the elements (constituent parts) of various socio-economic forms in our economy in May 1918. No one can deny the existence of all these five stages (or constituent parts), of all these five forms of economy—from the patriarchal, that is, semisavage, to the socialist system. That the small-peasant "form," partly patriarchal, partly petty-bourgeois, predominates in a small-peasant country is self-evident. Since there is exchange, the development of the small economy is petty-bourgeois development, it is a capitalist development—this is an incontrovertible truth, an elementary truth of political economy, confirmed, moreover, by the everyday experience and observation of even the ordinary man in the street.

What policy can the socialist proletariat pursue in the face of this economic reality? To give the small peasant *all* he needs of the goods produced by large-scale socialist industries in exchange for his grain and raw materials? This would be the most desirable and the most "correct" policy—and we have started on it. But we cannot give *all* the goods, very far from it; nor shall we be able to do so very soon—at all events not until we complete the first stage of the electrification of the whole country. What is to be done? One way is to try to prohibit entirely, to put the lock on all development of private, nonstate exchange, that is, trade, that is, capitalism, which is inevitable when there are millions of small producers. But such a policy would be foolish and suicidal for the party that tried to apply it. It would be foolish because such a policy is economically impossible. It would be suicidal because the party that tried to apply such a policy would meet with inevitable disaster. We need not conceal from ourselves the fact that some Communists sinned "in thought, word, and deed" in this respect and descended to just *such* a policy. We shall try to rectify these mistakes. They must be rectified without fail; otherwise things will come to a very sorry state.

The alternative (and this is the last *possible* and the only sensible policy) is not to try to prohibit or put the lock on the development of capitalism, but to try to direct it into the channels of *state capitalism*. This is economically possible, for state capitalism—in one form or another, to some degree or other—exists wherever the elements of free trade and capitalism in general exist.

Can the Soviet state, the dictatorship of the proletariat, be combined, united with state capitalism? Are they compatible?

Of course they are. This is exactly what I argued in May 1918. I hope I proved it in May 1918. Nor is that all. I then proved that state capitalism is a step forward compared with the small-proprietor (both small-patriarchal and petty-bourgeois) element. Those who juxtapose or compare state capitalism only with socialism commit a host of mistakes, for in the present political and economic circumstances it is essential to compare state capitalism also with petty-bourgeois production.

The whole problem—both theoretical and practical—is to find the correct methods of directing the inevitable (to a certain degree and for a certain time) development of capitalism into the channels of state capitalism; to determine what conditions to hedge it round with, how to ensure the transformation of state capitalism into socialism in the near future.

In order to approach the solution of this problem we must first of all picture to ourselves as distinctly as possible what state capitalism will be and can be in practice within our Soviet system, within the framework of our Soviet state.

Concessions are the simplest example of how the Soviet government directs the development of capitalism into the channels of state capitalism, of how it "implants" state capitalism, is concessions. We all now agree that concessions are necessary; but not all of us have given thought to what concessions mean. What are concessions under the Soviet system, viewed in the light of the above-mentioned forms of economy and their interrelations? They are an agreement, a block, an alliance between the Soviet, that is, proletarian, state power and state capitalism against the small-proprietor (patriarchal and petty-bourgeois) element. The concessionaire is a capitalist. He conducts his business on capitalist lines, for profit. He is willing to enter into an agreement with the proletarian government in order to obtain extra profits, over and above ordinary profits, or in order to obtain raw materials which he cannot otherwise obtain, or can obtain only with great difficulty. Soviet power gains by the development of the productive forces, by securing an increased quantity of goods immediately, or within a very short period. We have, say, a hundred concerns, mines and forest territories. We cannot develop all of these— we lack the machines, food, and transport. And this is also why we are doing almost nothing to develop the other territories. Owing to the poor and inadequate development of the large enterprises, the small-proprietor element is more pronounced in every aspect, and this is reflected in the deterioration of the surrounding (and later the whole of) peasant farming, the disruption of its productive forces, decline in its confidence in Soviet power, thieving and widespread, petty (the most dangerous) profiteering, and the like. By "implanting" state capitalism in the form of concessions, the Soviet government strengthens large-scale production as against petty production, advanced production as against backward production, machine production as against hand production. And it obtains a larger quantity of the products of large-scale industry (percentage deduction) and strengthens state-regulated economic relations as against petty-bourgeois anarchical relations. The moderate and cautious application of the concessions policy will undoubtedly help us quickly (to a modest extent) to improve the state of industry and the conditions of the workers and peasants—of course, at the cost of certain sacrifices, the surrender to the capitalist of many million poods of very valuable products. The degree and the conditions that will make concessions advantageous and not dangerous to us are determined by the relation of forces; they are decided by struggle; for concessions are also a form of struggle; they are the continuation of the class struggle in another form, and under no circumstances are they the substitution of class peace for class war. Practice will determine the methods of struggle.

Compared with other forms of state capitalism within the Soviet system, state capitalism in the form of concessions is, perhaps, the simplest, most distinct, clearest, and most precisely defined. Here we have a formal, written agreement with the most cultured, advanced, West-European capitalism. We know exactly our gains and our losses, our rights and obligations. We know exactly the periods for which we grant the concessions. We know the terms of redemption before the expiration of the agreement if the agreement provides for such redemption. We pay a certain "tribute" to world capitalism; we "ransom" ourselves from it by such-and-such arrangements and

obtain immediately the more stable position of Soviet power and better conditions for our economy. The whole difficulty with concessions
is the proper consideration and appraisal of all the circumstances when
concluding a concession agreement, and then seeing that it is fulfilled.
Undoubtedly, there are difficulties; and in all probability mistakes
will be inevitable at first. But these difficulties are minor ones compared with the other problems of the social revolution and, in particular, compared with the difficulties involved in other forms of
developing, permitting and implanting state capitalism.

The most important task that confronts all Party and Soviet workers in connection with the introduction of the tax in kind is to be
able to apply the principles, the fundamentals of the "concession"
policy (that is, a policy that is similar to "concession" state capitalism) to the other forms of capitalism—free trade, local exchange, etc.

Take the cooperatives. It is not surprising that the decree on the
tax in kind immediately necessitated a revision of the regulations governing the cooperatives and a certain extension of their "freedom"
and rights. The cooperatives, too, are a form of state capitalism, but
a less simple one; its outline is less distinct; it is more intricate and
therefore creates greater practical difficulties for our government. The
small commodity producers' cooperatives (and it is the latter, and
not the workers' cooperatives, that we are discussing as the predominant and typical form in a small-peasant country) inevitably give rise
to petty-bourgeois, capitalist relations, facilitate their development,
push small capitalists into the foreground, and benefit them most. It
cannot be otherwise, since the small proprietors predominate, and
exchange is possible and necessary. Under the conditions prevailing
in Russia at present, freedom and rights for the cooperative societies
mean freedom and rights for capitalism. It would be stupid or
criminal to close our eyes to this obvious truth.

But, unlike private capitalism, "cooperative" capitalism under the
Soviet system is a variety of state capitalism, and as such it is advantageous and useful for us at the present time—in a certain measure,
of course. Since the tax in kind means the free sale of surplus grain
(over and above that taken in the form of the tax), we must exert
every effort to direct *this* development of capitalism—for free sale,
free trade *is* the development of capitalism—into the channels of cooperative capitalism. Cooperative capitalism resembles state capitalism in that it facilitates accounting, control, supervision, and the
establishment of contract relations between the state (in this case, the
Soviet state) and the capitalist. Cooperative trade is much more advantageous and useful than private trade not only for the above-mentioned reasons, but also because it facilitates the association, the
organization of millions of the population, and later of the entire
population; and this in its turn is an enormous gain from the point of

view of the subsequent transition from state capitalism to socialism.

Let us compare concessions and cooperatives as forms of state capitalism. Concessions are based on large-scale machine industry; the cooperatives are based on small, handicraft, and partly even on patriarchal industry. Each individual concession agreement affects one capitalist, or one firm, one syndicate, cartel, or trust. The cooperative societies embrace many thousands and even millions of small proprietors. Concessions permit and even presuppose a definite agreement for a definite period. Cooperative societies permit of neither a definite agreement nor a definite period. It is much easier to repeal the law on the cooperatives than to annul a concession agreement. But the annulment of an agreement means a sudden rupture in the practical relations of economic alliance, or economic coexistence, with the capitalist, whereas the repeal of the law on the cooperatives, or the existence of any law for that matter, does not immediately break off the practical coexistence of Soviet power and the small capitalists, nor, in general, is it able to break off practical economic relations. It is easy to "watch" a concessionaire; it is difficult to watch cooperators. The transition from concessions to socialism is the transition from one form of large-scale production to another form of large-scale production. The transition from small-proprietor cooperatives to socialism is the transition from small production to large-scale production, that is, it is a more complicated transition, but, if successful, is capable of embracing wider masses of the population, is capable of pulling up the deeper and more tenacious roots of the old, presocialist and even precapitalist relations, which most stubbornly resist all "innovations." The concessions policy, if successful, will give us a few exemplary—compared with our own—large enterprises built on the level of modern advanced capitalism. After a few decades these enterprises will revert to us in their entirety. The cooperative policy, if successful, will result in raising small economy and in facilitating its transition, within an indefinite period, to large-scale production on the basis of voluntary association.

Take a third form of state capitalism. The state enlists the capitalist as a merchant and pays him a definite commission on the sale of state goods and on the purchase of the produce of the small producer. A fourth form: the state leases to the capitalist entrepreneur an industrial establishment, concerns, forest territories, land, etc., which belong to the state, the lease being very similar to a concession agreement. These two latter forms of state capitalism are not mentioned, thought about, or noticed at all. This is not because we are strong and clever, but because we are weak and foolish. We are afraid to look "vulgar truth" straight in the face, and too often we yield to "exalting deception." [4] We are constantly repeating that "we" are

4 The phrase is from Pushkin's poem, "The Hero." [*Ed.*]

passing from capitalism to socialism, but we forget to picture to ourselves precisely and distinctly who "we" are. We must constantly
have in mind the whole list—without any exception—of the constituent parts of our economy, of all the diverse forms of economy
in our country that I gave in my article of May, 1918, in order that
this clear picture may not be forgotten. "We," the vanguard, the
advanced contingent of the proletariat, are passing directly to socialism; but the advanced contingent is only a small part of the whole
of the proletariat, while the latter, in its turn, is only a small part of
the whole population. And in order that "we" may successfully solve
the problem of our immediate transition to socialism we must understand what *intermediary* paths, methods, means, and instruments are
required for the transition from *precapitalist* relations to socialism.
That is the whole point.

Look at the map of [Russia]. . . . To the north of Vologda, to the
southeast of Rostov-on-Don and Saratov, to the south of Orenburg
and Omsk, to the north of Tomsk, there are boundless areas big
enough to contain scores of large civilized states. And over all these
spaces patriarchalism, semisavagery, and real savagery reign. And
what about the out-of-the-way peasant districts of the rest of Russia,
wherever scores of . . . [miles] of country track, or rather of track-
less country, separate the villages from the railways, that is, from
material connection with culture, with capitalism, with large-scale industry, with the big cities? Do not patriarchalism, Oblomovism,[5]
and semisavagery also predominate in those places?

Is an immediate transition to socialism from the state of affairs
predominating in Russia conceivable? Yes, it is conceivable to a certain degree, but on one condition, the precise nature of which we
know now thanks to an enormous piece of scientific work that has
been completed. That condition is electrification. If we construct
scores of district electric power stations (we now know where and
how these can and should be constructed), if we transmit electric
power from these to every village, if we obtain a sufficient number of
electric motors and other machinery, we shall not need, or shall
hardly need, transition stages, intermediary links between patriarchalism and socialism. But we know perfectly well that at least ten years
will be required to complete only the first stage of this "one" condition; a reduction of this period is conceivable only if the proletarian
revolution is victorious in such countries as Britain, Germany, or the
U.S.A.

For the next few years we must learn to think of the intermediary
links that can facilitate the transition from patriarchalism, from small

5 "Oblomovism" refers to Oblomov, the central character in Goncharov's
novel of the same name. Oblomov was incapable of action. He symbolized all
that was dreamy, slothful and ineffectual in old Russia. [*Ed.*]

production, to socialism. "We" still often keep repeating the argument that "capitalism is evil, socialism is good." But this argument is wrong, because it fails to take into account all the existing forms of economy and singles out only two of them.

Capitalism is evil compared with socialism. Capitalism is good compared with medievalism, compared with small production, compared with bureaucracy, which is connected with the fact that the small producers are scattered. Inasmuch as we are as yet unable to pass directly from small production to socialism, capitalism is inevitable to a certain degree as the elemental product of small production and exchange; and so, we must utilize capitalism (particularly by directing it into the channels of state capitalism) as the intermediary link between small production and socialism, as a means, a path, a method of increasing the productive forces.

Take the question of bureaucracy and glance at it from the economic aspect. In May, 1918, bureaucracy was not within our field of vision. Six months after the October Revolution, after we had smashed the old bureaucratic apparatus from top to bottom, we did not yet feel this evil.

Another year passed . . . a new Party program was adopted, and in this program we spoke forthrightly—of *"a partial revival of bureaucracy in the Soviet system"*—not fearing to admit the evil, but desiring to reveal it, to expose it, to pillory it, to awaken the thought and will, energy, and action to combat it.

Another two years passed. In the spring of 1921, after the Eighth Congress of Soviets (December 1920), which discussed the question of bureaucracy, and after the Tenth Congress of the Russian Communist Party (March 1921), which summed up the controversies that were closely connected with the analysis of bureaucracy, we see *this* evil confronting us more clearly, more distinctly, and more menacingly. What are the economic roots of bureaucracy? The roots are mostly dual in character: on the one hand, a developed bourgeoisie needs a bureaucratic apparatus, primarily a military apparatus, and then a judiciary, etc., to be used against the revolutionary movement of the workers (and partly of the peasants). This we have not got. Our courts are class courts directed against the bourgeoisie. Our army is a class army directed against the bourgeoisie. Bureaucracy is not in the army, but in the institutions that serve it. Bureaucracy in our country has a different economic root—the atomized and dispersed character of small production with its poverty, lack of culture, the absence of roads, illiteracy, absence of *exchange* between agriculture and industry, the absence of connection and interaction between them. To a large extent this is the result of the Civil War. When we were blockaded, besieged on all sides, cut off from the whole world and from the grain-bearing South, from Siberia, from the coal-fields, we could not restore industry. We had, unhesitatingly, to introduce War Communism, to dare to go to the most desperate extremes, to suffer an existence of semistarvation and worse than semistarvation, but to hold on at all costs, in spite of unprecedented ruin and the absence of economic intercourse, in order to save the workers' and peasants' rule. We did not allow ourselves to be frightened. . . . But what was a condition of victory in a blockaded country, in a besieged fortress, revealed its negative side precisely in the spring of 1921, when the last of the whiteguard forces were finally driven from the territory of . . . [Russia]. In the besieged fortress, it was possible and imperative to "lock up" all trade; with the masses displaying extraordinary heroism this could be borne for three years. After that, the ruin of the small producer still further increased, the restoration of large-scale industry was still further delayed, postponed. Bureaucracy, as a heritage of the "siege," as the superstructure built over the isolated and downtrodden state of the small producer, fully revealed itself.

We must learn to admit an evil fearlessly in order to combat it the more firmly, in order, again and again, to start from the beginning —we shall many times and in all spheres of our work have to start all over again from the beginning, finish what was left undone, and choose different methods of approach to a problem. There is obviously a delay in the restoration of large-scale industry, and the "locking up" of exchange between industry and agriculture has become intolerable. Consequently, we must concentrate on what is more accessible— the restoration of small industry, helping things from that side, propping up that side of the structure that has been half-demolished by the war and blockade. We must do everything possible to develop trade at all costs, without being afraid of capitalism, because the limits we have put to it (the expropriation of the landowners and of the bourgeoisie in the economy, the rule of the workers and peasants in politics) are sufficiently narrow, sufficiently "moderate." This is the fundamental idea of the tax in kind; this is its economic significance. . . .

Private capital in the role of helper of socialism—does that not seem paradoxical?

It is not paradoxical in the least; it is an irrefutable economic fact. Since we are dealing with a small-peasant country in which transport is in an extreme state of dislocation, a country that has just emerged from war and blockade, that is politically guided by the proletariat—which controls the transport system and large-scale industry—it inevitably follows, first, that at the present moment local exchange acquires first-class significance, and, second, that there is a possibility of assisting socialism by means of private capitalism (not to speak of state capitalism).

Less argument about words! We still have too much of this sort of thing. More variety in practical experience and more study of this experience! Under certain circumstances, the exemplary organization of local work, even on the smallest scale, is of far greater national importance than many branches of central state work. And these are precisely the circumstances that at present prevail in peasant farming in general, and in regard to the exchange of the surplus products of agriculture for industrial goods in particular. Exemplary organization in this respect, even in a single [district] . . . , is of far greater national importance than the "exemplary" improvement of the central apparatus of any People's Commissariat; our central apparatus has been built up during the past three and a half years to such an extent that it has managed to acquire a certain amount of harmful routine; we cannot improve it quickly to any extent; we do not know how to do it. Assistance in the work of radically improving it, in securing an influx of fresh forces, in combating bureaucracy effectively, and in overcoming this harmful routine must come from the localities, from the lower ranks, with the exemplary organization of something "whole," even if on a small scale. I say "whole" advisedly, that is, not one industry, not one branch of industry, not one factory, but the *totality* of economic relations, the *totality* of economic exchange, even if only in a small locality.

Those of us who are doomed to remain at work in the center will continue the task of improving the apparatus and purging it of bureaucracy, even if in modest and immediately achievable dimensions. But the greatest assistance in this task is coming, and will come, from the localities. Generally speaking, as far as I can observe, things are better in the localities than at the center; and this is understandable, for, naturally, the evil of bureaucracy concentrates at the center. In this respect Moscow cannot but be the worst city, and in general the worst "place," in the republic. In the localities we have deviations from the average to the good and the bad sides, the latter being less frequent than the former. The deviation to the bad side is shown by the abuses committed by former government officials, landlords, bourgeois, and other scum who have attached themselves to the Communists and who sometimes commit abominable outrages and acts of tyranny against the peasantry. Here there must be a terrorist purge, summary trial, and the firing squad. Let . . . nonparty philistines . . . beat their breasts and exclaim: "I thank Thee, Lord, that I am not as one of 'these,' that I have never recognized, nor do I recognize, terror." These simpletons "do not recognize terror" because they chose for themselves the role of servile accomplices of the whiteguards in fooling the workers and peasants. The Socialist-Revolutionaries and Mensheviks "do not recognize terror" because under the flag of "socialism" they are fulfilling their function of *placing* the masses *at the mercy of the whiteguard terror.* . . .

The deviation towards the good side is shown by the success achieved in combating bureaucracy, by the great attention shown for the needs of the workers and peasants, the great care devoted to developing the economy, raising the productivity of labor, and developing local exchange between agriculture and industry. Although the good examples are more numerous than the bad ones, they are, nevertheless, rare. Still, they are there. New, young, fresh communist forces, steeled by civil war and privations, are coming forward in all localities. We are still doing far too little to promote these forces regularly from lower to higher posts. This can and must be done more persistently, and on a wider scale than at present. Some workers can and should be transferred from work at the center to local work. As leading men [in localities] . . . , where they can organize economic work *as a whole,* on *exemplary* lines, they will do far more good, and perform work of far greater *national* importance, than by performing some function at the center. The exemplary organization of the work will help to train new workers and provide examples that other districts could follow with relative ease. We at the center could do a great deal to encourage the other districts all over the country to "follow" the good examples and even make it mandatory for them to do so.

By the way. As a small but nevertheless significant circumstance, note should be taken of the necessary change in our attitude to the problem of combating profiteering. We must foster "proper" trade, trade that does not evade state control; it is to our advantage to develop it. But profiteering, taken in its political-economic sense, *cannot* be distinguished from "proper" trade. Free trade is capitalism; capitalism is profiteering. It would be ridiculous to close our eyes to this.

What should we do. Declare profiteering to be no longer punishable?

No. We must revise and redraft all the laws on profiteering and declare all *thieving* and every direct or indirect, open or concealed *evasion of state control, supervision, and accounting* to be a punishable offense (and in fact prosecuted with redoubled severity). It is by presenting the question in this way . . . that we shall succeed in directing the inevitable, to a certain extent, and necessary development of capitalism into the channels of *state* capitalism.

Political Summary and Deductions

. . . Our Communists still do not have a sufficient understanding of their real duties of administration: they should not strive to do "everything themselves," wearing themselves out and failing to cope with everything, undertaking twenty jobs and finishing none. They should check up on the work of scores and hundreds of assistants, arrange to have their work checked up from below, that is, by the real masses. They should *direct* the work and *learn* from those who have knowledge (the experts) and experience in organizing large-scale production (the capitalists). A wise Communist will not be afraid of learning from a military expert, although nine-tenths of the military experts are capable of treachery at every opportunity. A wise Communist will not be afraid of learning from a capitalist (no matter whether that capitalist is a big capitalist concessionaire, or a commission agent, or a petty capitalist cooperator, etc.), although the capitalist is no better than the military expert. Did we not in the Red Army learn to catch treacherous military experts, to single out the honest and conscientious, and, on the whole, to utilize thousands and tens of thousands of military experts? We are learning to do the same (in an unconventional way) with engineers and teachers, although we are not doing it as well as we did it in the Red Army. . . . We shall learn to do the same (again in an unconventional way) with the commission agents, with the buyers who are working for the state, with the petty capitalist cooperators, with the entrepreneur concessionaires, etc.

The masses of workers and peasants need an immediate improvement of their conditions. By putting new forces, including nonparty forces, to useful work, we shall achieve this. The tax in kind, and a number of measures connected with it, will facilitate this. By this we shall cut at the economic root of the inevitable vacillations of the small producer. As for political vacillations . . . , we shall fight them ruthlessly. The waverers are many; we are few. The waverers are disunited; we are united. The waverers are not economically independent; the proletariat is. The waverers do not know what they want: they want to do something very badly, but . . . [they are prevented from doing it]. We know what we want.

And that is why we shall win.

Conclusion

To sum up.

The tax in kind is a transition from War Communism to the proper socialist exchange of products.

The extreme ruin rendered more acute by the crop failure in 1920 made this transition urgently necessary owing to the fact that it was impossible to restore large-scale industry rapidly.

Hence, the first thing to do is to improve the condition of the peasants. The means to this are the tax in kind, the development of exchange between agriculture and industry, the development of small industry.

Exchange is free trade; it is capitalism. It is useful to us inasmuch as it will help us overcome the dispersal of the small producer, and to a certain degree to combat bureaucracy; to what extent, will be determined by practical experience. The proletarian regime is in no danger as long as the proletariat firmly holds power in its hands, as long as it firmly holds transport and large-scale industry in its hands.

The fight against profiteering must be transformed into a fight against larceny and against the evasion of state supervision, accounting, and control. By means of this control we shall direct capitalism, which is to a certain extent inevitable and necessary for us, into the channels of state capitalism.

The fullest scope must be given for the development of local initiative and independent action in encouraging exchange between agriculture and industry—this must be done to the fullest extent and at all costs. The experience gained must be studied; and this experience must be made as varied as possible.

Assistance for small industry which serves peasant agriculture and helps to improve it—to some extent this assistance may be given in the form of raw materials from the state stocks. The most criminal thing would be to leave these raw materials unprocessed.

We must not be afraid of Communists "learning" from bourgeois experts, including merchants, petty capitalist cooperators, and capitalists, learning from them in the same way as we learned from the military experts, though in a different form. The results of "learning" must be tested only by practical experience, by doing things better than the bourgeois experts at your side; try this way and that to secure an improvement in agriculture and industry, and to develop exchange between them. Do not begrudge the price for "tuition." No tuition fee will be too high if only we learn something.

Do everything to help the masses of the working people, to come closer to them, to promote from their ranks hundreds and thousands of nonparty people for the work of economic administration. But those "nonparty" people who are nothing more nor less than Mensheviks and Socialist-Revolutionaries disguised in fashionable, nonparty attire, . . . should be carefully kept in prison, or packed off to Berlin, . . . so that they may freely enjoy all the charms of pure democracy and freely exchange ideas with . . . [those we have ousted].

THE IMPORTANCE OF GOLD NOW AND AFTER THE COMPLETE VICTORY OF SOCIALISM (NOVEMBER 1921)

THE BEST WAY to celebrate the anniversary of a great revolution is to concentrate attention on its unsolved problems. It is particularly appropriate and necessary to celebrate the revolution in this way at a time when we are faced with fundamental problems that the revolution has not yet solved; when we must master something new (from the point of view of what the revolution has accomplished up to now) for the solution of these problems.

What is new for our revolution at the present time is the need to resort to a "reformist," gradual, cautious, and roundabout mode of operation in solving the fundamental problems of economic development. This "novelty" gives rise to a number of questions, perplexities, and doubts in both theory and practice.

A theoretical question. How can we explain the transition from a series of extremely revolutionary actions to extremely "reformist" actions in the same field at a time when the revolution as a whole is making victorious progress? Does this not imply a "surrender of positions," an "admission of defeat," or something of that sort? Of course, our enemies—from the semifeudal type of reactionaries to the Mensheviks . . .—say that it does. They would not be enemies if they did not shout something of this sort on every pretext, and even without any pretext. The touching unanimity that prevails on this question among all parties, from the feudal reactionaries to the Mensheviks, is only further proof that opposed to the proletarian revolution is the "one reactionary mass" of all these parties. . . .

But there is some "perplexity" among friends too.

Restore large-scale industry, organize the direct interchange of its output for the produce of small-peasant farming, and thus assist the socialization of the latter. For the purpose of restoring large-scale industry, borrow from the peasants a certain quantity of foodstuffs and raw materials by means of the surplus-appropriation system—this was the plan (or method, system) that we followed for more than three years, up to the spring of 1921. This was a revolutionary approach to the problem, namely, to proceed at once to break up the old social-economic system completely and to substitute a new one for it.

Since the spring of 1921, instead of this approach, plan, method, or mode of action, we have been adopting (we have not yet "adopted" but are still "adopting," and we have not yet fully realized this) a totally different method, a reformist type of method: not to *break up* the old social-economic system—trade, small production, small proprietorship, capitalism—but to *revive* trade, small proprietorship, capitalism, while cautiously and gradually getting the upper hand over them, or creating the possibility of subjecting them to state regulation *only to the extent* that they revive.

This is quite a different approach to the problem.

Compared with the previous, revolutionary, approach, this is a reformist approach (revolution is a change which breaks the old order to its very foundations, and not one that cautiously, slowly, and gradually remodels it, taking care to break as little as possible).

The question that arises is this. If, after trying revolutionary methods, you find they have failed and adopt reformist methods, does this not prove that you are declaring the revolution to have been a mistake in general? Does it not prove that you should not have started with the revolution but should have started with and confined yourselves to reforms?

This is the conclusion that is drawn by the Mensheviks and others like them. But this conclusion is either sophistry and simply a fraud perpetrated by hardened politicians, or the childishness of political tyros. The greatest, perhaps the only danger for the genuine revolutionary is that of extreme revolutionism, ignoring the limits and conditions in which revolutionary methods are appropriate and can be successfully employed. Genuine revolutionaries have come a cropper most often when they began to write "revolution" with a capital R, to elevate "revolution" to something almost divine, to lose their heads, to lose the ability to reflect, weigh, and ascertain in the coolest and most dispassionate manner at what moment, under what circumstances, and in which sphere of action it is necessary to act in a revolutionary manner, and at what moment, under what circumstances and in which sphere it is necessary to apply reformist action. Genuine revolutionaries will perish (not that they will be defeated from outside, but that their work will suffer internal collapse) only if they abandon their sober outlook and take it into their heads that the "great, victorious world" revolution can and must solve all problems in a revolution manner under all circumstances and in all spheres of action. If they do this, their doom is certain.

Whoever gets such ideas into his head, must perish, because he has foolish ideas about a fundamental problem; and in a fierce war (and revolution is the fiercest sort of war) the penalty for folly is defeat.

What grounds are there for assuming that the "great, victorious world" revolution can and must employ only revolutionary methods? There are none at all. It is absolutely untrue, and if we stick to Marxism it can be proved by purely theoretical propositions. The experience of our revolution also shows this is a fallacy. From the theoretical point of view—foolish things are done in time of revolution just as at any other time, said Engels, and he was right. We must try to do as few foolish things as possible and rectify those that are done as quickly as possible; we must estimate as soberly as possible which problems can be solved by revolutionary methods at any given time and which cannot. From the point of view of our own practical experience—the Brest Peace was an example of action that was not revolutionary at all; it was reformist, and even worse, because it was a retreat, whereas, as a general rule, reformist action advances slowly, cautiously, gradually, and does not move backwards. The proof that our tactics in signing the Brest Peace were correct is now so complete, is so evident to all and generally admitted, that there is no need to say any more about it.

Our revolution has completed only its bourgeois-democratic work; and we can be legitimately proud of this. The proletarian or socialist part of its work may be summed up in three main points: (1) The revolutionary emergence from the imperialist world war; the exposure and *halting* of the slaughter organized by the two world groups of capitalist predators. Our part of this we accomplished in full; it could have been accomplished in all parts only by a revolution in a number of advanced countries. (2) The creation of the Soviet system, the form in which the dictatorship of the proletariat is effected. This epoch-making change has been made. The era of bourgeois-democratic parliamentarism has come to an end. A new chapter in world history—the era of proletarian dictatorship—has been started. The Soviet system and all forms of proletarian dictatorship will have the finishing touches put to them and be completed only by the efforts of a number of countries. There is still a great deal we have not done in this field. It would be unpardonable to lose sight of this. Again and again we shall have to put the finishing touches to the work, re-do it, start from the beginning. Every step forward and upward that we take in developing our productive forces and our culture must be accompanied by the work of finishing and altering our Soviet system, for we are still low in the scale of economics and culture. Much will have to be altered, and to be "embarrassed" by this would be the height of folly (if not something worse than folly). (3) The creation of the economic basis of the socialist system. This has not yet been completed in the main, fundamental aspects, but it is our surest foundation, surest from the point of view of principle and from the practical point of view, from the point of view of [Russia] . . . today and from the international point of view.

Since the main features of this basis have not yet been completed, we must concentrate all our attention upon it. The difficulty here lies in the form of the transition.

In April 1918, . . . I wrote:

"It is not enough to be a revolutionary and an adherent of socialism or a Communist in general. You must be able at each particular moment to find the particular link in the chain which you must grasp with all your might in order to hold the whole chain and to prepare firmly for the transition to the next link; the order of the links, their form, the manner in which they are linked together, their difference from each other in the historical chain of events are not as simple and not as senseless as those in an ordinary chain made by a smith."

At the present time, in the sphere of activity with which we are dealing, this link is the revival of home *trade* under proper state regulation (direction). Trade—that is the "link" in the historical chain of events, in the transitional forms of our socialist construction in 1921–1922, which we, the proletarian state, we, the leading Communist Party, "*must grasp with all our might.*" If we "grasp" this link firmly enough *now* we shall certainly control the *whole* chain in the very near future. If we do not, we shall not control the whole chain; we shall not create the foundation for socialist social and economic relations.

Communism and trade?! It sounds strange. The two seem to be unconnected, incongruous, remote from each other. But if we study it from the point of view of *economics,* we shall find that the one is no more remote from the other than communism is from small-peasant, patriarchal agriculture.

When we are victorious on a world scale, I think we shall use gold for the purpose of building public lavatories in the streets of some of the largest cities of the world. This would be the most "just" and most educational way of utilizing gold for the benefit of those generations which have not forgotten how, for the sake of gold, ten million men were killed and thirty million maimed in the "great war for freedom," in the war of 1914–1918, in the war that was waged to decide the great question of which peace was the worst, the Brest Peace or the Versailles Peace; and how, for the sake of this gold, they certainly intend to kill twenty million men and to maim sixty million in a war, say, in 1925 or 1928, between, say, Japan and America, or between Britain and America, or something like that.

But however "just," useful, or humane it would be to utilize gold for this purpose, we nevertheless say: let us work for another decade or two with the same intensity and with the same success as in the 1917–1921 period, only in a much wider field, in order to reach this stage. Meanwhile, we must save the gold in [Russia] . . . , sell it at the highest price, buy goods with it at the lowest price. "When you live among wolves, you must howl like a wolf." As for exterminating all the wolves, as should be done in a rational human society, we shall act up to the wise Russian proverb: "Boast not before but after the battle."

Trade is the only possible economic link between the scores of millions of small farmers and large-scale industry *if* . . . *if* there is not alongside these farmers an excellently equipped large-scale machine industry linked up by a network of electric cables, an industry well enough equipped technically, with its organizational "superstructures" and accompanying accessories, to be able to supply the small farmers with the best goods in larger quantities more quickly and more cheaply than before. On a world scale this "if" *has already been achieved*, this condition already exists. But the country, formerly one of the most backward capitalist countries, which tried alone directly and at one stroke to create, to put into use, to organize practically the *new* links between industry and agriculture, failed to achieve this task by "direct assault" and must now try to achieve it by a number of slow, gradual, and cautious "siege" operations.

The proletarian state can control trade, direct it into definite channels, keep it within certain limits. I shall quote a small, a very small example: in the Donets Basin a slight, still very slight, but undoubted economic revival has commenced, partly due to an increase in the productivity of labor at the large state mines, and partly due to the leasing of small-peasant mines. As a result the proletarian state is receiving a small quantity (a miserably small quantity compared with what is obtained in the advanced countries, but an appreciable quantity considering our poverty-stricken condition) of extra coal at a cost of, say, 100; and it is selling this coal to various government departments at a price of, say, 120, and to private people at a price of, say, 140. (I must say in parenthesis that my figures are quite arbitrary, first because I do not know the exact figures, and, second, I would not now make them public even if I did.) This looks as if we are *beginning*, if only in very modest dimensions, to control *trade* between industry and agriculture, to control wholesale trade, to cope with the task of taking in hand the available, small, backward industry, or large-scale but enfeebled and ruined industry; of reviving trade on the *present* economic basis; of making the ordinary, average peasant (and this is the typical peasant, representative of the masses and the vehicle of anarchy) feel the benefit of the economic revival; of taking advantage of it for the purpose of more systematically and persistently, more widely and successfully, restoring large-scale industry.

We shall not surrender to "sentimental socialism" or to the old Russian, semiaristocratic, semimuzhik, and patriarchal mood, with their supreme contempt for trade. We can use, and, since it is necessary, we *must* learn to use, all transitional economic forms for the purpose of strengthening the link between the peasantry and the proletariat, for the purpose of immediately reviving the economy of our ruined and tormented country, of reviving industry, and facilitating future, more extensive, and more deep-going measures like electrification.

Only Marxism has precisely and correctly defined the relation of reforms to revolution. However, Marx was able to see this relation only from one aspect, namely, under the conditions preceding the first to any extent permanent and lasting victory of the proletariat, if only in one country. Under those conditions, the basis of the proper relation was: reforms are a by-product of the revolutionary class struggle of the proletariat. In the capitalist world this relation is the foundation of the revolutionary tactics of the proletariat—the ABC, which is being distorted and obscured by the corrupt leaders of the Second International. . . . After the victory of the proletariat, if only in one country, something new enters into the relation between reforms and revolution. In principle, it is the same as before, but a change in form takes place, which Marx himself could not foresee, but which can be appreciated only on the basis of the philosophy and politics of Marxism. Why were we able to carry out the Brest retreat successfully? Because we had advanced so far that we had room in which to retreat. At such dizzy speed, *in a few weeks*, from October 25, 1917, to the Brest Peace, we built up the Soviet state, withdrew from the imperialist war in a revolutionary manner and completed the bourgeois-democratic revolution so that *even* the great backward movement (the Brest Peace) left us sufficient room in which to take advantage of the "respite" and to march forward victoriously. . . .

Before the victory of the proletariat, reforms are a by-product of the revolutionary class struggle. After the victory (while still remaining a "by-product" on an international scale) they are, in addition, for the country in which victory has been achieved, a necessary and legitimate respite in those cases when, after the utmost exertion of effort, it becomes obvious that sufficient strength is lacking for the revolutionary accomplishment of some transition or another. Victory creates such a "reserve of strength" that it is possible to hold out even in a forced retreat, hold out both materially and morally. Holding out materially means preserving a sufficient superiority of forces to prevent the enemy from inflicting utter defeat. Holding out morally means not allowing oneself to become demoralized and disorganized, keeping a sober view of the situation, preserving vigor and firmness of spirit, even making a long retreat, but within bounds, and in such a way as to stop the retreat in time, and again return to the offensive.

We retreated to state capitalism, but we retreated within bounds. We are now retreating to the state regulation of trade, but we shall retreat within bounds. Signs are already visible that the retreat is coming to an end; the prospect of stopping this retreat in the not too distant future is dawning. The more conscious, the more unanimous, the more free from prejudice we are in carrying out this necessary retreat, the sooner shall we be able to stop it, and the more lasting, speedy, and extensive will our subsequent victorious advance be.

ON COOPERATION
(JANUARY 1923)

I

IT SEEMS to me that not enough attention is being paid to the cooperative movement in our country. Not everyone understands that now, since the time of the October Revolution and quite apart from NEP (on the contrary, in this connection we must say—because of NEP), our cooperative movement has become one of great significance. There is a lot of fantasy in the dreams of the old cooperators. Often they are ridiculously fantastic. But why are they fantastic? Because people do not understand the fundamental, the rock-bottom significance of the working-class political struggle for the overthrow of the rule of the exploiters. We have overthrown the rule of the exploiters, and much that was fantastic, even romantic, even banal in the dreams of the old cooperators is now becoming unvarnished reality.

Indeed, since political power is in the hands of the working class, since this political power owns all the means of production, the only task, indeed, that remains for us is to organize the population in cooperatives societies. With most of the population organized in cooperatives, the socialism which in the past was legitimately treated with ridicule, scorn, and contempt by those who were rightly convinced that it was necessary to wage the class struggle, the struggle for political power, etc., will achieve its aim automatically. But not all comrades realize how vastly, how infinitely important it is now to organize the population of Russia in cooperative societies. By adopting NEP we made a concession to the peasant as a trader, to the principle of private trade; it is precisely for this reason (contrary to what some people think) that the cooperative movement is of such immense importance. All we actually need under NEP is to organize the population of Russia in cooperative societies on a sufficiently large scale, for we have now found that degree of combination of private interest, private commercial interest, with state supervision and control of this interest, that degree of its subordination to the common interests which was formerly the stumbling-block for very many socialists. Indeed, the power of the state over all large-scale means of production, political power in the hands of the proletariat, the alliance of this proletariat with the many millions of small and very small peasants, the assured proletarian leadership of the peasantry, etc.—is this not all that is necessary to build a complete socialist society out of co-operatives, out of cooperatives alone, which we formerly ridiculed as huckstering and which from a certain aspect we have the right to treat as such now, under NEP? Is this not all that is necessary to build a complete socialist society? It is still not the building of socialist society, but it is all that is necessary and sufficient for it.

It is this very circumstance that is underestimated by many of our practical workers. They look down upon our cooperative societies and do not appreciate their exceptional importance, first, from the stand-point of principle (the means of production are owned by the state), and, second, from the standpoint of transition to the new order by means that are the *simplest, easiest, and most acceptable to the peasant*.

But this again is of fundamental importance. It is one thing to draw up fantastic plans for building socialism through all sorts of workers' associations, and quite another thing to learn to build so-cialism in practice in such a way that *every* small peasant may take part in it. That is the stage we have now reached. And there is no doubt that, having reached it, we are taking too little advantage of it.

We went too far when we introduced NEP, but not because we attached too much importance to the principle of free industry and trade—we went too far because we lost sight of the cooperatives, be-cause we now underrate the cooperatives, because we are already be-ginning to forget the vast importance of the cooperatives from the above two points of view.

I now propose to discuss with the reader what can and must at once be done practically on the basis of this "cooperative" principle. By what means can we, and must we, start at once to develop this "cooperative" principle so that its socialist meaning may be clear to all?

Cooperation must be politically so organized that it will not only generally and always enjoy certain privileges, but that these privileges should be of a purely material nature (a favorable bank-rate, etc.). The cooperatives must be granted state loans that are greater, if only by a little, than the loans we grant to private enterprises, even to heavy industry, etc.

Every social system arises only if it has the financial backing of a definite class. There is no need to mention the hundreds of millions of rubles that the birth of "free" capitalism cost. At present we must realize that the social system to which we must now give more than ordinary assistance is the cooperative system, and we must actually give that assistance. But it must be assistance in the real sense of the word, that is, it will not be enough to interpret it to mean assistance for any kind of cooperative trade; by assistance we must mean aid to cooperative trade in which *really large masses of the population really take part*. It is certainly a correct form of assistance to give a bonus to peasants who take part in cooperative trade; but the whole point is to verify the nature of this participation, to verify the awareness behind it, and to verify its quality. Strictly speaking, when a cooperator goes to a village and opens a cooperative store, the people take no part in this whatever; but at the same time, guided by their own interests, the people will hasten to try to take part in it.

There is another aspect to this question. From the point of view of the "civilized" (primarily, literate) European there is not much left for us to do to induce absolutely everyone to take not a passive but an active part in cooperative operations. Strictly speaking, there is *"only"* one thing we have left to do, and that is, to make our people so "civilized" that they understand all the advantages of everybody participating in the work of the cooperatives, and organize this participation. *"Only"* that. There are now no other devices needed to advance to socialism. But to achieve this "only," there must be a veritable revolution—the entire people must go through a period of cultural development. Therefore, our rule must be: as little philosophizing and as few acrobatics as possible. In this respect NEP is an advance, because it is adjustable to the level of the most ordinary peasant and does not demand anything higher of him. But it will take a whole historical epoch to get the entire population into the work of the cooperatives through NEP. At best we can achieve this in one or two decades. Nevertheless it will be a distinct historical epoch, and without this historical epoch, without universal literacy, without a proper degree of efficiency, without training the population sufficiently to acquire the habit of book-reading, and without the material basis for this, without a certain sufficiency to safeguard against, say, bad harvests, famine, etc.—without this we shall not achieve our object. The thing now is to learn to combine the wide revolutionary range of action, the revolutionary enthusiasm which we have displayed, and displayed sufficiently, and crowned with complete success—to learn to combine this with (I am almost inclined to say) the ability to be an efficient and capable trader, which is fully sufficient to be a good cooperator. By ability to be a trader I mean the ability to be a cultured trader. Let those Russians, or plain peasants, who imagine that since they trade they are good traders, get that well into their heads. This does not follow at all. They do trade, but that is far from being cultured traders. They now trade in an Asiatic manner, but to be a trader one must trade in the European manner. They are a whole epoch behind in that.

In conclusion: a number of economic, financial, and banking privileges must be granted to the cooperatives—this is the way our socialist state must promote the new principle on which the population must be organized. But this is only the general outline of the task; it does not define and depict in detail the entire content of the practical task, that is, we must find what form of "bonus" to give for joining the cooperatives (and the terms on which we should give it), the form of bonus by which we shall assist the cooperatives sufficiently, the form of bonus that will produce the civilized cooperator. And given social ownership of the means of production, given the class victory of the proletariat over the bourgeoisie, the system of civilized cooperators is the system of socialism. . . .

II

Whenever I wrote about the New Economic Policy I always quoted the article on state capitalism which I wrote in 1918. This has more than once aroused doubts in the minds of certain young comrades. But their doubts were mainly on abstract political points.

It seemed to them that the term state capitalism could not be applied to a system under which the means of production were owned by the working class, a working class that held political power. They did not notice, however, that I used the term "state capitalism," *first,* to connect historically our present position with the position adopted in my controversy with the so-called Left Communists; also, I argued at that time that state capitalism would be superior to our existing economy. It was important for me to show the continuity between ordinary state capitalism and the unusual, even very unusual, state capitalism to which I referred in introducing the reader to the New Economic Policy. *Second,* the practical purpose was always important to me. And the practical purpose of our New Economic Policy was to lease out concessions. In the prevailing circumstances, concessions in our country would unquestionably have been a pure type of state capitalism. That is how I argued about state capitalism.

But there is another aspect of the matter for which we may need state capitalism, or at least a comparison with it. That is the question of cooperatives.

In the capitalist state, cooperatives are no doubt collective capitalist institutions. Nor is there any doubt that under our present economic conditions, when we combine private capitalist enterprises—but in no other way than on nationalized land and in no other way than under the control of the working-class state—with enterprises of a consistently socialist type (the means of production, the land on which the enterprises are situated, and the enterprises as a whole belonging to the state), the question arises about a third type of enterprise, the cooperatives, which were not formerly regarded as an independent type differing in principle from the others. Under private capitalism, cooperative enterprises differ from capitalist enterprises as collective enterprises differ from private enterprises. Under state capitalism, cooperative enterprises differ from state-capitalist enterprises, first, because they are private enterprises, and, second, because they are collective enterprises. Under our present system, cooperative enterprises differ from private capitalist enterprises because they are collective enterprises but do not differ from socialist enterprises if the land on which they are situated and the means of production belong to the state, that is, the working class.

This circumstance is not considered sufficiently when cooperatives are discussed. It is forgotten that owing to the special features of our political system, our cooperatives acquire an altogether exceptional significance. If we exclude concessions, which, incidentally, have not developed on any considerable scale, cooperation under our conditions nearly always coincides fully with socialism.

Let me explain what I mean. Why were the plans of the old cooperators, from Robert Owen [1] onwards, fantastic? Because they dreamed of peacefully remodeling contemporary society into socialism without taking account of such fundamental questions as the class struggle, the capture of political power by the working class, the overthrow of the rule of the exploiting class. That is why we are right in regarding as entirely fantastic this "cooperative" socialism, and as romantic, and even banal, the dream of transforming class enemies into class collaborators and class war into class peace (so-called civil peace) by merely organizing the population in cooperative societies.

Undoubtedly we were right from the point of view of the fundamental task of the present day, for socialism cannot be established without a class struggle for political power in the state.

But see how things have changed now that political power is in the hands of the working class, now that the political power of the exploiters is overthrown and all the means of production (except those which the workers' state voluntarily abandons conditionally and for a certain time to the exploiters in the form of concessions) are owned by the working class.

Now we are entiled to say that for us the mere growth of cooperation (with the "slight" exception mentioned above) is identical with the growth of socialism, and at the same time we have to admit that there has been a radical modification in our whole outlook on socialism. The radical modification is this; formerly we placed, and had to place, the main emphasis on the political struggle, on revolution, on winning power, etc. Now the emphasis is changing and shifting to peaceful, organization, "cultural" work. I should say that

---

1   Robert Owen (1771–1858) British industrialist and social experimenter who was instrumental in establishing cooperative communities in Britain and the United States. [*Ed.*]

emphasis was shifting to educational work, were it not for our international relations, were it not for the fact that we have to fight for our position on a world scale. If we leave that aside, however, and confine ourselves to internal economic relations, the emphasis in our work is certainly shifting to education.

Two main tasks confront us, which constitute the epoch—to reorganize our machinery of state, which is utterly useless, and which we took over in its entirety from the preceding epoch; during the past five years of struggle we did not, and could not, drastically reorganize it. Our second task is educational work among the peasants. And the economic object of this educational work among the peasants is to organize the latter in cooperative societies. If the whole of the peasantry had been organized in cooperatives, we would by now have been standing with both feet on the soil of socialism. But the organization of the entire peasantry in cooperative societies presupposes a standard of culture among the peasants (precisely among the peasants as the overwhelming mass) that cannot, in fact, be achieved without a cultural revolution.

Our opponents told us repeatedly that we were rash in undertaking to implant socialism in an insufficiently cultured country. But they were misled by our having started from the end opposite to that prescribed by theory (the theory of pedants of all kinds), because in our country the political and social revolution preceded the cultural revolution, that very cultural revolution which nevertheless now confronts us.

This cultural revolution would now suffice to make our country a completely socialist country; but it presents immense difficulties of a purely cultural (for we are illiterate) and material character (for to be cultured we must achieve a certain development of the material means of production, must have a certain material base).

OUR REVOLUTION
(JANUARY 1923)

Apropos of N. Sukhanov's Notes

1

I HAVE lately been glancing through Sukhanov's [1] notes on the revolution. What strikes one most is the pedantry of all our petty-bourgeois democrats and of all the heroes of the Second International. Apart from the fact that they are all extremely faint-hearted, that when it comes to the minutest deviation from the German model even the best of them fortify themselves with reservations—apart from this characteristic, which is common to all petty-bourgeois democrats and has been abundantly manifested by them throughout the revolution, what strikes one is their slavish imitation of the past.

They all call themselves Marxists, but their conception of Marxism is impossibly pedantic. They have completely failed to understand what is decisive in Marxism, namely, its revolutionary dialectics. They have even absolutely failed to understand Marx's plain statements that in times of revolution the utmost flexibility is demanded and have even failed to notice, for instance, the statements Marx made in his letters—I think it was in 1856—expressing the hope of combining a peasant war in Germany, which might create a revolutionary situation, with the working-class movement—they avoid even this plain statement and walk round and about it like a cat around a bowl of hot porridge.

Their conduct betrays them as cowardly reformists who are afraid to deviate from the bourgeoisie, let alone break with it, and at the same time they disguise their cowardice with the wildest rhetoric and braggartry. But what strikes one in all of them even from the purely theoretical point of view is their utter inability to grasp the following Marxist considerations: up to now they have seen capitalism and bourgeois democracy in Western Europe follow a definite path of develop-

___

1   N. N. Sukhanov, Russian historian and member of the Menshevik faction of the Russian Social-Democratic Labor Party. [*Ed.*]

ment and cannot conceive that this path can be taken as a model only *mutatis mutandis*, only with certain amendments (quite insignificant from the standpoint of the general development of world history).

First—the revolution connected with the first imperialist world war. Such a revolution was bound to reveal new features, or variations, resulting from the war itself, for the world has never seen such a war in such a situation. We find that since the war the bourgeoisie of the wealthiest countries have to this day been unable to restore "normal" bourgeois relations. Yet our reformists—petty bourgeois who make a show of being revolutionaries—believed, and still believe, that normal bourgeois relations are the limit (thus far shalt thou go and no farther). And even their conception of "normal" is extremely stereotyped and narrow.

Second, they are complete strangers to the idea that while the development of world history as a whole follows general laws it is by no means precluded, but, on the contrary, presumed, that certain periods of development may display peculiarities in either the form or the sequence of this development. For instance, it does not even occur to them that because Russia stands on the borderline between the civilized countries and the countries which this war has for the first time definitely brought into the orbit of civilization—all the Oriental, non-European countries—she could and was, indeed, bound to reveal certain distinguishing features; although these, of course, are in keeping with the general line of world development, they distinguish her revolution from those which took place in the West-European countries and introduce certain partial innovations as the revolution moves on to the countries of the East.

Infinitely stereotyped, for instance, is the argument they learned by rote during the development of West-European Social-Democracy, namely, that we are not yet ripe for socialism, that, as certain "learned" gentlemen among them put it, the objective economic premises for socialism do not exist in our country. It does not occur to any of them to ask: but what about a people that found itself in a revolutionary situation such as that created during the first imperialist war? Might it not, influenced by the hopelessness of its situation, fling itself into a struggle that would offer it at least some chance of securing conditions for the further development of civilization that were somewhat unusual?

"The development of the productive forces of Russia has not attained the level that makes socialism possible." All the heroes of the Second International, including, of course, Sukhanov, beat the drums about this proposition. They keep harping on this incontrovertible proposition in a thousand different keys and think that it is the decisive criterion of our revolution.

But what if the situation, which drew Russia into the imperialist world war that involved every more or less influential West-European country and made her a witness of the eve of the revolutions maturing or already partly begun in the East, gave rise to circumstances that put Russia and her development in a position which enabled us to achieve precisely that combination of a "peasant war" with the working-class movement suggested in 1856 by no less a Marxist than Marx himself as a possible prospect for Prussia?

What if the complete hopelessness of the situation, by stimulating the efforts of the workers and peasants tenfold, offered us the opportunity to create the fundamental requisites of civilization in a different way from that of the West-European countries? Has that altered the general line of development of world history? Has that altered the basic relations between the basic classes of all the countries that are being, or have been, drawn into the general course of world history?

If a definite level of culture is required for the building of socialism (although nobody can say just what that definite "level of culture" is, for it differs in every West-European country), why cannot we begin by first achieving the prerequisites for that definite level of culture in a revolutionary way, and *then*, with the aid of the workers' and peasants' government and the Soviet system, proceed to overtake the other nations?

II

You say that civilization is necessary for the building of socialism. Very good. But why could we not first create such prerequisites of civilization in our country as the expulsion of the landowners and the Russian capitalists, and then start moving towards socialism? Where, in what books, have you read that such variations of the customary historical sequence of events are impermissible or impossible?

Napoleon, I think, wrote: "*On s'engage et puis . . . on voit.*" Rendered freely this means: "First engage in a serious battle and then see what happens." Well, we did first engage in a serious battle in October 1917 and then saw such details of development (from the standpoint of world history they were certainly details) as the Brest peace, the New Economic Policy, and so forth. And now there can be no doubt that in the main we have been victorious.

Our Sukhanovs, not to mention Social-Democrats still farther to the right, never even dream that revolutions could be made otherwise. Our European philistines never even dream that the subsequent revolutions in Oriental countries, which possess much vaster populations and a much vaster diversity of social conditions, will undoubtedly display even greater distinctions than the Russian revolution.

It need hardly be said that a textbook written on Kautskian lines was a very useful thing in its day. But it is time, for all that, to abandon the idea that it foresaw all the forms of development of subsequent world history. It would be timely to say that those who think so are simply fools.

BETTER FEWER, BUT BETTER
(MARCH 1923)

IN THE MATTER of improving our state apparatus, the Workers' and Peasants' Inspection [1] should not, in my opinion, either strive after quantity or hurry. We have so far been able to devote so little thought and attention to the quality of our state apparatus that it would now be quite legitimate if we took special care to secure its thorough organization, and concentrated in the Workers' and Peasants' Inspection a staff of workers really abreast of the times, that is, not inferior to the best West-European standards. For a socialist republic this condition is, of course, too modest. But our experience of the first five years has fairly crammed our heads with mistrust and scepticism. These qualities assert themselves involuntarily when, for example, we hear people dilating at too great length and too flippantly on "proletarian culture." For a start, we should be satisfied with real bourgeois culture, for a start, we should be glad to dispense with the cruder types of prebourgeois culture, that is, bureaucratic culture or serf culture, etc. In matters of culture, haste and sweeping measures are most harmful. Many of our young writers and Communists should get this well into their heads.

Thus, in the matter of our state apparatus we should now draw the conclusion from our past experience that it would be better to proceed more slowly.

Our state apparatus is so deplorable, not to say disgusting, that we must first think very carefully how to combat its defects, bearing in mind that these defects are rooted in the past, which, although it has been overthrown, has not yet been overcome, has not yet reached the stage of a culture that has receded into the distant past. I say culture deliberately, because in these matters we can only regard as

---

1 The People's Commissariat of Workers' and Peasants' Inspection was established early in 1920 to provide a broadly based instrument of state control. Its staff was elected from the ranks of the proletariat and the peasantry and its task was to "struggle with bureaucratism and corruption in Soviet institutions." Although Lenin supported the creation of the Commissariat, by 1922 he had become thoroughly disgusted with its operation in practice. [*Ed.*]

achieved what has become part and parcel of our culture of our social
life, our habits. We might say that the good in our social system has
not been properly studied, understood, and taken to heart; it has been
hastily grasped at; it has not been verified or tested, tried by experience, and not made durable, etc. Of course, it could not be otherwise
in a revolutionary epoch, when development proceeded at such break-
neck speed that in a matter of five years we passed from tsarism to
the Soviet system.

It is time we did something about it. We must show sound scepticism for too rapid progress, for boastfulness, etc. We must give
thought to testing the forward steps we proclaim every hour, take
every minute, and then prove every second that they are flimsy, superficial, and misunderstood. The most harmful thing here would be
haste. The most harmful thing would be to rely on the assumption
that we know at least something, or that we have any considerable
number of elements necessary for the building of a really new state
apparatus, one really worthy to be called socialist, Soviet, etc.

No, we are ridiculously deficient of such an apparatus, and even
of the elements of it, and we must remember that we should not stint
time on building it, and that it will take many, many years.

What elements have we for building this apparatus? Only two.
First, the workers who are absorbed in the struggle for socialism.
These elements are not sufficiently educated. They would like to build
a better apparatus for us, but they do not know how. They cannot
build one. They have not yet developed the culture required for this;
and it *is* culture that is required. Nothing will be achieved in this by
doing things in a rush, by assault, by vim or vigor, or in general, by
any other of the best human qualities. Second, we have elements of
knowledge, education, and training, but they are ridiculously little
compared with all other countries.

Here we must not forget that we are too prone to compensate (or
imagine that we can compensate) our lack of knowledge by zeal,
haste, etc.

To renovate our state apparatus we must at all costs set out, first,
to learn, second, to learn, and third, to learn, and then to see to it
that learning shall not remain a dead letter or a fashionable catch-
phrase (and we should admit in all frankness that this happens very
often with us), that learning shall really become part of our very
being, that it shall actually and fully become a constituent element of
our social life. In short, we must not make the demands that are
made by the bourgeoisie of Western Europe, but demands that are fit
and proper for a country which has set out to develop into a socialist
country.

The conclusions to be drawn from the above are the following:
we must make the Workers' and Peasants' Inspection a really exem-

plary institution as the instrument to improve our state apparatus.

In order that it may attain the desired high level, we must follow the rule: "Measure your cloth seven times before you cut."

For this purpose, we must utilize the very best of what there is in our social system and utilize it with the greatest caution, thoughtfulness, and knowledge to build up the new People's Commissariat.

For this purpose, the best elements that we have in our social system—such as, first, the advanced workers, and, second, the really enlightened elements for whom we can vouch that they will not take the word for the deed and will not utter a single word that goes against their conscience—should not shrink from admitting difficulties and should not shrink from any struggle in order to achieve the object they have seriously set themselves.

We have been bustling for five years trying to improve our state apparatus, but it has been mere bustle, which has proved useless in these five years, or even futile, or even harmful. This bustle created the impression that we were doing something, but in effect it was only clogging up our institutions and our brains.

It is high time things were changed.

We must follow the rule: Better fewer, but better. We must follow the rule: Better get good human material in two or even three years than work in haste without hope of getting any at all.

I know that it will be hard to keep to this rule and apply it under our conditions. I know that the opposite rule will force its way through a thousand loopholes. I know that enormous resistance will have to be put up, that devilish persistence will be required, that in the first few years at least, work in this field will be hellishly hard. Nevertheless, I am convinced that only by such effort shall we be able to achieve our aim; and that only by achieving this aim shall we create a republic that is really worthy of the name of Soviet, socialist, and so on and so forth. . . .

I think that the time has at last come when we must work in real earnest to improve our state apparatus, and in this there can scarcely be anything more harmful than haste. That is why I would utter a strong warning against inflating [statistics]. . . . In my opinion, we should, on the contrary, be especially sparing with figures in this matter. Let us say frankly that the People's Commissariat of the Workers' and Peasants' Inspection does not at present enjoy the slightest authority. Everybody knows that no other institutions are worse organized than those of our Workers' and Peasants' Inspection, and that under present conditions nothing can be expected from this People's Commissariat. We must have this firmly fixed in our minds if we really want to create within a few years an institution that will, first, be an exemplary institution, second, win everybody's absolute confidence, and third, prove to all and sundry that we have really justified the work of such a highly placed institution as the Central Control Commission. In my opinion, we must immediately and irrevocably reject all general figures for the size of office staffs. We must select employees for the Workers' and Peasants' Inspection with particular care and only on the basis of the strictest test. Indeed, what is the use of establishing a People's Commissariat which carries on no matter what, which does not enjoy the slightest confidence, and whose word carries scarcely any weight? I think that our main object in launching the work of reconstruction that we now have in mind is to avoid all this.

The workers whom we are enlisting as members of the Central Control Commission must be irreproachable Communists, and I think that a great deal has yet to be done to teach them the methods and objects of their work. Furthermore, there must be a definite number of secretaries to assist in this work, who must be put to a triple test before they are appointed to their posts. Last, the officials whom in exceptional cases we shall accept directly as employees of the Workers' and Peasants' Inspection must conform to the following requirements:

First, they must be recommended by several Communists.

Second, they must pass a test for knowledge of our state apparatus.

Third, they must pass a test in the fundamentals of the theory of our state apparatus, in the fundamentals of management, office routine, etc.

Fourth, they must work in such close harmony with the members of the Central Control Commission and with their own secretariat that we could vouch for the work of the whole apparatus.

I know that these requirements envisage extraordinarily big conditions, and I am very much afraid that the majority of the "practical" workers in the Workers' and Peasants' Inspection will say that these conditions are impracticable or will scoff at them. But I ask any of the present chiefs of the Workers' and Peasants' Inspection, or anyone associated with that body, whether they can honestly tell me the practical purpose of a People's Commissariat like the Workers' and Peasants' Inspection. I think this question will help them recover their sense of proportion. Either it is not worth while having another of the numerous reorganizations that we have had of this hopeless affair, the Workers' and Peasants' Inspection, or we must really set to work, by slow, difficult and unusual methods, and by testing these methods over and over again, to create something really exemplary, something that will win the respect of all and sundry for its merits, and not only because of its rank and title.

If we do not arm ourselves with patience, if we do not devote several years to this task, we had better not tackle it at all.

In my opinion we ought to select a minimum number of the highest labor research institutes, etc., which we have baked so hastily, see whether they are organized properly, and allow them to continue working, but only in a way that conforms to the high standards of modern science and gives us all its benefits. If we do that it will not be utopian to hope that within a few years we shall have an institution that will be able to perform its functions correctly, to work systematically and steadily on improving our state apparatus, an institution backed by the trust of the working class, of the Russian Communist Party, and the whole population of our Republic.

The spade-work for this could be begun at once. If the People's Commissariat of the Workers' and Peasant's Inspection accepted the present plan of reorganization, it could now take preparatory steps and work methodically until the task is completed, without haste, and not hesitating to alter what has already been done.

Any half-hearted solution would be extremely harmful in this matter. A measure for the size of staff of the Workers' and Peasants' Inspection based on any other consideration would, in fact, be based on the old bureaucratic considerations, on old prejudices, on what has already been condemned, universally ridiculed, etc.

In substance, the matter is as follows:

Either we prove now that we have really learned something about state organization (we ought to have learned something in five years), or we prove that we are not sufficiently mature for it. If the latter is the case, we had better not tackle the task.

I think that with the available human material it will not be immodest to assume that we have learned enough to be able systematically to rebuild at least one People's Commissariat. True, this one People's Commissariat will have to be the model for our entire state apparatus.

We ought at once to announce a contest in the compilation of two or more textbooks on the organization of labor in general and on management in particular. . . .

We ought to send several qualified and conscientious people to Germany, or to England, to collect literature and to study this question. I mention England in case it is found impossible to send people to America or Canada.

We ought to appoint a commission to draw up the preliminary program of examinations for prospective employees of the Workers' and Peasants' Inspection; ditto for candidates to the Central Control Commission. . . .

Simultaneously, a preparatory commission should be appointed to select candidates for membership of the Central Control Commission. I hope that we shall now be able to find more than enough candidates for this post among the experienced workers in all departments, as well as among the students of our Soviet higher schools.

It would hardly be right to exclude any category beforehand. Probably preference will have to be given to a mixed composition for this institution, which should combine many qualities and dissimilar merits. Consequently, the task of drawing up the list of candidates will entail a considerable amount of work. For example, it would be least desirable for the staff of the new People's Commissariat to consist of people of one type, only of officials, say, or for it to exclude people of the propagandist type, or people whose principal quality is sociability or the ability to penetrate into circles that are not altogether customary for officials in this field, etc.

I think I shall be able to express my idea best if I compare my plan with that of academic institutions. Under the guidance of their presidium, the members of the Central Control Commission should systematically examine all the papers and documents of the Political Bureau. At the same time they should divide their time correctly between various jobs in investigating the routine in our institutions, from the very small and privately owned offices to the highest state institutions. And last, their functions should include the study of theory, that is, the theory of organization of the work they intend to devote themselves to, and practical work under the guidance either of older comrades or of teachers in the higher institutes for the organization of labor.

I do not think, however, that they will be able to confine themselves to this sort of academic work. In addition, they will have to prepare themselves for work which I would not hesitate to call training to catch—I will not say rogues, but something like that—and working out special ruses to screen their movements, their approach, etc.

If such proposals were made in West-European government institutions, they would rouse frightful resentment, a feeling of moral indignation, etc.; but I trust that we have not become so bureaucratic as to be capable of that. NEP has not yet succeeded in gaining such respect as to cause any of us to be shocked at the idea that somebody may be caught. Our Soviet Republic is of such recent construction and there are such heaps of the old lumber still lying around that it would hardly occur to anyone to be shocked at the idea that we should delve into them by means of ruses, by means of investigations sometimes directed to rather remote sources or in a roundabout way. And even if it did occur to anyone to be shocked by this, we may be sure that such a person would make himself a laughing-stock.

Let us hope that our new Workers' and Peasants' Inspection will abandon what the French call *pruderie*, which we may call ridiculous primness, or ridiculous swank, and which plays entirely into the hands of our Soviet and Party bureaucracy. Let it be said in parentheses that we have bureaucrats in our Party offices as well as in Soviet offices.

When I said above that we must study and study hard in institutes for the higher organization of labor, etc., I did not by any means imply "studying" in the schoolroom way, nor did I confine myself to the idea of studying only in the schoolroom way. I hope that not a single genuine revolutionary will suspect me of refusing, in this case, to understand "studies" to include resorting to some semihumorous trick, cunning device, piece of trickery, or something of that sort. I know that in the staid and earnest states of Western Europe such an idea would horrify people and that not a single decent official would even entertain it. I hope, however, that we have not yet become as bureaucratic as all that and that in our midst the discussion of this idea will give rise to nothing more than amusement.

Indeed, why not combine pleasure with utility? Why not resort to some humorous or semihumorous trick to expose something ridiculous, something harmful, something semiridiculous, semiharmful, etc.?

It seems to me that our Workers' and Peasants' Inspection will gain a great deal if it examines these ideas, and that the list of cases in which our Central Control Commission and its colleagues in the Workers' and Peasants' Inspection achieved a few of their most brilliant victories will be enriched by not a few exploits of our future Workers' and Peasants' Inspection and Central Control Commission members in places not quite mentionable in prim and staid textbooks.

How can a Party institution be amalgamated with a Soviet institution? Is there not something improper in this suggestion? ·

I do not ask these questions on my own behalf but on behalf of those I hinted at above when I said that we have bureaucrats in our Party institutions as well as in the Soviet institutions.

But why, indeed, should we not amalgamate the two if this is in the interests of our work? Do we not all see that such an amalgamation has been very beneficial in the case of the People's Commissariat for Foreign Affairs, where it was brought about at the very beginning? Does not the Political Bureau discuss from the Party point of view many questions, both minor and important, concerning the "moves" we should make in reply to the "moves" of foreign powers in order to forestall their, say, cunning, if we are not to use a less respectable term? Is not this flexible amalgamation of a Soviet institution with a Party institution a source of great strength in our politics? I think that what has proved its usefulness, what has been definitely adopted in our foreign politics and has become so customary that it no longer calls forth any doubt in this field, will be at least as appropriate (in fact I think it will be much more appropriate) for our state apparatus as a whole. The functions of the Workers' and Peasants' Inspection cover our state apparatus as a whole, and its activities should affect all and every state institution without exception: local, central, commercial, purely administrative, educational, archive, theatrical, etc.— in short, all without the slightest exception.

Why then should not an institution whose activities have such wide scope, and which moreover requires such extraordinary flexibility of forms, be permitted to adopt this peculiar amalgamation of a Party control institution with a Soviet control institution?

I see no obstacles to this. What is more, I think that such an amalgamation is the only guarantee of success in our work. I think that all doubts on this score arise in the dustiest corners of our government offices, and that they deserve to be treated with nothing but ridicule.

Another doubt: is it expedient to combine educational activities with official activities? I think that it is not only expedient, but necessary. Generally speaking, in spite of our revolutionary attitude towards the West-European form of state, we have allowed ourselves to become infected with a number of its most harmful and ridiculous prejudices; to some extent we have been deliberately infected with them by our dear bureaucrats, who counted on being able again and again to fish in the muddy waters of these prejudices. And they did fish in these muddy waters to so great an extent that only the blind among us failed to see how extensively this fishing was practiced.

In all spheres of social, economic, and political relationships we are "frightfully" revolutionary. But as regards precedence, the observance of the forms and rites of office management, our "revolutionariness" often gives way to the mustiest routine. On more than one occasion, we have witnessed the very interesting phenomenon of a great leap forward in social life being accompanied by amazing timidity whenever the slightest changes are proposed.

This is natural, for the boldest steps forward were taken in a field which was long reserved for theoretical study, which was cultivated mainly, and even almost exclusively, in theory. The Russian, when away from work, found solace from bleak bureaucratic realities in unusually bold theoretical constructions, and that is why in our country these unusually bold theoretical constructions assumed an unusually lopsided character. Theoretical audacity in general constructions went hand in hand with amazing timidity as regards certain very minor reforms in office routine. Some great universal agrarian revolution was worked out with an audacity unexampled in any other country, and at the same time the imagination failed when it came to working out a tenth-rate reform in office routine; the imagination, or patience, was lacking to apply to this reform the general propositions that produced such "brilliant" results when applied to general problems.

That is why in our present life an astonishing degree of reckless audacity goes hand in hand with timidity of thought even when it comes to very minor changes.

I think that this has happened in all really great revolutions, for really great revolutions grow out of the contradictions between the old, between what is directed towards developing the old, and the very abstract striving for the new, which must be so new as not to contain the tiniest particle of the old.

And the more abrupt the revolution, the longer will many of these contradictions last.

The general feature of our present life is the following: we have destroyed capitalist industry and have done our best to raze to the ground the medieval institutions and landed proprietorship, and thus created a small and very small peasantry, which is following the lead of the proletariat because it believes in the results of its revolutionary work. It is not easy for us, however, to keep going until the socialist revolution is victorious in more developed countries merely with the aid of this confidence, because economic necessity, especially under NEP, keeps the productivity of labor of the small and very small peasants at an extremely low level. Moreover, the international situation, too, threw Russia back and, by and large, reduced the labor productivity of the people to a level considerably below prewar. The West-European capitalist powers, partly deliberately and partly unconsciously, did everything they could to throw us back, to utilize the elements of civil war in Russia in order to spread as much ruin in the country as possible. It was precisely this way out of the imperialist war that seemed to have many advantages. They argued somewhat as follows: "If we fail to overthrow the revolutionary system in Russia, we shall, at all events, hinder her progress towards socialism." And from their point of view they could argue in no other way. In the end, their problem was half-solved. They failed to overthrow the new system created by the revolution, but they did prevent it from at once taking the step forward that would have justified the forecasts of the socialists, that would have enabled the latter to develop the productive forces with enormous speed, to develop all the potentialities which, taken together, would have produced socialism; socialists would thus have proved to all and sundry that socialism contains within itself gigantic forces and that mankind had now entered into a new stage of development of extraordinarily brilliant prospects.

The system of international relationships which has now taken shape is one in which a European state, Germany, is enslaved by the victor countries. Futhermore, owing to their victory, a number of states, the oldest states in the West, are in a position to make some insignificant concessions to their oppressed classes—concessions which, insignificant though they are, nevertheless retard the revolutionary movement in those countries and create some semblance of "social peace."

At the same time, as a result of the last imperialist war, a number of countries of the East, India, China, etc., have been completely jolted out of the rut. Their development has definitely shifted to general European capitalist lines. The general European ferment has begun to affect them, and it is now clear to the whole world that they have been drawn into a process of development that must lead to a crisis in the whole of world capitalism.

Thus, at the present time we are confronted with the question—shall we be able to hold on with our small and very small peasant production, and in our present state of ruin, until the West-European capitalist countries consummate their development towards socialism? But they are consummating it not as we formerly expected. They are not consummating it through the gradual "maturing" of socialism, but through the exploitation of some countries by others, through the exploitation of the first of the countries vanquished in the imperialist war combined with the exploitation of the whole of the East. On the other hand, precisely as a result of the first imperialist war, the East has been definitely drawn into the revolutionary movement, has been definitely drawn into the general maelstrom of the world revolutionary movement.

What tactics does this situation prescribe for our country? Obviously the following. We must display extreme caution so as to preserve our workers' government and to retain our small and very small peasantry under its leadership and authority. We have the advantage that the whole world is now passing to a movement that must give rise to a world socialist revolution. But we are laboring under the disadvantage that the imperialists have succeeded in splitting the world into two camps; and this split is made more complicated by the fact that it is extremely difficult for Germany, which is really a land of advanced, cultured, capitalist development, to rise to her feet. All the capitalist powers of what is called the West are pecking at her and preventing her from rising. On the other hand, the entire East, with its hundreds of millions of exploited working people reduced to the last degree of human suffering, has been forced into a position where its physical and material strength cannot possibly be compared with the physical, material, and military strength of any of the much smaller West-European states.

Can we save ourselves from the impending conflict with these imperialist countries? May we hope that the internal antagonisms and conflicts between the thriving imperialist countries of the West and the thriving imperialist countries of the East will give us a second respite as they did the first time, when the campaign of the West-European counter-revolution in support of the Russian counter-revolution broke down owing to the antagonisms in the camp of the counter-revolutionaries of the West and the East, in the camp of the Eastern and Western exploiters . . . ?

I think the reply to this question should be that the issue depends upon too many factors, and that the outcome of the struggle as a whole can be forecast only because in the long run capitalism itself is educating and training the vast majority of the population of the globe for the struggle.

In the last analysis, the outcome of the struggle will be determined by the fact that Russia, India, China, etc., account for the overwhelming majority of the population of the globe. And it is this majority that, during the past few years, has been drawn into the struggle for emancipation with extraordinary rapidity, so that in this respect there cannot be the slightest doubt what the final outcome of the world struggle will be. In this sense, the complete victory of socialism is fully and absolutely assured.

But what interests us is not the inevitability of this complete victory of socialism, but the tactics which we, the Russian Communist Party, we, the Russian Soviet government, should pursue to prevent the West-European counter-revolutionary states from crushing us. To ensure our existence until the next military conflict between the counter-revolutionary imperialist West and the revolutionary and nationalist East, between the most civilized countries of the world and the Orientally backward countries, which, however, comprise the majority, this majority must become civilized. We, too, lack enough civilization to enable us to pass straight on to socialism, although we do have the political requisites for it. We should adopt the following tactics or pursue the following policy to save ourselves.

We must strive to build up a state in which the workers retain the leadership of the peasants, in which they retain the confidence of the peasants, and by exercising the greatest economy remove every trace of extravagance from our social relations.

We must reduce our state apparatus to the utmost degree of economy. We must banish from it all traces of extravagance, of which so much has been left over from tsarist Russia, from its bureaucratic capitalist state machine.

Will not this be a reign of peasant limitations?

No. If we see to it that the working class retains its leadership over the peasantry, we shall be able, by exercising the greatest possible economy in the economic life of our state, to use every saving we make to develop our large-scale machine industry, to develop electrification, the hydraulic extraction of peat, . . . etc.

In this, and in this alone, lies our hope. Only when we have done this will we, speaking figuratively, be able to change horses, to change from the peasant, muzhik horse of poverty, from the horse of an economy designed for a ruined peasant country, to the horse which the proletariat is seeking and must seek—the horse of large-scale machine industry, of electrification, . . . etc.

That is how I link up in my mind the general plan of our work, of our policy, of our tactics, of our strategy, with the functions of the reorganized Workers' and Peasants' Inspection. This is what, in my opinion, justifies the exceptional care, the exceptional attention that we must devote to the Workers' and Peasants' Inspection in raising it to an exceptionally high place, in giving it a leadership with Central Committee rights, etc., etc.

And this justification is that only by thoroughly purging our government offices, by reducing to the utmost everything that is not absolutely essential in them, shall we be certain of being able to keep going. Moreover, we shall be able to keep going not on the level of a small-peasant country, not on the level of universal limitation, but on a level steadily advancing to large-scale machine industry.

These are the lofty tasks that I dream of for our Workers' and Peasants' Inspection. That is why I am planning for it the amalgamation of the most authoritative Party body with an "ordinary" Peoples' Commissariat.

SUGGESTIONS FOR FURTHER READING

STUDENTS who are interested in learning more about Lenin's life and thought would do well to consult the following:

Louis Fischer, THE LIFE OF LENIN, New York, 1964

Leopold Haimson, THE RUSSIAN MARXISTS AND THE ORIGINS OF BOLSHEVISM, Cambridge, Mass., 1955

Alfred G. Meyer, LENINISM, Cambridge, Mass., 1957

Leonard Schapiro and Peter Reddaway (eds.), LENIN: THE MAN, THE THEORIST, THE LEADER, London, 1968

David Shub, LENIN: A BIOGRAPHY, Garden City, New York, 1948

Donald W. Treadgold, LENIN AND HIS RIVALS, New York, 1955

Adam Ulam, THE BOLSHEVIKS: THE INTELLECTUAL AND POLITICAL HISTORY OF THE TRIUMPH OF COMMUNISM IN RUSSIA, New York, 1965

——————, THE UNFINISHED REVOLUTION: AN ESSAY ON THE SOURCES OF INFLUENCE OF MARXISM AND COMMUNISM, New York, 1960

Bertram D. Wolfe, THREE WHO MADE A REVOLUTION, New York, 1948